Caribbean Sea

VENEZUELA

(GUYANA)

DUTCH GUIANA
(SURINAME)

FRENCH
GUIANA

COLOMBIA

ECUADOR

Amazon

Manáos
(Manaus)

Amazon

Madeira

River of Doubt
(Rio Roosevelt)

BRAZIL

José Bonifácio

Juruena

Utiarity (Utiariti)

Mato Grosso

Bahia
(Salvador)

PERU

Vilhena

Tapirapoan (Tapirapuã)

São Luis de Cáceres (Cáceres)

BOLIVIA

Corumbá

PARAGUAY

São Paulo

Pacific

Ocean

Tucumán

Asunción

Rio de Janeiro

Santiago

Mendoza

URUGUAY

Buenos Aires

Montevideo

CHILE

ARGENTINA

Valdivia

0 Miles   400   800

0 Kilometers   800

Theodore Roosevelt's South America Tour:
October 18, 1913, through December 12, 1913

Journey to the River of Doubt:
December 12, 1913, through February 25, 1914

Descent of the River of Doubt:
February 27, 1914, through April 26, 1914

Place names are spelled as they were in 1914.
Current spellings are in parentheses.

© 2005 Jeffrey L. Ward

The River of Doubt

The River of Doubt

THEODORE ROOSEVELT'S
DARKEST JOURNEY

Candice Millard

DOUBLEDAY

NEW YORK   LONDON   TORONTO   SYDNEY   AUCKLAND

PUBLISHED BY DOUBLEDAY
a division of Random House, Inc.

DOUBLEDAY and the portrayal of an anchor with a dolphin are
registered trademarks of Random House, Inc.

Book design by Lovedog Studio

Endpapers designed by Jeffrey L. Ward;
endpaper sketch map by Theodore Roosevelt, courtesy of the
Theodore Roosevelt Collection, Harvard College Library. See photo credits on p. 417.

Library of Congress Cataloging-in-Publication Data
Millard, Candice.
The river of doubt : Theodore Roosevelt's darkest journey /
Candice Millard.— 1st ed.
p.   cm.
Includes index.
ISBN 0-385-50796-8
1. Roosevelt River (Brazil)—Description and travel. 2. Amazon River Valley—
Description and travel. 3. Rain forests—Amazon River Valley.
4. Natural history—Amazon River Valley. 5. Roosevelt-Rondon Scientific
Expedition (1913–1914) 6. Roosevelt, Theodore, 1858–1919—
Travel—Brazil—Roosevelt River. 7. Presidents—United States—Biography. I. Title.
F2546.M587 2005
918.1'13045—dc22   2005046541

PRINTED IN THE UNITED STATES OF AMERICA

November 2005

7   9   10   8   6

For Mark

CONTENTS

Part Six
Deliverance

The River of Doubt

Prologue

"I DON'T BELIEVE HE CAN live through the night," George Cherrie wrote in his diary in the spring of 1914. A tough and highly respected naturalist who had spent twenty-five years exploring the Amazon, Cherrie too often had watched helplessly as his companions succumbed to the lethal dangers of the jungle. Deep in the Brazilian rain forest, he recognized the approach of death when he saw it, and it now hung unmistakably over Theodore Roosevelt.

Less than eighteen months after Roosevelt's dramatic, failed campaign for an unprecedented third term in the White House, the sweat-soaked figure before Cherrie in the jungle darkness could not have been further removed from the power and privilege of his former office. Hundreds of miles from help or even any outside awareness of his ordeal, Roosevelt hovered agonizingly on the brink of death. Suffering from disease and near-starvation, and shuddering uncontrollably from fever, the man who had been the youngest and most energetic president in his nation's history drifted in and out of delirium, too weak to sit up or even to lift his head.

Throughout his life, Roosevelt had turned to intense physical exertion as a means of overcoming setbacks and sorrow, and he had come to the Amazon in search of that same hard absolution. Deeply frustrated by the bitterness and betrayals of the election contest, he had sought to purge his disappointment by throwing himself headlong against the cruelest trials that nature could offer him. With only a handful of men, he had set out on a self-imposed journey to explore the River of Doubt, a churning, ink-black tributary of the Amazon that winds nearly a thousand miles through the dense Brazilian rain forest.

In a lifetime of remarkable achievement, Roosevelt had shaped his own character—and that of his country—through sheer force of will, relentlessly choosing action over inaction, and championing what he famously termed "the strenuous life." From his earliest childhood, that energetic credo had served as his compass and salvation, propelling him to the forefront of public life, and lifting him above a succession of personal tragedies and disappointments. Each time he encountered an obstacle, he responded with more vigor, more energy, more raw determination. Each time he faced personal tragedy or weakness, he found his strength not in the sympathy of others, but in the harsh ordeal of unfamiliar new challenges and lonely adventure.

On the banks of the River of Doubt, the same unyielding will and thirst for achievement brought him face to face with the absolute limits of his strength. The exotic splendor of the unexplored jungle had captivated Roosevelt and his men as the journey began. "No civilized man, no white man, had ever gone down or up this river, or seen the country through which we were passing," he wrote. "The lofty and matted forest rose like a green wall on either hand. The trees were stately and beautiful, the looped and twisted vines hung from them like great ropes."

After months in the wilderness, however, harsh jungle conditions and the river's punishing rapids had left the expedition on the verge of disaster. Roosevelt and his men had already lost five of their seven canoes and most of their provisions, and one man had perished. What lay around the next bend was anyone's guess. Even Colonel Cândido

Rondon, the expedition's Brazilian co-commander, who had explored more of the Amazon than any other man alive, had no idea where the uncharted river would take them.

For Roosevelt's men, fears for their own survival were eclipsed only by despair about the fate of their leader. As Roosevelt's fever soared to 105 degrees, Cherrie and Kermit, Roosevelt's second son, were certain that they were witnessing his final hours. "The scene is vivid before me," Kermit would later recall. "The black rushing river with the great trees towering high above along the bank; the sodden earth under foot; for a few moments the stars would be shining, and then the sky would cloud over and the rain would fall in torrents, shutting out the sky and trees and river."

As the fever-wracked former president drifted in and out of consciousness, he slipped into a trancelike delirium, reciting over and over again the opening lines to Samuel Taylor Coleridge's "Kubla Khan": "In Xanadu did Kubla Khan a stately pleasure-dome decree. In Xanadu did Kubla Khan a stately pleasure-dome decree. In Xanadu . . ."

PART ONE

Breaking Away

CHAPTER 1

Defeat

THE LINE OUTSIDE MADISON Square Garden started to form at 5:30 p.m., just as an orange autumn sun was setting in New York City on Halloween Eve, 1912. The doors were not scheduled to open for another hour and a half, but the excitement surrounding the Progressive Party's last major rally of the presidential campaign promised a packed house. The party was still in its infancy, fighting for a foothold in its first national election, but it had something that the Democrats had never had and the Republicans had lately lost, the star attraction that drew tens of thousands of people to the Garden that night: Theodore Roosevelt.

Roosevelt, one of the most popular presidents in his nation's history, had vowed never to run again after winning his second term in the White House in 1904. But now, just eight years later, he was not only running for a third term, he was, to the horror and outrage of his old Republican backers, running as a third-party candidate against Democrats and Republicans alike.

Roosevelt's decision to abandon the Republican Party and run as a Progressive had been bitterly criticized, not just because he was muddying the political waters but because he still had a large and almost fanatically loyal following. Roosevelt was five feet eight inches tall, about average height for an American man in the early twentieth century, weighed more than two hundred pounds, and had a voice that sounded as if he had just taken a sip of helium, but his outsized personality made him unforgettable—and utterly irresistible. He delighted in leaning over the podium as though he were about to snatch his audience up by its collective collar; he talked fast, pounded his fists, waved his arms, and sent a current of electricity through the crowd. "Such unbounded energy and vitality impressed one like the perennial forces of nature," the naturalist John Burroughs once wrote of Roosevelt. "When he came into the room it was as if a strong wind had blown the door open."

Not surprisingly, Roosevelt was proving to be dangerous competition for the Democratic candidate, Woodrow Wilson, to say nothing of President William Howard Taft, the lackluster Republican incumbent whom Roosevelt had hand-picked to be his successor in the White House four years earlier. It was a bitterly contested race, and Roosevelt hoped that this rally, strategically scheduled just a week before election day, could help swing the vote in his favor.

Before the doors even opened, more than a hundred thousand people were swarming the sidewalks and choking the surrounding cobblestone streets. Men and boys nimbly wove their way through the crowd, boldly hawking tickets in plain sight of a hundred uniformed policemen. The scalpers had their work cut out for them selling tickets in the churning throng. Days earlier the Progressive Party, nicknamed the Bull Moose Party in honor of its tenacious leader, had posted a NO MORE TICKETS sign, but brokers and street-corner salesmen had continued to do a brisk business. Dollar seats went for as much as seven dollars—roughly $130 in today's money—and the priciest tickets in the house could set the buyer back as much as a hundred dollars. On the chaotic black market, however, even experienced con men could not be sure what they had actually bought. When Vincent Astor, son of financier John Jacob Astor, arrived at his box, he found it already occupied by George Graham Rice, lately of Blackswell's Island—then one of New York's grimmest penitentiaries. When the police escorted him out, Rice complained bitterly that he had paid ten dollars for the two choice seats.

More than two thousand people tried to make it into the arena by bypassing the line and driving to the gate in a hired carriage or one of Henry Ford's open-air Model T's. But this tactic did not work for everyone. Even Roosevelt's own sister Corinne was turned away at the gate.

"For some unexplained reason the pass which had been given to me that night for my motor was not accepted by the policeman in charge, and I, my husband, my son Monroe, and our friend Mrs. Parsons were obliged to take our places in the cheering, laughing, singing crowd," she later wrote. "How it swayed and swung! how it throbbed with life and elation! how imbued it was with an earnest party ambition, and yet, with a deep and genuine religious fervor. Had I lived my whole life only for those fifteen minutes during which I marched toward the Garden already full to overflowing with my brother's adoring followers, I should have been content to do so." Caught up in the moment, fifty-one-year-old Corinne finally made it into the arena by climbing a fire escape.

Theodore Roosevelt, the object of all the furor, had nearly as much trouble trying to reach Madison Square Garden as his sister. The police had blocked off Twenty-seventh Street from Madison to Fourth Avenue for his car, but when his black limousine turned onto Madison Avenue at nine-fifteen, the excitement burning all night flamed into hysteria. A *New York Sun* reporter marveled at the chaos as swarms of people rushed Roosevelt's car, "yelling their immortal souls out. They went through a battery of photographers, tried to sweep the cops off their feet, tangled, jammed and shoved into the throng."

Roosevelt, a little stiff in his black suit, stepped out of the car, raised his hat to the crowd, and walked through a narrow, bucking pathway that the policemen had opened through the suffocating press of bodies. As Roosevelt passed by, his admirers "had their brief and delirious howls, their cries of greeting," one reporter wrote. When he opened a door that led directly onto the speaker's platform, the arena seemed to expand with his very presence, and the people outside "had to step back and watch the walls of the big building ripple under the vocal pressure from within, like the accordion-pleated skirt of a dancer."

* * *

INSIDE THE auditorium, Edith Roosevelt, every inch the aristocrat with her softly cleft chin and long, elegant neck, was seated in a box above the fray when a mighty roar rose up from the audience, heralding her husband's entrance. Four colossal American flags greeted Roosevelt, waving grandly from the girdered ceiling, and an entire, massive bull moose stood mounted on a pedestal and bathed in a white spotlight, its head raised high, its ears erect, as if about to charge.

Roosevelt, still famously energetic at fifty-four, greeted his admirers with characteristic vigor, pumping his left arm in the air like a windmill. His right arm, however, hung motionless at his side. The last time Roosevelt had given a speech—just two weeks earlier, in Milwaukee, Wisconsin—he had been shot in the chest by a thirty-six-year-old New York bartender named John Schrank, a Bavarian immigrant who feared that Roosevelt's run for a third term was an effort to establish a monarchy in the United States. Incredibly, Roosevelt's heavy army overcoat and the folded fifty-page manuscript and steel spectacle-case he carried in his right breast pocket had saved his life, but the bullet had plunged some five inches deep, lodging near his rib cage. That night, whether out of an earnest desire to deliver his message or merely an egotist's love of drama, Roosevelt had insisted on delivering his speech to a terrified and transfixed audience. His coat unbuttoned to reveal a bloodstained shirt, and his speech held high so that all could see the two sinister-looking holes made by the assailant's bullet, Roosevelt had shouted, "It takes more than that to kill a bull moose!"

Now, in Madison Square Garden as the boisterous cheering went on for forty-one minutes, Roosevelt still had one of Schrank's bullets in his chest. At 10:03 p.m., pounding on the flag-draped desk in front of him and nervously snapping his jaws, he finally convinced the crowd that he was in earnest, and the hall slowly quieted. Unaided by a loudspeaker, an invention that would revolutionize public speaking the following year, he began his speech. "Friends . . ." At the sound of his voice, the crowd erupted into a thunderous cheer that continued for two more minutes. When it tapered off, he began again. "My friends," he said, "perhaps once in a generation . . ." Suddenly, from seats close to the platform, a clamor arose as policemen tried to push back several people who had forced their way into the hall. Bending forward, Roosevelt bellowed, "Keep those people quiet, please! Officers, be quiet!"

Then, in a voice that filled the auditorium, Theodore Roosevelt launched into the last great campaign speech of his political career: "Friends, perhaps once in a generation, perhaps not so often, there comes a chance for the people of a country to play their part wisely and fearlessly in some great battle of the age-long warfare for human rights." He still had the old percussive rhythm, exploding his "p"s and "b"s with vigor, but his tone had lost the violence and his words the bitterness of the past. He did not attack his opponents—the coolly academic Wilson or the genial Taft. Instead, he talked in broad terms about character, moral strength, compassion, and responsibility. "We do not set greed against greed or hatred against hatred," he thundered. "Our creed is one that bids us to be just to all, to feel sympathy for all, and to strive for an understanding of the needs of all. Our purpose is to smite down wrong."

To the people in the hall, and to millions of Americans, Roosevelt was a hero, a leader, an icon. But even as he stood on the stage at Madison Square Garden, he knew that in six days he would lose not only the election but also this bright, unblinking spotlight. He would be reviled by many and then ignored by all, and that would be the worst death he could imagine.

"I know the American people," he had said prophetically in 1910, upon returning to a hero's welcome after an epic journey to Africa. "They have a way of erecting a triumphal arch, and after the Conquering Hero has passed beneath it he may expect to receive a shower of bricks on his back at any moment."

*   *   *

ON ELECTION day, November 5, 1912, Roosevelt's grim expectations about his candidacy were realized in full. Woodrow Wilson took the White House in a landslide victory, winning 2.2 million more votes than Roosevelt out of the fifteen million cast. Roosevelt did not lose alone, however. He brought Taft, the incumbent Republican president, down with him. Only three and a half million Americans had voted for Taft, some six hundred thousand fewer than voted for Roosevelt and nearly three million fewer than Wilson. The Socialist candidate, Eugene V. Debs, pulled in over nine hundred thousand votes, more than twice the number he had received during his presidential run four years earlier.

For Roosevelt, who was not used to losing, even his victory over Taft was cold comfort. He had long ago lost his respect for the three-hundred-pound president, dismissing him as "a flubdub with a streak of the second-rate and the common in him." Besides, everyone knew that Taft hadn't really been in the race from the beginning. Before the Republican convention, even Taft's own wife, the fiercely ambitious Nellie, had told him, "I suppose you will have to fight Mr. Roosevelt for the nomination, and if you get it he will defeat you."

She was right on both counts. Roosevelt had at first vied for the Republican nomination, and when party bosses ensured Taft's victory, he had struck back by ensuring their defeat in the general election. As a third-party candidate, Roosevelt could not count on winning, but he could certainly spoil. When backed by a united Republican Party in his earlier election bids, Roosevelt had swept easily to victory over the Democrats. By turning his enormous popularity against his former party, however, he merely split the Republican vote and handed the election to Wilson—a widely predicted result that, when it came to pass, provoked bitter criticism of his tactics. "Roosevelt goes down to personal and richly deserved defeat," spat an editorial in the *Philadelphia Inquirer.* "But he has the satisfaction of knowing that by giving vent to his insatiate ambition and deplorable greed for power he has elevated the democratic party to the control of the nation."

Roosevelt had never been willing to share his private pain with the public. In a formal statement, he announced, "I accept the result with entire good humor and contentment." In private, however, he admitted to being surprised and shaken by the scope of his crushing defeat. "There is no use disguising the fact that the defeat at the polls is overwhelming," he wrote to his friend the British military attaché Arthur Hamilton Lee. "I had expected defeat, but I had expected that we would make a better showing. . . . I try not to think of the damage to myself personally."

The Republican Party's Old Guard, once a bastion of Roosevelt's friends and backers, held him responsible for the debacle that had put a Democrat in the White House for the first time in sixteen years. Before the Republican convention, they had assured Roosevelt that if he would only accept the party's decision to let Taft run for a second term in 1912, they would happily hand him the nomination four years later. But his injured pride and his passion for what he believed to be a battle against the nation's great injustices had driven him out of the fold. "Many of his critics could account for his leaving the Republican Party and heading another, only on the theory that he was moved by a desire for revenge," William Roscoe Thayer, Roosevelt's friend and one of his earliest biographers, wrote in 1919. "If he could not rule he would ruin. The old allegation that he must be crazy was of course revived."

* * *

ROOSEVELT SPENT that winter hunkered down at Sagamore Hill with his wife and their younger daughter, Ethel. He took walks with Edith, answered letters, and worked quietly in his book-lined study. He had few interruptions.

"The telephone, which had rung like sleigh-bells all day and half the night, was silent," wrote Roosevelt's young literary friend and eventual biographer Hermann Hagedorn. "The North Shore neighbors who, in the old days, had flocked to Sagamore at every opportunity, on horseback or in their high fancy traps, did not drive their new shining motor-cars up the new, hard-surfaced road the Roosevelts had put in the year before. The Colonel was outside the pale. He had done the unforgivable thing—he had 'turned against his class.' "

Friends and colleagues who had once competed for Roosevelt's attention now shunned him. Roosevelt, like his wife, had been born into New York's highest society. From childhood, he had been not only accepted but admired and undoubtedly envied as a Roosevelt, the older son of a wealthy and respected man. As an undergraduate at Harvard, he had been a member of the exclusive and unapologetically elitist Porcellian Club. During the Spanish-American War, he had been glorified as a courageous colonel of his own regiment—Roosevelt's Rough Riders. And as president of the United States for nearly eight years, he had been at the apex of power and prestige. Now, for the first time in his life, he was a pariah, and he was painfully aware of it.

Holed up at Sagamore Hill, Roosevelt, who was famous for his almost overbearing optimism and confidence, suffered from what his family delicately referred to as a "bruised spirit." "Of course I am having a pretty hard time, in a way," he admitted to his son Kermit in early December. "The defeated are always held accountable in every way." Roosevelt's family was so concerned about his state of mind that they discreetly asked Dr. Alexander Lambert, Roosevelt's physician and a former friend of his father's, to come for a visit. Lambert immediately packed his bags for Oyster Bay. "You cannot imagine how glad I am to see you!" Roosevelt confessed to Lambert. "I have been unspeakably lonely. You don't know how lonely it is for a man to be rejected by his own kind."

* * *

IF REJECTION was new to Roosevelt, loss and disappointment were not. Although he was only fifty-four years old, he had already lived an extraordinarily full life. Perhaps even more striking than the peaks and valleys of Roosevelt's life was the clear relationship between those extremes—the ex-president's habit of seeking solace from heartbreak and frustration by striking out on even more difficult and unfamiliar terrain, and finding redemption by pushing himself to his outermost limits. When confronted with sadness or setbacks that were beyond his power to overcome, Roosevelt instinctively sought out still greater tests, losing himself in punishing physical hardship and danger—experiences that came to shape his personality and inform his most impressive achievements.

The impulse to defy hardship became a fundamental part of Roosevelt's character, honed from earliest childhood. Frail and sickly as a child, and plagued by life-threatening asthma, Roosevelt forced himself into a regimen of harsh physical exercise in an effort to conquer his weakness. His sister Corinne remembered her brother as a "fragile, patient sufferer . . . struggling with the effort to breathe" in their nursery on East Twentieth Street in New York City. But before Theodore had reached adolescence, he had already resolved to free himself from invalidism and frailty. Through what Corinne described as "regular, monotonous motion"—swinging from horizontal bars, struggling with heavy, awkward barbells—Teedie, as his family called him, slowly broadened his chest, strengthened his arms, and transformed himself into a young man whose body was as strong and sure as his mind.

Although it was Theodore's own iron discipline that brought about this transformation, it was his father's encouragement that sparked his resolve. Theodore Senior loomed large in the lives of all of his children, but for his older son he was idol, hero, and savior. "One of my memories," Roosevelt wrote later in life, "is of my father walking up and down the room with me in his arms at night when I was a very small person, and of sitting up in bed gasping, with my father and mother trying to help me." Desperate for their child to breathe, Theodore and Martha Roosevelt tried anything, making Teedie drink strong black coffee, forcing him to vomit by coaxing syrup of ipecac down his throat, or hovering over him while he miserably smoked a cigar. Finally, Theodore Sr. sat his son down and told him that he had the power to change his fate, but he would have to work hard to do it. "Theodore, you have the mind but you have not the body," he said, "and without the help of the body the mind cannot go as far as it should. You must make your body. It is hard drudgery to make one's body, but I know you will do it." Teedie, then only about eleven years old, flashed his famous teeth, and, accepting the challenge, cried, "I'll make my body."

Roosevelt did make his body, and he never again allowed it to grow weak or idle. On the contrary, what began as drudgery soon became a compulsion. Throughout his adult life, Roosevelt would relish physical exertion, and he would use it not just as a way to keep his body fit and his mind sharp but as his most effective weapon against depression and despair.

At Harvard, Roosevelt grew steadily stronger and more vigorous and finally outpaced his asthma. He even began boxing, starting with lessons and working his way up to matches. Early in 1879, Roosevelt won his first boxing match and made a name for himself on campus—not for his strength but for his honor. William Roscoe Thayer, a contemporary of Roosevelt's at Harvard, would never forget that match. "When the referee called 'time,' Roosevelt immediately dropped his hands," Thayer later wrote, "but the other man dealt him a savage blow on the face, at which we all shouted, 'Foul, foul!' and hissed; but Roosevelt turned towards us and cried out 'Hush! He didn't hear,' a chivalrous act which made him immediately popular."

During his sophomore year at Harvard, his father—"the best man I ever knew"—died from stomach cancer at the age of forty-six. Blindsided, Roosevelt reeled from the greatest loss of his young life. "If I had very much time to think," he wrote in his diary, "I believe I should go crazy."

After his father's funeral, Roosevelt fought back. Upon finishing the school year, he fled to Oyster Bay to wrestle with his grief and anger in seclusion. In the small, heavily wooded village where his family had long spent their summers, he swam, hiked, hunted, and thundered through the forest on his horse Lightfoot, riding so hard that he nearly destroyed her. Then, before returning to Harvard, he disappeared into the Maine wilderness with an ursine backwoodsman named Bill Sewall. "Look out for Theodore," a doctor traveling with Roosevelt advised Sewall. "He's not strong, but he's all grit. He'll kill himself before he'll even say he's tired."

Roosevelt emerged from that summer determined to survive any loss. And loss would come. Following his father's death, Roosevelt had a string of successes. He graduated from Harvard with honors, married Alice Lee—a pretty blonde who he was certain would never have him, "but," he insisted, "I am going to have her!"—and, at twenty-three, was elected New York State's youngest assemblyman. In 1884, however, when he was only twenty-five years old, Roosevelt was called home by an ominous telegram. When he arrived, he found that the two most important women in his life—his mother and his young wife—were dying. At 3:00 a.m. on February 14, Valentine's Day, Martha Roosevelt, still a vibrant, dark-haired Southern belle at forty-six, died of typhoid fever. Eleven hours later, her daughter-in-law, Alice Lee Roosevelt, who had given birth to Theodore's first child just two days before, succumbed to Bright's disease, a kidney disorder. That night, in his diary, Roosevelt marked the date with a large black "X" and a single anguished entry: "The light has gone out of my life."

Desperate to conquer his despair, Roosevelt resorted to the only therapy he knew: physical hardship and danger. He left his infant daughter with his sister Anna and boarded a train for the Dakota Badlands, where he hoped to find the kind of hard existence that might keep his body and mind too busy to ache for Alice. Roosevelt rarely spoke about that terrible night or about his first wife—even to their daughter, who was named for the mother she would never know. He was a different man when he finally returned east for good two years later. He was filled with vigor and perspective after mastering an entirely unfamiliar world of danger on the American frontier—and defeating, by sheer energy and physical exertion, the grief that had threatened to overwhelm him. "Black care," he explained, in a rare unguarded comment on the subject, "rarely sits behind a rider whose pace is fast enough."

Black care again descended on Roosevelt in 1909, the year he left the White House. It was a transition that was entirely of his making—he had inherited his first term after William McKinley's assassination in 1901, and so could easily have run again seven and a half years later—but giving up the presidency left him feeling empty and adrift. Though he had done great things during his two presidential terms—from negotiating an end to the Russo-Japanese War to making possible the construction of the Panama Canal—Roosevelt felt that he had not had an opportunity for greatness. "Of course a man has to take advantage of his opportunities, but the opportunities have to come," he told an audience in Cambridge, England, in the spring of 1910. "If there is not the war, you don't get the great general; if there is not the great occasion, you don't get the great statesman; if Lincoln had lived in times of peace, no one would know his name now." The disappointment of stepping down before he was ready, before he had been tested by some catclysmic event, was so great that, two days before leaving office, Roosevelt had admonished his friend Paul Martin, "My dear fellow, for Heaven's sake don't talk about my having a future. My future is in the past."

As difficult as Roosevelt's departure from the White House had been, however, it was mild compared with the pain of his electoral defeat in 1912. His second wife, Edith, who had known her husband her entire life and had witnessed firsthand his reactions to sorrow and disappointment, could not have doubted what now lay in store. It was just a matter of time before Roosevelt would break away again, and there was nothing she could do to prevent it. Edith was a private person, and her quiet life at Sagamore Hill was precious to her. But she knew that it was not enough for Theodore. He would not rest until he found some physically punishing adventure that would take him far from home and, Edith feared, place him in grave danger.

CHAPTER 2

Opportunity

IN FEBRUARY 1913, THREE months after Roosevelt's election defeat, the postman who delivered first-class mail to Sagamore Hill on a horse-drawn wagon arrived with a letter from Argentina. The formal, three-page letter, carefully typed in English on the stationery of the Museo Social in Buenos Aires, was merely one of many invitations from around the globe that arrived regularly for the ex-president. Within a matter of months, however, it would prove to be the very opportunity that Roosevelt had been longing for.

Founded by a group of forward-thinking businessmen and political figures, Argentina's Museo Social was an institution devoted to the kind of progressive intellectual agenda that most appealed to the former American leader. Although it was only two years old, the social-history museum was ambitious in its lofty goal of "bringing together men and ideas." It wanted Roosevelt as a guest lecturer, and its president, a man named Emilio Frers, was determined to get him. With the instincts of a seasoned diplomat, Frers aimed directly for Roosevelt's Achilles' heel, his vanity, making clear that the former president could define all the terms of this visit if he would only consent to come.

"Your presence in this country will be greatly appreciated by our countrymen who have heard so much about you, about your public career and the high ideals you stand for," he wrote.

Frers's words must have been a cool balm to Roosevelt's wounded pride, but the Argentinian did not stop there, offering to pay the ex-president more than $13,000 ($250,000 in today's money) for three lectures. Although Frers could not have known it, the question of money was very much on Roosevelt's mind. He had inherited a substantial fortune from his father, a fortune that had enabled him to go into politics without worrying about supporting his family. After a long, successful political career, however, he could hope to leave little but a famous name to his own children.

*   *   *

BEYOND THE money, the recognition, and the opportunity to advise a fledgling democracy, Roosevelt also had a very personal reason for wanting to take this trip: It would give him a chance to see his twenty-three-year-old son, Kermit, who had been living and working in South America for more than a year. Kermit was a quiet middle child, the third of Roosevelt's six children. He was smart, disciplined, and a skilled athlete, and he had inherited his father's passion for far-flung places and physically challenging adventures.

Kermit's first great adventure had been a gift from his father: a chance to join him on his post-presidency African safari in 1909. Kermit was only eighteen years old at the time and had just begun Harvard as a freshman. Roosevelt had hesitated to take his son on a trip that he himself had waited a lifetime for, but in the end he put his faith in Kermit's serious demeanor and rigorous discipline, concluding that he would not risk spoiling the young man. "You blessed fellow, I do not think you will have to wait until your ship comes in before making that African trip," Roosevelt wrote Kermit from the White House that spring. "The only question that gives me concern in connection with it is whether letting you take it will tend to unsettle you for your work afterwards. I should want you to make up your mind fully and deliberately that you would treat it just as you would a college course; enjoy it to the full; count it as so much to the good, and then when it was over turn in and buckle down to hard work; for without the hard work you certainly can not make a success of life."

Kermit justified his father's trust in him by returning to his studies as soon as the expedition ended and completing his four years at Harvard in two and a half. As soon as he graduated in the summer of 1912, however, he dived headlong into another adventure—in a new country, on a new continent, and entirely on his own. His first job in South America had been with the Brazil Railway Company, but after some shakeups in the management he had taken a job building bridges for the Anglo Brazilian Iron Company. Although he suffered from what Roosevelt referred to as "intermittent fever," he was thriving in this rough, unfamiliar environment and was making his father proud. "I am greatly pleased at the way that Kermit has gone on," Roosevelt had written to his sister-in-law, Emily. "He appears to be making good down in Brazil."

Kermit's decision to go to Brazil could hardly have been better calculated to impress his father. Not only had the young man struck out on his own, but he had chosen South America, a continent that, in the early part of the twentieth century, was still considered remote, mysterious, and dangerous. In fact, at that time less was known about the interior of South America than about any other inhabited continent.

If the idea of traveling to a South American city was unusual for most Americans in 1913, venturing into the dense jungles of the Amazon was simply out of the question. With the exception of a few large and widely spaced rivers, each more than eight hundred miles long, there was a blank, unexplored spot on the map of South America the size of Germany, and within it lay the vast, tangled expanse of the Amazon rain forest.

So remote and unknown was the Amazon that the first substantial effort to penetrate it had ended in failure only the year before, when the final wooden ties were laid on the Madeira–Mamoré railroad. The railroad, which ran little more than two hundred miles along the

Madeira and Mamoré rivers in western Brazil, had been designed to carry the highly prized sap of the rubber tree from the depths of the Amazon to the coast, where it could be shipped to overseas markets. Any promise that the railroad held, however, was eclipsed by the horrors of building it. In *The Sea and the Jungle,* his classic 1912 book on the Amazon, British author H. M. Tomlinson described meeting some of the men who worked on the railroad. "They were bearded like Crusoe, pallid as anaemic women, and speckled with insect bites," he wrote. "These men said that where they had been working the sun never shone, for his light was stopped on the unbroken green which, except where the big rivers flowed, roofed the whole land." Nicknamed "Mad Maria" by the engineers who designed it, the railroad took five years to finish, and by the time it was ready in 1912, the South American rubber trade had gone bust, and the estimated six thousand men who had died of disease and starvation trying to build it had lost their lives for nothing.

For Roosevelt, South America's vast, largely unknown, and unexplored interior was perhaps the most important factor of all in shaping his decision to accept the Museo Social's invitation. With its primordial jungles and broad savannas, its soaring mountains and harsh extremes of climate and terrain, the continent offered the kind of unbounded, unfamiliar frontier and harsh physical adventure that had attracted Roosevelt throughout his life. There were few places on earth that were of greater interest to the former president than the Amazon—not just because it promised adventure but because it was a naturalist's Shangri-La.

* * *

BEFORE HE was a president, before he was a Rough Rider, a cowboy, or even a Harvard man, Roosevelt was a naturalist. From his earliest childhood, the sickly, privileged young man from New York City had been fascinated to the point of obsession with plants, animals, and insects, thrilling to the stories of famous adventurers and longing for the day when he could join the ranks of the pioneering natural scientists he read about so intently. As a boy, he filled his house and pockets with spiders, mice, and snakes, studying and sketching them with discipline and talent that far exceeded his age. As a young politician, he broke free from his official duties at every opportunity to pursue his passion, plunging into the nearest wilderness in search of new or uncatalogued species. By the time he was in the White House, Roosevelt was not merely the most powerful elected official in the country, but one of its most knowledgeable and experienced naturalists.

Looking back, Roosevelt could name the exact day on which, as he put it, "I started on my career as zoölogist." He was just a boy walking up Broadway in New York City, headed to the market to buy some strawberries, when he spied a dead seal that had been killed in the harbor and stretched out on a wooden plank. "That seal filled me with every possible feeling of romance and adventure," he later recalled. As long as the seal lay there, rotting, Roosevelt visited it every day, measuring it—with a folding pocket ruler because he did not have a tape measure—and carefully writing his first natural history, with the dead seal as the star.

Captivated by the thrill of discovery, the young Theodore, along with two cousins, founded the Roosevelt Museum of Natural History. "The collections were at first kept in my room," he remembered, "until a rebellion on the part of the chambermaid received the approval of the higher authorities of the household and the collection was moved up to a kind of bookcase in the back hall upstairs." When Roosevelt was only fourteen years old, he began contributing specimens to New York's American Museum of Natural History, the museum that his father had helped found in 1869. After a family vacation in the Adirondacks, he proudly donated a bat, a turtle, four birds' eggs, twelve mice, and a red-squirrel skull to the two-year-old museum, which was then modestly housed in the Arsenal on the east side of Central Park.

Roosevelt's dream of becoming a naturalist burned brightly until he began his studies at Harvard. He entered college "devoted to out-of-doors natural history," dreaming of following in the footsteps of men like the world-renowned ornithologist John James Audubon, but he quickly became disgusted with the university's curriculum for aspiring naturalists, which focused on laboratory experiments to the exclusion of, and disregard for, fieldwork. "In the entirely proper desire to be thorough and to avoid slipshod methods, the tendency was to treat as not serious, as unscientific, any kind of work that was not carried on with laborious minuteness in the laboratory," he wrote. "My taste was specialized in a totally different direction, and I had no more desire or ability to be a microscopist and section-cutter than to be a mathematician. Accordingly, I abandoned all thought of becoming a scientist."

Although Roosevelt chose politics over science, he never lost his passion for natural history, and his ascent to high office afforded him ever-expanding opportunities to follow his obsession. During his last term in the White House, he had invited the naturalist John Burroughs to Pine Knot, his presidential retreat in rural Virginia, to help him name the local birds. It was a day that Burroughs would never forget. "Together we identified more than seventy-five species of birds and wild fowl. He knew them all but two, and I knew them all but two," Burroughs later recalled. "A few days before he had seen Lincoln's sparrow in an old weedy field. On Sunday after church, he took me there and we loitered around for an hour, but the sparrow did not appear. Had he found this bird again, he would have been one ahead of me. The one subject I do know, and ought to know, is the birds. It has been one of the main studies of a long life. He knew the subject as well as I did, while he knew with the same thoroughness scores of other subjects of which I am entirely ignorant."

Roosevelt's collecting trip through East Africa in 1909 had been a great boon to the American Museum of Natural History and the Smithsonian Institution—indeed, the entire scientific world. In fact, according to the then-president of the American Museum of Natural History, Henry Fairfield Osborn, it had been "by far the most successful expedition that has ever penetrated Africa."

The trip to South America that Roosevelt began to consider on the strength of the Argentine museum's invitation would not cover uncharted territory. But it would, he hoped, offer the chance to do something of scientific importance. To expand his itinerary beyond a mere speaking tour, he again turned to the American Museum of Natural History to discover where and how he might find the opportunity to indulge his passion for natural science during the trip. Although he did not contemplate anything too difficult or dangerous, the sheer scale of the continent's natural wonders promised a rich and absorbing adventure, crowned by the chance to have a firsthand look—however casual—at the wonders of the Amazon.

In looking to the museum for advice, Roosevelt was turning to the epicenter of American natural science. The museum, encompassing four city blocks between Seventy-seventh and Eighty-first Streets, had grown during Roosevelt's lifetime to become not only one of the world's leading natural-history museums, but also a renowned sponsor of expeditions to all corners of the earth, from the North Pole to the Gobi Desert to the lush jungle of the Congo.

Foremost among Roosevelt's friends at the museum was Henry Fairfield Osborn, the articulate young paleontologist who, five years earlier, had become the first scientist to be named president of the museum, a position he would hold for twenty-five years. Roosevelt had known "Fair" Osborn most of his life. "I can hardly express to you how much your offer to cooperate with the American Museum of Natural History pleases me," Osborn wrote Roosevelt when he heard about his plans for a trip to the Amazon, "both for your own sake and because of the historical association of your Father in the foundation of the Museum." Osborn, who would earn a place in history for naming the Tyrannosaurus Rex, did not have the specialized regional knowledge necessary to help the former president with his plan, but he pledged the full support of the museum staff, and offered the assistance of Frank Chapman, head of the museum's ornithology department, whom Roosevelt knew and respected from his own detailed study of birds. A veteran scientist and experienced traveler who knew

South America well, Chapman quickly arranged a luncheon with Roosevelt at the museum to discuss the details of the expedition.

Though the Museo Social's letter—as well as subsequent invitations from Brazil and Chile—served to catalyze many different motives that Roosevelt had for embarking on a trip to South America, it was not the first time that the former president had entertained the idea of such an adventure. Roosevelt's decision to make the journey was likely due in large part to the fact that just such a trip had been urged on him for many years by an old acquaintance from the University of Notre Dame named Father John Augustine Zahm.

A slight, balding man with heavily lidded blue eyes and cup-handle ears, Father Zahm was a strange pastiche of seemingly incongruent interests and passions, which had placed him at the crossroads of religion, science, and politics. A priest since the age of twenty-three, Zahm had begun training for the position when he was only sixteen and had developed, as his friend Father John Cavanaugh put it, "an intense zeal for the glory of God and the triumph of the Church." But, paradoxically, Father Zahm, who had taught chemistry and physics at Notre Dame, was also a proponent of evolution, a theory that—although Charles Darwin had published *On the Origin of Species* more than half a century earlier—was still shunned by many Americans as sacrilege and derided by most Catholics as, in the words of one journalist, "the 'philosophy of mud' and the 'gospel of dirt.' " In 1896, while still at Notre Dame, Zahm had even taken the extraordinary step of publishing a book defending evolution. The book, titled *Evolution and Dogma*, bravely argued that evolution "explains countless facts and phenomena which are explicable on no other theory," and that, rather than being religion's enemy, was its ally.

Father Zahm's contradictions, however, went beyond science and religion. While he was a devoted priest and a serious scholar, he was hardly an ascetic, and had a deep appreciation and affinity for the good things in life. Now that he was at Holy Cross Academy in Washington, D.C., he had become a member of the exclusive Cosmos Club, a luxurious club that the American writer Wallace Stegner would call "the closest thing to a social headquarters for Washington's intellectual elite." Zahm was also a skilled self-promoter—"keep yourself before the public always," he advised his brother, Albert, "if you wish the public to remember you or do anything for you"—and he reveled in his friendship with Roosevelt, crowing to Albert that he and the former president were "the chummiest of chums."

Father Zahm had fallen under the spell of South America in 1907, when he had traveled, with a guide, through the northern reaches of the continent. At the end of his trip, as he had sailed east on the Amazon River, toward the Atlantic Ocean and home, Zahm had promised himself that he would return, but the next time he wanted company. The problem was finding a suitable companion. "Where was I to find the kind of a companion desired—one who was not only a lover of wild nature but one who was also prepared to endure all the privations and hardships incident to travel in the uninhabited jungle?" Zahm wrote. "I had not, however, pondered the matter long before I bethought me of a man who would be an ideal traveling companion, if he could find the necessary leisure, and could be induced to visit the southern continent. This man was Theodore Roosevelt."

With high hopes, Zahm had visited the Oval Office in 1908, during Roosevelt's last year in the White House, to propose the trip to his friend. Roosevelt had been intrigued by the invitation, but since he had already planned his yearlong hunting trip to East Africa with his son Kermit, he had turned the priest down. Disappointed but not discouraged, Zahm had decided to wait for Roosevelt. He waited through Roosevelt's trip to Africa, his controversial campaign, his electoral defeat, and his brooding isolation on Oyster Bay. He waited until, on the cusp of sixty-two and in failing health, he felt that he could not wait any longer.

Finally, in the summer of 1913—the same summer that Roosevelt accepted the invitation to speak at the Museo Social—Father Zahm, in his own words, reluctantly began to "cast about" for someone else to accompany him to the Amazon. In an extraordinary stroke of luck, Zahm decided to seek advice not just from the same institution that

Roosevelt had turned to for help, but from the exact same man—Frank Chapman, the bird curator at the American Museum of Natural History. In describing his long-dreamed-of trip to the Amazon, Zahm happened to mention to the curator that he was planning to visit Roosevelt at Oyster Bay. Zahm had "no hope," he wrote, "that the Colonel would finally be able to go to South America," but he felt certain that he would be interested in hearing about the journey that they had long discussed, and which would soon take place without him.

"You may save yourself the trip to Oyster Bay, if you have anything else to do," Chapman replied. "For Colonel Roosevelt is going to take luncheon with me here tomorrow and I shall be glad to have you join us." Surprised and delighted, Zahm immediately accepted, and Chapman added him to the guest list—apparently without warning Roosevelt.

*   *   *

"BY GEORGE! You here!" Roosevelt cried when he blew into the museum's dining room for his luncheon with Chapman and found Father Zahm in the midst of the scientists and staff who were to be his own expedition advisers. Zahm's unexpected appearance caught Roosevelt off guard, but, with a veteran politician's skill, he recovered nicely. "You are the very man I wish to see," he boomed. "I was just about to write you to inform you that I think I shall, at last, be able to take that long-talked-of trip to South America."

The abrupt reappearance of the priest and his dreams of South American adventure both accelerated the preparations for the ex-president's own trip and gave it an energetic, full-time advocate and organizer in the person of Zahm. The elderly priest quickly assumed responsibility for planning the journey, and placed himself in charge of choosing a route, organizing transportation, and ordering provisions and equipment—details that Roosevelt was content to leave in the hands of others.

Zahm's grasp of the actual requirements of such a journey, however, was far from certain. Zahm had billed himself as something of an expert on South America. In addition to his travels through the continent, he had also written several books on the subject. However, both *Up the Orinoco and Down the Magdalena* and *Along the Andes and Down the Amazon*—which Zahm had published under the pen name H. J. Mozans, Ph.D.—had generated skepticism within the country's relatively small circle of South American travelers. "With a wide knowledge of the history of the regions traversed," Frank Chapman would later write, "he seemed to have seen so little of the countries themselves that it was suggested he had never visited them."

If Roosevelt had concerns about his friend's abilities, he did not express them, perhaps because he did not expect the trip—conceived initially as a simple speaking tour—to prove too taxing. Rather, in a rare reference to his own age and mortality, Roosevelt merely cautioned the priest to be mindful of the potential risks inherent in such travel, and avoid imprudent choices in his planning. "[I] would like to get a fairly good idea of . . . the amount of mischance to which we would be exposed," he wrote Zahm. "I don't in the least mind risk to my life, but I want to be sure that I am not doing something for which I will find my physical strength unequal."

CHAPTER 3

Preparation

ALTHOUGH ROOSEVELT REMAINED MILDLY interested in his pending South American journey during the months before his departure, he viewed the expedition as little more than a "delightful holiday" that would provide "just the right amount of adventure." In fact, he was so certain that the trip would be uneventful that he left the planning almost entirely to Father Zahm, whom he affectionately though condescendingly referred to as "a funny little Catholic priest." In July, Roosevelt left New York for five weeks to go cougar hunting in Arizona with his two youngest sons, Archie and Quentin. The only instruction he offered Zahm before leaving was to say that, in regard to the expedition's proposed route, he refused to be the "thousandth American to visit Cuzco."

Having at last realized his long-standing ambition to return to South America, Father Zahm was now faced with the job of turning his dream into reality. Looking for assistance, he headed to the sporting-goods section of Rogers Peet & Company, the New York City department store, and fell into conversation with the head sporting-goods clerk, a man named Anthony Fiala. On the strength of

Fiala's evident interest in exploration, Father Zahm wasted no time in inviting him to join the Roosevelt party, quickly delegating the logistical burdens of the trip by placing his new friend in charge of selecting and ordering the expedition's provisions and equipment.

As convenient as it may have seemed to Zahm, however, the selection of Fiala as the expedition's quartermaster was less than auspicious for the expedition as a whole. For while the forty-four-year-old clerk did indeed have a background in exploration, the details of that experience arguably made him the last person on earth to be entrusted with the planning or provisioning of a scientific expedition. Despite his current job as a department-store clerk, nearly every explorer at the turn of the twentieth century knew who Anthony Fiala was. Indeed, his story was a cautionary tale of what can happen when an expedition goes terribly wrong and its commander survives to face derision from his peers and exclusion from his profession.

Ten years earlier, Fiala—tall and thin, with a prominent nose and a small, angular face—had been in a high-stakes race with an elite group of men for one of history's greatest geographical prizes: the North Pole. Fiala's first trip to the Arctic had been as the photographer for the Baldwin-Ziegler Expedition in 1901. When that mission failed to reach the pole, its leader, Evelyn Baldwin, was fired, and Fiala was promoted from photographer to commander of a second expedition in 1903. The renamed Fiala-Ziegler Expedition never made it farther north than 82 degrees. Its ship, crushed in the Arctic ice, sank, and Fiala and his men, out of the reach of rescue ships, were stranded in the icy north for two excruciating years. On Fiala's orders, the expedition's provisions were bundled together for safekeeping on the ice, which gave way one night as Fiala and his thirty-eight men slept. They awakened in horror to find half of their food supply and all of their coal lost; only the discovery of supplies from another expedition kept the entire party from perishing. Back in New York, Fiala had had to face his fellow explorers' brutal assessment of his leadership skills. They wasted no time on sympathy. On hearing details about the expedition, the renowned British naturalist and explorer

Henry Feilden excoriated it as "an ill conceived, badly managed, undisciplined venture," and its commander as "utterly incompetent." Fiala, Feilden wrote, "may be a fairly good cook but not a leader of men." It was clear that no one would be sending Anthony Fiala on another expedition anytime soon.

When Father Zahm happened into Rogers Peet a decade later looking for supplies for his trip with Roosevelt, his story of an impending journey into the Amazonian jungle tapped a wellspring of hope in Fiala. "I would give anything in the world to go with you," he told Zahm. Had Roosevelt been concerned about the trip he was about to take, he certainly would have hesitated to hire a man whose sole exploring experience had been in the Arctic—a region that had almost nothing in common with the Amazon—and who, while there, had led his men to a disaster of legendary proportions. But, given Zahm's enthusiasm about Fiala, Roosevelt, almost in passing, agreed to hire him—not merely as an extra hand, but as the man in charge of equipping the entire expedition.

*   *   *

ZAHM WAS thrilled. With Fiala now in the picture, the priest could simply delegate and pontificate, both of which he happily did. "A better man . . . could hardly have been found for our purposes," he wrote. "Thenceforward I had little more to do with the outfitting of the expedition than to tell Fiala what my experiences in the tropics had taught me was necessary for our undertaking, and everything was attended to with rare intelligence and dispatch."

The expedition's tentative plan was to start in Buenos Aires, Argentina, and then travel by boat northward up the length of the continent along well-known navigable rivers to the Amazon, giving Roosevelt a chance to observe a wide range of landscapes and animal life in relative comfort. After reaching the Amazon River, Roosevelt was considering traveling up the Rio Negro, whose black waters famously mix with the café-au-lait–colored Amazon at the junction of the two great rivers in north-central Brazil, then down the broad

Orinoco River, crossing Venezuela to the Atlantic Ocean. While such an itinerary would take the expedition into sparsely populated areas, and promised a fascinating tour of the continent's wilderness and wildlife, it would not be particularly taxing or dangerous, and was limited to well-charted rivers that could be expected to offer adventure without risk.

One of the earliest disagreements of the fledgling expedition was a dispute over the selection of boats to carry Roosevelt and his men along the rivers of South America. Despite the central role of river travel in the planned route, the specific requirements of that travel were largely a matter of mystery to those charged with outfitting the expedition. Apart from Father Zahm, whose time in South America had been primarily limited to sightseeing, none of the men involved in planning the trip had ever been to South America, or had any knowledge whatsoever of its rivers. Despite, or perhaps because of, that inexperience, each man developed a different idea about the type and characteristics of boat the expedition would need to complete its journey.

Fiala was looking forward to using the expedition to test a pet theory he had developed about canoes, and took the initiative to order two craft similar to those traditionally built by the native peoples of North America. He was convinced that the lightweight Northern canoes were much better suited for the Amazonian tributaries than the inflexible, heavy dugouts that they would find in South America. The canoes he ordered were nineteen feet long, built with a cedar frame, and covered in canvas. Where the rivers were navigable, each one could carry a ton of cargo and three to four men. Even better, they weighed only 160 pounds each, so four men—two if necessary— could pick them up and easily haul them for miles if the rivers became impassable.

Frank Harper, Roosevelt's British-born private secretary, concerned about Roosevelt's safety but otherwise lacking a clear professional basis for his opinion, favored instead a variety of stamped-steel boats manufactured by the W. H. Mullins Company of Salem, Ohio. Father

Zahm, meanwhile, had sent a check to the Rift Climbing Boat Company in Athens, Pennsylvania, in payment for a matching pair of eight-hundred-pound steel-hulled motorboats. Characteristically, Zahm also managed to prevail upon the company to make some improvements to the boats at the company's own expense, for the "glory" of it. He also ordered two custom pennants to announce the expedition with appropriate pomp and ceremony: one with an "R" for Roosevelt and the other with a "Z"—for Zahm.

While the chaos and costs surrounding the expedition's boats grew, Fiala set about providing for the rest of their needs, procuring the food and provisions the men would require, as he understood them. The quantity and variety were impressive, but the question of what items to include was something else entirely. Nearly as much thought seemed to have been put into the purchase of luxuries and incidentals as necessities. Fiala ordered pancake flour, sliced bacon, boned chicken, dehydrated potatoes, safety matches, and soap, but he also stocked up on smoking pipes (three dozen), two kinds of tobacco, malted milk, and twenty-four rolls of Challenge toilet paper. One heavy zinc-lined case included nothing but spices and gourmet condiments: tins of ground mustard, celery salt, poultry seasoning, paprika, cinnamon, nutmeg, chutney, orange and grapefruit marmalade, Tabasco sauce, and olive zest. Ever mindful that the expedition would be led by a former president, Fiala even sent Roosevelt a variety of teas so that he could select his favorite kind. "I am sending you five samples of tea," he wrote in early September, "and would appreciate it very much if you would test these and let me know which variety you prefer for your jungle trip."

* * *

BACK AT the American Museum of Natural History, Frank Chapman was looking for someone to accompany Roosevelt into the Amazon who actually had firsthand experience in that part of the world. Chapman and the museum's president, Henry Fairfield Osborn, were concerned about Roosevelt's safety, not only because he was an old friend but because they had the interests of their institution to consider. A former president of the United States was about to travel through the Amazon under the museum's auspices. If the expedition did not go well, or if Roosevelt was injured or became ill—or if the unthinkable happened and he was killed—the museum's reputation could be damaged beyond repair.

Roosevelt expected the journey to be safe and uneventful, but he was not deterred by the possibility that he could be wrong. Osborn could not have been happy to hear Roosevelt say, as he often did, that he did not mind risking his life on this expedition. After being told that he might encounter hostile Indians, white-water rapids, and deadly, disease-carrying insects, Roosevelt had said, "I'll reply to you as I did to the doctors who said they would not be responsible for the consequences if I delivered my address after being shot and wounded in Milwaukee: 'I'm ahead of the game and can afford to take the chances.' "

The museum, however, could not afford to take chances, so Chapman was determined to find a naturalist who not only was talented and experienced but could be counted on to ensure that Roosevelt returned from the Amazon—alive. In making his choice, Chapman knew that he could have his pick of the finest scientists and explorers in the country: Few scientists would pass up an opportunity to work for the American Museum of Natural History. As fate would have it, however, the man Chapman had picked for the job—a nearly forty-eight-year-old ornithologist and veteran explorer named George Cherrie—was also the only man who was likely to turn it down.

George Cherrie had spent the past quarter-century, more than half his life, collecting birds in South America. Although he had the lean, carved muscles of a jaguar and skin that looked as if it had been soaked in tannin and left to dry in the sun, Cherrie also had the refined features of a venerated statesman. His hair was closely clipped and graying, and he had a handsome face, a modest mustache, and a calm, dignified expression that unfailingly inspired trust and respect. If you were about to go into the Amazonian jungle, George Cherrie was the man you wanted by your side. Chapman had known Cherrie for more than thirty years and had recently accompanied him on an "exceptionally trying" collecting trip in Colombia. "He speaks Spanish like a native, is accustomed to roughing it, and is, besides, a capital traveling companion," Chapman told Father Zahm.

Cherrie received Chapman's letter on a scorching-hot day in July, while he was "lounging in comfortable fashion" in the speckled shade of an apple tree on his Vermont farm—Rocky Dell. Tearing open the envelope postmarked "New York" with his leathery hands, he found an invitation to join Roosevelt's expedition—a journey that would begin in the fall and, he knew, last well into the spring. "Having just returned from my twenty-fifth trip to that country," he later observed dryly, "my enthusiasm did not break bounds." Besides his reluctance to leave his family and his farm, which had been obliged to struggle on without him far too long and too often, Cherrie had little interest in tagging along with an official entourage or spending time, as he put it, "camping with royalty."

Despite such misgivings, Cherrie agreed to make the trip to New York in ten days to learn more about the expedition. Once he was at the museum, Chapman was able to remind him of the excitement of their recent adventures and the possibility of collecting specimens that were new to science. Chapman also offered the naturalist a salary of $150 per month, guaranteeing that he would be making nearly three times the average American worker's wage, and far more than he could have expected to receive from his own farm. By the end of the visit, Cherrie had agreed to repack the luggage he had so recently put down and to leave behind his family and farm for yet another long trip through the South American wilderness.

As extra insurance, Chapman also recruited another museum scientist, Leo Miller, who at twenty-six was already highly regarded by his colleagues, to accompany Roosevelt. Miller, who was already in South America collecting both birds and mammals for the museum, would be the designated mammalogist on the Roosevelt expedition, leaving the birds to Cherrie. This division of labor, Chapman reported to Osborn, would have the effect of "practically doubling the efficiency of the collecting force."

With the addition of Cherrie and Miller to the expeditionary team, Osborn relaxed, secure in the knowledge that Roosevelt would come home safely. Although the museum president would later insist that his friend had "prepared with the utmost intelligence and thoroughness for what he knew would be a hazardous trip," the truth was that at this point Roosevelt viewed the expedition as neither hazardous nor deserving of much time or thought. Osborn, however, had two reasons to feel confident. He had hired tough, experienced naturalists to accompany Roosevelt. Even more important, the expedition's intended route, although strenuous, was relatively well known and not particularly dangerous.

There was no cause for concern—so long as Roosevelt's plans did not change.

CHAPTER 4

On the Open Sea

O N THE MORNING OF October 4, 1913, the day he was to set sail for South America, Roosevelt arrived at Pier 8 in Brooklyn, New York. As he stepped from his car, he could see the *Vandyck*—a two-year-old, ten-thousand-ton steamship—towering, tall and majestic, above the farewell party that had gathered on the dock to wish him bon voyage. It was a bright, crisp, blue-sky morning, the perfect day for slipping away.

As soon as Roosevelt boarded the *Vandyck,* joking as he scaled the steep gangplank that "this is where I commence my mountaineering," he went straight to his suite of rooms to put away the belongings he had packed for the roughly two-and-a-half-week-long sea voyage ahead of him. Among those waiting patiently to shake hands with Roosevelt were three South American ambassadors who had come to Pier 8 to wish him a successful and, they dared to hope, uncontroversial journey. For the ambassadors—from the so-called ABC Powers of Argentina, Brazil, and Chile—Roosevelt's visit to their countries was as much a subject of concern as of pride, and with good reason. As president, Roosevelt had provoked more controversy in South

America than in any other region of the world, and although four years had passed since he had left the White House, South Americans had not forgotten his policies or his unapologetic imperialism.

Roosevelt was an avid proponent of the Monroe Doctrine, and he had even attached his own, imperialistic twist to it. Enunciated by President James Monroe in 1823, the doctrine sent a clear message to any European powers with colonial ambitions in South America that the United States would not stand idly by and allow the oppression, control, or colonization of any country in its hemisphere. On the contrary, such an act would, by definition, be considered hostile to the United States. The doctrine was put to the test in 1904, when Germany threatened to use military force against the Dominican Republic in an effort to collect unpaid debts. The small Latin American country turned to Roosevelt, who was then in the last year of his first term in the White House, for protection. In response, the president not only upheld the doctrine but added to it, creating what became known as the Roosevelt Corollary.

Whereas the Monroe Doctrine barred Europe from intervening in the affairs of any country in the Western Hemisphere, the Roosevelt Corollary asserted America's right to intervene whenever it felt compelled. "If a nation shows that it knows how to act with reasonable efficiency and decency in social and political matters, if it keeps order and pays its obligations, it need fear no interference from the United States," Roosevelt declared as he defined his corollary to Congress on December 6, 1904. "Chronic wrongdoing, or an impotence which results in a general loosening of the ties of civilized society . . . may force the United States, however reluctantly, in flagrant cases of such wrongdoing or impotence, to the exercise of an international police power." Roosevelt went on to add that the colossus to the north would intervene "only in the last resort," but that did little to reassure South Americans, or temper their outrage.

Nearly a decade later, South America still bristled at the inherent condescension and implied threat of the doctrine and its corollary. A few weeks before his departure, Roosevelt had received a letter from former New York Congressman Lemuel Quigg—a longtime supporter of Roosevelt's who had traveled through much of South America as a journalist—warning him that, if he planned to talk about the Monroe Doctrine on his trip, he could expect the political equivalent of being tarred, feathered, and ridden out of the continent on a rail.

The controversy surrounding the Roosevelt Corollary to the Monroe Doctrine had become even more acute in the months preceding Roosevelt's departure for South America, because the corollary was about to be tested. As Roosevelt prepared to set sail, Mexico was, as he had written to Kermit, "bubbling like a frying-pan," and Woodrow Wilson faced the unwelcome possibility of being forced to put Roosevelt's theory into action. The Mexican Revolution had been raging since 1910 and had already brought about the forced resignation and exile of one of the country's presidents and the imprisonment and assassination of another. The United States government was concerned about the revolution not only because Mexico was its closest neighbor to the south, or even because thousands of American expatriates were living there at the time, but because Americans had invested millions of dollars in the country. If the revolution continued to spin out of control, Wilson could decide at any moment to intervene—a step that South Americans expected, and bitterly resented.

* * *

IF THE United States did go to war with Mexico, Roosevelt was confident that his two oldest sons would be among the first to enlist. Theodore Jr. and Kermit had been raised by a father who was almost obsessed by war. Their grandfather, whom Roosevelt had idolized, had paid another man to fight for him during the Civil War, and Roosevelt had never gotten over it. It was relatively common at that time for wealthy men to pay poor men to take their place on the battlefield, and Roosevelt's father had taken this route not out of fear but out of respect for his wife, who was a Southerner and whose brothers were fighting in the Confederate Army. But Roosevelt could never understand what he saw as the one flaw in his father's otherwise irreproachable character. He would never miss a war, and neither would his sons. "I should regard it as an unspeakable disgrace if either of them failed to work hard at any honest occupation for his livelihood, while at the same time keeping himself in such trim that he would be able to perform a freeman's duty and fight as efficiently as anyone if the need arose," Roosevelt had written to the British historian and statesman George Otto Trevelyan after a post-Africa tour of Europe with Kermit in 1910.

The importance of a Latin American conflict loomed particularly large for Kermit, who had embraced the region and was quickly earning a reputation for himself in Brazil as a disciplined and high-minded young man. Thin and fair, with high cheekbones and deep-set eyes, Kermit did not look much like his heavy-featured father, nor did he have the elder Roosevelt's big, boisterous personality, but it was often said that he was, in many ways, more like his father than any of Roosevelt's other children. Not only did he love adventure, he loved to learn. He was a voracious reader, and he had an uncanny ability with languages. By the end of his life, Kermit spoke Arabic, Urdu, Hindustani, and Romany, not to mention French, German, and Spanish. He read Greek in the original, had earned his porters' respect and gratitude in Africa by learning Swahili, and was now speaking Portuguese like a native Brazilian.

Kermit also had, as his sister Ethel often said, "the soul of a poet." Before going to South America, Kermit had made a quick tour of Europe, stopping in England to stay with Rudyard Kipling. "He is very interested in South America, and wants to go there, as I suppose he will someday," Kermit wrote to a friend from Kipling's house. Kipling talked to Kermit about his poetry, explaining when and with what inspiration he wrote such immortal lines as those that had hung over the platform the night that the Progressive Party had nominated Roosevelt and Hiram Johnson to run for president and vice-president:

For there is neither East nor West,
Border nor breed nor birth,
When two strong men stand face to face,
Though they come from the ends of the earth.

No longer a boy—he would turn twenty-four in just six days—
Kermit was showing every sign of growing into the man that his
father had always hoped he would be. He had not only carved out a
life for himself under tough circumstances in Brazil, but he was earning his own way and was steadily establishing his independence.
Concerned that his son was getting "down to such a very simple diet
as a result of having no money at the end of the month," Roosevelt
had resolved in April to send him two hundred dollars each quarter.
By late July, however, Kermit was proudly tearing up his father's
checks. "Unless things go very badly I shan't need money unless I happened to marry. I'm now getting something more than a living wage,
and have about three hundred and fifty dollars in the bank," Kermit
told his father. "I wrote you that I had torn up the first check and I
have now torn up the second."

Although Kermit's pay had improved since he had first arrived in
Brazil, the conditions under which he was working had not. Not only
did he suffer from recurring bouts of malaria—a disease that he had
endured since childhood, having first succumbed to it in Washington,
D.C., in the days before the swamps on which the capital was built had
been drained—but he worked in remote, sparsely populated locations
near Indians who had had little interaction with white men beyond
occasional, violent clashes. Kermit took the dangers in stride. In a letter he wrote home the previous fall, while he was working for the
Brazil Railway Company, he had mentioned offhandedly that they
had had three derailments in a single week. "Twice it was a big box
car that went off, and once it was the engine," he wrote. "Only one of
them amounted to anything, and there we very nearly killed our
cook." A few weeks later, he mentioned that he did not think he

would be able to do much hunting for a while, "for the Indians are up, and have killed several engineers with their long arrows."

Kermit was now building bridges in the Xingu Valley, a job that, if possible, was even more dangerous than the work he had done for the railroad. The Xingu Valley, which covers 195,000 square miles of northeastern Brazil, had not been explored until 1884, and there were still far more native inhabitants in that stretch of the country than settlers. The job paid well, and it had the added benefit of pleasing and impressing Roosevelt, but it came at a cost. That summer, Kermit had nearly been killed when a bridge had collapsed while he was working on it and he had fallen thirty-five feet into a dry, rocky ravine. It wasn't anyone's fault, he had written to his parents, just "the chances of the game," but even he had to admit that it had been an incredibly close call. "I was bounced about like a ball," he wrote. "I didn't think I had a chance in a million nor did anyone else." From the bottom of the ravine, injured and stunned, Kermit had watched as the massive bridge, trailing steel guy wires, plummeted toward him, but he could not move fast enough to get out of its way. He lived to tell the story only because the bridge miraculously fell just short of him. He walked away from the accident with two broken ribs, two missing teeth, and a partially dislocated knee, and was, he told his father, "somewhat scarred on head and hands which looks bad and means nothing."

Kermit was tough, fearless, and independent, but, as his parents well knew, he was not invulnerable to setbacks or disappointment. Of all of Roosevelt's children, Kermit was the most sensitive. Even in childhood he had had a quiet, brooding disposition that gave him a gravitas that was startling for his age. "Kermit was a very solemn little boy," his older brother, Theodore Jr., recalled. "He was not talkative. As a result when he said anything it gave the impression of a carefully weighed accurate statement." Although he did not mind the difficult and dangerous conditions under which he worked in Brazil, the isolation from everything and everyone he knew had begun to wear on him. He even admitted to his father that just the sight of his parents' proposed itinerary for South America had made him "tremendously homesick."

Perhaps it was this loneliness, as much as anything else, that had led Kermit to fall in love with a girl he hardly knew—and had not laid eyes on for more than a year. Her name was Belle Willard, and she was, as one admiring newspaper account put it, "fortunate in having been able to live up to her name." Petite and blonde, with what the *New York Times* referred to as "clear-cut features," Belle was an heiress to a family fortune and the oldest daughter of Joseph Willard, the newly appointed American ambassador to Spain.

Kermit had met Belle when his sister Ethel invited her to Sagamore Hill one summer. Belle seemed to share all of Kermit's interests— from reading to traveling to even hunting—and they struck up a flirtatious friendship that survived in spite of Kermit's quick departure for Brazil. For the past year and a half, their relationship had grown by small, tentative steps through letters that followed Belle from her home state of Virginia, to New York, and then to Europe, and Kermit to Europe and South America. With each letter, the two young aristocrats grew warmer toward each other, more familiar, and more willing to show interest and even affection.

Kermit enjoyed his "gypsy life" in Brazil, but he never forgot Belle. On the contrary, he often worried that she would forget him. "No letter from you for ever so long. I'm afraid you've got engaged or married," he had written only half jokingly from Piracicaba, Brazil, in March. "I suppose I shall have the formal announcement the next time I get mail." Although he was looking forward to seeing his father, Kermit was saving his vacation time for Belle. "I don't want to ask for any holiday," he had written to her, "so that when you come I can have a good right to ask for one."

Kermit planned to meet his father in Bahia, a beautiful coastal town in central Brazil, but he did not plan to join him on his trek into the Amazon, nor did Roosevelt expect him to. Kermit had been the perfect companion in Africa, hardworking, uncomplaining, and independent, but he was a man now, and he had responsibilities that precluded such lighthearted excursions as this. Besides, Roosevelt did not think his son would be missing much. "It won't be anything like our Africa trip," he had assured Kermit in June. "There will be no hunting and no adventures so that I shall not have the pang I otherwise would about taking it and not taking you along—which of course would never do."

* * *

THE PROSPECT of seeing Kermit had helped persuade his father to make a visit to South America, but it was even more important in convincing Roosevelt's wife, Edith, to join him on the trip. After Kermit's fall, Ted Jr. had written his brother that their father had taken "a sort of grim pride in the fact that you are doing dangerous work in which you could be injured." Their mother, on the other hand, had felt Kermit's absence from her life even more deeply. Kermit and his mother had always had a close relationship, at times the envy of her other children, and since his move to Brazil, Edith had mourned not only his physical distance but his growing emotional independence. "I have not been able to help Father," she would confess to her daughter, Ethel, "and Kermit does not need me now." Edith, however, had decided to span those thousands of miles that separated her from her second son by accompanying her husband to South America. Although she would only stay for the first few months of Roosevelt's trip, she would be on the continent long enough to get a good, long look at Kermit and judge for herself whether or not he was indeed "all right again," as he had assured her from his hospital bed in São Paulo.

The real driving force behind Edith's decision to go to South America, however, was concern not for her son but for her husband. For Roosevelt, this journey was an opportunity to escape the doomed Progressive Party, his own humiliating defeat, and the self-doubt that had haunted him for the past year. For his wife, it was just another long, lonely separation—as painful as it was familiar. Edith had spent half her life waiting for Theodore to come home—from the battlefield, the campaign trail, hunting trips, and grand adventures. After the election, she had been hurt when he had decided to set sail once again, but she had not been surprised. "Father needs more scope," she had written to Ethel, "and since he can't be President must go away from home to have it."

Edith was also worried about Roosevelt's safety. He was no longer a young man, and he had driven his body too hard for too long. Worse, he had become secretive. She complained that Theodore had maintained a "sphinx-like silence" about his expedition into the Amazon. If he thought that his reticence might spare her worry, he was wrong. "I can but hope that the wild part of his trip is being more systematically arranged than is apparent," she had written Kermit just a few weeks before they sailed.

* * *

ON BOARD the *Vandyck,* while Roosevelt fielded reporters' questions and attempted to calm the South American ambassadors' fears, Father Zahm and Fiala desperately tried to tie up loose ends. It was only with much frantic telephoning and telegraphing that they got the last of the equipment and provisions on board and safely stored in the ship's hold. Roosevelt was getting nervous, because it was nearly 1:00 p.m., the time the *Vandyck* was scheduled to set sail, and no one had seen George Cherrie, the naturalist whom Frank Chapman had hand-picked for the expedition.

To add to the chaos, Father Zahm had decided at the eleventh hour to hire another man, a Swiss handyman named Jacob Sigg. Although Zahm had first met Sigg only a short time earlier, he envisioned the handyman as a perfect jack-of-all-trades—and, perhaps more important, as a capable personal assistant for the priest himself. These qualities, real or imagined, persuaded Zahm to overlook what even he himself acknowledged to be the handyman's "checkered career." In offering his services, Sigg had told Zahm, who had no real ability to check out his story, that he had been the chief engineer of an electrical power plant, had operated steam engines, served as a courier in

Europe, mined for gold in the Andes, helped build a railroad in Bolivia, and, incredibly, been the interpreter for an Indian princess. He could also drive a motorboat and an automobile (still a relatively rare skill at that time), speak Spanish and Portuguese, and shoot a gun. "And with all these qualifications," Zahm wrote enthusiastically, "he was brave and trustworthy, devoted and ready for any emergency, from extracting an ulcerated tooth and amputating a crushed finger to making an anchor for a disabled launch."

Roosevelt's team was becoming larger and more eclectic with each passing hour, but he knew that it would be seriously, and dangerously, incomplete without George Cherrie. At 1:00 p.m., the final gong sounded, warning anyone who was not a passenger to head quickly to shore or find himself steaming toward Barbados. Just as Roosevelt was beginning to think that his ornithologist was not going to make it, Cherrie raced up the pier and bounded on board. Although he had had his colleagues' hearts in their throats, Cherrie was casually but completely prepared for his twenty-sixth expedition to South America when the *Vandyck* slipped its moorings and plowed through the muddy East River en route to the sea.

* * *

THE MOMENT Manhattan melted into the horizon, Roosevelt was reborn. "I think he feels like Christian in *Pilgrims Progress* when the bundle fell from his back," Edith wrote her sister-in-law Bamie from her stateroom. "In this case it was not made of sins but of the Progressive Party." Although the real expedition had yet to begin, the Rooseveltian therapy of adventure and danger in a strange land was already working. Roosevelt had put the Progressive Party and his failed campaign behind him, and his thoughts and energy were focused on achieving something significant, something important in the Amazon. "If we have reasonably good luck we shall accomplish something worth accomplishing," he wrote to his daughter Ethel. "But of course there is enough chance in it to make me reluctant to prophesy."

Zahm, on the other hand, not only confidently predicted the expedition's success, he was already busy trying to negotiate a potentially lucrative little deal with one of the country's best-respected and best-funded institutions: The National Geographic Society. "Ask [Gilbert] Grosvenor [the editor-in-chief of *National Geographic* magazine] if he would like a series of first-class photographs—with a suitable description—of the heart of South America," he instructed his brother, Albert. "They will be the best and rarest ever taken and will possess a special value for his magazine. Try, diplomatically, to learn what he would give for a good, illustrated article with absolutely new and unique photographs. But do not let him know that I have written you about the matter. Act as if you were doing it spontaneously and in his interest."

In her suite on the *Vandyck*'s B deck, which had been reserved for the Roosevelts' private use, Edith pursued rest and relaxation. Most days she did not even get dressed until the afternoon, when she would pull on long white gloves and a veil and sit on the ship's deck to listen to her cousin Margaret Roosevelt, who had volunteered to accompany her to South America, read aloud. Margaret, the daughter of Theodore's cousin Emlen, was a vibrant young woman who radiated health and enthusiasm. Twenty-five years old, she was an athlete—equally skilled at golf, tennis, and riding—and she loved adventure. Lately, she had become one of Edith's favorite companions.

Theodore also approved of Margaret and was prepared to let his young cousin and his wife have an adventure of their own. "Margaret has proved a delightful companion," he wrote to Ethel. "I am now quite at ease about having Mother and her go up the West Coast from Chile together." Margaret and Edith had planned to make a trip to Panama after Roosevelt set off for the Brazilian interior. Margaret was looking forward to it, but there were plenty of distractions on board the *Vandyck* to keep her amused until they reached South America, including the flattering attentions of a fellow passenger, a man named Henry Hunt.

The men of the Roosevelt South American Scientific Expedition—

newly christened during a last-minute meeting at the Harvard Club in New York City—spent most of their time thinking about and planning for the Amazon. Fiala could usually be found hunched over his sextant and theodolite, examining the surveying tools he had used ten years earlier in the Arctic. Cherrie busied himself with his collecting equipment, and Frank Harper studied his new Kodak camera—an invention that was fast becoming a national craze—which he had bought for the trip.

Six days out of New York, the *Vandyck* picked up the young naturalist Leo Miller in Barbados. It was too early to tell what kind of camp companion he would be, but Roosevelt liked what he saw in Miller, and in all of his men. "I am pleased with the entire personnel of the trip," he wrote to Chapman. "Evidently Cherrie and Miller will more than justify your choice of them." Roosevelt's men were equally pleased with their commander. Most of them had known Roosevelt only as a remote and exalted president of the United States, but he soon put them at ease with his tales of hunting grizzlies and stalking lions and his sincere interest in their own lives. "The Colonel's friendly interest in each member of the party and his almost boyish enthusiasm for the project in hand won our confidence and loyalty at the outset," Cherrie wrote.

During the voyage to sun-soaked Bahia, the day-to-day routine of eating, reading, and sleeping gave way to more unusual activities. One particularly rowdy event was a pillow fight between two men straddling a spar laid across a tank of water. The match was a great spectator sport, but it rarely ended in a decisive victory. The combatants were not allowed to lock their feet beneath the pole, so both men usually ended up pitching headfirst into the tank. There was also a tug-of-war contest, in which, Cherrie reported, Roosevelt's "two hundred and twenty pounds of avoir-dupois were the deciding factors," and then, at night, there was dancing. One evening, after dinner, even the former president made his way onto the floor. Arms crossed and legs flying, he danced a rousing hornpipe "in true sailor fashion," Cherrie recalled, and brought down the house.

* * *

WHILE ROOSEVELT set his cares aside and enjoyed himself for the first time in a long time on the *Vandyck,* his son Kermit sat alone, brooding in his cabin aboard the SS *Voltaire,* which was carrying him northward to Bahia. He was looking forward to seeing his parents again, but his mind was somewhere else entirely. The longer he had remained in Brazil, and the more lonely and isolated he had become, the more perfect Belle Willard had seemed. Finally, Kermit had come to the conclusion that he simply could not live without her. His heart bursting, he picked up a piece of the ship's stationery and sat down to write the most important letter of his life.

Dear Belle,

I've been thinking about this letter for a very long time and have thought that I had no right to send it, but fools rush in where angels fear to tread, and I suppose that's what I'm doing; for I don't think that I have any right to write, but Belle I love you very much and want you to marry me. . . . Belle, I couldn't go on writing to you and not tell you for I do love you so very much, and tho' I know how very unworthy I am of you, I can't help writing you this. Oh I would give anything to be able to go over and see you and tell you this, but I've got my way to make in the world, and I couldn't ask you unless I had work which looked as if I could make it; and I couldn't keep my position here if I just went away with no explanation. I would do anything in the world for you Belle, leave anything, or go anywhere if I felt you wanted me to, but you wouldn't have wanted me to do that; for I must try to prove myself in some way worthy of you, no matter in how small a way. But oh Belle if we were we could go anywhere and succeed, I know that. Please, please forgive me if this is all wrong to you, and I should never have spoken, but it was more than I could do not to write for I love you so, that all the time that you were so far away just seems so much time when I'm not living but perhaps might be. It's so very hard to put this in writing and you must read a lot that I have not written and would never know how to write. I've wished and prayed so much that you might love me, and perhaps you might tho' I can't seem to believe that you could.

Good night Belle and please forgive me if I'm doing wrongly.

Kermit

A Change of Plans

I T   T O O K   E I G H T   D A Y S for the *Vandyck,* trailing a white ribbon of foam, to steam from Barbados to Bahia, Brazil, roughly a third of the way down South America's Atlantic seaboard. It would have been a much shorter trip but for the continent's enormous northeastern coastline, which juts into the ocean like a broad shoulder, forcing ships to travel hundreds of miles east before resuming their southward journey. Three days before reaching Bahia, the steamer crossed the equator, an event that the crew and passengers celebrated with practical jokes and deck games, in keeping with nautical tradition. But for Roosevelt and his men, crossing from the Northern to the Southern Hemisphere was especially significant, because it meant that they were passing the natural wonder that was to be the ultimate object of their journey: the Amazon River.

From the deck of the *Vandyck,* out of sight of shore as they steamed along the Brazilian coast, Roosevelt and his men could not see the Amazon. But even at sea there was no escaping the sheer size and power of the giant river, a nonstop deluge that by itself accounts for approximately 15 percent of all fresh water carried to sea by all of the planet's rivers put together. The river's mouth is so vast that the island that rests in the middle of it, Marajó, is nearly the size of Switzerland, and the muddy plume that spills into the Atlantic reaches some hundred miles out into the open sea.

For Roosevelt, the prospect of exploring such a magnificent, unfamiliar phenomenon of nature was irresistible. The ex-president was no doubt also thrilled that the mighty Amazon was intimately related to another region he had explored and come to love so well—Africa. As reflected by the very route that the *Vandyck* was following around the bulging coastline of South America, the continent had once been connected to Africa, fitting neatly under the chin of West Africa, just below what is today the string of small countries that reaches from Liberia to Nigeria.

Floating upon the planet's underlying core of molten rock, the plates that make up the earth's outer shell have shifted slowly but continuously throughout the planet's history—a process known as plate tectonics. Hundreds of millions of years ago, the South American continent was part of a single primal "protocontinent" known as Pangaea, which covered half the earth. During the Triassic period, Pangaea began to separate into two independent continents—a northern continent, known as Laurasia, and a southern continent, Gondwanaland.

Approximately ninety million years ago, Gondwanaland, which encompassed Africa, Australia, Antarctica, peninsular India, and South America, also broke apart. The South American landmass drifted westward until it collided with the Nazca Plate, which underlies much of the Pacific Ocean. When the two enormous plates met, the momentum of the impact thrust the western edge of South America over the edge of the Nazca Plate. The result was a continent-long spine of rock and stone that formed what are known today as the Andes Mountains.

The creation of the Andes dramatically altered South America's rainfall patterns and river system. Prior to the rise of the Andes, the Amazon River had flowed in the opposite direction from its present course, descending northwestward and separated from the Atlantic

Ocean to the east by a high stone ridge. The rise of the Andes blocked that westward route to the Pacific, leaving the continent's rivers and streams no outlet to the sea on east or west. Cut off by the narrow cordon of mountains, rain that fell as little as a hundred miles from the Pacific Ocean could no longer reach it, and instead flowed back eastward, flooding the center of the landmass.

Beyond merely redirecting the drainage of rain that fell upon the continent, the towering mountains also changed the location of the rainfall itself. By creating a barrier that reaches as high as twenty thousand feet, the Andes serve as a trap for moisture-laden winds from the interior, forcing clouds high into the atmosphere, where they condense and bathe the Andes' eastern slopes and the basin's lowland forests in nearly constant precipitation.

For millions of years, the Amazon River was a vast inland sea that covered the central part of the continent. Finally, during the Pleistocene epoch, which began approximately 1.6 million years ago, the rising waters broke through the continent's eastern escarpment and poured into the Atlantic Ocean. In their wake, they left behind the world's greatest river system and the former inland seabed—a vast basin of rich sediments and fertile lowlands perfectly suited to support an array of plant and animal life almost without parallel on the face of the earth.

For all its exotic allure and potential riches, the great Amazon River Basin in 1913 remained a vast and remarkably mysterious place, untouched by modernity and repelling all but the most determined attempts to explore its hidden secrets. Although more than two-thirds of the Amazon Basin rests within Brazilian borders, the vast majority of Brazilians in the early twentieth century, crowded along the sun-soaked eastern coast, had little interest in knowing what lay within the basin and no way to find out even if they had.

Communication between the coastal cities and the country's largely unexplored interior was difficult, and travel was nearly impossible for the average person. The country's sheer size was one impediment; its dense forests and rapids-choked rivers were another. The world's fifth-largest nation, Brazil encompasses 3.3 million square miles, making it more than two hundred and fifty thousand square miles larger than the contiguous United States. The approximately four-thousand-mile-long Amazon River slices through the northern section of the country and is navigable for almost three-quarters of its length—roughly the distance from Bangor, Maine, to San Francisco, California—but its thousands of tributaries, which reach like tentacles into every corner of Brazil, are fast, twisting, and wild. Until very late in the nineteenth century, the only alternative for entering the interior was by mule, over rutted dirt roads and through heavy jungle and wide, barren highlands.

The potential political consequences of such a vast, unknown territory in the heart of their country had been brought home to Brazilian leaders in 1865, when Paraguay invaded Brazil along its southern boundary and more than a month passed before the emperor, Pedro II, knew anything about it. Before he abdicated the throne twenty-five years later, Pedro II, who had reigned over Brazil since he was five years old, committed part of his military to the monumental task of linking Brazil's coast with its interior by telegraph line. Stringing the line through the jungle had since cost the Strategic Telegraph Commission the lives of countless men, but the battalion had explored thousands of miles of wilderness and was slowly mapping large swaths of the northern and southern highlands and the wide Amazon Basin.

Despite the progress the telegraph commission had made, however, vast stretches of Brazil remained unknown and unmapped, and its promise of adventure and discovery would soon prove too strong for Roosevelt to resist. The route that Father Zahm had drawn up entailed travel along five of the best-known rivers on the continent: the Paraná, the Paraguay, the Tapajos, the Negro, and the Orinoco, each of which appeared on even the most rudimentary maps of South America. Within days of his arrival in Brazil, however, Roosevelt would abandon Zahm's tame itinerary and commit himself to an expedition that was much more interesting—and exponentially more dangerous.

* * *

ON OCTOBER 18, 1913, the *Vandyck* landed in Bahia, Brazil, where Kermit Roosevelt was waiting for his parents on a flag-draped launch that the city's governor had sent into the harbor to welcome the former president of the United States to South America. It was a flawless day, and the passengers of the *Vandyck* were all gathered on the deck for their first glimpse of Bahia, one of the country's oldest and most beautiful cities.

Thousands of Brazilians waited on shore to greet Roosevelt, but he stayed in the city only long enough to take a tour, meet the governor, and pick up Kermit. He wanted to make sure that he was in Rio de Janeiro, then Brazil's capital, by October 21, in time for a meeting he had arranged with Lauro Müller, Brazil's minister of foreign affairs. A week earlier, aboard the *Vandyck*, Roosevelt had written to the minister gently reminding him that Ambassador Don Domicio da Gama had volunteered the Brazilian government's help in transporting the expedition's unwieldy boats and five tons of baggage overland from the Paraguay River to where they planned to begin their descent of the Tapajos.

Da Gama had also offered to provide Roosevelt with a guide, but not just any guide. He had promised him Colonel Cândido Mariano da Silva Rondon, the heroic commander of the Strategic Telegraph Commission. The forty-eight-year-old Rondon had spent half his life exploring the Amazon and had traversed roughly fourteen thousand miles of wilderness that was not only unmapped but largely unknown to anyone but the indigenous peoples who lived there. On October 4, the day that Roosevelt had set sail for South America, Rondon had just completed an inspection trip to Barra dos Bugres, the farthest point south on his telegraph line. Upon returning to one of his less remote outposts, he had found a telegram from Müller, an old military-academy classmate of his, waiting for him. Rondon had not been surprised to receive a cable from Rio—he had instructed the Central Office to send him regular telegrams with news of the outside world, messages that the telegraph operators had nicknamed "the Rondon newspaper"—but he was surprised by its contents: an order to travel with Theodore Roosevelt into the Amazon.

Rondon had accepted the assignment, but, like Cherrie, he had done so with reservations. He had made it clear to his superiors that he would join this expedition only if it was a serious scientific endeavor. He would not be a tour guide, nor would he join a hunting safari. "The fact is," one of Rondon's soldiers later wrote, "after Roosevelt made his expedition to Africa, the general assumption was that he was motivated exclusively by hunting concerns."

Unknown to Rondon, the type of trip that he demanded was increasingly what Roosevelt had in mind. The ex-president had come to the Amazon for neither tourism nor sport but for scientific exploration, and he held the deepest disdain for anyone who wanted anything less. "The ordinary traveller, who never goes off the beaten route and who on this beaten route is carried by others, without himself doing anything or risking anything, does not need to show much more initiative and intelligence than an express package," Roosevelt sneered. "He does nothing; others do all the work, show all the forethought, take all the risk—and are entitled to all the credit. He and his valise are carried in practically the same fashion; and for each the achievement stands about on the same plane."

Müller, a sophisticated, cosmopolitan man who reminded Roosevelt of his own secretary of state, John Hay, quickly understood that what his distinguished guest really wanted was an expedition that had much more potential for scientific discovery and historical resonance than the journey that Father Zahm had laid out for him. With a single question—startling for its simplicity in light of the series of events that it set in motion—Müller made Roosevelt an offer. "Colonel Roosevelt," he asked, "why don't you go down an unknown river?"

*   *   *

THE RIVER that Müller had in mind was one of the great remaining mysteries of the Brazilian wilderness. Absent from even the most accurate and detailed maps of South America, it was all but unknown to the outside world. In fact, the river was so remote and mysterious that its very name was a warning to would-be explorers: Rio da Dúvida, the River of Doubt.

Even Rondon, who had discovered and named the river, had been able to tell Müller very little about its course or its character. Rondon had stumbled upon its source five years earlier while on a telegraph line expedition in the Brazilian Highlands, the ancient plateau region south of the Amazon Basin, and he and his men had followed it just long enough to realize that they would need a separate expedition, one solely devoted to mapping its entire length, to know anything of substance about it. When he was told that Roosevelt's objective was to "unravel the unknown aspects of our wilds," Rondon himself had proposed the descent of the River of Doubt as one of five possible alternatives to Zahm's more conventional route. No one who knew Roosevelt would have been surprised to learn that, of the five alternatives, he quickly chose the one that, in Rondon's words, "offered the greatest unforeseen difficulties."

Even in a time when great feats of discovery were almost commonplace, a descent of the River of Doubt would be audacious. Not only was the river unmapped—its length and direction unknown and each whirlpool, rapid, and waterfall a sudden and potentially deadly surprise—but it coursed through a dense, tangled jungle that had a dark history of destroying the men who hoped to map it.

One of the Amazon's earliest explorers, the first nonnative to descend the Amazon River, Francisco de Orellana, suffered more than most. Orellana, who had lost one of his eyes during the conquest of the Incas in Peru, plunged into the Amazon rain forest in 1541, in the hope of discovering the legendary kingdom of El Dorado, whose ruler was said to coat his body in gold dust and then wash it off in a sacred lake. Orellana's expedition, however, soon changed from a search for gold to a battle for survival. According to a friar who traveled with the expedition and chronicled its journey, before the men even reached the Amazon River, they were reduced to "eating nothing but leather, belts and soles of shoes, cooked with certain herbs." Once on the river, they fought nearly every Indian tribe they encountered, eventually losing roughly a dozen men to starvation and three others to poisonous arrows. Incredibly, Orellana survived to repeat the ordeal just three years later, this time losing 172 men to starvation and Indian attacks before himself succumbing to disease and, some said, heartbreak at the disastrous collapse of his ambitions.

Thirteen years later, another ill-fated Spanish expedition, this one led by thirty-four-year-old Pedro de Ursúa, set out to find El Dorado, which was rumored to lie at the headwaters of the Amazon River. Although Ursúa had had many successes in his young life, on this expedition he made the fatal mistake of hiring Lope de Aguirre, a man whose name would later become practically synonymous in South America with deceit and brutality. As soon as the expedition reached the Amazon's headwaters, Aguirre led a mutiny, murdering Ursúa in his hammock and installing another man, Fernando de Guzmán, as the expedition's commander. Guzmán then met his own end one morning when Aguirre and a band of men awakened him at dawn and, after reassuring him—"Do not be alarmed, Your Excellency"— shot him at point-blank range with their heavy matchlock guns, known as arquebuses. Aguirre then took command of the expedition and tore through what is now Venezuela, ransacking towns, killing inhabitants, and burning homes. Spanish royalists finally caught up with him in Peru in late October 1561. In a bloody standoff, Aguirre was shot to death by two of his own men. He was then beheaded and his body quartered, gutted, and tossed into the road.

The stories of death and disaster in the Amazon did not end with the withdrawal of the colonial powers from South America. As long as there was a wilderness in the heart of the continent, it seemed, men would be willing to risk their lives to find its riches, or at least discover what lay within. Less than twenty-five years before Roosevelt arrived in South America, a Brazilian engineer officer, Colonel Teles Pires, hoping to chart the course of an unmapped river that, like the River of Doubt, poured out of the Brazilian Highlands, lost all of his provisions in a descent through whitewater rapids. The expedition was then beset with fever and starvation, and in the end only three men survived. Pires was not one of them.

The very idea of Theodore Roosevelt on a river that was as remote and unknown as the one that had killed Pires and his men was enough to make Foreign Minister Müller quickly regret his impulsive suggestion that Roosevelt change his trip. "Now, we will be delighted to have you do it, but of course, you must understand we cannot tell you anything of what will happen," Müller hastened to warn Roosevelt. "And there may be some surprises not necessarily pleasant."

If Müller was nervous about Roosevelt's decision to descend an unmapped river, Henry Fairfield Osborn was thunderstruck. The news, which Frank Chapman delivered to Osborn after receiving a letter from Roosevelt, set off alarm bells at the American Museum of Natural History. Horrified, Osborn immediately sent a blistering message to Roosevelt that he would "never consent to his going to this region under the American Museum flag." This was not remotely the journey they had agreed on, and Osborn fumed that he "would not even assume part of the responsibility for what might happen in case [Roosevelt] did not return alive."

Roosevelt's admission that his new plan was "slightly more hazardous" than the original was, according to Frank Chapman, the understatement of the century. "In a word," the bird curator later wrote, "it may be said with confidence . . . that in all South America there is not a more difficult or dangerous journey than that down the [River of Doubt]." Roosevelt was more than willing to accept that danger for himself, but he would not force his men to do the same. Turning to his naturalists, his secretary, and his old friend Father Zahm, Roosevelt assured them that they were free to leave the expedition if they wished. "If they had the slightest hesitation I would take them with me to the headwaters of the unknown river and then go down it myself with Col. Rondon and my son Kermit, and I would send them back with the collections to the Paraguay and then home," he later wrote Chapman. To Roosevelt's surprise, each of the men—even Zahm, who had drafted the original route—agreed to the drastic change of plans.

The journey that Roosevelt had lightheartedly described as his "last chance to be a boy" had suddenly turned into his first chance to be something that he had always dreamed of being: an explorer. "The little boy of six in the nursery on 20th Street had read with fervent interest of the adventures of the great explorer Livingstone," Roosevelt's sister Corinne would later write. "He had achieved his ambition to follow those adventures as a mighty hunter in Africa; he had achieved many another ambition, but none was more intense with him than the desire to put [the] 'River of Doubt' on the map of the world."

Roosevelt lived during the last days of the golden age of exploration, a time when men and women of science roamed the world, uncovering its geographical secrets at a breathtaking pace and giving rise to bitter international competitions. The year he was born, the earnest young explorer John Hanning Speke, traveling with the famed Orientalist Richard Burton, discovered the source of the White Nile. In 1909, the year that Roosevelt left the White House, Americans Robert Peary and Matthew Henson won the race to reach the North Pole—the race that had nearly cost Fiala his life and the lives of all his men. Just two years later, in late December 1911, Norwegian explorer Roald Amundsen became the first man to reach the South Pole. Robert Scott, a renowned explorer and British hero, made it to the pole a month later, only to find the Norwegian colors flapping in the polar wind where he had planned to plant the British flag. Shocked and dispirited, Scott and his men froze to death on their long, bitter journey back to their ship. Sir Ernest Shackleton and his men, in a legendary attempt to cross Antarctica, narrowly escaped the same fate two years later, the same year that Roosevelt would set off down the River of Doubt.

To Osborn, Roosevelt's decision to descend this river seemed insane if not suicidal, and he ordered Chapman to tell the former president that the American Museum of Natural History expected him to adhere to his original plan. However, when Chapman's letter, with all the weight of the museum behind it, reached Brazil, it had less effect than a leaf falling in the rain forest. Having found the challenge he had been yearning for, Roosevelt was beyond the reach of Osborn's persuasion. In a letter to Chapman, Roosevelt wrote, "Tell Osborn I have already lived and enjoyed as much of life as any nine other men I know; I have had my full share, and if it is necessary for me to leave my bones in South America, I am quite ready to do so."

* * *

OSBORN'S OBJECTION to Roosevelt's new expedition was not only that it would take him through one of the most remote and least known regions of the Amazon rain forest, but that it was based on a sudden decision. The months of planning that had taken place in New York the past summer had been for a completely different kind of journey, one that could not be easily, much less quickly, adapted to fit the new route. Even Roosevelt had to admit that the man he had originally entrusted with planning his Amazon expedition was far out of his league when it came to the descent of the River of Doubt. "Father Zahm is a perfect trump," he wrote to Chapman on November 4. "But he knows nothing of any of the country which we have planned to go through, and in practice can give us no help or advice as to methods of travelling and what we will or will not be actually able to accomplish."

Zahm put on a brave face, writing to his brother, Albert, that he was "most eager to begin the strictly scientific part of our trip—the exploration of an unknown river and an unknown region," but the abrupt change of plans must have been deeply disappointing. After little more than a week in South America, he was already beginning to lose control of his trip—a journey that he had conceived of, waited five years for, and lovingly planned. Zahm must have known that it would be unlikely that he would play a central role in the new expedition, if any role at all.

It was becoming apparent to everyone in the expedition that they were not as well prepared for a journey, of any kind, into the Amazon as they had allowed themselves to believe. One of the most essential items for their trip—the motorboats that Father Zahm had ordered—not only were unsuitable for the new expedition, they would have been inappropriate even for the original route. Brazilians who had traveled in the Amazon took one look at the massive boats and bluntly told Roosevelt that it would be impossible to transport them through the jungle.

Also, the provisions that Fiala had so carefully chosen and packed were more of a burden than a blessing in the eyes of the other men on the expedition. When Roosevelt's party reached Buenos Aires, the sheer volume of baggage that was unloaded from the *Vandyck* drew a crowd of curious onlookers. There were mountains of crates: guns and ammunition, chairs and tables, tents and cots, equipment for collecting and preserving specimens, surveying the river and cooking meals. After one of the baggage handlers, soaked in sweat, carried the final item from the steamer to the dock, a customs officer asked him if everything was now accounted for. Mopping his brow, the stevedore replied, "Nothing lacking but the piano!" and the crowd erupted in laughter. Even worse for Fiala and Sigg, soon after they disembarked, the two men found themselves the lone custodians of this mountain of bags, boxes, and crates. Leo Miller and Cherrie promptly excused themselves, explaining that they needed to start doing some collecting, and fled to Asunción, Paraguay, leaving their companions to struggle with what Miller referred to as the expedition's "appalling amount of luggage."

* * *

ROOSEVELT, FOR his part, would have no opportunity to help get his expedition on track. From the moment he set foot in South America, he was plunged into a nonstop whirlwind of political commitments and controversies. His speaking tour through Brazil,

Uruguay (a last-minute addition), and Argentina would follow a fishhook-shaped course down the Atlantic coast and then westward to Chile, before returning to Brazil and the Amazon.

Frankly, Roosevelt was not looking forward to any of it. "I loathe state-traveling and speechmaking! Ugh!," he wrote to his daughter Ethel in early December. He knew that his expedition through the Amazon would be difficult, but he suspected that it would be "less unhealthy than a steady succession of dreary 'banquets,' and of buckets of sweet tepid champagne." Zahm, on the other hand, delighted in the endless parade of banquets and dinners and basked in the glow of Roosevelt's reflected fame. "As you will see from the papers sent you, I have covered much ground since I wrote you and have been lionized everywhere, notwithstanding the fact that there has been a very big lion with me," he wrote his brother. "If I were young enough to be spoiled, I should now be beyond redemption."

The excitement with which Roosevelt was met in nearly every city he visited—in countries whose governments and citizens supposedly feared and hated him—was testimony to the Rough Rider's legendary charm. Not everyone in South America admired Theodore Roosevelt, however, and he soon found that his detractors were as loud and passionate in their derision as his supporters were in their praise. Although Father Zahm would later refer to the tour as one "continuous ovation," Chile was a notable exception. Students at the university in Santiago disagreed with Roosevelt on several serious issues, not the least of which was the Panama Canal.

Roosevelt considered the Panama Canal to be one of the greatest achievements of his presidency, and he believed that the canal's architectural genius and the indelible mark that it—and, through it, he—would leave on the world more than justified the small South American revolution he had had to foment in order to make it a reality. In 1903, Roosevelt's third year in the White House, the United States government decided, after much heated debate, that Panama rather than Nicaragua would be the best location for a canal that would connect the Atlantic and Pacific Oceans. At that time, Panama was a state within Colombia, and so Roosevelt had offered Colombia twelve million dollars for the right to build the canal. When the Colombian Senate countered with restrictive treaty language and a demand for more money, Roosevelt's response was impatience and contempt. He wrote to his secretary of state, John Hay, that the United States should not allow the "lot of jackrabbits" in Colombia "to bar one of the future highways of civilization," and he proceeded quietly to encourage and support a Panamanian revolution that had been bubbling under the surface for years.

On November 3, 1903, with U.S. Navy ships lined up in nearby waters, Panama declared its independence. Fifteen days later, John Hay and Philippe Bunau-Varilla, a Frenchman who had been the canal's chief engineer, signed the Hay-Bunau-Varilla Treaty, which gave the United States control of the Canal Zone, a five-mile-wide swath of land on either side of the waterway. A decade later, the Colombians were still fuming. When asked by a Brazilian official why he had left Colombia off of his South American itinerary, Roosevelt had replied, "Don't you know, my dear friend, that I am not a 'persona grata' in Colombia?"

Although Roosevelt had steered clear of Colombia, he would not be able to avoid a hostile encounter in Chile, where Colombian students had organized protests against him. When his train pulled into Chile's capital, Santiago, in late November, he was greeted by a crowd that at first seemed to mirror the friendly masses that had welcomed him to Brazil, Uruguay, and Argentina. But the moment he leapt from his Pullman to the train-station floor, with the triumphal strains of the American and Chilean national anthems echoing around him, his welcoming party suddenly transformed into an angry protest rally. "The human multitude, showing marked hostility, shouted with all their might vivas!—to Mexico and Colombia, and Down with the Yankee Imperialism!" a journalist for Lima's *West Coast Leader* excitedly reported.

The Chilean government went to great lengths to shield Roosevelt from the demonstrations, even buying and destroying newspapers that covered anti-Roosevelt rallies, but their guest had no desire to hide from any assault on himself or his country. On the contrary, he took every opportunity to face down his attackers, ready to explain in no uncertain terms why he was right and they were wrong. At a state reception welcoming him to Chile, he vigorously debated Marchial Martínez, a former Chilean ambassador to the United States, about the continued relevance of the Monroe Doctrine. Days later, in an electrifying speech, he gave an impassioned, utterly unapologetic defense of the Panama Canal.

The speech was Roosevelt's last in Chile, and it left the country, if not convinced of Roosevelt's righteousness, at least impressed by his conviction. "As soon as he began to advert to the subject everyone was attention, and the silence that prevailed was almost painful," Zahm later recalled. "The large auditorium in which he spoke seemed to be surcharged with electricity and everyone seemed to be prepared for a shock or an explosion. Everything—the environment, the speaker, the subject, the great historical event under review—was dramatic in the extreme, and everyone felt that it was dramatic."

Drama was Roosevelt's forte, and few subjects stirred him to greater emotion than did the Panama Canal. Whatever animosities may have been harbored against him when he began speaking, he had his audience in his pocket by the time he walked out the door. "I love peace, but it is because I love justice and not because I am afraid of war," Roosevelt told the spellbound crowd. "I took the action I did in Panama because to have acted otherwise would have been both weak and wicked. I would have taken that action no matter what power had stood in the way. What I did was in the interest of all the world, and was particularly in the interests of Chile and of certain other South American countries. I was in accordance with the highest and strictest dictates of justice. If it were a matter to do over again, I would act precisely and exactly as I in very fact did act." As these words rang through the hall, the audience leapt to its feet, cheering and applauding the Yankee imperialist.

* * *

WHILE ROOSEVELT was distracted from his pending expedition by a thousand different commitments, his son and young cousin had only one thing on their minds: love. While in Buenos Aires, Margaret Roosevelt had received bunches of white roses every day from Henry Hunt, her admirer from the *Vandyck*.

Kermit, for his part, was still waiting miserably for a reply to the marriage proposal he had sent Belle a month earlier. He was a confident young man, but Belle had always seemed elusive, and Kermit was far from certain that she would agree to marry him. Not only was he thousands of miles away from her, but he had been so for more than a year. He also was not living in the kind of place that would necessarily appeal to a girl like Belle. While working on the railroad, Kermit had lived in a retired day coach that could barely accommodate him and his few belongings. Perhaps worst of all, in the rural areas where he worked, there was a nearly constant threat of disease.

Kermit had had so many recurring bouts of malaria since he had moved to Brazil that the disease had become almost commonplace for him. It would not, however, seem commonplace to Belle, nor did it to Kermit's parents. When Roosevelt had first seen his son in Bahia, he had written to his sister Bamie that Kermit was not "in quite as good health as I should like to see him." On the other hand, Roosevelt wrote, "He has matured very much. He earns $2,500 a year [the equivalent of about forty-five thousand dollars today], is deeply interested in his work, and it looks as if he has a future."

Kermit hoped that that future would be solid enough to impress Belle, but he could not be sure. She was a beautiful, wealthy girl who was surrounded by America's and Europe's most eligible young bachelors. He knew that she could have any man she wanted. What he did not know was whether she wanted him. On November 14, he finally got his answer:

> Dear Kermit,
> I'm very glad you did send the letter, because, I do love you, and will marry you. I don't know how, or why you should love me—

perhaps because I too have prayed,—& been unhappy—and now you love me and my heart is very full—What have I done that God should choose me out of all this world for you to love—but as He has done this, so perhaps He will make me a little worthy of your love. May He keep you safe for me! I love you, Kermit, I love you

　　Belle

When Kermit read Belle's reply, all of his worrying, all of the excruciating weeks of waiting, were forgotten. He was obliged to attend a formal luncheon and an elaborate dinner that day, but he floated through both events in a joyous fog. "I don't remember a word I said tho' I remember all I thought for I was with you the whole time," he wrote her. "It just seems like a dream, dearest, and I get so afraid that I may wake, for if it's a dream I want to stay asleep forever."

Roosevelt was thrilled for his son. "Kermit is as much in love as any one could desire," he wrote his daughter-in-law Eleanor. "And I am pleased beyond measure that he should be about to marry. Belle is a dear girl." Edith, however, seemed less enthusiastic about the match. She remembered Belle from the summer before Kermit left for Brazil, and now that her quiet, serious son was engaged to the young socialite, a girl Edith had nicknamed "the Fair One with Golden Locks," she wrote Ethel that she felt "a trifle down."

Although his mother seemed to have reservations about his impending marriage, Kermit himself had none. He wanted nothing more than to board the next boat to Europe and, at long last, be reunited with his fiancée. While they were still in Bahia, however, Edith had pulled her son aside at the first opportunity and urged him to take a leave of absence from work so that he could look after his father in the Amazon. Kermit had no interest in joining the expedition, but he felt that he had little choice in the matter. He could see that his mother was worried, and he had to admit that he too was concerned about his father's health and safety.

Roosevelt had always seemed invincible to his children, as though the great heart in his barrel chest would never stop beating. But the assassination attempt in 1912 had, with a shocking suddenness, changed all of that. Kermit, already living and working in Brazil at that time, had been hit perhaps hardest of all by the reality of his father's mortality. "It was a bad time to be far away," he admitted to Belle. "And the way in which I was told didn't help matters. I guess the man must have been worrying how to tell me, and got mixed up. He's a big up-from-the-soil sort of foreman; and looked rather embarrassed, and then said, 'Well I guess that they've shot Roosevelt all right.' . . . It was almost impossible to get anything more out of him. It was exactly like one of those 'breaking the news' anecdotes; but it doesn't amuse you very much when it happens to you."

Roosevelt had at first welcomed the addition of his son to his expedition, but the news of Kermit's engagement made him hesitate. He did not want Kermit to accompany him on an unavoidably dangerous journey when he had a fiancée who was anxiously awaiting his return. "I did not like Kermit to come on this trip with me," Roosevelt wrote his daughter-in-law Eleanor, "but he did not wish to be married in my absence, and moreover felt that this semi-exploration business was exactly in his line." However, in a letter to Belle, Kermit confessed that he was determined to go on this expedition not for his own sake but for his father's, and he would count the days until the journey's end. "It just doesn't seem as if I could live so long without seeing you, but I feel so very sure that I am doing what you would want me to do," he wrote her. "Yesterday mother gave me another long talk about father, and about some other ways I must look after him. She's dreadfully worried about him, and there's nothing for me to do but go."

Kermit's commitment to his father's expedition was painfully tested on November 26, when he watched his mother and cousin set sail for the Panama Canal from Valparaiso, on Chile's Pacific coast. The thought of the months ahead of him without Belle made Kermit miserable. Yet he stood resolutely by his father's side as the ship carrying Edith and Margaret disappeared in the distance.

"We would have both felt that I must go with father," he wrote to Belle that night. "If I weren't going I should always feel that when my chance had come to help, I had proved wanting, and all my life I would feel it."

PART TWO

Into the
Wilderness

CHAPTER 6

Beyond the Frontier

O N THE MORNING OF December 12, 1913, Colonel Cândido
Rondon—five feet three inches tall, with dark skin, a shock of
black, slightly graying hair and a ramrod-straight posture—was looking crisp and starched in his dress whites as he anxiously paced the
deck of the *Nyoac,* a shallow-river steamer that was anchored at the
juncture of the Paraguay and Apa Rivers on Brazil's southern border.
Peering into the distance, Rondon searched for a column of smoke, a
tall steel mast, anything that would herald the arrival of the *Adolfo
Riquielme,* the Paraguayan president's gunboat-yacht that was carrying Theodore Roosevelt to meet him.

After almost two months in South America, Roosevelt had finally
completed his official duties, and could now devote himself entirely
to his long-anticipated expedition into the Amazon. So remote was
the region he had agreed to explore, however, that even getting to
the River of Doubt would require a journey of at least two more
months—first by boat and then on muleback. Crossing into Brazil on
the broad Paraguay River, Roosevelt and his men would continue upstream as far as possible, disembarking at a telegraph station and

frontier town called Tapirapoan. They would then make their way across four hundred miles of the Brazilian Highlands, passing through open plains, scrub forest, barren desert, and dense jungle to reach the river, and launch their boats down its black, fast-moving waters.

With every mile of this journey, the expedition would be moving farther from populated areas, and closer to the edge of the unknown. Although the initial leg of boat travel offered a last opportunity for relative comfort and safety, the grueling overland journey would take them well past the frontier of settled lands, and into dangerous wilderness regions where the first outposts of military and governmental authority had only recently been established, and where harsh terrain and fierce indigenous tribes still posed a grave threat to intruders.

Even for the most hardened, ambitious Brazilian frontiersmen, the territory that Roosevelt was preparing to cross was considered too difficult and dangerous to settle or explore. Indeed, except for indigenous tribesmen, only a handful of men in the history of Brazil had ever reached the headwaters of the River of Doubt and survived to tell the tale. Those men had been led by Cândido Rondon.

* * *

BORN IN the remote western-Brazilian state of Mato Grosso, in a little town called Mimoso that was twenty miles south of the state's capital, Cuiabá, Rondon had grown up in painful isolation from the rest of Brazil. His earliest memories were of war and irreparable loss. His father, Cândido Mariano da Silva, a *caboclo*, or man of mixed Indian and European descent, died from smallpox six months before his son was born. Just days later, the Paraguayan dictator Francisco Solano López invaded Mato Grosso in retaliation for Brazil's military intervention in the Uruguayan civil war. Since there were no lines of communication at that time between Mato Grosso and the Brazilian capital, the remote, impoverished people of Mato Grosso could not look to the government for aid.

The War of the Triple Alliance, a bloody five-year war that pitted

Paraguay against an alliance of Brazil, Uruguay (run by a puppet government controlled by Brazil), and Argentina, officially began in 1865, the year that Rondon was born. Under constant siege, the people living in Mato Grosso's far-flung towns fled to Cuiabá in search of protection. Rondon's mother, who was one-quarter Terena Indian and one-quarter Borôro Indian, snatched up her infant son and ran. All she found in Cuiabá, however, was the same deadly disease that had killed her husband. In 1867, half the refugees in Cuiabá, roughly six thousand people, died from smallpox. In the midst of famine, widespread disease, and war, Rondon survived. His mother did not.

Survival against great odds was to become a hallmark of Rondon's life, but so too were loneliness and isolation. Orphaned at the age of two, Rondon was cared for by his grandparents until they too died while he was still a boy. He was then sent to live with his mother's brother, a man who adopted him, gave him his surname, and educated him until, at the age of sixteen, Rondon moved to Rio de Janeiro. The city must have seemed utterly alien to a young man who had grown up in the backwoods of Mato Grosso. It is no surprise that he gravitated toward the only semblance of a family that was available to him: the Escola Militar, Rio's military school.

Rondon, however, was not like the other boys at the military school, and nearly a year passed before he began to feel comfortable there. Even as a teenager, Rondon was serious and driven; he was also poor beyond anyone's understanding. He woke up at 4:00 a.m. every day to swim in the sea and was back in his dark room by 5:00 a.m., studying by the thin light of a whale-oil lamp while the other students, most of whom had been out late the night before, burrowed deeper into their beds, dreading the 6:00 a.m. reveille. Besides his extraordinary discipline, Rondon's extreme poverty and rural background made him an outcast. Too poor even to afford textbooks, he never left campus with the other boys on the weekends, and he was nicknamed "the hairy brute" because he was so awkward in social situations. The earnest young man's isolation was so complete that no one around him noticed that he was starving. Living on a meager diet of rice and beans, and working night and day in an effort to complete a two-year degree in only one year, he became so malnourished that he finally collapsed while descending a flight of stairs on his way to a math class.

Rondon lost an entire year of school while he slowly recovered, but he spent the time tutoring other students and never gave up his ambitions for a military career. After returning to school, he earned a bachelor's degree in mathematics and the physical and natural sciences, and, while still in his early twenties, was promoted to military engineer, a title that ensured him a lifelong professorship or a well-respected position as an intellectual at the military headquarters in Rio—positions that would have been the culmination of a dream for many men, especially a poor *caboclo* from remote Mato Grosso.

Rondon, however, had other plans. He wanted to serve not just his country but its most disenfranchised and endangered inhabitants: the Indians. "I want to bring the civilization which I have acquired to my Mato Grosso and my Amazonia," he said, "to the jungle and its tribes." His determination to protect South American Indians and incorporate them into mainstream Brazilian society—a passion that would come to override all others in his life—grew less out of his ethnic background than his philosophical convictions. Rondon was a member of Brazil's Positivist movement, which, founded by the French philosopher Auguste Comte in the mid-nineteenth century, had its foundations in the French Enlightenment and British Empiricism. Although Positivists claimed to be, as one historian put it, "the respectful heirs of Catholicism," the country's dominant faith, their beliefs were in direct contradiction to that religion. Largely a philosophy of humanity, Positivism chose scientific knowledge and observed facts over mysticism and blind faith, putting its trust in the inevitable pull of progress, a type of Darwinian evolution toward civilization.

Rondon was first exposed to the tenets of Positivism while he was a student at the military school. His math teacher, Benjamin Constant—a man known as a "mathematical sleepwalker" because he could sit for hours in perfect silence, ruminating on the mysteries of math while the chaotic world went on around him—was a vocal member of the movement and did not hesitate to indoctrinate his students. Although he was a personal friend of Emperor Pedro II, Constant, through the military, played a pivotal role in the overthrow of the monarchy and the establishment of the Federal Republic of Brazil in November 1889. After the relatively bloodless coup—Pedro II, like countless fallen monarchs before and after him, sought exile in Paris—the leaders of the Republic created a new flag for Brazil, choosing a green background with a bright-blue globe resting on a gold diamond. On the globe they scattered twenty-seven five-pointed stars, one for each of Brazil's states and for the Federal District, and stretched a white banner across its face that today still proudly bears the Positivist motto: *Ordem e Progresso,* Order and Progress—not just for Brazilians but also for the country's native inhabitants.

Less than six months after the founding of the Republic, Rondon was given an unexpected opportunity to put his Positivist beliefs to work for the good of Amazonian Indians. He was chosen as the head of the Strategic Telegraph Commission—thereafter known as the Rondon Commission—a job that would put him in direct contact with the Amazon's most isolated tribes. Rondon accepted the assignment and returned to Mato Grosso in April 1890 as a local hero. He was not yet twenty-five years old, but, just eight years after leaving Cuiabá, he was the commander of a small arm of the military, and he had been entrusted with arguably the Republic's most difficult assignment.

The Rondon Commission's expeditions into the Brazilian interior were infamous. At best, they were long, exhausting, lonely treks through unfamiliar territory. At worst, they were terrifying forced marches that subjected the soldiers to disease, starvation, and relentless Indian attacks. Rondon was supposed to have between 100 and 150 men for his expeditions, but he rarely had a full unit. In 1900, Rondon began an expedition with eighty-one men. By the end of the year, only thirty were left. Of the missing, seventeen had deserted, and the rest were either hospitalized or dead. Time passed, and Rondon gained more experience, but the conditions under which his men labored did not improve. In 1903, only fifty-five men returned from an expedition that had begun with a hundred. Assignment to Rondon's unit became a punishment, reserved for those enlisted men who had proved themselves to be lazy, violent, or, frequently, both. Many of his men were recruited directly from Rio de Janeiro's prisons. Had they known what hardship they would face on one of Rondon's expeditions, most of them would have likely begged to remain in jail.

The most harrowing trip that Rondon's men had endured was in 1909, the year that their commander discovered the River of Doubt. He had started out in early June of that year from Tapirapoan—the same town that would serve as the launching point for Roosevelt's overland journey—with forty-two men, including two Indian guides. A supply train of five hundred oxen and 160 mules was supposed to meet him at the next telegraph station, Juruena, but only forty animals survived the journey. A few days later the expedition's geologist and its pharmacist, as well as several military recruits and civilian workers, had to be sent back because they were too sick to travel any farther. Rondon himself was so ill with malaria that the expedition's doctor finally convinced him to ride on an ox. After riding just a quarter of a mile, however, he insisted on walking with his men, explaining later that, "with every step, my self-respect was reduced a little more."

In early August, the men, struggling through a dense, tangled jungle that Rondon described as "monstrously fecund," stumbled upon a strange, twisting stream. In some places the stream plunged underground. In others it spread out to nearly forty feet in width. It seemed to flow in a general north-northwest direction, but it twisted so wildly that it was impossible to be sure where it would lead. After following it briefly, the men, their provisions perilously low, gave up. They had neither the strength nor the time to solve the mystery of the river, prompting Rondon to christen it Rio da Dúvida—the River of Doubt.

As the men hacked their way through the deepening jungle, their suffering began in full force. By late August, they had exhausted all their supplies and were surviving on Brazil nuts, hearts of palm, wild honey, and an occasional fish. The rivers teemed with piranha, but they sliced through the men's fishing line and hooks with knife-blade teeth. So difficult were they to catch that, out of desperation, one lieutenant, a man named Pyrineus, finally threw dynamite into a pond above a waterfall. As he splashed through the water below, eagerly gathering his spoils, he made the mistake of holding a piranha in his mouth while his hands were busy scooping up others. The fish had at first been stunned by the dynamite and so lay slack between his teeth, but as soon as it recovered, it attacked. Before Pyrineus had time to react, the piranha had taken a bite out of his tongue. He would have bled to death had the expedition's doctor not stanched the wound with moss.

By the time the expedition emerged from the jungle in late December 1909, the men who were still alive were so weak that many of them could hardly crawl. All of them had parasitic insects wriggling under their skin. Those who were not completely naked were wearing only rags, and all were on the brink of starvation. However, over the course of 237 days, they had covered six hundred miles of unmapped territory, and Rondon took great satisfaction in the tremendous leap forward that he and his men had made toward the understanding of Brazil's mysterious interior. Then he set about planning his next expedition.

* * *

RONDON WAS not, as he later put it, "tormented with nervousness" when, at 11:30 a.m., the *Adolfo Riquielme* finally pulled up alongside the *Nyoac* and he and his officers stepped aboard the yacht to meet Roosevelt. Although Rondon had spent the better part of the past twenty-five years in the jungle, "frequenting the Ministries of the Borôro, Pareci and Nhambiquara Indians, perfecting . . . the etiquette of their respective Courts," he was confident that he would know how to greet a former president of the United States. "If, when we greet in the Borôro fashion, we are immediately prepared for the sharp odour of naked bodies painted with urucum," he wrote, referring to the pungent red pigment used by Amazon tribes, "in compensation, when we exchange amiabilities in the language of Corneille and Molière, we are insensibly drawn to gentleness and refinement."

In fact, the language of Corneille and Molière was the only language that Rondon and Roosevelt—now officially co-commanders of the expedition—had in common. Roosevelt had learned only two words of Portuguese—*mais canja,* which means "more soup"—and Rondon, although he knew ten different Indian dialects, did not speak English. Unless Kermit was around to translate, the two men had to rely on French—a language that Roosevelt admitted to speaking "as if it were a non-Aryan tongue, having neither gender nor tense." Despite this barrier, the two colonels seemed to have little difficulty communicating, and by the time their combined party reached the Brazilian river town of Corumbá on December 15, they had already developed a deep and lasting respect for each other.

For Roosevelt, Rondon represented the kind of man he had championed and admired throughout his life: a disciplined officer who thrived on physical challenges and hardship, and accomplished great feats through sheer force of will. It would be a measure of his profound respect for Rondon that, years later, Roosevelt would count the Brazilian officer among the four greatest explorers of his time—alongside Roald Amundsen, Richard Byrd, and Robert Peary.

A conspicuous contrast between the two men was in the philosophical conclusions that each drew from his experiences. For Roosevelt, the lessons of nature and human history proved the need to vindicate principles with assertive action—even when that action entailed bloodshed or conflict. Along with that passionate belief in action came a politician's pragmatism—a flexibility in tactics that favored results over process.

For Rondon, however, a life spent at the edge of Brazil's frontier—and at the margins of its society—had instilled a powerful mistrust of imposed solutions and a determination to respect the workings of law and rationality even when none appeared to exist. In keeping with his Positivist beliefs, Rondon did not welcome conflict but, rather, sought to avoid it at all costs. Although a military officer, Rondon approached his duties with a pacifist's idealism that would ultimately secure him a place not merely as Brazil's greatest explorer, but as one of its pioneering social thinkers.

Devotion to their principles would become part of the legend of both Roosevelt and Rondon. Both had developed their beliefs over a lifetime of experience and thought, and both would be remembered for the passion with which they put those beliefs into practice. From the very beginning, however, their contrasting approaches and personalities ensured that the newly renamed Roosevelt-Rondon Scientific Expedition would reflect its leaders' powerful and divergent views about life and leadership. The beliefs of both men, moreover, would soon be put to the test on the River of Doubt.

*   *   *

CORUMBÁ, THE town in which Miller, Cherrie, Fiala, and Sigg had been waiting for Roosevelt for three weeks, was larger than most along the Paraguay River. Cherrie had been impressed by his first glimpse of the town, seeing it "bathed in the early morning sunshine, the red tiled roofs and white walls in pleasing contrast to the rich green of banana trees and the fronds of waving palms." It had not taken long, however, for the romance to wear thin. Although Corumbá, which had been founded as a military outpost in 1778, had ten thousand citizens, it did not have streetcars or even hirable carriages. "For ambulance service," Cherrie noted, "a hammock was swung from a long pole that was borne on the shoulders of a couple of porters."

After a side trip to a nearby ranch where Roosevelt hunted jaguars, the *Nyoac* left Corumbá on Christmas Day, 1913. "It was a brilliantly clear day," Roosevelt wrote. "We sat on the forward deck, admiring the trees on the brink of the sheer river banks, the lush, rank grass of the marshes, and the many water-birds. The two pilots, one black and one white, stood at the wheel. Colonel Rondon read Thomas à

Kempis. Kermit, Cherrie, and Miller squatted outside the railing on the deck over one paddle-wheel and put the final touches on the jaguar-skins. Fiala satisfied himself that the boxes and bags were in place. It was probable that hardship lay in the future; but the day was our own, and the day was pleasant."

Rondon had gone to great lengths to try to manufacture Christmas cheer, even sending his men to gather palm leaves and other greenery along the shore so that they could decorate the boat. His American guests, however, could not help feeling homesick. "What a Xmas Eve!" Cherrie had written in his diary the night before. "Could anything be less Christmas like. How I wish I might be at home tonight." Kermit confessed in a letter to Belle that he was not feeling "a bit Christmassy," either. He missed her, he missed civilization, and he was worried about his father, who he feared had gotten in over his head—a situation for which he blamed Father Zahm. "The priest is a foolish well meaning little fellow, who mislead [sic] father greatly as to the conditions of travel and life down here," he wrote. "He had never been off the beaten track and saw everything through a golden haze."

The *Nyoac* chugged along at a sluggish pace, leaving the men little choice but to settle back on the side-wheel steamer, jammed tight with men, dogs, crates, and reeking animal skins, and spend the next few weeks getting to know the land and one another. Everyone aboard the *Nyoac*, with the exception of Kermit, was understandably curious about Roosevelt. He had already surprised them by being warm and affable, more interested in hearing about their achievements and ambitions than in talking about his own, but they, like the men who had planned Roosevelt's speaking tour, knew his reputation for physical vigor and must have wondered if now, at the age of fifty-five, he could still live up to it. It was not long before they had their answer.

Not only could Roosevelt withstand extreme tests of physical endurance, but he relished them—to the distress of anyone who was unfortunate enough to be along for the ride. In the White House,

Roosevelt used to torture the members of his Cabinet with long "point-to-point" walks through Rock Creek Park, the enormous forested park that runs through Washington, D.C. The walks went on any time of day or night and in any season. "On several occasions we thus swam Rock Creek in the early spring when the ice was floating thick upon it," Roosevelt remembered. "If we swam the Potomac, we usually took off our clothes. I remember on one such occasion when the French Ambassador, [Jules] Jusserand . . . was along, and, just as we were about to get in to swim, somebody said, 'Mr. Ambassador, Mr. Ambassador, you haven't taken off your gloves,' to which he promptly responded, 'I think I will leave them on; we might meet ladies!' "

Five years after leaving the White House, Roosevelt still had the endurance of a man half his age, and he proved it on New Year's Day, 1914. After a 5:00 a.m. breakfast of sardines, ham, coffee, and hardtack, Roosevelt, Kermit, some Brazilian officers, and a handful of camaradas—the Portuguese word for "comrades" and the name given to poor laborers in Brazil—headed out for a jaguar hunt near the banks of the São Lourenço, a small river that the *Nyoac* had steamed into the day before. This was Roosevelt's second jaguar hunt, but it would later become emblematic among the Brazilians aboard the *Nyoac* as the true measure of the former American president.

Anthony Fiala, who witnessed the hunting party's mounting exhaustion from the expedition's base camp along the river, would never forget that day. He later told a reporter for the *New York Times*:

> We did not hear from the party until late in the afternoon, when a big Indian came running into camp, shouting "Burroo-Gurra-Harru," which meant "Plenty work, tired." He fell down in a corner and went to sleep. Twenty minutes later another Indian ran in, apparently all used up. He said, "Gurra-Harru," and he went to sleep. The third Indian arrived then and said, "Harru," as he threw up his arms and went off into a trance.

This caused me to become anxious about the safety of the Colonel and his son, and we started to look for them, as it was getting toward sundown. After walking through the forest for a short distance we came to a small open space, where we found one of the Brazilian officers lying on the ground so dead tired that he could go no further. His clothes were torn and his face and neck were covered with dust and blood.

Leaving him in the care of three of the natives to carry him back to the camp, I pushed on farther and in another clearing I saw Colonel Roosevelt and Kermit dragging the other Brazilian officer after them through the jungle. I shall never forget the awesome appearance of the intrepid Colonel as the falling rays of the sun streamed through the trees and lit up his dusty and begrimed features. His clothes were torn to tatters and Kermit was in the same condition, but had not his father's warlike look.

I called out to him, "Are you all right, Colonel?" and he replied, "I'm bully," and then went to camp with the used-up officer. Next day the Colonel and Kermit were about the camp as if nothing had happened out of the ordinary, but the Brazilians were laid up for two days. The Indians regarded the Colonel with awe after that trip.

CHAPTER 7

Disarray and Tragedy

W HEN THE EXPEDITION REACHED Tapirapoan just before
noon on January 16, Roosevelt stepped off his boat expecting
to find a well-organized army of oxen and mules prepared to carry
heavy loads and make a quick departure for the River of Doubt. To
his amazement and dismay, what awaited him in the little riverside village was not military precision but utter chaos.

Set into low scrub forest on the river's edge, Tapirapoan consisted
of little more than a collection of small, mud-walled huts and a central square flanked by the offices of the Rondon Commission. It had
been swathed in bunting, colorful flags from all the countries of
North and South America, and even Chinese lanterns in celebration
of Roosevelt's arrival. "However, if Tapirapoan bore a festive outward
appearance," Miller wrote, "it acted merely as a mask to cover up the
general confusion that even a casual inspection could not fail to
disclose." Among a scattering of wagons, carts, and telegraph line
trucks, a variety of animals, from oxen to mules to milch cows and
beef cattle, wandered, Roosevelt wrote, "almost at will."

Rondon had arranged ahead of time for 110 mules and seventy

pack oxen to be on hand for the expedition's overland journey. He had also put Captain Amilcar Botelho de Magalhães, a trusted friend who had traveled with him on several previous expeditions, in charge of the baggage train. The problem was that the Americans had brought with them much more baggage than Rondon had expected. Rather than risk embarrassment by explaining the situation to Roosevelt, the colonel scrambled to find additional animals.

Although extra mules and oxen were located, they were far from tame. Amilcar, despite his extensive experience with pack animals, had little control over his wild, willful charges. Most of the animals were "apparently fresh from the ranges and had never been broken to work of any kind," Miller observed. "The corrals reminded one of a Wild West show. Gauchos, wearing fringed leather aprons, and wicked, keen-edged knives in their belts, and who swore fluently in two or three different languages, lassoed the panicky animals, blind-folded them, and adjusted the packs. When the covering was removed from the animals' eyes they frequently gave a few sharp snorts, and then started through the corral in a series of rabbit-like leaps, eventu-ally sending the packs, saddles, and all flying in every direction."

Roosevelt and his men had expected to stay in Tapirapoan for only one or two days. They quickly realized, however, that they would not be leaving anytime soon. Miller and Cherrie did not mind the delay because it gave them an opportunity to collect more specimens. Father Zahm too was "constantly engaged in congenial occupations," and so relatively content. Kermit, however, had no patience with the bum-bling antics that layered day after day onto his already unbearable ab-sence from Belle. As he watched the camaradas struggle to control the animals, he silently seethed. "The oxen aren't used to be carrying packs and won't let themselves be loaded and when they are loaded they buck until the[y] fall down or throw off the packs," he railed in a letter to Belle. "I have been ready to kill the whole lot and all the members of the expedition."

Perhaps the only man as anxious as Kermit to get to the River of Doubt and get home was Roosevelt himself. Although the opportu-

nity to descend an unmapped river had seemed exciting and adventurous when he was in Rio de Janeiro, it now paled in comparison with
what was happening on the world stage. While Woodrow Wilson was
making high-stakes decisions about the United States' role in the
Mexican Revolution, Roosevelt was headed into one of the few places
left on earth where his opinions would go unheard.

Since taking office, Wilson had been doing his best to stay out of
Mexico, but it had not been easy. The country's current president,
Victoriano Huerta, once the commander of the federal troops, had
achieved his position nearly a year earlier by arresting and, a few days
later, ordering the assassination of the acting president, Francisco
Madero. Repelled by tales of Huerta's ruthless and repressive regime,
Wilson determined to help remove him from power—by diplomatic
means. "Intervention must be avoided until a time comes when it is inevitable, which God forbid!" he told his wife. After sending two en-
voys in unsuccessful attempts to persuade Huerta to step down,
Wilson had announced that United States policy toward Mexico
would consist of "watchful waiting."

Such a passive policy was anathema to Roosevelt, who was consti-
tutionally incapable of watchful waiting. As he had made clear in his
1912 campaign speech at Madison Square Garden, his ambition—
more personal even than political—was to "smite down wrong." With
the political situation in Mexico continuing to unravel, Roosevelt,
Kondon noticed, walked around Tapirapoan in a state of "constant
preoccupation." At a time when he should have been preparing for the
expedition before him, Roosevelt was distracted by a situation that
was beyond his control and thousands of miles away.

To Roosevelt's growing frustration, the expedition remained practically immobile. Not only were the pack animals recalcitrant, but
the already massive amounts of baggage—360 enormous boxes and
countless smaller ones—had been increased significantly by a set of
beautiful, elaborate, and completely impractical gifts that the Brazilian
government had waiting for the former American leader in Tapirapoan.
Roosevelt's only success in speeding up the expedition's departure was

to convince Rondon to divide the nearly two hundred pack animals into two separate detachments: Roosevelt and Rondon would lead the mule train, and Amilcar would lead the larger baggage train, made up of both mules and oxen.

On January 19, the baggage train at last set off across the Brazilian Highlands with the camaradas that Rondon had hired in Tapirapoan—porters and future paddlers—and most of the expedition's baggage, including the provisions that Fiala had packed in New York as well as his Canadian canoes, drawn on a cart pulled by six oxen. Amilcar's early departure would help give the overburdened baggage train a head start on the mules, which would doubtless be moving at a much faster pace. But Rondon also wanted Amilcar and his men to ride ahead of the mule train so that they could remove any obstacles from the telegraph road and repair any sagging bridges that might impede Roosevelt's progress.

The expedition's route called for the men on muleback to follow the supply train north until they reached an outlying telegraph station in Utiarity, where they would turn west and travel for another month, until they encountered the dark, snakelike upper reaches of the River of Doubt. They were still in the state of Mato Grosso, but they were now crossing a corner of a vast, ancient plateau known as the Brazilian Highlands.

These highlands encompass 580,000 square miles—more than twice the area of Texas—but they were once even larger still. For millions of years, the Brazilian Highlands were connected to the Guiana Highlands in the north, and were separated only after the Amazon River formed twelve million years ago, splitting the enormous, contiguous plateau into northern and southern halves. The crystalline massifs of both plateaus thus rank among the oldest rock formations on earth, dating back to the Precambrian era billions of years ago. In fact, the Brazilian Highlands are so ancient and have endured such extensive erosion that the highest elevation on the plateau is less than ten thousand feet—half the height of the tallest mountains in the geologically young Andes—and their jagged expanse is marked by steep cliffs, deep ravines, and rolling hills.

The highlands, as Roosevelt soon learned, are as varied as they are vast. On the first day out of Tapirapoan, the expedition passed through an open pastureland that was dotted with widely spaced trees. On the second day, the men plunged into dense tropical jungle. "Away from the broad, beaten route every step of a man's progress represented slashing a trail with the machete through the tangle of bushes, low trees, thorny scrub, and interlaced creepers," Roosevelt wrote. By the next morning, however, the mule train had climbed a steep slope into the cool, dry air of a high plateau that rested roughly two thousand feet above sea level—a region that the Brazilians refer to as *chapadão,* or tableland. The men were surprised by the region's aridity, its conspicuous lack of wildlife, even mosquitoes, and the nights that turned so cold that, for the first time since beginning their journey, they had to wrap themselves in blankets while they slept.

In the early twentieth century, modern maps of the Brazilian Highlands, drawn up by the world's most respected and experienced cartographers, were strikingly wrong. "The whole region," Lauro Müller, Brazil's minister of foreign affairs, had told Roosevelt, "would have to be remapped after the discoveries of the telegraph commission." It was in exploring the Brazilian Highlands that Rondon and his men had lost all their oxen and had nearly starved to death. Rondon knew the region better now, but it was no more settled or welcoming to travelers than it had been on his first journey across it. In fact, his knowledge of the highlands only served to underscore for Rondon how difficult and dangerous their journey to the River of Doubt would be.

*   *   *

WITHIN DAYS of leaving Tapirapoan, Roosevelt and the rest of his men could for the first time clearly see signs of the hardships that lay ahead of them. Although they were still hundreds of miles away from the River of Doubt, the fabric of their expedition was beginning to unravel.

The men were already obliged to get by with much simpler and less frequent meals. "Until Tapirapoan, our food was abundant, very good, and quite varied," the expedition's Brazilian doctor wrote. "Nevertheless, due to the conditions of the backland, we presently had to change the eating habits we had heretofore adopted, despite the great interest Colonel Rondon had placed on providing our guests with the same privileges granted to them up to that time."

Meals usually consisted of fresh meat from one of the oxen, black beans, rice, biscuits, and coffee, but in an effort to save provisions as well as time, Rondon had ordered that their midday meal be omitted completely. Breakfast was served anytime between 6:00 and 8:00 a.m., but then the men did not eat again until 8:00 p.m. at the earliest, and, on some nights, not until 11:00 p.m. For the men, the sometimes seventeen-hour stretch between the two meals was difficult. Even Cherrie, the consummate experienced explorer, complained in his diary one night, after a long ride without anything to eat until 10:00 p.m., that they were "all nearly famished."

More troubling than their own growing hunger was the visibly deteriorating condition of their mules and oxen. The open, sandy stretch of the Brazilian Highlands was extremely inhospitable for the pack animals. "It was rarely that we saw here a tree more than fifteen or twenty feet high," Father Zahm recalled. "And certain areas were as treeless as the desert lands of New Mexico or Arizona. . . . During our first day in this arid land we did not find a drop of water for a stretch of twenty miles." There was no way to carry heavy bags of grain, so the mules and oxen were simply set free at night to wander in an often fruitless search for grass and water. Then, as the rainy season downpours began in earnest, the dry dirt trail on which they were traveling turned to mud, forming a slick hazard for the animals.

Worse trouble lay ahead. For the men in the mule train, the first warning signs appeared when they began to see the skeletons of oxen and mules that had starved to death or been eaten during previous expeditions, most likely Rondon's. Although their startlingly white bones, bleached by the sun to a ghostly hue, indicated that they had died many months, if not years, earlier, that knowledge was of little comfort to Roosevelt and his men as they encountered unharnessed oxen from their own baggage train staggering slowly along the road. Having grown too weak from hunger and hard use to keep up with the rest of the train, the unfortunate beasts had simply been released and left to die.

The men were stunned by the sight they encountered next: Strewn across their path, settling into the thick mud, were unopened supply crates, all clearly marked "Roosevelt South American Expedition." The pack animals, who were still making their weary way across the plateau ahead of the mule train, had begun bucking off their heavy loads.

As the officers in the mule train rode slowly past the boxes on their tired mounts, they wondered what they were leaving behind and how precious it might seem to them in the months to come. "What became of this food which we had so carefully selected in New York, and which we had looked after so solicitously for thousands of miles, it would be interesting to know," Zahm wrote. "It was impossible for anyone to collect it and add it to our other stores which had been sent ahead, and impossible for our pack animals to carry it, for their burdens were already as great as they could bear."

The men also began to show signs of strain. Three Brazilians—a doctor, a lieutenant, and a botanist—had already resigned their posts, having lost all faith in what they now believed was a fatally unorganized and mismanaged expedition. Worse than the malcontent officers, however, was a volatile camarada who had been assigned to Amilcar's baggage train in Tapirapoan. Julio de Lima, a full-blooded Portuguese from Bahia, had already given his captain good reason to worry. Just a few weeks into the overland journey, he viciously attacked another camarada with a knife and was prevented from injuring or even killing him only because Amilcar and one of his lieutenants, Vieria de Mello, stepped in and wrenched the weapon from his hand. Amilcar punished Julio—the only time he was forced to punish one of his men during the overland journey—but he was left with a foreboding about the violent camarada that he could not shake.

* * *

DRAWN TOGETHER by their ordeal, the men of the expedition quickly grew to know one another well. After riding together all day long, they shared tents at night and during pounding rainstorms—which were now all too frequent—and they ate every meal together. Each night, after erecting tents, organizing baggage, and peeling off their drenched clothes, the men would gather around two oxhides that had been spread over the damp ground and laid with rations of rice, beans, pork, and beef. The men, Rondon noted, "squatted in the Yedo and Tokyo fashion, some with a certain amount of elegance and others in a very clumsy posture; but they honoured our table with that joviality which can only be prepared by the exercise of long marches in the open, breathing the fresh and oxygenated air of the virgin forests and drinking from the running waters of the rivers."

It was during these dinners, and afterward, as they sat under the bright Southern stars, that the Brazilians and Americans began to forge the mutual respect and friendship that often develops between men who camp together for long periods of time in rough conditions—even men who do not share a common language. They relied on expressions, gestures, and an international amalgam of tongues that, in Roosevelt's words, consisted of "English, Portuguese, bad French, and broken German." Their conversation often centered on the river toward which they were riding—its length, its character, where it would take them, and when they would reach its end. But the River of Doubt still seemed impossibly far away, and their past lives were ever present in vivid, and often disturbing, memories.

It was not long before the men began to tell stories from their former expeditions into the wilderness—whether South American, North American, African, or Arctic. Although Roosevelt was widely considered the best raconteur, the competition from this group of well-traveled, adventurous, and courageous men was impressive. Rondon enthralled his audience with memories of long expeditions through uncharted land. Roosevelt and his son shared stories from their year-long hunting safari in Africa, during which they had earned the nicknames Bwana Makubwa, or "Great Master," and Bwana Mardadi, "Dandy Master." And Miller, Roosevelt recalled, "told of the stone gods and altars and temples he had seen in the great Colombian forests, monuments of strange civilizations which flourished and died out ages ago, and of which all memory has vanished."

Cherrie, who had had perhaps a wider range of experiences than any man present, remained relatively silent until one night, when the conversation turned to cavalry battles. Despite himself, the taciturn naturalist nodded somberly when someone mentioned the powerful psychological effect of a shining, razor-sharp lance. Their curiosity aroused by Cherrie's obvious firsthand knowledge of the subject, the men would not leave him alone until he told his story.

"It was while he was fighting with the Venezuelan insurgents in an unsuccessful uprising against the tyranny of Castro," Roosevelt wrote of Cherrie's involvement in the effort to topple Venezuelan tyrant Cipriano Castro. "He was on foot, with five Venezuelans, all cool men and good shots. In an open plain they were charged by twenty of Castro's lancers, who galloped out from behind cover two or three hundred yards off. It was a war in which neither side gave quarter and in which the wounded and the prisoners were butchered. . . . Cherrie knew that it meant death for him and his companions if the charge came home; and the sight of the horsemen running in at full speed, with their long lances in rest and the blades glittering, left an indelible impression on his mind. But he and his companions shot deliberately and accurately; ten of the lancers were killed, the nearest falling within fifty yards; and the others rode off in headlong haste. A cool man with a rifle, if he has mastered his weapon, need fear no foe."

Few tales of exploration or even warfare, however, could compete with Anthony Fiala's memories of spending two years trapped in the frozen north. The supply ship that was supposed to relieve the expedition never appeared, and if it had not been for seal blubber, an unlucky polar bear, and the frozen caches of food left behind by earlier expeditions, he and his men would have starved.

As they listened to Fiala's stories of disaster and near-death in the polar north, Roosevelt and the other officers could not have helped but reflect on the fact that the commander of that expedition was the quartermaster of theirs. Fiala was not leading them into the Amazon, but he had chosen and packed everything that they would rely on to keep themselves alive during the months to come.

* * *

ON JANUARY 25, some good news arrived for Roosevelt and his men in the almost surreal form of three huge all-terrain trucks. The "auto vans," as Zahm called them, rattled into camp that night on their way to the Utiarity telegraph station, the expedition's next stop, and the point at which it would turn west and head directly toward the River of Doubt. The trucks, which belonged to the Rondon Commission, each carried two tons of freight and had been outfitted with wide, slatted belts that wrapped around the wheels on each side like tank treads, forming what Miller referred to as an "endless trail" through the thick mud. This invention, which anticipated the use of the first military tank two years later, during World War I, amazed and elated the explorers. "It was a strange sight to see them racing across the uninhabited chapadão at a speed of thirty miles an hour," Miller wrote. "Surely this was exploring *de luxe.*"

No member of the expedition appreciated *de luxe* travel more than Father Zahm. The next morning, he secured two seats on one of the trucks for himself and the Swiss handyman Jacob Sigg, whom he had long since appropriated as his personal assistant. Cherrie and Miller also decided to ride in one of the trucks so that they would have a chance to do some collecting before the rest of the expedition caught up with them.

Father Zahm, however, was unhappy with his ride in the auto van.

According to Rondon, the priest was deeply offended that he had had to ride "beside the driver, a black man—which [he] never forgave." While in Bahia, Father Zahm had been impressed with the successful mingling of the races. "Truth to tell," he wrote, "there is not a little to say in favor of the fusion of the European and African races in Brazil. For some of the most distinguished men the country has produced have had a strain of Negro blood in their veins." However, whatever his intellectual and theoretical opinions about racial integration, he clearly believed that the United States was not ready to take such a drastic step—and neither was he.

In Brazil, Zahm wrote, "Whites, Indians, and Negroes associate together in a way which would be quite impossible with us, and which an old Virginian planter would condemn as an abomination unutterable." Father Zahm, on the other hand, had no problem voicing his complaints about the "ignorant and careless negro" who, as a favor to Rondon, had driven him to Utiarity. And he thereafter, Rondon wrote, referred to that truck ride as a "measure of how much he had suffered during the expedition."

It would have been difficult for Father Zahm to find a better or faster way to alienate Rondon than to make a racist comment about one of his men. Not only was Rondon proud of his soldiers, but he was a humanist and a champion of minority rights. He had also been a victim of racism himself, and would continue to be for most of his life, in spite of all that he had achieved. "The colonel possesses the temperament of the savage," a Brazilian journalist would write four years later. "In the centers of civilization he feels out of place. . . . [He] is a lost cause . . . because he has a high percentage of Indian blood mixed with the worst habits the centers of civilization have to offer."

Father Zahm was also openly scornful of Rondon's philosophical beliefs and the deferential treatment he accorded Brazil's indigenous peoples. In the introduction to his book *Evolution and Dogma*, Zahm had made it clear that he considered Positivism to be dangerous and subversive. "Our great, or more truthfully our greatest enemy, in the intellectual world to-day," he wrote, "is Naturalism—variously known as Agnosticism, Positivism, Empiricism—which, as [the British statesman] Mr. [Arthur J.] Balfour well observes, 'is in reality the only system which ultimately profits by any defeats which theology may sustain, or which may be counted on to flood the spaces from which the tide of religion has receded.'"

The priest made a point of baptizing both Brazilian settlers and Indians at several stops along the way on both their river journey up the Paraguay and Sepotuba Rivers and their mule ride through the highlands. While he bristled at the implication that Zahm was saving savage souls, Rondon never tried to stop him. "Although the Indian Service would not catechize, respecting the spiritual freedom and the way of life of the Indians under its protection," he wrote, "it would not prevent others from trying to convert them to their beliefs, provided that they didn't force them."

*　*　*

COMPOUNDING THE growing frictions caused by harsh terrain, meager rations, and personality clashes was the ever-present risk of accident and illness. In early January, when the men had reached Saõ Luis de Cáceres, a small town on the Paraguay River, Rondon had learned that four of the soldiers that he had posted there were now dead. Three had drowned while trying to ascend the Gy-Paraná, a five-hundred-mile-long river in western Mato Grosso, and another man, Captain Cardoso, had succumbed to beriberi—a disease brought on by a thiamine deficiency—along the same route that Roosevelt's expedition was traveling.

A few weeks later, in Tapirapoan, illness had cost Roosevelt the assistance of his right-hand man, Frank Harper. As Roosevelt's personal representative during the planning and equipping of the expedition, Harper had worked to protect the ex-president's interests and was the only member of the expedition other than Zahm and Fiala with knowledge about the specific content of the crates and boxes that the baggage train was now laboring to deliver to the River of Doubt.

Harper had contracted malaria early in the journey, and had been miserable ever since. He was not the only man on the expedition to suffer from the mosquito-borne infection, but he had gotten a vivid preview of the miseries that awaited him on the River of Doubt, and he wanted out. On January 18, three days before the other men left on their overland journey, Harper announced that he had had enough and had decided to return home.

Beyond the additional logistical burdens it imposed on Roosevelt, Harper's departure pointed up the acute vulnerability, in medical terms, that the expedition could expect to face for the duration of the journey. For, despite the gravity of his illness, Harper had nevertheless had the option of returning with relative speed and safety to well-equipped medical facilities and, ultimately, the comfort of his own home. Once embarked upon their overland journey, however, Roosevelt and his men no longer had that safety net, and even otherwise minor illnesses acquired in the wilderness or on the river itself could have fatal consequences.

The expedition did have a doctor—a tough, serious, and highly competent man named José Cajazeira, whom Rondon had hired in Corumbá—but, as Roosevelt knew, Dr. Cajazeira was only a thin line of defense against the dangers of the Amazon. "A good doctor is an absolute necessity on an exploring expedition in such a country as that we were in, under penalty of a frightful mortality among the members," Roosevelt wrote. "The necessary risks and hazards are so great, the chances of disaster so large, that there is no warrant for increasing them by the failure to take all feasible precautions."

Unbeknownst to anyone in the expedition but Kermit and Roosevelt himself, having a doctor on hand for the former president was more than an ordinary precaution. More than a decade earlier, while he was campaigning in Pittsfield, Massachusetts, Roosevelt's carriage had been struck by a runaway trolley. One of his secret-service agents had been killed instantly, and he had been thrown thirty feet. The accident had left Roosevelt with loosened teeth, a swollen and bruised cheek, a black eye, and a severe injury to his left leg. The infection that followed had nearly led to blood poisoning, a disease that, in a time before antibiotics, often proved deadly. Even six years after the accident, when Roosevelt was in his second term in the White House, he wrote Kermit that he had "never gotten over the effects of the trolley-car accident . . . when, as you will remember, they had to cut down to the shin bone. The shock permanently damaged the bone, and if anything happens there is always a chance of trouble which would be serious."

Kermit, realizing that he had come close to losing his father that day, had been traumatized by the accident. Afterward, he had declared that, from then on, he "must be on hand to protect his Father." In fact, that accident, and the threat that it would forever after pose to Roosevelt's life, was one of the principal reasons Kermit had felt compelled to join this expedition into the Amazon. "You see he has never quite recovered from the accident he had when the wagon he was driving in got run over by a trolley," he had explained to Belle. "One of his legs is still pretty bad and needs a lot of care."

Right now, however, it was Kermit rather than his father who needed a lot of care. To Roosevelt's deep dismay, even before Harper prepared to return home, Kermit also fell ill with malaria. As his father looked on, "utterly miserable with worry," the younger Roosevelt became so ill with fever and chills that he could not manage to rise from his hammock. Arguing that he had long since become accustomed to the rigors of the tropics, Kermit refused to yield to his illness or to consider returning in Harper's footsteps. But the specter of his son's suffering made a powerful impression on the elder Roosevelt, who was left to ponder, amid the rapidly mounting difficulties the expedition was facing, how heavy a toll he might ultimately be forced to pay for his decision to descend the River of Doubt.

*   *   *

IN LATE January, upon reaching Utiarity, the remote telegraph station that constituted one of the last, tentative outposts of official exploration into Brazil's dark interior, Roosevelt learned that his fears about the risk of illness had already been realized. Thousands of miles away, in New York City, the deadly diseases of the tropics had claimed their first victim from his expedition: his young cousin Margaret Roosevelt.

Waiting for Roosevelt at the lonely telegraph office was a short, devastating message informing him that Margaret had died three weeks before, from typhoid fever contracted on her journey to South America. It was the same infectious disease that had killed his mother thirty years earlier. The young woman had first begun to show signs of illness in early December, a few days after she and her aunt left Panama. Edith was baffled. "Margaret drank only bottled water and ate no salad," she had written despondently in her diary after Margaret's death. "Can't imagine how she got the typhoid." Edith, shaken by the sudden loss of her cousin and young companion, had attended the funeral two days later. "Poor Henry Hunt there," she had written that night. She felt pity for the man who had fallen in love with Margaret on the *Vandyck* and had lost her before he had even had a chance to win her.

A hemisphere away from New York, in the remote wilderness of Brazil, the delayed news of Margaret's death had an unusually powerful and unsettling impact, casting a pall over the entire expedition that had started in her youthful, vibrant company nearly four months before. Having looked forward to their arrival in Utiarity as one of their last contacts with civilization, and a reason for festivities, Roosevelt's men found even that small pleasure stolen from them, and quickly forgot any thought of celebration. The men of the Roosevelt-Rondon Scientific Expedition somberly returned their thoughts to the trip before them, and to very real concerns about their own mortality in the months to come.

CHAPTER 8

Hard Choices

H EAVY SHEETS OF RAIN swept over Utiarity the day after
Roosevelt reached it, drenching the muddy little village and its
population—which was more than doubled by the arrival of the mule
train. Even in such a squall, however, the town offered a welcome
respite for Roosevelt and his men.

Little more than a clearing in the rough, scrubby forest that surrounded it, Utiarity was divided into two parts. One section was composed of the buildings of the Rondon Commission, and the other,
where the Pareci Indians lived, was a set of twelve rectangular huts
with steeply pitched palm-thatch roofs held up by roughly hewn
wooden poles. In a sense, the village was a triumph of man over
nature, having been carved out of the wilderness just a few years earlier by a handful of telegraph line soldiers. But it was a temporary victory at best. Utiarity's grounds were nothing but forlorn-looking
stretches of stone-pocked dirt encircled by a seemingly endless green
expanse of trees and vines. Wherever the citizens of Utiarity looked,
there was wild nature, waiting to reclaim what was rightfully her own.

The Pareci Indians, who had made their peace with Rondon and his men some years earlier, had been convinced to abandon their nearby forest villages to work at, and help protect, the telegraph station. Unlike the men of the expedition, the Pareci were accustomed to the sweltering heat and driving rain of their native climate, and did not see why the deluge should inhibit their celebrations in honor of the expedition's presence. Whenever the downpour let up, the Pareci would quickly gather in the square to play a rousing ball game that fascinated their visitors. The ball, which the Pareci made themselves, was a light, hollow sphere of rubber about eight inches in diameter. The players, of whom there were eight or ten on each team, would line up facing one another with the ball on the ground between them. Then, suddenly, to the joy of the small crowd, one player would run into the middle, dive headfirst at the ground, and butt the ball with his head as hard as he could. A player from the other team would then butt the ball back, this time sending it high enough into the air that one of his opponents could catch it on his head, Roosevelt wrote, "with such a swing of his brawny neck, and such precision and address that the ball bounds back through the air as a football soars after a drop-kick."

The game continued until one player was able to connect with the ball so successfully, never using any part of his anatomy but his head, that it flew high over the heads of his opponents for an obvious and thrilling goal that sent the fans of the winning team into shrill, elated cries of victory. The Americans were impressed by the skill and dexterity of the players, but taken aback by the wild abandon with which they threw themselves headfirst toward the hard, rock-studded ground. "Why they do not grind off their noses I cannot imagine," Roosevelt marveled.

* * *

As welcome as it was, the distraction offered by the Indians' enthusiastic games could not outpace the deepening foreboding among the men. With each passing day, it was becoming increasingly clear to Roosevelt that he was going to have to take drastic measures if the expedition hoped to descend—and survive—the River of Doubt.

Even before reaching Tapirapoan, the men had agreed that not all of them would be able to descend the river. While they made their way across the highlands, they had been steadily adding men to their expedition, men who would be indispensable to their safety and the success of their journey. In Tapirapoan alone, they had added 148 camaradas to the contingent of eleven officers. Of greatest importance to the expedition were the additions of Dr. Cajazeira and a man named Lieutenant João Salustiano Lyra. A military engineer and skilled surveyor, Lyra had accompanied Rondon on three of his previous expeditions, including the 1909 journey during which he discovered the River of Doubt, and had helped map large swaths of the Amazon. Although he had come close to losing his life several times while following Rondon, Lyra had never hesitated to venture back into the jungle with his colonel.

It was immediately apparent to everyone in the expedition that the cuts would have to come from within the American contingent, not the Brazilian. The first difficult decision had centered on the two American naturalists, Cherrie and Miller. Although both men were hardworking and experienced explorers, their skills overlapped to a large degree, and having two naturalists was a luxury that the expedition could no longer afford. Only one of the men would continue with the expedition; the other would descend the Gy-Paraná, which Rondon had already mapped but which would offer good opportunities for collecting. This was a less dangerous journey (though not significantly so, judging from the recent drowning deaths of Rondon's soldiers on the same river), and could be made in a *batelão*, a large wooden boat with a tree-trunk keel and arched palm-leaf roof, that Rondon had arranged to have sent up the river to meet them. Scientifically, however, it was also much less important than the descent of the wild, unknown River of Doubt, and neither the hard-bitten, middle-aged Cherrie nor the ambitious young Miller had much interest in it.

Rather than choose between his two naturalists, Roosevelt had suggested that they draw lots or find some other way to make the decision themselves. After giving the matter some thought, however, Miller had simply fallen on his sword. "It seemed to me that, as Cherrie was the older and more experienced man," he wrote, "he was justly entitled to accompany the colonel on the journey down the new river." Roosevelt agreed with Miller's decision, but sought to ease the young man's disappointment. "When I get back I am anxious to help you send Miller to complete his work around Mount Duida," he wrote to Osborn. "He ought to have $5,000 for the trip. I will subscribe $1,000, and do my best to help raise the remainder. . . . I wish to give this as a kind of consolation prize to Miller!"

Roosevelt had also concluded that his old friend Father Zahm was not suited to the treacherous passage down the uncharted river. Zahm, like Miller, would continue with the expedition until it reached the River of Doubt, but at that point he would be shunted off to another, less challenging journey. "Father Zahm has now been definitely relegated from the Rio da Duvida trip and goes down the Gy [-P]araná," Kermit wrote to his mother. Even though the trip had been Zahm's idea in the first place and, at his age and with his failing health, he was unlikely to return to the Amazon, few members of the expedition shed any tears for him. "All for each, and each for all, is a good motto," Roosevelt had once written, "but only on condition that each works with might and main to so maintain himself as not to be a burden to others."

Kermit certainly would not miss the elderly priest. He had thought Zahm unfit for this type of expedition from the moment he met him in Bahia, and this impression had only been confirmed as the expedition progressed. Zahm had "no real harm to him," Kermit wrote. "He's just a very commonplace little fool." Even Roosevelt had placed increasingly less stock in his old friend. "Of our whole expedition every one works hard except good little Father Zahm," he wrote to Edith. But, though he would not excuse Zahm's flaws, Roosevelt always treated the priest kindly, never forgetting that he had been one of his few faithful friends in 1912. Throughout the campaign, Zahm had carefully monitored the political pulse of the Catholic laity, and at a time when nearly everyone else was abandoning Roosevelt, he had made it clear that his own support was unwavering. Borrowing from Psalm 44, Zahm had encouraged his friend to *"Prospere procede et regna"*—proceed prosperously and reign. "Win or lose, Father," Roosevelt had answered, "there are certain friendships I have tested in this campaign . . . and among these friendships is my friendship with you."

Zahm must have been humiliated to find himself pushed out of the expedition that he had planned to lead with Roosevelt. But, characteristically rebounding, he sought to make the best of it, asserting that the change in plans had actually been his own idea. Indeed, Zahm, the master of self-promotion, could do even better than that. After reaching Manáos, he assured his brother, Albert, he then planned to set off on an expedition that would outshine nearly any other in its feats of exploration. If his health held up, he wrote, he hoped to travel "through the heart of South America from Patagonia to the Caribbean. It will be the first time the trip has ever been made, and will in the estimation of every one that has heard of it be an extraordinary achievement and one that will contribute more towards making the southern continent known to the world than any similar undertaking in South American history. This is the opinion of some of the most eminent men in South America, all of whom are enthusiastic about the enterprising 'sacerdote Norte Americano,' as they are pleased to call me."

Any prospect that Father Zahm might have had for reviving his hopes of glory with his new itinerary, however, was soon undone by his worsening relations with the rest of the men, and his concern for his own comfort. Even now, Father Zahm came up with a new idea for the remainder of his journey with the expedition, and proposed it to Rondon.

Given the discomforts of traveling, the priest explained, the best solution would be for him to ride in a divan chair on the shoulders of four strong Indians. This suggestion seemed straightforward and practical to Zahm. But Roosevelt and Rondon must have been rendered almost speechless by the image of Father Zahm riding across the highlands like Montezuma on the bent backs of his subjects. While the Brazilian colonel kept his composure, he made it perfectly clear to Zahm that no Pareci would submit to such degrading and subservient work.

Surprised that Rondon had recoiled at his suggestion, Father Zahm reassured him that, in Peru, carrying a member of the Roman Catholic clergy in such a fashion was "an honour worth disputing." "Father Zahm called our attention to the noteworthy fact that such a great difference should exist in the natures of men of an almost identical degree of civilization," Rondon later wrote, restraining his contempt for Zahm, but just barely. "We, however, did not share in our friend's astonishment, inasmuch as we consider this and other differences as natural consequences of the methods adopted for the education of the Indians. . . . If we propose to educate men, so that they may incorporate themselves into our midst and become our co-citizens, we have nothing more to do than to persevere in applying the methods up to the present adopted in Brazil: if, however, our intention is to create servants of a restricted and special society, the best road to follow would be the one opened by the Jesuitic teachings."

When it was clear that Rondon would not relent, Zahm appealed to Roosevelt, a decision that proved to be his undoing. "Indians are meant to carry priests," he explained to his old friend, "and I have resorted to such transportation several times." Roosevelt, who was well aware that Rondon was an Indian and a Positivist and had witnessed firsthand the mistreatment of Indians in the Dakota Territories, chose his words carefully before replying to Father Zahm. "But you will not commit such an affront to my dear Colonel Rondon's principles," he said in measured tones.

Since the day he had met Rondon on the Paraguay-Brazil border,

Roosevelt had gone to great lengths to show his Brazilian co-commander every courtesy and mark of respect that his experience and position, as well as his character, deserved. Not only did Roosevelt admire Rondon's accomplishments as an explorer and a military man, but he respected his philosophical beliefs. "The colonel's Positivism was in very fact to him a religion of humanity," Roosevelt wrote, "a creed which bade him be just and kindly and useful to his fellow men, to live his life bravely, and no less bravely to face death, without reference to what he believed, or did not believe, or to what the unknown hereafter might hold for him."

Roosevelt also insisted that he and Rondon be treated as equals in every way. One night during their overland journey, as the men sat on the damp ground around their oxhide dinner table, Rondon had ceremoniously produced two chairs: one for Roosevelt and the other for Father Zahm. Zahm surely welcomed the simple luxury, but Roosevelt refused to take a seat unless Rondon also had a chair. "Mr. Roosevelt positively declared to me, that as long as he was in the wilderness he would accept nothing, and do nothing, that might have an appearance of special attention to his person," Rondon recalled. "And consequently just as he saw me sit so would he sit himself."

Father Zahm, however, apparently did not have the same qualms about demanding special treatment. Finally, after what Rondon described as a heated exchange over Zahm's request to be carried in a divan chair, Roosevelt invited the priest to step into his tent. By the time the two men reappeared, Zahm was on his way home. "Since you cannot ride a horse," Roosevelt told him, "you will go back to Tapirapoan, accompanied by Sigg."

No one was happier to hear the news of Zahm's departure than Kermit. "Father Zahm is being sent back from here," he wrote Belle. "He showed him[self] so completely incompetent and selfish that he got on everyone's nerves, and then he tried a couple of things that made it easy to send him back."

The next day, Roosevelt sat down with a blank piece of paper and, aware that his friend would arrive home ahead of him, took the unusual step of handwriting a brief but formal record of Zahm's dismissal, which everyone but the camaradas signed.

Utiarity

Feb. 1st   1914

Every member of the expedition has told me that in his opinion it is essential to the success and well being of the expedition that Father Zahm should at once leave it and return to the settled country.

Theodore Roosevelt

The above statement is correct.

Candido Mar. Rondon	Jacob Sigg
Leo E. Miller	Euzebio Paul
J. S. Lyra	L. Oliveira
Geo K. Cherrie	Anthony Fiala
José A. Cajazeira	Kermit Roosevelt

Even Sigg, whom Zahm had hired and whose fate was tied to the priest's, stepped forward to sign the document.

* * *

AFTER LEAVING Utiarity, the mule train resumed its grueling progress toward the headwaters of the River of Doubt, adhering closely to the crude trail blazed by the Rondon Commission. An astronomical effort had gone into simply erecting the poles that supported the telegraph line. First a team of about twenty men would map the area, cutting down and stripping the branches from trees deemed straight and tall enough to hold up their raw copper wires. Then an oxcart would deliver a newly dismembered tree to the eight men whose job it was to erect the telegraph pole. Two men would slip a rope around the pole and then strain to pull it toward them from one side, while the other six men struggled to lift the pole from the opposite direction. It was dirty, exhausting work that was usually done in blazing heat or a thunderous downpour, and on an empty stomach.

Following in the path of the telegraph builders, Roosevelt and his men were spared the exhausting and often deadly toil that had gone into building the lines, but even so their progress was still painfully slow and their daily routine was defined by the same strict military regimentation and discipline that were the hallmark of all Rondon's explorations. Every morning the men were startled out of their sleep by a sharp bugle. As they awoke, Juan, a black camarada whom Miller described as being "as big-hearted and obliging as he was tall and powerful," would duck his head into their tent with a pot full of coffee, which he poured, black and steaming, into aluminum cups.

In the tender light of the early morning, the camaradas would saddle their mules so that they would be ready to ride as soon as the officers finished their breakfast. Roosevelt would usually try to duck away at this time, to get in some writing before the long day's ride began. This was often his only opportunity to work on the series of articles he was writing for *Scribner's* magazine: Once the men mounted their mules, they did not stop until late in the afternoon, and then usually had to wait four or five hours more for the mule train to arrive with their baggage.

Before they left camp each morning, Rondon would announce how many kilometers they would ride that day. There were eleven telegraph line poles per kilometer, and a consecutive number had been carved onto each pole, so, by watching the poles pass by, the men could easily estimate how far they had to go until they reached the next campsite. Even a short day, however, could seem unbearably long. Kermit had developed sores on his legs, and they became so inflamed that at one point he had to spend almost an entire day standing straight up in his stirrups. Early in the overland journey, Cherrie had driven a palm thorn into one of his legs, and the point remained buried a half-inch deep in the muscle, partially paralyzing his foot. They were all tormented by hordes of gnats, sand flies, horseflies, and small, stingless bees that the Brazilians call *lambe-olho,* or "eye lick-ers." These bees swarmed around their hands and faces, congregating at the corners of their eyes and buzzing about their lips with madden-ing persistence. Not even the most thundering swat would dissuade them. As described by H. M. Tomlinson, who had traveled through the Amazon in 1909 and 1910, and had suffered their ceaseless atten-tions, the stingless bees preferred "death to being dislodged from [their] enjoyment."

The most difficult part of every day's ride, however, was the rain, which had begun mildly enough at the beginning of their journey but was now falling, Kermit wrote his mother, "mournfully, dismally, and ceaselessly; in a sort of hopeless insistent way." Their mules slipped and stumbled in the slick, thickening mud, and collecting specimens for the museum had become, Cherrie complained, "a practical impos-sibility." One day, the Americans and the Brazilian officers were obliged to stand, without shelter of any kind, for hours in a heavy downpour while they waited for the mule train to arrive with their tents. "Everything became mouldy," Roosevelt wrote, "except what became rusty."

The weather only deepened Roosevelt's concern about Kermit, whose malaria had continued to worsen, leaving him with a debilitat-ing fever that now reached as high as 102 degrees. For Roosevelt, worry about his second son had become as familiar as the swelling pride he felt when he reflected on all that the young man had already accomplished.

As proud as Roosevelt was of his son's physical stamina and vigor-ous work ethic, he feared that Kermit might one day push himself too far. In Africa, Roosevelt had watched with growing alarm as Kermit threw himself into increasingly dangerous situations. "It is hard to re-alize that the rather timid boy of four years ago has turned out a per-fectly cool and daring fellow," Roosevelt had written his oldest son, Ted Jr. "Indeed he is a little too reckless and keeps my heart in my throat, for I worry about him all the time; he is not a good shot, not even as good as I am, and Heaven knows I am poor enough; but he is a bold rider, always cool and fearless, and eager to work all day long. He ran down and killed a Giraffe, alone, and a Hyena also, and the day before yesterday he stopped a charging Leopard within six yards of him, after it had mauled one of our porters."

Now, in a remote corner of the Brazilian interior, Roosevelt worried less about Kermit's aim than about his ability to fight off the deadly diseases of the Amazon or survive the River of Doubt. He could not bear the thought of facing Belle and Edith if anything happened to Kermit. Kermit had joined the expedition so that he could protect his father, but it was Roosevelt who now feared for his son.

*   *   *

ON FEBRUARY 4, Roosevelt, perhaps shaken by the provisions the expedition had already lost, the lonely telegraph workers' graves he had seen, Margaret's death, and his son's illness, decided that it was imperative to the success of the expedition that he cut another man from his team. Unfortunately, that man was the member of the expedition who, with the possible exception of Father Zahm, had hung the greatest hopes on this journey into the Amazon.

After they made camp near the Burity—a swift, deep river that afforded them the luxury of a much-needed bath—Roosevelt called Anthony Fiala aside. With deep regret, he gave him the painful news that he would not be descending the River of Doubt with the rest of the expedition. Although Fiala had done his best to please Roosevelt, his knowledge of Arctic exploration, and the hard lessons he had learned there, had failed to translate to the Amazon.

Miller dismissed Fiala out of hand, writing to Chapman that their quartermaster was "quite incompetent to do a single thing," and Cherrie readily agreed. "I have not written anything about the organization of our expedition, but now I'm going to record my opinion that a greater lack of organization seems hardly possible!" he had written in his diary on November 25, while he and Miller were still in Corumbá. "There is no head no chief of the expedition. Fiala in a way is the temporary head but utterly incompetent for the work he has to do without previous experience in the tropics without any knowledge of the character of the people with whom he must treat and the almost insurmountable handicap of not having any knowledge of the language."

Of the trio of adventurous Americans whom Roosevelt had nicknamed the "three Buccaneers"—Cherrie, Miller, and Fiala—only Cherrie would actually go on the expedition that they had all planned to take together. But, as he had for Miller, Roosevelt made an effort to find another river journey for Fiala so that he would have some compensation for the months he had already devoted to the expedition. His plan was for the photographer to descend the Papagaio River, much of which had yet to be explored, even though its source and mouth were relatively well known. Fiala accepted the offer, but his heart clearly wasn't in it.

Although the men had had little sympathy for Father Zahm, they could not help pitying Fiala, whose cherished opportunity to redeem himself as an explorer was now lost. "Fiala left us and started back toward Utiarity at 10 p.m.," Cherrie wrote in his diary that night. "I think his going had a saddening effect on all of us; and Fiala himself was almost in tears."

CHAPTER 9

Warnings from the Dead

"THE OXEN HAVE GIVEN out," Kermit recorded in the cream-colored pages of his bound Letts of London journal on February 6, 1914. As drastic as Roosevelt's cutbacks in men and equipment had been, it had quickly become apparent that they were not enough. The expedition was faltering again. Not only were the oxen collapsing, the mules were dying at an alarming rate. Since Tapirapoan, the expedition had lost more than half of its ninety-eight mules and of those that remained, ten could barely walk. If the men hoped to reach the banks of the River of Doubt, their only option was to make more sacrifices—gambling that the provisions and equipment that they abandoned now would not be desperately needed later on.

Before the overland journey had even begun, Roosevelt had insisted that they leave behind half of the tents that the Brazilian government had given them as gifts in Tapirapoan, and which, he later confided to the Royal Geographical Society's John Scott Keltie, were "enormously heavy" and "utterly unsuited for the work." He now urged Rondon to get rid of half of the tents that remained. "I had to exercise real tact," he wrote Keltie, "because it almost broke the heart of good Colonel Rondon. . . . Our companions cared immensely for what they regarded as splendor." Two oxcarts, groaning with the weight of their cargo, were abandoned, as were two trunks of specimens that Miller and Cherrie had collected and preserved for the museum. The naturalists were even forced to part with most of their collecting equipment.

Each man then cut his personal baggage in half, keeping, Roosevelt wrote, only "the sheer necessities." Kermit faithfully did his part to throw out what he did not absolutely need. He counted as necessities, however, his packet of letters from Belle—including a small picture of her that he always carried in his shirt pocket, and which he feared she would not recognize, "what with [it] being wet through so many times"—and his books, which were heavy, but essential. "Through all the lightening of the baggage I have kept my books," he wrote Belle. "It means a lot to go to a quiet place to read the poems that we both like, and those that I always associate with you." The poems were from *The Oxford Book of French Verse*. Besides this volume and *The Oxford Book of English Verse*, the rest of Kermit's books were written in Portuguese—with the notable exception of his copies of *The Iliad* and *The Odyssey*, which were in the original Greek.

As crucial as it was for the expedition to lighten the pack animals' loads, however, much of what they were carrying was not expendable. Before they began jettisoning crates of food and other critical supplies, Roosevelt, using all of his diplomatic skills so as not to offend his co-commander, questioned Rondon about the expedition's preparedness for the River of Doubt. If there was any possibility that they might not have all that they needed to make a safe descent, he told Rondon, they should walk, reserving every able-bodied animal for carrying provisions rather than passengers. Rondon "would not have minded the walk at all from the physical standpoint," Roosevelt wrote, "but he simply could not bear to have us take action which he regarded as an admission that we were not doing the thing in splendid style." He assured Roosevelt that there was no need to take such a drastic step. Everyone in the expedition would be well provided for on the River of Doubt.

On February 8, the American and Brazilian officers finally reached the Juruena River, the site of another of Rondon's remote and isolated telegraph stations. Pausing on a hilltop, the men looked back over the miles of rolling landscape that they had crossed, shrouded in low, thick forest. Farther north, the six-hundred-mile-long Juruena widens significantly, but even here, in its relatively narrow southern reaches, it was broad and deep enough to force the mules to cross it on a rickety raft composed of a wooden platform lashed onto three dugout canoes. When they reached the other side, pulling themselves across the rushing current with a wire trolley, the men were, as always, relieved to stop at a telegraph station. Their accommodations would again be a simple wattle-and-daub hut with a thatched roof and plenty of cracks and chinks for the sand flies to find their way inside and torment them throughout the night, but it was better than spending another miserable night in rain-soaked tents.

As it had in Utiarity, however, bad news awaited the expedition in Juruena. This time, it was about Fiala. From a telegram that was handed to Roosevelt, the men learned that the first day of their friend's descent of the Papagaio River had nearly been his last. Fiala's expedition, which had begun just the day before without any of the provisions he had packed for Roosevelt's journey, had met with immediate and almost complete disaster. Not long after they had launched their three dugout canoes, two of them, including the one in which Fiala was riding, were sucked into a churning pocket of the river known as the Rapids of the Devil. Most of the nine men had managed to fight their way back to the bank, but Fiala, along with half of the expedition's food and most of its equipment, was swept helplessly down the river.

"I just saved myself by snatching hold of a tree-bough that overhung the stream about thirty feet from the bank, and then pulling myself in," Fiala told a reporter for the *New York Times* after returning home. The Brazilians whom Rondon had assigned to accompany

Fiala, however, told their colonel a very different story. It was true that the boats had capsized, they said, but Fiala did not save himself—in fact, he very nearly caused the drowning death of the man who ultimately rescued him from the rapids.

Even if Fiala had once again led his men into a disaster, with new doubts about his own actions, the ill-starred explorer had at least been proved right on one count: his insistence that North American canoes were the proper means for descending the Amazon's dangerous tributaries. Fiala blamed his near-death in the Papagaio rapids on the heavy, clumsy South American dugouts. After his first disastrous day on the Papagaio, Fiala refused to trust the dugouts a second time. He returned to Utiarity and retrieved the Canadian canoes that he himself had handpicked, and which Roosevelt's expedition had left behind because they could not afford the additional weight.

The Brazilians on his team thought that their commander had lost his mind and balked at the idea of boarding such an insubstantial-looking canoe, especially since Rondon held them responsible for Fiala's safety. However, when they saw "how buoyantly the canoe rode the rapids," Fiala later proudly recalled, "how a twist of the paddle would deflect it around a rock on which a dugout would crash and smash, they gave cries of delight." Fiala's selection of his Canadian canoes had been vindicated.

Miles away, on his journey to the River of Doubt, however, Roosevelt had no way to know that and could do nothing about it even if he had.

* * *

OUTSIDE OF Juruena, moreover, the men's concern about accidental mishaps, dying mules, and low supplies were compounded by a new fear: calculated attack. The hum of the telegraph wires, as familiar now as the weary clop-clop-clop of their mules' hooves on the wet clay and sand soil, was the only sign of civilization in the broad scrub forest before them. They felt as isolated as if they were traveling across an uninhabited planet. They were not alone, however, and they knew that there was rarely a moment of the day or night when they were not being watched.

They were now, Roosevelt wrote, "in a still wilder region, the land of the naked Nhambiquaras." Rondon had made first contact with this tribe, one of the most isolated and primitive of the Amazon, only six years earlier. They had welcomed him with a fusillade of poison-tipped arrows. Hoping to make a clear gesture of friendship, Rondon and just three of his men, including Lyra, had ridden single-file toward a Nhambiquara camp, their mules heaped high with gifts. But before they had even reached the camp, Rondon had felt something fly past his face that was so light and fast that for a moment he thought it was a bird. In the millisecond it took him to realize that it was an arrow, a second one slammed into his helmet. The third arrow struck his chest and lodged in his thick leather bandolier. Ordering his men not to return fire, Rondon calmly turned his mule around and rode back to his own camp, sitting straight in his saddle with the arrow—five feet long with a ten-inch macaw feather, split in two, on one end and a serrated, curare-coated tip on the other—still sticking out of his chest.

For weeks, the Nhambiquara had terrorized Rondon's men, disappearing during the day and attacking at night, when the soldiers were most vulnerable. The men were so frightened that they refused even to build a campfire after the sun went down, in the hope that the Nhambiquara would not be able to find them on the black plateau. Gradually, however, Rondon had won the Indians over, by first wooing them with gifts and then luring them to his campsite by playing a phonograph at night, sending the strains of a Wagnerian opera into the forest like a beautiful, incorporeal siren. Through persistent kindness, compassion, and patience in the face of relentless and often deadly attacks, he had forged a simple peace, but it was tentative at best and had met with varying degrees of success within the tribes' scattered and independent bands.

For the telegraph-station workers, the men whom Rondon left behind to guard and repair the poles after the rest of the expedition had moved on, the Nhambiquara remained a constant threat. In general, long-term peace between the telegraph-station workers and the Indians was rare. Although the relationship usually started out on a friendly footing—Rondon having ordered the workers to be kind to the Indians, not meddle in their affairs, and give them plenty of gifts—it almost always devolved into resentment and distrust. The telegraph-station workers, moreover, were utterly alone, with no hope of help from any quarter, and with a store of coveted weapons and metal tools that made them enticing targets. In the late 1930s, the French anthropologist Claude Lévi-Strauss traveled along Rondon's telegraph line and heard many stories of telegraph workers who had died grisly deaths at the hands of the Nhambiquara. "Someone may recall," Lévi-Strauss wrote in his seminal book *Tristes Tropiques,* "how a certain telegraph operator was found buried up to the waist, with his chest riddled with arrows and his morse-key on his head."

Even missionaries, who were ostensibly there to help the Indians, body and soul, had difficulty staying alive in Nhambiquara territory. The seemingly simplest of misunderstandings could lead to the slaughter of an entire missionary community. Lévi-Strauss told the story of one such massacre that happened in the very region through which Roosevelt and his men were now traveling:

A Protestant mission came to settle not far from the post at Juruena. It would seem that relations soon became embittered, the natives having been dissatisfied with the gifts—inadequate, apparently—that the missionaries had given them in return for their help in building the house and planting the garden. A few months later, an Indian with a high temperature presented himself at the mission and was publicly given two aspirin tablets, which he swallowed; afterwards he bathed in the river, developed congestion of the lungs and died. As the Nambikwara are expert poisoners, they concluded that their fellow-tribesman had been murdered; they launched a retaliatory attack, during which six members of the mission were massacred, including a two-year-old child. Only one woman was found alive by a search party sent out from Cuiaba.

* * *

EVEN WHERE relationships appeared to be well established, there was still a good chance that things could go disastrously wrong. Rondon did his best to "civilize" the Indians who lived near his telegraph stations—a perhaps misguided effort for which he would be criticized in later years—but he did not control them, and he never would. In Utiarity, he taught the Pareci Indians, one of the region's most sophisticated and peaceful tribes, how to build more substantial houses; he helped them grow potatoes, corn, and manioc; and he gave them clothing. He even hired some of them to work for the Rondon Commission, paying the average worker sixty-six cents a day, particularly valuable employees a dollar, and chiefs $1.66.

The Nhambiquara, however, had proved impervious to Rondon's efforts. They were still largely nomadic hunter-gatherers, settling down only during the rainy season. For most of the year, they slept under the most temporary and fragile of shelters—a half- or quarter-circle of palm branches that they had driven into holes dug into the sand. They would set up these shelters in the direction from which they expected to receive the most sun, wind, or rain, but they would disassemble them every morning and build new ones the next night. Unlike neighboring tribes, the Nhambiquara also slept on the ground rather than in a hammock—a practice for which the Pareci despised them.

The Nhambiquara were also wholly uninterested in clothing. Some of the Pareci who worked for the telegraph stations had begun to wear shirts and even pants, but the Nhambiquara men still wore nothing more than a string around their waist with, at the most, a tuft of dried grass or a scrap of cloth that served no purpose beyond pure ornamentation. The Nhambiquara women did not even wear that much. This determined nakedness never ceased to worry Rondon, who did not trust his soldiers around the Indian girls, and who knew that, if his men succumbed to this particular temptation, they would likely pay for it with their lives.

An even greater danger to the telegraph line soldiers—and to all the progress that Rondon had made in his relationship with the Indians—was tribal warfare. Rondon had strictly forbidden his men ever to take sides in a tribal battle, no matter how seemingly brutal or unjust. In Utiarity, however, one man had recently defied this order, with potentially disastrous results. Shortly before the expedition had arrived there, a group of Nhambiquara had descended on the Pareci's village while their men were gone. Hearing the screams of their wives and mothers, the Pareci had rushed home, and a battle had broken out in full view of the telegraph station. The Nhambiquara were better, more experienced warriors than the Pareci, but the Pareci had a powerful ally: a telegraph line employee, the only man for nearly a hundred miles who had a gun. Having grown fond of the Pareci, and having watched the Nhambiquara prey on them time and again, the man had stepped into the melee, raised his gun, and fatally shot a Nhambiquara warrior, enraging Rondon and putting at risk the precarious peace he had worked so long to achieve.

Rondon's injunction against violence directed toward an Indian— any Indian, for any reason—was categorical. In fact, he valued the lives of the Amazonian Indians above his own life—or the lives of his men. Surely there was not a soldier in the Rondon Commission who could not recite by heart his colonel's now famous command: "Die if you must, but never kill." Rondon's success in the Amazon had depended on this dictum. It was the only reason the Indians had ever dared to trust him.

As they had in the United States, Native Americans in Brazil had been exploited, enslaved, and slaughtered for centuries—since 1500, the year the Portuguese explorer Pedro Álvares Cabral is said to have discovered the region. In 1908, Hermann von Ihering, the German-born director of the São Paulo Museum, argued that it was a shame, but the Indians would surely not survive Brazilian ambitions, and they should not be allowed to stand in their way. "I feel for them as a man," he wrote, "but as a citizen in keeping with my political belief, I cannot stand by and watch the march of our culture halted by Indian arrows. And certainly the life of the backwoodsman and colonist is worth more to us than the life of the savage. The fate of the Indians is certain. Many of them will accept our culture, the remainder will continue to be our enemies and, as such, will gradually disappear."

Unwittingly, however, von Ihering had ignited the greatest advancement in the cause of Indian rights that Brazil had ever witnessed. Outraged by the museum director's blatant disregard for Indian lives—von Ihering had even gone so far as to note in an article that it was "worth registering here what the American General Custer said: 'the only good Indian is a dead Indian' "—Rondon engaged him in a public debate. In 1910, the momentum generated by this debate resulted in the formation of Brazil's Indian Protection Service—SPI—the country's first agency devoted to the protection of its native inhabitants, and Rondon was named its first director.

Rondon's brave and unyielding advocacy of the Amazonian Indian was to become his most important legacy—outshining even his achievements as an explorer. Whatever the merits of his philosophy, however, his approach was cold comfort to the soldiers he forced to practice it. In fact, so infamous were Rondon's expeditions into the interior that he had to pay his men seven times what they made anywhere else. Even the cook aboard the *Nyoac* had known Rondon's reputation for losing his men's lives as he forged a path through Indian territory. When the Brazilian colonel invited him to join the descent of the River of Doubt, the cook had replied in horror, "Sir! I have done nothing to deserve such punishment!"

Rondon refused even to let his men retaliate when they had been attacked. It was not unusual for his soldiers to have to watch helplessly while their friends died brutal deaths at the hands of Indians, and then have no ability to avenge their loss, no recourse but tears. "Let us weep," Rondon would tell them, "for I loved this man who has perished for my sake. But I command you to do as he did. Never shoot."

Rondon believed that his mission in protecting and pacifying the Indians was larger than his own life, larger than any of their lives. He would rather die than surrender his ideals, and he obliged his men to follow suit.

* * *

ROOSEVELT, FOR his part, was not planning on sacrificing his expedition or the lives of any of his men on the altar of Rondon's ideals. As a young rancher in the Dakota Territories, Roosevelt had barked, "I don't go so far as to think that the only good Indians are dead Indians, but I believe nine out of every ten are, and I shouldn't like to inquire too closely into the case of the tenth." By the time he became president, his views had tempered, and he, like Rondon, believed that the country's "aim should be [the Indians'] ultimate absorption into the body of our people." However, the man he appointed as commissioner of Indian Affairs, Francis Leupp, made no effort to hide his belief that Indians would never be seamlessly integrated into the world of the white man. In fact, he argued that Indians should not be made United States citizens. "They are not fitted for [citizenship's] duties," he declared, "or able to take advantage of its benefits."

Roosevelt would never completely shake off the model of the American Western frontier with which he had grown up. When he was in Dakota, the battles between the Indians and the pioneers were only just ending. "There were still sporadic outbreaks here and there, and occasionally bands of marauding young braves were a menace to outlying and lonely settlements," he recalled, but "many of the white men were themselves lawless and brutal, and prone to commit outrages on the Indians." Though Roosevelt had sympathy for the Indians and understood the injustices and cruelties that they had endured, in South America as well as in North America, Rondon's passive, pacifist approach was alien to his entire way of thinking. He was much more inclined to conquer than to be slaughtered.

The stakes were rising, moreover, because, with each passing day, the expedition was intruding deeper into Nhambiquara territory, and the Indians were becoming increasingly bold with Roosevelt and his men. Their gestures were friendly, as they clearly knew and liked Rondon, but the expedition members understood that the slightest insult or injury, whether real or simply perceived, could turn the Indians against them before they even realized what had happened.

The Nhambiquara lived by the laws of the wilderness, which demanded that, as Roosevelt explained, "friends proclaim their presence; a silent advance marks a foe." During war, the Nhambiquara had perfected the art of the surprise attack. "When preparing for a war the chief of the band takes the men into the woods and tells them that there are bad people to the north which they must kill," observed Kalvero Oberg, a Smithsonian anthropologist who studied the tribe in the mid-1940s.

> Then after singing a war song they set about making many arrows and war clubs. The night before the attack they camp near the village of the enemy. The men paint their bodies with the sap of some latex tree and their faces with urucú and charcoal. They then take leaves and stuff them into any holes in the ground or in trees around their camp. After all the holes are stopped up, they take the skin of an anteater, the skin of a toad, and the leaves of a tree, which are used in preventing rain, and burn them. The stopping of the holes is believed to prevent the enemy from hearing them. . . . The Chief remains at his spot and sings all night with the shamans. At dawn the young men approach the huts of the enemy, stand in the doorway and shout, and when the occupants awaken they are shot down or clubbed. No one is spared.

Conversely, to show their good intentions when they visited the expedition, the Indians would leave their weapons behind and call out to Roosevelt and his men from hiding places in the forest that surrounded the telegraph road. The members of the expedition would answer, inviting the Indians to visit their camp. The Indians would then shout again. The expedition would answer. Shout. Answer. Shout.

Answer. Until, finally, the Indians were certain that they were welcome, and the expedition was certain that they were coming as friends and not as attackers.

Once in the camp, the Nhambiquara would get as close as physically possible to the white men, whom they found curiously pale, tall, and hairy. While Roosevelt was trying to write, they would gather around him so tightly that he would have to gently push them away so that he could move his arms. The Nhambiquara were taller and darker than the Pareci, with longer heads and hair cut into distinctive bowl-like bangs. Around Rondon, they were smiling and relaxed. Kermit liked them. They are "a very pleasant set," he wrote Belle, "and didn't look at all as if they had given Rondon all the trouble they have. . . . They have small hands and feet, and really nice faces. It's melancholy to think how they will change when civilization comes here." Leo Miller, however, who, perhaps of all the members of the expedition, had the lowest opinion of Indians, was repelled by the quills and thin pieces of bamboo that the Nhambiquara men threaded through holes pierced into their upper lips and the septum of their noses—especially since the Indians clearly had no appreciation for the American concept of personal space. "They had the unpleasant habit of coming close up to one and jabbering at a furious rate of speed," Miller wrote. "This caused the labrets to move uncomfortably near one's eyes, and it was necessary at times to retreat a short distance in order to get out of range of the menacing ornaments." Roosevelt marveled that these sticks, which were roughly six inches long, did not bother the Indians, even when they ate. "They laughed at the suggestion of removing them," he wrote. "Evidently to have done so would have been rather bad manners—like using a knife as an aid in eating ice cream."

The Nhambiquara intrigued Roosevelt, and he enjoyed their company, but he would not let his guard down around them. He had heard vivid tales of their brutality toward the Pareci in Utiarity, and he had spent a night watching them dance in Juruena, only to wake up and find that they had left in the wee hours, taking with them two of the expedition's dogs. These Indians were, he wrote, "light-hearted robbers and murderers."

While he was on this expedition, Roosevelt felt obliged to follow Rondon's lead. This was his country and his territory, and Roosevelt respected Rondon's authority as a colonel in the Brazilian military. However, nothing he saw suggested that Rondon's approach would produce anything but tragedy. His concerns were dramatically illustrated on February 11, when the men made camp near the remains of an abandoned Indian village. After dinner, a few of the men wandered over to see what was left. Not far from the sagging and crumbling palm-thatch huts, the men stumbled upon the graves of two Brazilian soldiers and an army officer who had been murdered by Nhambiquara and then buried vertically, with their heads and shoulders sticking out of the ground.

The most frightening aspect of these lonely graves was that the Indians who had killed these men were much further along the road of pacification, civilization, and friendship with the outside world than were the unknown Indians who lived on the banks of the River of Doubt. The Nhambiquara were violent and unpredictable, but at least they had forged a semblance of peace with Rondon. The Indians of the River of Doubt, in contrast, were utterly unknown even to Rondon, and there was no reason to think that they would welcome the expedition into their territory with any more tolerance or self-restraint than the Nhambiquara had shown when they had rained arrows down on Rondon at his first approach. Roosevelt and his men may have regarded themselves as explorers, but the Indians would know them only as invaders.

*   *   *

WITH ALL of these worries weighing on his mind, Roosevelt was struck one last heavy blow just as he reached the River of Doubt. Throughout the overland journey, Rondon had assured the ex-president that the expedition would have enough provisions for every man who was to descend the river. When they took stock of their supplies, however, Rondon and Roosevelt together learned that the haphazard preparations for the journey, and the grueling month since leaving Tapirapoan, had taken a far greater toll than anyone had fully realized.

Even in the best of circumstances, the remaining rations would not come close to feeding the sixteen camaradas who were to do the hardest work of paddling the expedition's boats and portaging its equipment. At the very outset of their descent of an unmapped river, Roosevelt was forced to cut his own and the other officers' rations in half so that the camaradas on whom they depended could have any chance of surviving the journey. The expedition had now turned into a race against time. The survival of every man would depend on their collective ability to master the churning river, evade its ever-present dangers, and discover a route out of the deepest rain forest before their supplies ran out.

PART THREE

The Descent

The Unknown

IF ROOSEVELT AND HIS men could have soared over the rain forest like the hawks that wheeled above them, the River of Doubt
would have looked like a black piece of ribbon candy nestled in an
endless expanse of green. Here, at the start of its tortuous journey
northward, the river was so tightly coiled that at times it doubled
back on itself, and in every direction the jungle stretched—dense,
impenetrable, and untouched—to the horizon. The expedition was finally preparing to descend into the Amazon Basin from the highland
plateau that it had just crossed. Even from the air, however, the river's
path into the jungle lowlands was so capricious, and the terrain so uneven, that it frequently disappeared entirely beneath the dense green
canopy, making it nearly impossible to follow.

Rondon believed that the River of Doubt ultimately poured into
the Madeira, the principal tributary of the Amazon River. On the basis of that educated guess, he had, before departing, sent a detachment of men to travel up the Madeira to the point where he calculated
that he and Roosevelt would eventually emerge. The detachment, led
by Lieutenant Antonio Pyrineus—the man who had nearly lost his

tongue and his life to a piranha during Rondon's harrowing 1909 tele-graph expedition—was ordered to set up camp at the confluence of the two southern branches of a tributary of the Madeira called the Aripuanã. The Madeira, which is so large that its basin is more than twice the size of France, winds for more than two thousand miles through western Brazil and has more than a dozen tributaries. As the Madeira's largest tributary, the Aripuanã was well known in its final, lower reaches, but rapids and Indians had prevented even the most in-trepid and ambitious rubber-tappers from traveling more than a few hundred miles up its course. Rondon had instructed Pyrineus to take a steamer up the Aripuanã as far as he could, and then to go by canoe to the point at which the river was known to split into two long arms. He was to wait at this fork in the river in the hope that, two or even three months after starting down the River of Doubt, the Roosevelt-Rondon Scientific Expedition would appear on the horizon.

If Rondon was right, and the expedition eventually reunited with Pyrineus on the Aripuanã, it would mean two things: First, it would mean that Roosevelt had placed on the map of South America a river that was nearly a thousand miles long—as long as the Ohio or the Rhine. There would then be no question but that the River of Doubt was, in Rondon's words, a "river whose importance would justify the idea of giving it [Roosevelt's] name." The scale of that achievement, however, would be directly proportional to the sacrifices it would re-quire. If the expedition emerged where Rondon predicted, it also would mean that Roosevelt, Rondon, and their men had survived a journey as perilous as any in the history of Amazon exploration.

In contrast to the broad, sweeping grandeur of the Amazon River itself, the thousands of tributaries that stream into it are wild and capricious. They tear through the jungle like wounded animals, thrashing their banks and spitting white foam into the branches of overhanging trees. The rivers' ferocity is caused not solely by the great volume of water they carry (taken by itself, the Madeira is equal in volume to the powerful Congo—the world's second-largest river by volume after the Amazon itself), or even by their plunge from high-

land plateau to lowland basin. Instead, the principal reason these
rivers are nearly impossible to navigate is that they are studded with
rapids that are produced as water flows over rock formations of contrasting degrees of hardness. The softer the rock, the more easily it
erodes, exposing bars of hard bedrock that form ever-steeper steps in
the riverbed, making the water roil and churn as if a fire were blazing
beneath it. The Madeira, which starts its journey near the Bolivia-
Brazil border in the Brazilian Highlands, has at least thirty major waterfalls and rapids, with sixteen powerful cataracts in one 225-mile
stretch alone.

Everyone in the expedition understood that the River of Doubt, if
it followed the path Rondon suspected, would be just as rapids-
choked as the Madeira, if not more so. The difference between
Roosevelt's expedition and those of the countless rubber tappers who
had tried unsuccessfully to negotiate the Amazon's wild tributaries
was that Roosevelt was going to descend the River of Doubt, not attempt to fight his way up it. This strategy would allow him to harness
the river's great strength rather than oppose it. But it represented a
gamble of life-or-death proportions, because, from the moment the
men of the expedition launched their boats, they would no longer be
able to turn around. The river would carry them ever deeper into the
rain forest, with whatever dangers that might entail. When they
reached a series of rapids, they would have to portage around them—
or mumble a prayer and plunge ahead. In either case, the option of
returning the way they came was no longer available to them. They
would find a way through, or they would perish in the attempt.

*   *   *

ON THE spot where Rondon had abandoned his exploration of the
River of Doubt five years earlier, the Rondon Commission had built a
simple wooden bridge to straddle the river's roughly sixty-five-foot
expanse. As Roosevelt at last stood on that bridge, listening to the
swift, muddy water slap against the warped planks beneath his feet,
he peered into the dark stretch of jungle ahead of him. This world,

which he was about to enter for better or worse, was strange and utterly unfamiliar, and while his first glimpse into it was exciting, it was also deeply sobering. No one, not even the inscrutable Rondon, could predict what was around the next bend. Roosevelt was about to become an explorer in the truest, and most unforgiving, sense of the word. It was an opportunity he had dreamed of from his earliest childhood. Now, however, he realized that he would be called on to pay the full cost of his ambitions—and he found himself gravely unprepared for what might lie ahead.

After months of inattention, Roosevelt had now come face to face with the acute logistical shortcomings and rapidly escalating risks that his own casual approach to the expedition and its route had produced. Roosevelt, Rondon, and their men were about to begin the most difficult leg of their journey, but they were already at the limits of their endurance. After spending more than a month slogging through the muddy highlands, with long days on muleback, nearly constant downpours, illness, worry, death, and sorrow, the men were exhausted, homesick, and wary—not just of the river they were about to descend but also of one another. To the Americans, the overland journey had appeared chaotic and shockingly disorganized. To the Brazilians, on the other hand, the Americans must have seemed selfish and demanding. Father Zahm had certainly been the worst offender, but the comfort of all the Americans had always come first—even before the Brazilians' basic needs. Unknown to Roosevelt, Rondon had not only ordered his men to eat less so that the Americans could eat more, but had intentionally overloaded the pack oxen and abandoned entire crates of the camaradas' provisions in the hope that he would not have to ask the Americans to leave behind any of their ponderous baggage.

Until now, the wrangling over provisions and equipment had all seemed vaguely theoretical in nature, revolving around a river journey that was always distant in both time and geography. At the river's edge, however, the immense difficulties and uncertainties of the task that Roosevelt had taken on were suddenly transformed into urgent realities. Everything that the men of the expedition knew about the journey ahead underscored the dangers that they would face from this point forward.

Even more disturbing than what they knew was what they did not know. The obvious riddle of the river's course was only one of a thousand potentially lethal mysteries that now surrounded them. As they plunged deeper and deeper into the jungle, the riot of nature that enveloped them—from the crowded canopy overhead to the buzzing, insect-laden air around their faces to the unseen depths of the black river—became increasingly strange, unfamiliar, and threatening, to say nothing of the constant threat of Indian attack, which transformed every shadow into a potential enemy.

The most immediate problem was how to negotiate the river itself. Shifting whirlpools and whitewater rapids were obvious dangers, but even a seemingly benign ripple could be deadly. The danger was in the eddy line, the point at which the current, which is running downstream, collides with the eddy, which is heading upstream, causing a powerful and chaotic swirl of water just under the surface.

To deal with the unpredictable dangers of powerful rapids, American river explorers had tried a variety of specialized boats, eventually developing unusual swayback drift boats, with a shallow draft and high aft and stern, which made it possible to ride out the churning white water. The remoteness of the River of Doubt and the chaos of the overland journey, however, meant that Roosevelt and his men would have no such equipment. Although Roosevelt had left New York with more boats than he would possibly need in the Amazon, he had, incredibly enough, arrived at the river with no boats at all. He had chosen to leave Father Zahm's eight-hundred-pound motorboats—the *Edith* and the *Notre Dame*—in Rio de Janeiro after it had become clear that they were far too heavy to haul through the rain forest. Then, during the overland journey, the men had agreed to abandon Fiala's Canadian canoes in Utiarity when their failing oxen could no longer carry even those light watercraft. Now that the expedition had finally reached the River of Doubt, it found itself with twenty-two men, hundreds of pounds of supplies, and not a single boat.

Forced to find a local substitute for such vital equipment, the men were obliged to make do with a set of seven roughly hewn dugouts that Rondon purchased from a group of Nhambiquara Indians, and which were now tethered to the base of the telegraph bridge. Rondon assured Roosevelt that these dugouts were all "recently built," but they had been built by one of the Amazon's most primitive tribes, a group that was reviled by other tribes for its lack of even the most rudimentary hammock.

There was no comparison between these massive, clumsy dugouts and the sleek 160-pound canvas-covered canoes that Fiala had ordered for the expedition and which were now carrying him safely down the Papagaio River. Little more than hollowed-out tree trunks, the dugouts would be nearly impossible to maneuver when the expedition encountered rapids. In contrast to drift boats, which are designed to ride high through bucking waters and to facilitate the agile changes of direction needed to avoid submerged boulders and other lethal obstacles, the dugouts provided only minimal flotation and had little or no capacity for steering, obliging their occupants to plow through—or into—whatever lay ahead. Even their buoyancy left much to be desired, as the men of the expedition quickly discovered: The fully loaded dugouts left them sitting only a few inches above the surface, and were quickly swamped in rough water. These particular dugouts, moreover, were in questionable condition. In fact, Roosevelt's recounting of them sounded ominously like a description of the Seven Dwarfs. "One was small, one was cranky, and two were old, waterlogged, and leaky," he wrote. "The other three were good."

* * *

THE EXPEDITION's unanticipated reliance on such primitive boats had implications far beyond mere efficiency or comfort, or even the increased risk of drowning and other disasters. In the jungle, the boats were not simply a form of transportation, but the expedition's principal refuge from a broad variety of natural enemies. Every time the men of the expedition were forced to leave the relative sanctuary of the boats, they would have to expose themselves to the dangerous, unseen, and unpredictable creatures that surrounded them—on land and in the water.

At up to twenty-five hundred pounds apiece, the dugouts were also enormously heavy. Should the river prove so impassable that the expedition was forced to portage around it, the boats would be an excruciating burden and distraction as the men, vulnerable and exhausted, tried to haul them through the forest. The weight of the craft also greatly increased the stakes of even a minor mishap. Any slip with the heavy, waterlogged boats during a portage, in the rushing current, or merely during routine loading and unloading as they bobbed near the shore, could easily crush a man's hand or leg if it did not kill him outright. In the harsh, primitive conditions that lay ahead, the prospect of such accidents took on grave significance; the men understood that on the River of Doubt the difference between any injury and death was likely just a matter of time.

From their rough, wet seats just above the waterline, Roosevelt and his men could see many of the predators that surrounded them in the river, and could only imagine those that waited below the inky surface. In the tangled vines that shrouded the shoreline, what appeared to be partially submerged logs suddenly blinked and slid beneath the surface, revealing themselves as caimans—South American alligators. Rhythmic eddies in the water betrayed the passage of anacondas, which can weigh as much as five hundred pounds. The men were by now well acquainted with the razor-toothed piranha; every time they were forced to wade while maneuvering their sluggish dugouts, they would be at risk of attack.

If the rapids on the River of Doubt proved impassable and the men were driven ashore, they would face even greater dangers than on the river. The insects had already begun to swarm, brought out in droves by the ceaseless rain. The gravest threat came from mosquitoes, which carried everything from malaria to yellow fever, but perhaps the worst

torment came from piums. These minuscule black flies gorge themselves on blood like mosquitoes but descend by the hundreds, inflict-
ing red pinpoint bites that not only itch but leave their victims looking
as if they have been shot with buckshot.

In the rain forest, it seemed that every living thing—from animals
to insects to bacteria—was ready to attack, whether in offense or self-
preservation. Some of the world's deadliest serpents were coiled on
the forest floor and in the low branches of trees. There were poisonous frogs; lithe, stealthy jaguars; and collared peccaries, wild pigs
known to run in packs of more than three hundred animals. Then
there were the Indians, who could easily remain invisible to Roosevelt
and his men, even if they chose to attack.

Compounding all these dangers was the critical factor of time. The
kind of delays that they had experienced during the overland journey
would be more than frustrating while they were on the river: They
would be deadly. Not only would each extra day they were forced to
spend on the river leave the men more vulnerable to predators, disease, and Indian attack, but it would bring them that much closer to
starvation. Every time their clumsy dugouts obliged them to portage
around rapids, the men would expend more precious calories and
would have to spend more time attempting to hunt or find food, slowing the expedition even further.

In the face of such evident flaws in the expedition's preparations,
and the potential risks associated with any delay, the differences between its American and Brazilian leaders grew wider. Roosevelt and
Kermit wanted nothing more than to move ahead quickly. Having put
his life on hold for this expedition, all that Kermit asked of it was
swift, uneventful progress. Even for Roosevelt, this trip, which was a
rare opportunity for both adventure and achievement, was simply another trophy, one that he could keep next to his memories of his
ranching days in the West, the Battle of San Juan Hill, and his seven
years in the White House. If he survived, he would return as quickly
as possible to the United States and the hectic political life that he had
led before he had even set foot on South American soil.

For Rondon, however, the descent of the River of Doubt was not an isolated event. It was an integral part of a quarter-century of extraordinary effort and sacrifice. When Lauro Müller asked him to accompany Roosevelt into the Amazon, Rondon had been in the midst of one of the most difficult periods of a notably difficult career. He had been fighting to keep his sick soldiers alive and his telegraph line moving forward while at the same time desperately trying to prepare for what he hoped would be the line's November 1914 inauguration. Rondon had accepted the assignment because he knew that Theodore Roosevelt could give his commission the kind of public attention that it needed in order to maintain its funding and political support from the Brazilian government. But if he was going to descend this river, he intended to carry out his work with the same discipline and rigorous attention to detail that he had applied to each of his expeditions, no matter how grueling or dangerous. This expedition was an opportunity to write history, and Rondon was not going to rush through it—whatever the cost.

* * *

CAMPED AT the water's edge, the men made their final preparations for the start of their river journey. A few days earlier, they had divided their provisions between the River of Doubt expedition and the separate Gy-Paraná expedition, which Miller and Amilcar would lead. Now, under Lyra's direction, the camaradas did their best to organize the remaining boxes of rations, coils of rope, bags of survey equipment, tents, cooking supplies, and hunting gear and then pack them in a way that they hoped would protect them from rain, sun, and rapids.

As the men inventoried their baggage, their concern about Fiala's preparations began to turn into alarm. "Most of his equipment was useless, or as it has been appropriately termed 'doodle-dabs,' " Miller wrote to Frank Chapman at the American Museum of Natural History. The rations were an even larger, and more critical, problem than the equipment. When the men pried open several of Fiala's crates, they were stunned by what they found. "We discovered here whole cases of olive oil, cases of mustard, malted milk, stuffed olives, prunes, applesauce, etc., etc. Even Rhine wine," Miller told Chapman. Such gourmet condiments were "all nice enough in their place," he wrote, but "on such a tremendous journey" they were useless.

Even if they had begun the expedition with full rations, Fiala had assumed that the men would rely heavily on hunting to supplement their diet. "For meat," he wrote, "the rubber hunter and explorer depends upon his rifle and fish-hook." Each food tin weighed twenty-seven pounds, and it would have been nearly impossible for the expedition's dugout canoes to carry enough tins to feed every man, every day. With no experience in the rain forest, however, Fiala had no basis for his assumption that the expedition would be able to find enough game to sustain itself, and his expectations would prove to be wildly unrealistic.

Having come this far, Roosevelt and his men now had no choice but to make the best of what they had. They spent most of February 26, the day before their departure, repairing the dugouts. They finally decided to lash the two "old, waterlogged, and leaky" boats together to form a more stable balsa, or raft, and they tied the cranky dugout to one of the three good ones. Since balsas are able to safely carry more weight than are single canoes, these four dugouts would haul the preponderance of the expedition's provisions, equipment, and men. Each boat, however, would have to carry a heavy load.

Even though Roosevelt and Rondon had repeatedly reduced the size of the expedition and the amount of its baggage since the pack trains left Tapirapoan more than a month earlier, they still had twenty-two men to feed, clothe, and equip for a journey that could last several months. To keep the baggage as light as possible, the officers agreed to share tents—Roosevelt, Kermit, and Cherrie under one fly, and Rondon, Lyra, and Dr. Cajazeira under another—and the sixteen camaradas would sleep wherever they could find a spot for their hammocks and shelter from the rain. They did pack one other light tent, but that was reserved for anyone who became too ill to walk.

Despite all of these efforts, the loaded dugouts still sank so low in the river that the camaradas had to tie long bundles of burity-palm branches to their sides to help improve their buoyancy. Roosevelt was concerned about riding so heavily in the swift water, but he had adopted a philosophical attitude about the danger that he faced on the River of Doubt. "If our canoe voyage was prosperous we would gradually lighten the loads by eating the provisions," he wrote. "If we met with accidents, such as losing canoes and men in the rapids, or losing men in encounters with Indians, or if we encountered over-much fever and dysentery, the loads would lighten themselves."

* * *

WHILE THE members of the River of Doubt team loaded the last of their belongings into their long, heavy canoes, Amilcar and Leo Miller, the naturalist who had been relegated to the descent of a different river, stood on the bridge, listening to their shouts and grunts of effort and watching the general commotion that accompanies the commencement of any long journey. "We had looked forward in eager anticipation to the end of the long ride across the Brazilian chapadão and the beginning of river work," he wrote. "But now that the goal had been attained . . . the division of the expedition seemed to have come all too soon."

In a gesture of confidence in the successful outcome of his expedition, Roosevelt borrowed $520 from Miller's museum money so that he could treat his men to a feast at the first semblance of a store that they found near the mouth of the River of Doubt, wherever that might be. He promised to pay Miller back in Manáos, the rubber boom city on the Rio Negro, where they all hoped to meet at the end of their respective journeys. That same day, Roosevelt also asked a favor of Cherrie. "Roosevelt asked me to cut his hair!" the naturalist wrote his wife, shocked that he had just groomed a former president of the United States. "I did the job but the Colonel refused to let me take his picture after I had finished!"

Finally, everything was in place, and, just after twelve noon on

February 27, 1914, Roosevelt carefully climbed inside his narrow dugout and found a seat on a bag that had been stuffed as tight as a sausage. As soon as the camaradas pushed off the banks, he immediately felt himself being swept up in the river's rushing current. The last thing he heard before he was carried too far down the river for Miller's voice to reach him, was a hearty "Good luck!"

"For several minutes we stood upon the fragile structure that bridged the unexplored river and stared at the dark forest that shut our erstwhile leader and his Brazilian companions from view," Miller would later write. "And then, filled with misgivings as to whether or not we should ever see them again, we turned our thoughts to the task before us."

CHAPTER 11

Pole and Paddle, Axe and Machete

CARRIED ALONG BY THE swift water, the expedition's seven dugouts snaked through the forest single-file. The jungle was thickest at the river's edge, where the trees crowded along the banks in a timeless battle for sunlight. They were matted together with vines and epiphytes that trailed in the water like heavy curtains and completely obscured the muddy bank. From his position in the last and largest canoe, which had a carrying capacity of one and a quarter tons, Roosevelt, along with Cherrie, Dr. Cajazeira, and their three paddlers, could see the other six dugouts floating in a long, broken chain ahead of him. Directly in front of him were the two balsas, which carried eight camaradas and most of the expedition's baggage, but were even more difficult to steer than the rest of the boats. Rondon, Lyra, and three paddlers rode in the second dugout, and Kermit and two camaradas sat in the smallest canoe at the head of the expedition.

"As we drifted and paddled down the swirling brown current, through the vivid rain-drenched green of the tropic forest, the trees leaned over the river from both banks," Roosevelt wrote. "There were many palms, both the burity with its stiff fronds like enormous fans, and a handsome species of bacaba, with very long, gracefully curving fronds. In places the palms stood close together, towering and slender, their stems a stately colonnade, their fronds an arched fretwork against the sky."

Roosevelt reveled in the beauty and variety of the plant life and the "fragrant scents [that] were blown to us from flowers on the banks," but he was puzzled by a distinct and eerie absence of sound. In the midst of all this lush life was a seemingly incongruent stillness. "Rarely we heard strange calls from the depths of the woods," he wrote, but "for the most part the forest was silent." Cherrie too was struck by how empty the jungle seemed. "Very little animal life was seen along the shore," he scribbled in his diary.

While Roosevelt and Cherrie studied the rain forest, their paddlers kept their eyes on the river. Pulling the dugout through the water with their long wooden paddles, they searched for a telltale ripple, their only warning that a fallen tree lay just below the surface. The rainy-season downpours that had been such a source of misery to the men on their overland journey had caused the river to swell to such a height that most of the sunken trees and boulders were safely buried under several feet of water. Some, such as the water-loving boritana palms, continued to grow and thrive although they were fully submerged, the current shaking their broad crowns like a strong wind. Other fallen trees, however, still lay close to the surface, and, whenever they appeared, the current seemed invariably to drive the expedition's canoes straight down on top of them. It was then, Roosevelt wrote, that "the muscles stood out on the backs and arms of the paddlers as stroke on stroke they urged us away from and past the obstacle."

The strength and skill of the camaradas was evident as they maneuvered their craft down the river. Rondon had hired rugged young men in Tapirapoan to be their paddlers and porters. They were a "strapping set," Roosevelt wrote admiringly. "They were expert rivermen and men of the forest, skilled veterans in wilderness work. They were lithe as panthers and brawny as bears. They swam like water-dogs. They were equally at home with pole and paddle, with axe and machete."

Roosevelt realized, however, that great difficulty often brought out the worst in a man. Deep in the Amazon, the expedition was utterly isolated and far from help of any kind. The camaradas—who out-numbered the officers nearly three to one—could mutiny as easily as sailors at sea. They were all capable men, and most of them were brave, but they had lived a hard life. They looked, Roosevelt wrote, "like pirates in the pictures of Howard Pyle and Maxfield Parrish." One glance at them revealed the almost unbridgeable difference be-tween their hardscrabble world and Roosevelt's refined and privileged one. For clothing, they had brought along nothing more than the thin shirts and ragged pants that they wore, and most of them were bare-foot. Their feet and hands were as hard and gnarled as their rough-hewn paddles. Their faces, some bright and cheerful, others dark and glowering, were usually obscured by their slouching and soiled hats. It would take time for the officers, especially the Americans, to get to know their paddlers and to learn those on whom they could rely, even trusting them with their own lives, and those on whom they should never turn their backs.

Even Roosevelt's own boatmen represented the extremes of good and bad among the camaradas. His steersman, a black man from Mato Grosso named Luiz Correia, and his paddler, Antonio Pareci, a member of the peaceful Pareci Indian tribe that the expedition had met in Utiarity, were two of the best men in the expedition. Over the course of the journey, both of them would earn Roosevelt's respect by proving that they not only knew the rain forest but were willing to work hard for the success of the expedition. The third camarada in Roosevelt's boat, however, was Julio de Lima, the broad-shouldered, hot-tempered Brazilian who had attacked another man with a knife during the overland journey. Apparently Amilcar had not shared his concerns about Julio with Rondon, because not only had the volatile camarada been chosen among the select group of men who were to descend the River of Doubt, but he was now Roosevelt's own bowman.

* * *

FROM THE moment their boats were swept into the unknown, Rondon set his plan for the expedition into motion. The Brazilian colonel was interested not in adventure but in geographical precision, and he was determined to survey the river carefully and completely, from its headwaters to its mouth. Little more than a century earlier, Alexander von Humboldt, the world-renowned German naturalist and explorer, had conducted the first thorough cartographical survey of South America, producing hundreds of maps based on seven hundred observations. Filling in these maps with the detail necessary to make them truly useful was an ongoing project, one that had met with varying degrees of success over the ensuing century. By the early twentieth century, the existing maps of the Brazilian interior were largely, and notoriously, wrong, indicating mountains where none existed and rivers misplaced by hundreds of miles. A significant part of Rondon's job over the past twenty-four years had been not only adding to the cartographic knowledge of his continent but correcting these mistakes.

There were no reference points in the vast jungle, so the men would have to rely on celestial navigation to tell them where they were. To determine latitude and longitude, they used the same instrument that Humboldt himself had used—a sextant, which measures the angle between the horizon and the sun, moon, or stars. To chart the river from point to point, Rondon instituted a fixed-station method of survey, one of the most accurate methods but also the most labor-intensive. Not only did it require repeated, detailed measurements, but it also demanded frequent stops, especially on a river that wound as tightly as the River of Doubt.

For the sake of accuracy, Rondon was more than willing to endure the tedium, grueling work, and danger that the fixed-station survey demanded. However, as in many great undertakings, the expedition's commander would not suffer alone. In the lead canoe, Kermit had accepted the unenviable job of placing the sighting rod that Lyra and Rondon would use to make their measurements. Kermit and his paddlers would find a spot that afforded the longest unimpeded view both upstream and downstream—usually at a bend in the river—land their boat, and, using a machete, cut away the thick branches and vines that covered the bank. Fighting off swarms of biting ants and angry wasps, Kermit would plant his sighting rod—a slim pole on which a red disk and a white disk had been positioned one meter apart—in the thin, black leaf litter under his feet. Lyra would then use a telemeter to establish the distance between his canoe and the sighting rod, and Rondon would consult his compass and record the river's direction.

The river twisted and turned so capriciously—curving "literally toward every point of the compass," Roosevelt remarked—that Kermit had to land, cut away the vegetation, and set up the sighting rod 114 times that first day alone. Roosevelt was not pleased with the fixed-station survey. Not only did it slow the expedition to a glacial pace—the boats traveled only six miles in five hours—but it placed his son in a particularly dangerous position. If there were sunken trees, hidden whirlpools, sudden waterfalls, or hostile Indians, Kermit would encounter them first. In spite of his concerns, however, Roosevelt refrained from asking Rondon to adopt a faster method of survey. This was Rondon's country and Rondon's expedition, more than his own, and Roosevelt was determined to respect his co-commander's wishes as long as he could. He planned, he wrote, simply to keep an eye on the expedition, maintaining a "close supervision over everything that was done but being more than courteous and polite and friendly with my Brazilian companions."

After only two hours on the river, Roosevelt, whose canoe had long since passed the two slow surveying boats, instructed his paddlers to pull over. Leaning over the sides of the dugout to grasp leafy branches that overhung the river, the camaradas pulled as close to the overgrown shore as they could and then used a rope to tether the boat to a tree. The six men then settled in to wait for their companions, their boat rocking in the current, the rain and sun alternately drenching and drying them. Finally, after two more hours had passed with no sign of the surveying canoes, Roosevelt ordered the camaradas to make camp. It was only 4:00 p.m., but they could not go forward without the rest of the expedition, and they had no idea when they would all be reunited.

* * *

THE EXPEDITION'S first camp on the River of Doubt was little more than a crude clearing on the river's edge. After making their way through the dense bushes and trees that crowded every inch of the shoreline and leaned far out over the river itself, the men were able to find a dry, level patch of ground at the top of a steep, hundred-yard incline. But fighting back the jungle was no easy task. With axes and machetes, the camaradas slowly began to cut away small trees and heavy vines, all crawling with a wide array of stinging, biting insects. Eventually they were able to form a little open island in the sea of trees, and they began hauling up bags from the dugouts, setting up the officers' two tents, and tying their own simple hammocks to sturdy trunks.

By the time Kermit, Rondon, Lyra, and their six paddlers appeared, filthy and exhausted, the sun was already setting, and Franca the cook had, as he had time and again for the past month, miraculously started a fire from sodden wood. As the men sat around the sputtering campfire, the rain tapered off, leaving a clear, star-scattered sky above them. Beyond their little circle of light, however, the jungle was so black that, had a sudden rain doused their fire, the men would not have been able to see their own hands, much less one another. Only six miles into their expedition, they could already feel their isolation. But as they sank into their hammocks that night, their first on the banks of the River of Doubt, little time was wasted on worry. Exhaustion descended, as heavy and inescapable as the tropical humidity, and the men quickly fell asleep.

CHAPTER 12

The Living Jungle

WHEN ROOSEVELT EMERGED FROM his thin balloon-silk tent on the morning of February 28, 1914, he stepped into the narrow clearing that his men had carved between water and forest. Before him rushed the River of Doubt, dark, swollen, and littered with debris from fallen trees. Having overflowed its banks, it coursed through the forest on either side in wayward streams and rivulets, picking up clots of leaves and displaced birds' nests, and filling the jungle with a glasslike floor of water that mirrored the canopy above. The expedition's dugouts rocked uneasily at their moorings, looking as unreliable at dawn as they had the afternoon before.

Although Roosevelt had hunted and camped in forests throughout the United States, marveling at California's enormous redwoods, he had never seen anything like the prodigy of nature that surrounded him now. The massive trees rose so high that their crowns disappeared in the tangle of branches and flicker of sunlight above his head. Branches of neighboring trees wound around one another like interlaced fingers, and heavy epiphytes unfurled from the treetops like a ship's rigging.

In the early-morning light, the scene that Roosevelt beheld was a breathtaking tableau of timeless nature—tranquil and apparently unchanging. That impression, however, could hardly have been more dangerous or deceiving. For, even as the men of the expedition gazed in awe at the natural beauty surrounding them, the creatures of the rain forest were watching back, identifying them as intruders, assaying their potential value, surveying their weaknesses, and preparing to take whatever they might have to give.

Far from its outward appearance, the rain forest was not a garden of easy abundance, but precisely the opposite. Its quiet, shaded halls of leafy opulence were not a sanctuary but, rather, the greatest natural battlefield anywhere on the planet, hosting an unremitting and remorseless fight for survival that occupied every single one of its inhabitants, every minute of every day. Though frequently impossible for a casual observer to discern, every inch of space was alive—from the black, teeming soil under Roosevelt's boots to the top of the canopy far above his head—and everything was connected. A long, linked mat of fungi under the soil consumed the dead and fed the living, completing an ever-changing cycle of remarkable life and commonplace death which had throbbed without pause for millions of years—and of which Roosevelt and his men, knowingly or not, had now become a part.

* * *

UNLIKE THE woods of New England, where Roosevelt had spent years exploring and learning about nature, the rain forest floor was not covered with thick leaf litter or plant life, but appeared largely empty, characterized only by a shallow layer of soil shot through with thin white threadlike fibers. Just as unusual, each tree in the Amazon rain forest appeared to be nearly unique. Many trees had commonly shaped leaves, but stands or groupings of a single tree species were very rare, and after identifying one tree the men could search for hours before finding another of the same kind. The trees themselves

"Such unbounded energy and vitality impressed one like the perennial forces of nature," the naturalist John Burroughs wrote of Roosevelt, who, in an unsuccessful bid for a third term as a third-party candidate, used his legendary magnetism to persuade millions of voters to abandon the Democratic and Republican parties in 1912.

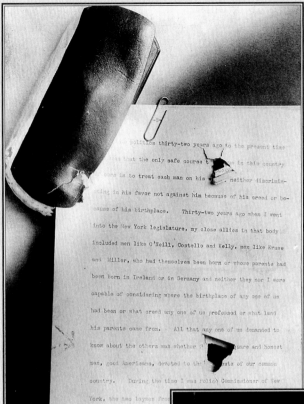

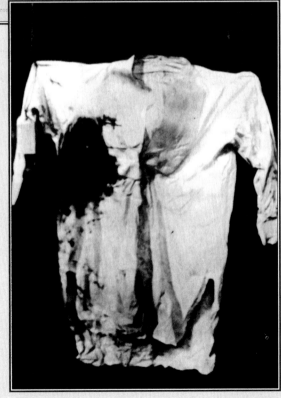

The folded manuscript and steel spectacle case that Roosevelt carried in his right breast pocket saved his life when he was shot by a would-be assassin before giving a campaign speech in 1912. Roaring that it "takes more than that to kill a Bull Moose!" Roosevelt insisted on giving his speech—still wearing his bloody shirt and with the bullet lodged five inches deep in his chest.

Even as a child, "Kermit was ...
very solemn," his older brother,
Theodore Jr., would recall. Quiet
and brooding by nature, Kermit was
both the most introverted of
Roosevelt's six children and the
most fearless. During a year-long
African hunting trip in 1909,
Roosevelt worried about his second
son's recklessness, complaining that
Kermit, shown below standing over
a lion he had killed, "keeps my
heart in my throat."

Kermit's introspective character was
hauntingly reminiscent of that of his
father's only brother, Elliott—First Lady
Eleanor Roosevelt's father. Although full
of promise as a young man, Elliott (right,
with Theodore in 1880) succumbed to
alcoholism and morphine addiction later
in life and died at the age of thirty-four.

When Roosevelt decided to undertake an expedition into the Amazon, the American Museum of Natural History hired two of its best naturalists to accompany him: George Cherrie (*top*) and Leo Miller (*bottom*).

Of the seven Americans who planned to descend the River of Doubt—from left to right, Anthony Fiala, George Cherrie, Father John Zahm, Theodore Roosevelt, Kermit Roosevelt, Frank Harper, and Leo Miller—only Roosevelt, Kermit, and Cherrie would make the journey.

Just before the expedition began, Kermit became engaged to Belle Willard, daughter of the American ambassador to Spain. After hearing that her quiet, serious son planned to marry the young socialite, Edith Roosevelt, who had nicknamed Belle "the Fair One with Golden Locks," confessed that she felt "a trifle down."

Signaling the commencement of their expedition, Roosevelt and his Brazilian co-commander, Colonel Cândido Rondon, met for the first time on December 12, 1913, on the Paraguay River. As head of the Strategic Telegraph Commission—commonly known as the Rondon Commission—Rondon had already spent nearly a quarter of a century, half his life, mapping the Amazon.

Renowned, and later criticized, as a big-game hunter, Roosevelt—posing here with Rondon and a bush deer he killed before reaching the River of Doubt—would find that, once on the river, he and his men were more often prey than predator.

For much of their month-long overland journey, Roosevelt (right), Rondon (left), and their men rode under the humming wires of the telegraph poles that the Rondon Commission had erected, at the cost of countless lives, across eight hundred miles of the Brazilian interior.

Overloaded and underfed, the expedition's pack oxen died at an alarming rate during the trip to the River of Doubt. In a futile attempt to save themselves, many of the oxen bucked off their loads, abandoning crates of provisions that the men would desperately need on the river.

"Why they do not grind off their noses I cannot imagine," Roosevelt marveled after watching a group of Pareci Indians at a telegraph station play a game that required them to butt a ball, a hollow sphere of rubber, by diving headfirst at the ground.

The Nhambiquara Indians, whom Roosevelt considered "light-hearted robbers and murderers," had answered Rondon's first attempt at contact in 1909 with a fusillade of curare-tipped arrows. Rondon had ordered his soldiers not to return fire, obliging them, as always, to live by his admirable if suicidal motto: "Die if need be, but kill never."

During the overland journey, the members of the expedition—from left to right, Father Zahm, Rondon, Kermit, Cherrie, Miller, four members of the Brazilian contingent, Roosevelt, and Fiala—gathered for their evening meal around two ox hides spread over the damp ground. Refusing to sit in a chair unless Rondon also had one, Roosevelt told his co-commander that "he would accept nothing, and do nothing, that might have an appearance of special attention to his person. And consequently just as he saw me sit so would he sit himself."

were often strange and complex, characterized by huge buttresses, flowering trunks, or apparent branches that plunged back into the earth or were wrapped in enormous looped or curled vines. Most important, other than insects, which teemed everywhere, the forest seemed virtually empty, with little or no sign or sound of any inhabitants.

These odd characteristics were not mere natural curiosities or local quirks, but direct reflections of the deadly, exquisitely efficient competition for survival that was taking place all around Roosevelt and his men. They also reflected the profound impact of that evolutionary competition on all forms of life in the Amazon, where it has produced some of the most phenomenally diverse and specialized plants and creatures anywhere on earth.

While the process of evolution has continuously altered and selected the features of life everywhere on the planet, in few places have its workings been as conspicuous or its results as refined as in the Amazon. The extraordinary range of forms that characterizes the Amazon rain forest has been attributed to many causes, all of which are likely to have played some role in creating the immense cornucopia of living things that surrounded the expedition.

Perhaps the most frequently cited factor in the species richness of the Amazon is the region's latitude, which has for millions of years produced generally stable temperatures and moist environmental conditions that have favored the uninterrupted development of the jungle and its inhabitants. Another prominent explanation is the repeated isolation and reconnection of the jungle to other continents and habitats over the broad sweep of time. Whereas some regions, such as Africa, have undergone fewer changes, and reflect a comparatively lower number of unique plant and animal species, the South American continent has at different points been cut off from, or rejoined to, other landmasses. The separation of South America from the rest of Gondwanaland, for example, created opportunities for the development of new indigenous species. That isolation was then interrupted by the rise of the Panamanian Land Bridge, which permitted the arrival of new species from North America, and started new rounds of selection.

Within the Amazon itself, some scientists believe, localized changes of climate created shifting patterns of so-called refugia, or rain forest pockets, whose isolation offered unusual opportunities for the emergence of specialized plants, birds, insects, and other animals. New variants of life, particularly fish life, were also fostered by the long presence of an inland sea at the heart of the continent. Distinct new species are also thought to have emerged within enclaves set off by natural boundaries such as mountains and, of course, the channels and tributaries of the giant Amazon river system itself.

As in the development of a modern economy, with its everincreasing specialization of labor and markets, each increase in competition among the inhabitants of the rain forest has itself been a powerful source of further speciation, rewarding entrepreneurial variations of life that can exploit skills and opportunities that previously went unrecognized or did not exist.

In the presence of such highly refined evolutionary pressures, every natural advantage and source of potential sustenance becomes an object of competition and is consequently used to its fullest. Despite the lush green vistas and overgrown shores that the expedition could see from the river, for example, the soil of many lowland rain forests is not rich or fecund but, rather, has adapted to recycle nutrients with extraordinary speed. The same abundant precipitation and steady temperatures that support life also leach minerals from the soil, and intense tree-and-plant growth exploits every available nutrient, leaving the floor of many tropical jungles, including the Amazon, permanently hovering at the margin of exhaustion.

For plants and trees, competition for available soil nutrients is paired with competition for sunlight, which is essential for the photosynthesis that green plants use to create carbohydrates from carbon dioxide and water. Every kind of plant or tree therefore represents a unique trade-off between the quest for water and soil nutrients on one hand, and the quest for sunlight on the other.

Soaring more than 150 feet above Roosevelt's head and out of sight in the green canopy were giant emergent tree species that had secured their survival by putting all their resources into the effort to outrace their competitors to the sunshine. For fast-growing trees, the trade-off for speed is inadequate defenses against insects and vulnerability to storms that cannot reach the lower, more sheltered layers of the forest. Unable to sink deep roots in the thin forest floor, canopy trees are also generally obliged to develop elaborate support systems at their base, either with giant triangular buttresses that surround the bole, or tree-trunk, or so-called flying buttresses that look like inverted branches.

On the forest floor, where the sky is all but obscured by such tall canopy trees, smaller plants or trees with limited resources must develop increasingly refined strategies to find a place in the sun. The most obvious of these strategies is to avoid the cost of building a structure capable of reaching the canopy by simply climbing a tree that has already done so. This opportunistic strategy, adopted by vines and lianas, can permit a newcomer to remain anchored in the forest floor while growing rapidly to the canopy. But since even vine construction requires substantial resources, it entails complex choices about which tree to climb—a requirement that has produced astonishingly sophisticated traits. Some Amazonian plants, for example, can shift as necessary between treelike form, when they receive sunlight, and a climbing vine, when they find themselves in shade. Others can transform themselves into trees once they reach the canopy, abandoning their host and winding their viny stems together into a trunk. While most plants naturally seek the sun, other Amazonian vines have adapted to seek out the dark bases of large canopy trees that might offer reliable support, and only then to turn upward toward the light.

With an alacrity that can seem almost human, rain forest vines send out tendrils that reach out delicately to encounter a potential host, then curl to grasp it once it is found. A principal risk of the vine strategy is the danger that the host tree will sway and break the vine, so many vine species have adapted by developing slack in the form of elaborate loops, curls, and coils, lending the rain forest the distinctive draping character that Roosevelt could so easily see and admire. Another adaptation to this and other dangers is for the vine simply to abandon its connection to the ground and to derive its water and nutrients entirely in the canopy, becoming an air plant or epiphyte, a category of plant that has generated literally thousands of species, including bromeliads and orchids. After establishing themselves in the canopy, some epiphytes, in their turn, then reverse the entire process, sending aerial roots downward to establish a connection to the forest floor.

In reaction to the attempts of freeloading vines and epiphytes to benefit from their hard-won position in the canopy—and to protect themselves from being shaded over by such parasites—trees have developed many protection methods of their own. Some have developed smooth bark that keeps tendrils from attaching, and still others have adapted to slough off bark, leaves, or indeed entire branches to send epiphytes and vines crashing to the forest floor. Throughout the jungle, moreover, trees have adapted to prevent multiple deaths from tree falls or blights by separating themselves at regular distances from trees of the same species.

From his vantage point on the shaded forest floor, Roosevelt stood far below much of this unceasing evolutionary combat. Crowded with broad-leaved trees, crowning vines, and epiphytes, as well as the hundreds of insect and animal species that rely upon them, the upper canopy is difficult to see from the ground, except in the rooflike function that its name implies. By shading everything below it, the canopy helps to obscure much of the activity that takes place in the understory, or middle level of the rain forest. Its shading action also contributes importantly to the relative absence of undergrowth on the forest floor, where the men of the expedition found that they could move about with surprising ease. While sunlight from the open river made the shoreline an almost impassable wall of trees, vines, and dense underbrush, once that barrier was breached the dark interior of the jungle, broken only by occasional gaps in the canopy and a scattered, speckled light, revealed a labyrinth of tree trunks and vines, but little else.

As the men of the expedition arose and started their morning routine, Roosevelt was able to admire the complexity of the jungle before him, but could only guess at the mysteries that it held beyond his view. So complex and interdependent was the ecosystem he and his men had entered that the jungle itself could appear to take on the attributes of a living being. If Roosevelt had been able to see the rain forest from a distance, he could have watched it breathe. As the trees transpire, or, in a sense, sweat, they pump water into the atmosphere from their leaves. In the warm air, the water quickly evaporates and is recycled as rain. As the ex-president stood at the river's edge, surveying the jungle he hoped to master and explore, the forest surrounding him met the dawn by exhaling thin white clouds of condensing moisture that rose over the canopy above him like the breath of a wolf on a winter morning.

* * *

As HE had during his telegraph line expeditions, Rondon approached the camp routine on the River of Doubt with military formality. To the task he brought not only strict discipline but even pomp and ceremony. Every morning, the men would gather in front of their Brazilian commander, who was dressed in his army khakis, to hear his Orders of the Day, laid out as formally as if he were addressing a regiment at war. Then, after a search through the surrounding forest for a piece of hardwood that would make a suitable marker, they would smooth one side of the wood with an adze, paint the camp number and the date on it, and drive it into the forest floor. They knew that rain, sun, and insects would likely destroy the markers long before they would be discovered by anyone who could read them, but they felt compelled nonetheless to leave behind a historical record of their journey.

This routine, which they planned to carry out every morning until they reached the mouth of the River of Doubt, was more than an empty ritual. It was a tangible connection to civilization and a constant reminder of who they were and why they were there. Rondon had learned through excruciating hardship how important routine, discipline, and military ritual were in maintaining morale during an expedition into the Amazon. Even on his 1909 journey, when he and all of his men nearly starved to death, Rondon had never deviated from his routine. "The ragged bugler had his bugle," Roosevelt wrote, recording the last, traumatic days of the expedition as Rondon described them to him. "Lieutenant Pyrineus had lost every part of his clothing except a hat and a pair of drawers. The half-naked lieutenant drew up his eleven fever patients in line; the bugle sounded; every one came to attention; and the haggard colonel read out the orders of the day."

As important as Rondon's routine had proved to be during a crisis, however, it could also appear inflexible and dogmatic to his men. Rondon expected the same rigorous discipline from his soldiers that he demanded from himself, and his was not an easy model to live up to. The colonel still woke at four o'clock every morning and swam in whatever pond or river was nearby. He shaved without a mirror and had a simple breakfast, never allowing himself any indulgences—even if he had access to them. He never drank alcohol, or allowed his men to do so, and he even abstained from coffee, drinking only water or herbal tea.

Roosevelt, in contrast, was much more flexible than his co-commander and, as a result, better liked. Roosevelt had endured some cold nights hunting down runaway cattle in the Dakota Badlands, and he had led a regiment to war, but he had never had to bring a band of starving, desperate men out of the jungle. Even on this expedition, he was more figurehead than commander, and when there were decisions to be made, he deferred to Rondon. Roosevelt's job had, in a way, become that of expedition raconteur. He regaled the men every night with stories of his days in the Wild West or on the African savanna.

He was, Rondon wrote, "the life of the party." In contrast to the reserved, taciturn Brazilian colonel, Roosevelt must have seemed peculiarly fun and lighthearted. Rondon himself was stunned by his loquacious co-commander. "And talk!" he wrote. "I never saw a man who talked so much. He would talk all of the time he was in swimming, all of the time during meals, traveling in the canoe and at night around the camp fire. He talked endlessly and on all conceivable subjects."

* * *

ALTHOUGH THEY had risen well before dawn, it was almost noon by the time Roosevelt, Cherrie, Dr. Cajazeira, and their three paddlers finally climbed into their dugout on the morning of February 28 and headed off down the river in pursuit of the rest of the expedition, which had left camp nearly four hours earlier. Sympathetic to how difficult it had been, and likely would continue to be, for his naturalist to collect specimens for the museum while they were on the River of Doubt, Roosevelt had ordered the other two dugouts and two balsas to go ahead without them when Cherrie heard some birdcalls near camp that morning. Cherrie had made it worth Roosevelt's while, capturing six birds, including a red-headed woodpecker and a brilliant turquoise-blue cotinga.

Once back on the twisting river, Roosevelt and Cherrie resumed their search for signs of life. Hour after hour passed, however, and their efforts were rewarded only by a few deserted game trails, an otter splashing across the river, and two tropical birds called guans. His face cast in shadow beneath his deep sun helmet, Roosevelt watched as the jungle glided past him, its towering trees and blue sky reflected, like a trembling, inverted world, in the water's dark surface. He drank in the rich array of beauty, admiring the many-colored butterflies that "fluttered over the river," and marveling at how a spark of sunlight could cloak the electric green jungle. "When the sun broke through rifts in the clouds," he wrote, "his shafts turned the forest to gold."

Despite the beauty they were witnessing, nearly constant rain and an onslaught of insects made the men miserable. The Amazon Basin gets as much as a hundred inches of rain each year, three times as much as New York City. The rain forest itself generates 60 percent of the precipitation through the transpiration process, and most of it falls during the months of March and April. The temperature was consistently high, usually in the mid-to-high eighties, but the heat was powerless to counteract the effects of the relentless rain. "There would be a heavy downpour," Kermit wrote. "Then out would come the sun and we would be steamed dry, only to be drenched once more a half-hour later."

The forest either steamed with thick humidity or sagged under a heavy downpour. Rain drummed on the river, ran off their hats, dripped down their backs, and pooled in their shoes. It soaked their tents and filled their canoes. Their clothes hung in heavy, clinging folds, and they never completely dried. "Our clothes were usually wet when we took them off at night, and just as wet when we put them on again in the morning," Roosevelt wrote. Within a few days, they would all forget what it felt like to pull on a dry pair of socks.

* * *

COMPOUNDING THE misery wrought by the rain was an overarching sense of isolation and uncertainty, a feeling that was magnified by strange noises that shattered the forest's silence and set the men's nerves on edge. That afternoon, as Roosevelt and the men in his dugout paddled quietly down the river, a long, deep shriek suddenly ripped through the jungle. It was the roar of a howler monkey, one of the loudest cries of any animal on earth. The sound, which can be heard from three miles away, is formed when the monkey forces air through its large, hollow hyoid bone, which sits between its lower jaw and voice box and anchors its tongue. The result is a deep, resonating howl that vibrates through the forest with strange, inhuman intensity, and echoes so pervasively that its location can be nearly impossible to identify.

Worse even than the noises they could recognize were those that none of them could explain. These strange sounds, which disappeared as quickly as they came and were a mystery even to those who knew the rain forest best, had made a strong impression on the British naturalist Henry Walter Bates fifty years earlier. "Often, even in the still hours of midday, a sudden crash will be heard resounding afar through the wilderness, as some great bough or entire tree falls to the ground," the naturalist wrote. "There are, besides, many sounds which it is impossible to account for. I found the natives generally as much at a loss in this respect as myself. Sometimes a sound is heard like the clang of an iron bar against a hard, hollow tree, or a piercing cry rends the air; these are not repeated, and the succeeding silence tends to heighten the unpleasant impression which they make on the mind."

There was activity all around the men, both human and animal, but they could not see it, and they could only guess at what it was. This blindness left them uniquely vulnerable as they fought their way through a tangled swath of submerged trees that evening—"hacking and hewing," Roosevelt wrote—in search of dry ground for their second camp. This was a different kind of fear altogether, something that even their grueling, worry-plagued overland journey had not prepared them for, and no man seemed immune to the change in mood that occurred as the river carried them ever deeper into the jungle.

The Amazon's sudden, inexplicable sounds were especially terrifying at night, when they were all in the pitch-black forest, with no way to see a potential attacker and no sure means of escape. While the jungle in daylight could sometimes appear completely devoid of inhabitants, the nightly cacophony left no doubt that the men of the expedition were not alone. Even for veteran outdoorsmen like George Cherrie, the setting of the sun came to mark an unnerving threshold between the relative familiarity of a long day on the river, and sleepless nights in the jungle, spent trying to imagine the source of the spine-chilling noises that echoed in the darkness around him. "Frequently at night, with my camp at the edge of the jungle," he wrote, "I have lain in my hammock listening, my ears yearning for some familiar sound—every sense alert, nerves taut. Strange things have happened in the night."

The screams, crashes, clangs, and cries of the long Amazon night were all the more disturbing because they often provoked apparent terror among the unseen inhabitants of the jungle themselves. In the fathomless canyons of tree trunks and the shrouds of black vines that surrounded the men at night, the hum and chatter of thousands of nocturnal creatures would snap into instant silence in response to a strange noise, leaving the men to wait in breathless apprehension of what might come next.

"Let there be the least break in the harmony of sound," Cherrie observed, "and instantly there succeeds a deathlike silence, while all living things wait in dread for the inevitable shriek that follows the night prowler's stealthy spring."

CHAPTER 13

On the Ink-Black River

F ROM THE MOMENT THEY launched their boats upon the River
of Doubt, Roosevelt and his men knew that the river would be
their only guide. Even when they were on land—hunting, portaging,
or making camp for the night—they would never stray far from its
shores. They needed it for drinking water, cooking, and bathing. They
needed it to escape from the oppressive heat of the rain forest, which
clung to them like a wet wool blanket. Most of all, they needed it to
carry them home.

As important as the river was to the expedition, however, it was a
capricious and unreliable ally. Like many South American rivers, the
River of Doubt could change character quickly and dramatically over
a very short distance, and with profound consequences for an expedition. Swollen and swift during the rainy season, it was cluttered with
dangerous debris and pocked with shifting whirlpools that could flip
a canoe and trap a man under the surface of the water in a matter of
seconds.

Even more complex and dangerous than the river itself were the
fishes, mammals, and reptiles that inhabited it. Like the rain forest

that surrounds and depends upon it, the Amazon river system is a prodigy of speciation and diversity, serving as home to more than three thousand species of freshwater fishes—more than any other river system on earth. Its waters are crowded with creatures of nearly every size, shape, and evolutionary adaptation, from tiny neon tetras to thousand-pound manatees to pink freshwater boto dolphins to stingrays to armor-plated catfishes to bullsharks. By comparison, the entire Missouri and Mississippi river system that drains much of North America has only about 375 fish species.

Able to swim freely through large swaths of the jungle during the rainy season, for example, certain Amazonian fish, such as the tambaqui, have evolved teeth that look like sheep molars and are tough enough to crack open even the hard, cannonball-sized shell of the Brazil nut. The ancient, eellike South American lungfish has lungs as well as gills. Unless it surfaces every four to ten minutes for a gulp of air, it will drown. During the dry season, however, while other fishes around it die as the ponds and streams dry up, the lungfish survives by burrowing into the mud and taking oxygen from the air. Still another species, the so-called four-eyed-fish, has eyes that are divided in two at the waterline by a band of tissue. With two separate sets of corneas and retinas, the fish can search for predators in the sky above and at the same time look for danger in the water below.

Many of these strange adaptations are geared toward self-defense. Others are designed to help the fish become better, faster, smarter predators. There are electric fishes that eat nothing but the tails of other electric fish, which can regenerate their appendages, thus ensuring the predator a limitless food supply. Other fish have evolved to eat prey that live outside of their own immediate ecosystem. The three-foot-long arawana, for example, has a huge mouth and a bony tongue and can leap twice its body length. Nicknamed the "water monkey," it snatches large insects, reptiles, and even small birds from the low branches of overhanging trees.

The riverine creatures that the members of the expedition were most interested in, however, were those that were dangerous to man.

The most visible threats were the fifteen-foot-long black caimans, which lay low near their nests of rotting debris and vanished into the water as the expedition's canoes passed by. Cherrie in particular had great respect for the South American alligator. He had nearly lost his life to one while on an expedition on the Orinoco. The river had been low, and the mud flat that bordered it studded with flat, exposed stones. He was stepping from stone to stone, his mind and eyes on the birds that lined the river, when he suddenly felt an impulse to look down. In mid-stride, with his foot still dangling in the air, he realized that he was just about to step not on a stone but on the back of a large caiman. "Had I done so," he later wrote, "the creature would have instantly whirled about and had me in his jaws before I could possibly have escaped."

The river's other inhabitants were largely invisible from the expedition's dugouts, but the fact that they could not be seen only heightened the oppressive sense of danger they instilled in the men. Aboard their crude, heavily loaded boats, they sat at most just six inches above the water, and courted danger whenever one of them dangled his foot overboard or trailed his fingers in the current. If one of their boats tipped over in a whirlpool or rapid, the men would find themselves dumped into the middle of the river with no option but a frightening swim to shore.

Launching and landing the boats, often chest-deep in water amid the heavy underbrush that lined the riverbank, the men were constantly vulnerable to the predatory fish, waterborne snakes, and other creatures they were disturbing. Even the mundane necessity of bathing was a source of ongoing concern, although, in the mud and sweltering jungle heat, the men grew willing to take their chances. Roosevelt himself cooled off in the river at every opportunity. Floating in the shallow water near the bank, the 220-pound former president looked to Rondon "like some sort of a great, fat fish which had come to the surface," defying the dangers that surrounded him.

The fish that inspired the greatest fear among the men was the piranha. Attracted by blood and drawn to the kind of commotion that a bathing man might make, piranha have been known to swim in groups of more than a hundred, spreading out to scout for prey and then alerting the others, probably by sound, when they find it. Of the approximately twenty piranha species, most prefer to attack something their own size or smaller, and they are happy to scavenge, especially during the rainy season, when there is more to choose from. However, their muscular jaws and sawlike teeth, which look as if they have been filed to tiny spear points, can make quick work of a living creature of any size and strength, from a waterbird to a monkey to even an ox. During telegraph line expeditions, Rondon and his soldiers regularly offered up their weakest ox to a school of piranha so that the rest of their herd could safely cross a river.

Even Rondon, who had faced down mutinous soldiers and ridden on horseback into hostile Indian territory, showed extreme caution when bathing in the river. Having seen his co-commander barefoot, Roosevelt could easily guess at the reason. One morning during a telegraph line expedition, Rondon had found a shallow pool to bathe in at the edge of a river. He had carefully inspected it first, but the moment he slipped a foot into the water, a piranha had attacked, clipping off one of his toes with a single bite.

More painful to Rondon was the loss of a friend to piranhas in 1904. While crossing a river on a wounded mule, the man, who, like Rondon, had been a top cadet at the Military Academy, was attacked by piranhas drawn to the mule's blood. By the time his companions found him, there was nothing left on his skeleton but the feet in his boots.

Roosevelt referred to piranha as "the fish that eats men when it can get the chance." By the time he had reached the River of Doubt, he had heard dozens of horrifying stories of piranha that had left nothing but white bones on a riverbed after seizing upon a wounded soldier or an unfortunate child. Astounded by their blood lust, he called the fish "ferocious little monsters," and his vivid retelling of catching them on the Paraguay River caused a sensation in the United States when his *Scribner's* articles began to hit the newsstands. "The [piranha's] rabid, furious snaps drive the teeth through flesh and bone," he wrote. "The head with its short muzzle, staring malignant eyes, and gaping, cruelly armed jaws, is the embodiment of evil ferocity; and the actions of the fish exactly match its looks. I never witnessed an exhibition of such impotent, savage fury as was shown by the piranhas as they flapped on deck. When fresh from the water and thrown on the boards they uttered an extraordinary squealing sound. As they flapped about they bit with vicious eagerness at whatever presented itself. One of them flapped into a cloth and seized it with a bulldog grip. Another grasped one of its fellows; another snapped at a piece of wood, and left the teethmarks deep therein."

Piranha had already left their teeth marks on several members of Roosevelt's own expedition. They had bitten off part of one of Leo Miller's hands while he and Cherrie were collecting in the Gran Chaco during Roosevelt's speaking tour. "Suddenly I heard an outburst of considerable profanity," Cherrie later recalled, "and he [Miller] came running to show me his hand, from which a good sized piece had been torn by a piraña, the most bloodthirsty inhabitant of tropical waters." Cherrie himself had been nearly devoured alive on another expedition, when he had fallen from a tree branch and landed in the middle of a piranha feeding frenzy—a frenzy that he had incited by tossing into the river pieces of another piranha that he had caught earlier in the day. Even years after the incident, Cherrie shuddered at the memory of that extraordinarily close call.

As I fell I made a wild grab at the limb and, in so doing, I struck my arm against a small projection, tearing a long gash in the flesh. Even in the fraction of a second it took me to fall I realized that I was bleeding and that my blood would instantly incite an attack by the murderous fish. To be sure, the bank was only a few yards distant; but the lightning-like rapidity of the piranha left me little chance to escape unhurt. My whole instinct was to strike out instantly for the shore. Even a poor swimmer would have made it in a dozen strokes. But I retained enough of my reason to know that my one chance of escape lay in keeping the fish at bay before they became crazed with the taste of blood. So not only did I strike out for the shore but I set up a violent motion of twisting and splashing with my arms and legs. Even then I felt a blow and a sharp pain in my shoulder that told me one of the fish had struck. All I could do was to continue my furious splashing. Luckily I succeeded in reaching the shore, though badly bitten before I dragged myself out of the water. The physical effort of my contortions had exhausted me. It was some time before I could get up strength enough to start back to camp. I still bear the scars of that encounter. And I know that had I been even slightly stunned by my fall I should never have lived to tell the tale.

As terrifying as the piranha were, many of those who lived in the settled areas of the Amazon would have preferred them to the tiny, almost transparent catfish known as the candiru. This sharp-spined fish is the only other animal besides the vampire bat that is known to survive solely on blood. Most species of candiru are only about an inch long, and they usually make their living by swimming into the gill chambers of larger fish. To other fish, the candiru is relatively harmless, because, when full to capacity, it simply swims back out of the gill chamber and burrows into a riverbed to digest its blood meal. To humans, however, the miniature catfish is a potentially lethal menace.

When it comes to parasitizing people, a very rare occurrence, the candiru's modus operandi is to enter through an orifice—from a vagina to an anus. It is most famous, however, for wiggling its way into a urethra. The most widely discussed, if highly controversial, theory is that candirus are attracted to urine streams, mistaking them for the gill streams of fish. Before the unsuspecting bather knows what is happening, the candiru has followed the stream to its source, slipped inside, sunk its spines in the soft tissue, and begun to gorge on its host's blood. For the candiru, this is a fatal move. While it can easily swim out of a fish's gills, it cannot find its way out of a human urethra. Even if it could swim backward, its stiff spines prevent it from going in any direction but forward.

For the person whom the candiru has parasitized, the situation is potentially just as dire, and the cure can be as bad as the affliction. The candiru soon dies where it is, but its body continues to block the urethra, causing excruciating pain and, if not removed, death. Candiru removal, however, is difficult, especially in the remote tropics. In 1897, George Boulenger, a Belgian ichthyologist and herpetologist, presented a candiru to the Zoological Society of London and related a gruesome story, told to him by a doctor named Bach, of the extreme measures to which men in outlying villages were willing to go in order to rid themselves of a candiru. "The only means of preventing it from reaching the bladder, where it causes inflammation and ultimately death, is to instantly amputate the penis," Boulenger told his no doubt horrified audience. "Dr. Bach had actually examined a man and three boys with amputated penis [sic] as a result of this dreadful incident." Dr. Bach was later discredited because he had not personally witnessed either the attacks or the amputations, but his was not the first, or the last, story of a penectomy performed on a man whose urethra had been blocked by a candiru.

The potential danger for the men on the River of Doubt came not just when they swam in the river but even when they urinated in its shallow waters. Instances of candirus parasitizing people are rare, but in the one case in which a doctor fully documented his removal of a candiru from a young man, the victim's explanation of how the fish had entered his urethra was nearly as shocking as the fact that it was there at all. Up to that point, most scientists had assumed that, in order for the fish to find its way into a urethra, that part of the victim's anatomy had to be submerged in the water. In this case, however, the victim reported that, just before the attack, he had been standing in a river urinating, but the water had reached only to his upper thighs, and his penis had not even touched the river, much less been submerged in it. The candiru, he claimed, had abruptly leapt out of the

water, shimmied up his urine stream, and disappeared into his urethra. He had made a desperate lunge for the fish, but it was too fast
and too slippery. The incident occurred in a small town more than a
hundred miles from Manáos, and the local doctors had been at a loss
to help the man. By the time he was finally moved to Manáos for
treatment, he had been unable to urinate for more than a week, and
his stomach had become so distended that he looked six months preg-
nant. The doctor who eventually operated on him was able to successfully remove the candiru—without resorting to amputation.

*   *   *

ON THE morning of March 1, the expedition's third day on the River
of Doubt, the survey canoes once again got an early start, and the rest
of the expedition followed around 11:00 a.m. The rain began almost
as soon as they shoved off the bank.

Carried relentlessly forward by the swift current, the boats had just
started to round a bend when the forested riverbank on both sides
abruptly began to change. Out of the mist and rain, a collection of
clearly manmade structures materialized before them, and the men
suddenly realized that they were being propelled—without warning
or preparation—into the middle of an Indian village. With no opportunity to retreat, and dangerously exposed, they braced themselves in
their low-riding dugouts.

As they moved swiftly toward the village, however, they could see
that it showed no signs of activity. Perched on both banks of the river,
the village appeared to be devoid of life. Its population had vanished,
and the jungle had already begun to reclaim the land. The palm-
thatch roofs on the huts were rotting, and what appeared to have been
small cultivated areas were overgrown—"studded," Roosevelt wrote,
"with the burned skeletons of trees." At the river's edge, a fish trap
bobbed in the current, little left beyond a few hewn sticks to distinguish it from the mass of vegetation growing on the banks.

Around another bend in the river lay the remains of a bridge that
dangled a couple of feet above the water, just a few stout poles that

had been driven into the riverbed, and a long rope of liana that had been twisted for strength and stretched from one bank to the other to form a handrail. The rest of the bridge was gone, swept away by the swollen river.

The village—the first sign of human life that they had seen since launching their boats—was irrefutable proof that Indians lived on the banks of the River of Doubt. While this knowledge doubtless thrilled Rondon, it must have been sobering to the rest of the men in the expedition. They had no way to know if these Indians were hostile, but for the sake of their own safety, and judging by the Nhambiquara's initial reaction to Rondon, they had to assume that they were. In fact, Rondon speculated that these Indians were a subgroup of the Nhambiquara called the Navaité. Rondon nominally had a treaty with the Nhambiquara, but there was no reason to believe that this group would honor that treaty—or even that they knew anything about it, or Rondon. The only certainty was that, if they were still alive, the Indians who once lived in this village would see the expedition before the members of the expedition would see them.

There was nothing to explain why the Indians had deserted their village. Perhaps they had moved into the interior as the river began to rise, or had found better land for planting or hunting elsewhere and so set out to establish a new home. But they also could have been massacred by another tribe, or even another group within their own tribe. Whatever the explanation, on this gray day, with the light dwindling in the silent forest, the village had the eerie unease of a ghost town— the dwelling place of spirits rather than of men of flesh and bone.

* * *

THE GLOOM of the day's events lifted somewhat when Cherrie, from his seat in Roosevelt's canoe, heard the very real and tantalizingly close sound of game. His ears—an ornithologist's most finely tuned collecting tool—caught the distinctive "eeolk, eeolk" of the woolly monkey coming from the branches of a tree just overhead. Woolly monkeys are highly intelligent, extremely sensitive animals. In captivity, they have even been known to weep when upset. But when Cherrie raised his rifle, took aim, and fired, he was not thinking about adding an interesting specimen to his museum collection; he was thinking about dinner. Moments later, a monkey with dense gray fur, a long prehensile tale, and a round, protruding belly pitched forward and fell heavily out of the trees. As they watched the monkey tumble through the branches, the men briefly forgot their worries and concentrated on the prospect of fresh meat for dinner.

Their excitement, however, nearly turned to catastrophe a few hours later, when, in their haste to make camp, they forgot one of the most fundamental rules of the rain forest: Watch your step. With their dinner in hand, the men searched for a dry stretch of shore on which they could spend the night. Finally finding a level spot a few feet above the river, they landed, moored their boats to some trees, and began clearing a site for their third camp. As usual, they did not venture far from the water's edge, but what they did not realize that night was that the brush they were clearing concealed a coral snake.

Of all the creatures of the rain forest, none are more reliably lethal to man than snakes. Naturalists complain that venomous snakes are hard to find in the jungle. They disappear in a mat of branches and leaves, or hide beneath a fallen tree. But they are there, and when they strike, they are deadly.

The most infamous of South America's poisonous snakes are the ringed coral snake and the pit viper. A relative of North American rattlesnakes and copperheads, pit vipers have long horizontal fangs that snap into place like switchblades when they are ready to strike. Within seconds, their victims begin to sweat, vomit, and swell. Death comes from renal failure or intracranial bleeding. In 1931, Clodomiro Picado, a Costa Rican biologist and snakebite expert, described the horrors of a pit-viper bite: "Moments after being bitten, the man feels a live fire germinating in the wound, as if red-hot tongs contorted his flesh; that which was mortified enlarges to monstrosity, and lividness invades him. The unfortunate victim watches his body becoming a corpse piece by piece; a chill of death invades all his being, and soon bloody threads fall from his gums; and his eyes without intending to, will also cry blood, until, beaten by suffering and anguish, he loses the sense of reality."

The coral snake, which lurked under the brush as Roosevelt and his men waded ashore to make camp that night, had venom as deadly as that of the pit viper. A member of the Elapidae family, which includes cobras and mambas, the coral snake is not as aggressive as a pit viper and has much shorter fangs, but its venom is just as potent and certainly as painful. Once injected, the venom immediately attacks the victim's nervous system, causing excruciating and irreversible paralysis. Eventually the respiratory system collapses, and the victim, acutely aware of what is happening to him, slowly suffocates to death.

So lethal is the bite of a coral snake that, in rural Brazil at the time of Roosevelt's expedition, local people did not even attempt to treat it. No antivenom existed, and the moment someone was bitten, he was given up for dead. In North America, naturalists use an old adage—"Red touching yellow, dangerous fellow"—to help distinguish between nonvenomous snakes and the lethal coral snake, with its distinctive black, red, and yellow bands. This adage, however, is useless in the Amazon, where many of the more than fifty species of coral snakes have red and yellow bands that do not touch, but are deadly nevertheless.

While the camaradas noisily cleared a space in the overgrown shoreline for their campsite, they at first did not notice the three-foot-long coral snake, which had darted out of its hiding place. As their callused and dirt-streaked bare feet moved upon the thin layer of leaf litter, the snake slithered by, growing increasingly agitated. When threatened, a coral snake thrashes its body and tail, often in prelude to an attack. Perhaps it was this whiplike movement that finally attracted the attention of one of the camaradas, just as he was about to plant his foot squarely on the venomous snake. Terrified, the man grabbed an ax and swung wildly, driving the snake away from his feet—and toward Roosevelt.

Roosevelt reacted quickly, although perhaps not with his usual athletic grace. "Despite his two hundred and twenty pounds avoirdu-pois," Cherrie later recalled, "he [Roosevelt] did a much livelier dance in attempting to set his foot on the snake than he did when he danced the hornpipe on shipboard." When Roosevelt's foot finally came thundering down, it missed its mark, crushing the snake's body rather than its lethal head. Rearing back, the snake attacked. Roosevelt, still wearing his heavy, hobnailed boots, watched as the snake's short fangs plunged into the tough leather and spilled its venom down the side of his boot. He had been spared an agonizing, certain death by a quarter-inch of leather.

CHAPTER 14

Twitching Through the Woods

A FTER THREE DAYS ON the River of Doubt, not one of the men in the expedition would have disputed Rondon's choice of name for this winding, enigmatic river. Not only did it continue to keep its ultimate destination a mystery, but it defied even the most experienced rivermen among them to predict where it would take them in the course of a single day. "The number of twists and turns and doublings back and forth of the river were almost incredible," Cherrie wrote. As far as the men could see, the River of Doubt had only one virtue: It was as placid as a lowland stream. It moved just quickly enough to relieve the paddlers of some of their work, but it rarely showed any more signs of life than a gentle current that rocked their canoes like a hand on a cradle. When they set off on the morning of March 2, the river was reassuringly familiar, lazily spreading through the forest and carrying them in a northwesterly direction. By the middle of the afternoon, however, the paddlers felt a subtle but disturbing change. The current had begun to quicken.

Each of the Amazon's thousands of tributaries starts at a high point—either in the Andes, the Brazilian Highlands, or the Guiana

Highlands—and then steadily loses elevation and picks up speed until it begins to approach the Amazon Basin. Scientists have divided
these tributaries into three broad categories—milky, black, and
clear—in reference to the color that they take on while carving their
way through three different types of terrain. Alfred Russel Wallace,
British naturalist and friend of Henry Walter Bates and Charles
Darwin, made the distinction widely known in the mid-nineteenth
century when he published his *Narrative of Travels on the Amazon
and Rio Negro*. Wallace noted the striking difference between the
milky Amazon and the black waters of the Negro where they collide
on the northern bank of the Amazon. Seen from above, the meeting
of these two colossal rivers looks like black ink spilling over parch-
ment paper. The visual effect is heightened because the Negro, which
is warmer and thus lighter in weight, rides on top of the Amazon, and
the rivers do not fully blend until they have traveled dozens of miles
together downstream.

Milky rivers, such as the Amazon and the Madeira, generally have
their origins in the west and are clouded by the heavy sediment load
that they carry down from the youthful Andes. Blackwater rivers,
on the other hand, usually come from the ancient Guiana Highlands
in the north and so wash over nutrient-poor, sandy soils. Scoured by
millions of years of hard rains, these soils cannot retain decomposing
organic matter—mostly leaves—which, when swept into a river, literally stains the water black like tea.

Although during the rainy season the River of Doubt is nearly as
black as the Negro and as murky as the Amazon, it is technically a
clearwater river. Like the Amazon's largest clearwater rivers, the
Tapajos and the Xingu, it has its source in the Brazilian Highlands,
and so it picks up very little sediment as it flows over ancient and
highly eroded soil. Clearwater rivers are also less acidic than blackwater rivers. Some, most notably the Tapajos, are so clear that they look
blue, perfectly mirroring the sky above them. But most, like the River
of Doubt, mix with either blackwater or milky tributaries as they

snake through the rain forest, and so look neither blue nor clear by the time they reach their mouth.

For Roosevelt and his men, the color of the River of Doubt was of interest primarily for what it revealed about the speed and character of its course. The same eroded crystalline plateau that kept the river largely sediment-free was also banded with alternating layers of soft young rock and hard ancient rock, each of which had been exposed by the carving force of the river, creating a perfect breeding ground for waterfalls and rapids.

At around three-thirty that afternoon, the men heard a low roar that traveled upstream like distant thunder before a rainstorm. Over the ensuing weeks, this roar would become for them one of the most alarming sounds in the Amazon: the sound of rapids. With a heightened sense of expectation, they allowed themselves to be swept along on the swift current until they reached the first rapid. Although lively, it was small, and the expedition's three canoes and two balsas easily bumped through its turbid water. The men's relief at having successfully navigated this first obstacle, however, was short-lived. "Instead of finding quiet waters at the foot," Cherrie wrote, "the current ran faster and faster until we were whirled along as though through a mill race."

Suddenly the river made a sharp turn, and when they rounded the bend, the men saw a seething cauldron of white water, the prelude to world-class rapids. Surprised by the stark transformation of their placid river, they quickly drove their canoes ashore so that they could decide what to do next from the relative safety of the bank. It was impossible from this vantage point to tell exactly what was whipping the river into such a frenzy, but they did not want to find out while they were still in their clumsy dugouts. Leaving the camaradas behind to set about clearing a spot for their camp, the officers cut a path along the bank so that they could see for themselves what awaited them downstream.

They were disheartened by what they found. Stretching before them for nearly a mile was a series of rapids that included two roughly six-foot waterfalls. The river sped, Rondon wrote, "with enormous velocity" through rocks of friable sandstone that had been "deeply cut out, smashed to pieces and thrown one on the top of the other by the rushing force of the waters." Once over the falls, the river briefly divided into two branches as it swept past a small island—"the last stronghold of resistance which that ruined ground offered," Rondon noted—but then came together again to perform a feat that none of them had ever expected to see. The water channel that had been at least a hundred yards wide and proportionally deep just a mile above the rapids now churned through a passage that, at one point, was less than two yards across, transforming the quiet river into a water cannon.

"It seemed extraordinary, almost impossible, that so broad a river could in so short a space of time contract its dimensions to the width of the strangled channel through which it now poured its entire volume," Roosevelt marveled. In fact, so narrow was this gorge that Kermit took a picture of Cherrie kneeling at its chipped and worn edge and spanning it with his rifle. "No canoe could ever live through such whirlpools," the naturalist would later write. "Only one glance at the angry waters was necessary for us to realize that a long portage would have to be made."

*   *   *

THE PORTAGE around the River of Doubt's first serious set of rapids lasted for two and a half days. Rondon put everyone to work except Franca, the cook, and an ill camarada, who had already begun to sweat and shiver with fever. Even Kermit, who was suffering from a renewed attack of the boils that had tortured him during the overland journey, helped move their camp to the foot of the falls and, with Lyra, hauled the expedition's heaviest, waterlogged dugout up from the river. It was only by applying block and tackle that the camaradas were able to get all of the dugouts out of the water, up the bank, and onto level ground. There must have been few men in the portage team who did not recall with deep regret the expedition's abandonment of Fiala's 160-pound canvas-covered canoes.

The camaradas had already prepared a corduroy road of heavy logs upon which they would drag the canoes. With axes and machetes, they had hewn a rough path through the jungle's tangle of trees and snaking vines. Then they began chopping down trees, a job made infinitely more difficult by the broad, load-bearing buttresses that supported most large boles. These trees were cut into hundreds of thick, six-foot-long poles, which were placed on the ground at two-yard intervals to serve as rollers for the unwieldy canoes.

Once the road had been laid, the real work could begin. Harnessing themselves to a drag rope, the camaradas lined up two by two like draft horses to pull the dugouts over the crude skidway. The only help came from one man who stood behind them with a lever and tried to pry the canoes over the gnarled, uneven logs. It was in this way—"bumping and sliding," Roosevelt wrote—that the seven dugouts painfully "twitched through the woods." For the camaradas, the pain was not limited to their massive, awkward loads, or even to the rough rope that blistered their sweat-slick hands and sawed heavily into their shoulders. As they cut through the jungle, twisted vines and sharp, grasping branches tore at their clothes and slashed their skin. The hot, humid air felt thick in their throats, and they fought off a dizzying sensation of claustrophobia as they fumbled through the close, dense, and seemingly endless fortress of trees along the riverbank.

As the men had feared, the price of encountering impassable rapids was prolonged, intimate exposure to a jungle that seemed increasingly dangerous and enigmatic. Common sense and scientific respect for the jungle told them that there must be an abundance of animal life in this part of the Amazon, as in every part, but there was very little to be seen. The men frequently saw trails left by tapirs and peccaries, piglike mammals, but they were always empty. So far, they had had little opportunity to hunt, and no luck even fishing. The only creatures in evidence were the insects, which seemed to grow increasingly bold and aggressive the deeper the men traveled into the rain forest.

In fact, as the men of the expedition labored to build their portage road, the jungle around them was teeming with life. While on land, the members of the expedition could not sit, step, lean, or stand without entangling themselves in the predatory ambitions of some creature or, more often, hundreds of creatures of the Amazon. Yet the same evolutionary competition that filled each branch, shadow, and muddy puddle with an unparalleled diversity of living things also ensured that those forms of life were virtually invisible to Roosevelt and his men. Those glimpses of activity that they did manage to see, moreover, were often calculated for the specific purpose of confusing and misleading them.

Rarely in the rain forest do animals or insects allow themselves to be seen, and any that do generally do so with ulterior motives. In a world of endless, life-or-death competition, the need to hide from potential predators and deceive sophisticated prey is a fundamental requirement of longevity, and it has produced a staggering range of specialized attributes and behavior aimed at manipulating—or erasing entirely—any visible form that an enemy or victim might see. So refined is the specialization of life in the rain forest that every inch of the jungle, and each part of the cycle of day and night, has plant, animal, and insect specialists that have adapted to exploit the unique appearance-altering potential it offers.

The most common defensive tactic, used by many or most of the animals that Roosevelt and his men had expected to see, is simply to hide, biding time in hollow trees, carefully constructed burrows, or camouflaged nests high in the canopy, and emerging only under cover of darkness. The tent-making bat painstakingly makes small bites along the centerline of large leaves so that they will droop on each side, creating small tentlike shelters that protect them from rain, wind, and sun and render them all but invisible. The lumbering armadillo, on the other hand, laboriously digs a burrow that it inhabits

for as little as a single day, only to abandon it in the interest of finding even greater safety and invisibility elsewhere.

To make the job of hiding easier, some creatures develop camouflage, or cryptic coloration, to help them disappear even in the plain
view of potential predators. A ten-foot-long gold-and-brown-striped
boa constrictor can all but vanish on the dappled forest floor.
Caterpillars of the geometrid moth are almost indistinguishable from
twigs, and katydids look like nothing more than green leaves. Fishes
of the Aspredinidae and Anabantidae families also specialize in looking like twigs and leaves, blending in with the detritus carried along
by the river's current.

When protective coloration does not come to them naturally, some
creatures have developed relationships with plants or insects that can
do the job for them. The three-toed sloth, for example, a long-limbed,
short-bodied mammal that lives in high trees, can nearly vanish while
hanging upside down from its clawed feet. As a mammal that is typically grayish-brown in color, the sloth has no natural way of blending
into the green coloration of the forest canopy. Each of its hairs has
therefore evolved to contain microscopic grooves that become filled
with algae, giving the sloth a greenish sheen that allows it to disappear when viewed from the ground.

Given their high numbers and stealthy habits, it is virtually certain
that sloths were a constant presence as the men of the expedition
fought their way through the forest below. Yet they remained undetected. In a world in which most animals have to fly, run, swing, or
scurry in order to elude predators, the sloth has made a virtue out of
immobility. The mere fact that it moves slowly and rarely—its head
can rotate more than ninety degrees, so that every other part of its
body can remain motionless—makes it almost impossible to see. So
perfectly has the sloth adapted to its strange treetop life-style that its
hair grows forward to allow the rain to drip effectively from its inverted body, and its sharp, curved claws are so specialized for the job
of clinging to branches that the female cannot even pick up her young

to carry them on her back—they must climb on by themselves after they are born.

To the degree that some creatures cannot avoid being seen, many adopt disguises to confuse, startle, or mislead potential enemies. The wings of many butterflies bear round, eye-shaped patterns which flash into view at the moment of flight, frightening potential predators by suggesting the face of an owl or a bird and buying a precious second of confusion for the butterfly to escape. The caterpillar of certain sphinx moths can contract its muscles so that it looks convincingly like the head of a small viper. To complete the illusion, it even sways slowly back and forth, much like a viper ready to strike.

The value of disguise and deception is not limited to defense against predators, and can also become a centerpiece of offensive strategies, like the remarkable Trojan Horse ploy used by the South American crab spider to capture the carpenter ants on which it feeds. After killing an ant, the crab spider, which is only a fifth of an inch long, carefully consumes the contents of the ant's body without harming the outer skeleton. It then carries the empty carcass over its own body so that, visually and chemically, the spider "looks" like its prey—allowing it to approach new victims undetected. Some plants also assume disguises to fool their evolutionary foes and accomplish their reproductive mission. Certain orchids, for example, attract male tachnid flies by mimicking females; when the male tries to copulate with what it believes to be a female fly, it ends up polinating the orchid.

For some species that deter attack by being poisonous, the goal of their physical appearance is not to hide or confuse other forest creatures, but to be noticed. In order to stay alive, they advertise their toxicity to potential predators through bright, vivid markings known as warning coloration. Some of the most famous practitioners of warning coloration in the Amazon are poison-dart frogs of the species *Phyllobates terribilis,* which can carry enough toxin to kill a hundred people and need only be touched to be deadly. These frogs, whose toxin is used on the blowgun darts of some Amazon Indian tribes, are

as small as a half-inch long. But their bold patterns and vivid color-
ing are as effective as a neon sign in warning their natural predators
of their lethal potential. For outsiders such as the men of the expedition, however, such signals meant little or nothing, and merely ensured that the only creatures they could see as they pushed through
the forest were likely to be especially dangerous or even lethal.

* * *

ROOSEVELT AND Kermit had come to the Amazon with the expectation that they would hunt wild game, much as they had done in the
wilderness of the Western United States and in Africa. But the relentless advance of evolutionary competition—together with the arrival
of human beings on the South American continent thousands of years
before—had largely eliminated the big, conspicuous game animals
that Roosevelt had become famous for hunting elsewhere.

For much of its history, South America was home to a striking array of large animals like those Roosevelt would have associated with
Africa or Asia. Although the reasons for the abrupt and dramatic loss
of life are not certain, many scientists believe that the impact of human migration was decisive. In contrast to Africa and parts of Asia,
where animals evolved alongside early humans and learned to fear
them, South America was the last continent to be populated by humans, who by that time had become sophisticated hunters. With no
understanding of their new predator, the large animals of South
America were prime prey for the arriving humans, and most of them
were soon driven to extinction.

Of the mammals that remain, the jaguar is the undisputed king.
Cherrie would never forget an earlier expedition along the Paraguay
River, when his party had been terrorized by a single jaguar. "Few
people have heard a horse scream," Cherrie wrote, still bothered by
the memory of the sound. "When the jaguar started in the direction
of our horses they literally screamed with fear and lunged about
fiercely. Several broke their hitchings and went tearing away into the
forest!"

For all its ferocity, however, the jaguar was too wary and elusive to constitute a real danger, and while other jungle mammals, such as peccaries, could be dangerous, they, too, were so scarce that the men would have welcomed the chance to encounter one in return for the possibility of a good meal. As they were quickly learning, the greatest challenge they faced from the rain forest came not from any creature or adversary that they could confront and defeat, but from the jungle as a whole—in the ruthless efficiency with which it apportioned food and nutrients, in the bewildering complexity of its defense mechanisms, in the constant demands that it placed upon every one of its inhabitants, and in the ruthlessness with which it dealt with the weak, the hungry, or the infirm.

To witness the devastating impact of this kind of danger, the men needed to look no further than the insects that filled the air around their faces, and swarmed over every tree, vine, and leaf they touched. Rondon, who had for decades watched his men be tortured, infected, and driven to the brink of madness by the jungle's multitude of insect pests, knew better than most what power such small creatures could wield. The Brazilian colonel, Roosevelt wrote, regarded the threat that even jaguars posed as "utterly trivial compared to the real dangers of the wilderness—the torment and menace of attacks by the swarming insects, by mosquitoes and the even more intolerable tiny gnats, by the ticks, and by the vicious poisonous ants which occasionally cause villages and even whole districts to be deserted by human beings. These insects, and the fevers they cause, and dysentery and starvation and wearing hardship and accidents in rapids are what the pioneer explorers have to fear."

So important and ubiquitous are insects in the ecology of the Amazon that, notwithstanding their generally small size, ants alone make up more than 10 percent of the biomass of all the animals in the rain forest. From tiny parasitic red mites to cyanide-squirting millipedes to giant six-inch beetles with legs so powerful that they require two men to pry them off if they grip a human arm, the insects of the rain forest have achieved an unparalleled degree of specialization, seeking out every possible source of sustenance and advantage. They accomplish this through adaptations that extend far beyond mere physical attributes and individual behavior, and reach into the realm of complex social relationships that involve not only other members of their own species but sophisticated alliances with other forms of life as well.

Like that of other rain forest organisms, the physical form of insects has evolved to accomplish a spectacular range of survival-related feats, from living upside down on canopy leaves to flying almost invisibly on transparent wings to biting with pincerlike mandibles so large that they are sometimes used by Indians to suture wounds. The Brazilian wasp *Mischocyttarus drewensi* secretes a chemical repellent from its abdomen that, when slathered onto the stem that holds its nest, forces marauding ants to turn back and abandon their plans of attack. Ants of the neotropical genus *Basiceros* have made themselves all but invisible on the forest floor both by camouflaging their bodies in fine particles of soil that collect in two layers of hair and by learning the value of slothlike immobility. When foraging, the ants move extremely slowly, and if disturbed, they stand perfectly still for minutes at a time, disappearing into the rotting litter around them.

More than any other rain forest creatures, insects have extended and refined their individual capabilities through elaborate social structures. As Roosevelt and his men discovered from their first moments on the River of Doubt, the powerful influence of ants, termites, wasps, and other highly regimented insects comes not only from the particular traits of any single individual, but from the collective, coordinated activities of colonies and hives that can number as many as a million members. Acting in concert, but with highly specialized roles, columns of hundreds of thousands of army ants can fan out in raiding parties fifty feet across at their front lines, harvesting huge numbers of tarantulas, roaches, beetles, scorpions, snakes, lizards, birds, and nearly anything else in their path before returning at dusk with the bodies of their prey to their common bivouac.

Insects have also developed highly refined, mutually beneficial relationships with other rain forest organisms. Many tropical trees and plants have special sheltering cavities or nectar-producing structures for the benefit of ants, which in return then patrol them vigilantly, defending them against herbivores, tending their leaves, and eating the eggs and larvae of other potentially damaging insects. As a result of such relationships, virtually every growing thing teems with insects; a single tree in the Amazon can serve as home to more than forty different species of ant, rendering even the most casual contact with it a nightmare of painful bites.

At this early point in the Roosevelt-Rondon Expedition, the insects had already become the bane of the men's existence. On the morning of March 4, Cherrie woke up to find that the poncho that he had spread underneath his hammock the night before was "literally alive with termites." Unfortunately for the expedition, termites swarm during the rainy season. The mass swarming may be an effort to increase their chances for reproducing, or it may better their odds for surviving their countless predators. Whatever the reason for this invasion, every man suffered because of it. The termites ate Cherrie's duffle bag, the red lining of Roosevelt's helmet, and even one leg of the former president's underwear. "When the Colonel held them up for our inspection there was a shout of laughter," Cherrie recalled. "But I don't believe he relished our mirth."

Roosevelt might have found more humor in the situation if he had had underwear to spare. As it was, he had precious few pairs left. Not only had he left some of these essential items behind in an effort to reduce his personal belongings during the overland journey, but he had also lost some to another, earlier attack. One night near Utiarity, while he and Kermit were sleeping, one of the expedition's pack oxen had gotten into their tent and feasted on their underwear.

The insects were more than destructive. Their bites were maddening and painful, forcing even strong men to seek shelter. "Our hands and faces were swollen from the bites and stings of the insect pests," Roosevelt complained. Each night when he sat down at his little portable table to work on his *Scribner's* articles, Roosevelt had to pull long, fringed gauntlets over his hands and arms and drape his sun helmet in mosquito netting that hung heavily over his face.

To fight off the insects, the men had at least one useful weapon besides clothing and netting: fly dope. Developed in the late nineteenth century, fly dope was one of the first chemical insect repellents to be introduced in the United States. "I had never before been forced to use such an ointment, and had been reluctant to take it with me," Roosevelt admitted. "But now I was glad enough to have it, and we all of us found it exceedingly useful. I would never again go into mosquito or sand-fly country without it."

As welcome a relief as it had been, however, the small quantity of fly dope that Roosevelt had brought with him was hardly sufficient compared to the sheer scale of the insect life that the expedition encountered as it made its way down the River of Doubt.

* * *

FOR EVERY plant and creature that surrounded Roosevelt and his men as they toiled to build their first portage road, the qualifications for survival in the rain forest were essentially the same: the ability to find food, the ability to find their way through the labyrinth of nature around them, and the ability to protect themselves and their offspring from predators.

In every part of the jungle, those requirements had produced miracles of adaptation and efficiency. In their hunt for food, the birds overhead enjoyed eyesight roughly eight times as acute as the best human vision. Some of the hawk moths that fluttered across their campsite at night could unfurl six-inch-long tongues to drink from the deep-throated flowers that sustained them. The leaf-cutting ants that paraded by in long lines, carrying proportionally huge bits of foliage, could not eat that leaf matter outright, but painstakingly transported it back home to cultivate the underground fungus on which their colony survived.

Although the men of the expedition couldn't discern them, the apparent chaos around them was actually organized into sophisticated paths that led throughout the jungle. Pink-faced capuchin monkeys swung along rapidly on carefully defined arboreal pathways at heights where the smallest miscalculation could mean a fatal fall. Millions of bats, following intricate sounds shaped by the strange fleshy protrusions, or nose leaves, on their faces, swooped confidently through the crowded, pitch-black forest on the basis of sound alone, alighting blindly but precisely on their nectar-filled blossoms, fruit, or insect prey, and even taking delicate sips of water from the river in midflight. Snakes, spiders, millipedes, mice, and lizards—to say nothing of their amazing ant neighbors—followed chemical pathways of taste and smell across the thin forest floor, ranging far each night before returning with flawless navigation to their carefully hidden sanctuaries.

At every step, any resources that did not go to finding sustenance were devoted to securing protection from predators. Everything in the rain forest, even the trees, had adapted to protect itself and its progeny from predation. The rubber tree, which had made the Amazon Basin a center of frenzied commercial attention, produced its sticky resin not for the purpose of building automobile tires, but to choke its insect predators. The army ants that flooded out of the trees and plants that the expedition disturbed were genetically programmed to give their own lives to save the one to three hundred thousand offspring carried by their one queen.

Within such an intricate world of resourcefulness, skill, and ruthless self-interest, refined over hundreds of millions of years, Roosevelt and his men were, for all their own experience and knowledge, vulnerable outsiders. Most of the men were veteran outdoorsmen, and many of them considered themselves masters of nature. They were stealthy hunters, crack shots, and experienced survivalists, and, given the right tools, they believed that they would never find themselves in a situation in the wild that they could not control. But as they struggled to make their way along the shores of the River of Doubt, any basis for such confidence was quickly slipping away. Compared with the creatures of the Amazon, including the Indians whose territory they were invading, they were all—from the lowliest camarada to the former president of the United States—clumsy, conspicuous prey.

CHAPTER 15

The Wild Water

THE LONG, DIFFICULT PORTAGE around the first set of rapids,
which Rondon had named Navaité Rapids in honor of the
Indians who he believed lived at their foot, finally ended on the morning of March 5. By early afternoon, the men had relaunched their canoes and were back on the river. Riding on the smooth current, they
noticed that the forest on either side of them grew denser and
denser—"and therefore more picturesque," Rondon wrote—as they
pushed deeper and deeper into the Amazon. The rain forest that
flanked the River of Doubt was the definition of a primordial jungle.
It was lush, vivid green, and absolutely pristine.

At night, gathered close to their campfire after a simple dinner, the
men unfailingly talked about the river's undecipherable course, won-
dering aloud where it would lead them and what the next day would
hold. "We held endless discussions and hazarded all kinds of guesses
on both subjects," Roosevelt would later recall. Regarding the river's
final destination, they had whittled the multitude of possibilities
down to only four: It could swing westward and feed into the Gy-
Paraná, the same river that Miller and Amilcar were now descending.

It could curve to the east and enter the Tapajos, the river that Roosevelt had originally planned to descend with Father Zahm. It could straighten out and head directly north to pour into the Madeira, the principal tributary of the Amazon River, as Rondon had gambled. Or it could turn out to be a direct tributary of the Amazon.

"We did not know whether we had one hundred or eight hundred kilometers to go," Roosevelt wrote, "whether the stream would be fairly smooth or whether we would encounter waterfalls, or rapids, or even some big marsh or lake." Roosevelt did not have long to wait for the answer to his second question. Around three o'clock the next afternoon, the men again felt the current quicken and heard the ominous roar of rapids ahead. They stopped, tied their canoes to some trees, and made their way down the bank by using a narrow trail blazed by a tapir. What they saw just a quarter-mile downstream— two waterfalls carved out of red porphyritic rock followed by a series of treacherous rapids—left no doubt in anyone's mind that they would again have to haul their heavy dugouts from the water and drag them through the jungle.

* * *

THE EXPEDITION'S second portage took three full days. The men were nervous not only about the time and rations that they were losing by carrying the equipment and hauling the canoes over the rough terrain, but about the damage that they were doing to their dugouts in the process. During the first portage, Roosevelt's canoe, battered by the crude corduroy road, had cracked. They had managed to patch it, but they did not know how long it would last or what yet another long portage would do to it or the other canoes. The dugouts—heavy, clumsy, and sagging though they were—were as precious to the men as the provisions that they carried.

The men had no hope that this series of rapids might be the last that they would encounter. On the first full day of the portage, the expedition got more bad news. Kermit had gone about four miles downstream that day to hunt with his dog, Trigueiro, and Antonio Pareci, one of Roosevelt's paddlers. As a hunt, the outing had been a success. Kermit returned with a jacu—a turkeylike bird—for Franca's pot, and Antonio brought back a big monkey. Roosevelt himself had even developed a taste for monkey meat, pronouncing his first mouthful "very good eating." But, as excited as the men had been to see Antonio Pareci holding a monkey in his hands when he walked back into camp, the news that Kermit carried deflated their spirits. If they made it through this series of treacherous rapids, he reported, another one awaited them not far downriver.

The men were defeated before they had even finished their first day of muscle-wrenching, bone-jarring work portaging around this second series of rapids. Lyra and Kermit divided the camaradas into two divisions. While Lyra and his men cut and laid the corduroy road, Kermit's team began dragging the dugouts up from the river. Together they then strained to pull the boats through the jungle and down the steep bank at the foot of the rapids.

On March 10, the men finally completed their three-day, 750-yard portage and relaunched their boats. Only a mile later, however, they reached the rapids that Kermit had warned them about. This time the prospect of another overland struggle was too much for them to bear. On the theory that the risk to their canoes from another haul through the jungle was even greater than the threat of smashing them to matchsticks in the roiling river, they decided to plunge ahead and take their chances on the water. One group of camaradas was assigned to carry the provisions to the foot of the falls by means of a hastily cut forest trail, while the rest of the men worked to get the empty dugouts through the rapids. The three individual canoes were then run straight through the boulder-strewn water by a couple of naked and intrepid paddlers, who managed to bring them through undamaged. The smaller of the two balsas, however, did not make it. It was swamped, and before they could do anything to save it, it sank.

Desperate not to lose the canoes, the camaradas tore into the river and wrenched them free from the rapids. In the process, one camarada was momentarily carried away by the rushing water. He fought his way to the bank, but not before slashing his face open on the unforgiving rocks that lined the riverbed. Shaken by the near-catastrophe, the men were not willing to risk the second, larger balsa. They secured it to ropes and slowly lowered it down the river.

No one worked harder than Kermit to get the expedition past these rapids and back onto the river. He was at his best when he had a mission. Left to his own devices, he had a tendency to brood, even to fall into a quiet depression, but, given a cause, he worked harder than anyone around him. He thrived on the challenge, and Roosevelt marveled at his son, who had grown a heavy beard and was "dressed substantially like the camaradas themselves," as he worked tirelessly to defeat the rapids that stood between him and home.

* * *

AFTER TWELVE days on the river, the expedition had only managed to cover seventy-five miles—an average of less than seven miles a day. Exhausted and hungry, the men decided to make camp immediately, directly below the last rapid. As usual, they searched for a high, level stretch of ground and then moored their canoes to some trees at the river's edge. Perhaps Fiala's stories of losing his provisions to the icy waters of the Arctic had stayed with them, because that night, as beaten by the river and jungle as they were, they hauled their provisions out of the canoes and up the slippery, overgrown bank. At the time it seemed like nothing more than a mild precaution.

As the men slept that night in their hammocks—the camaradas beneath twelve-foot-long wild banana-tree leaves that gave them some meager shelter from the rain—the river rose. Slowly, inch by inch, water began to seep into the old and leaky dugout that had been tied to the expedition's largest canoe. At some point during the night, the leaky dugout took on so much water that it began to sink, dragging the big canoe down with it. Since the men had chosen a campsite close to the tail of the rapids, the river was not only high, it was rough, and the two boats rolled and twisted in the current until they finally snapped their moorings and were swept downriver.

The members of the expedition had endured a week of painful portages because they could not imagine losing even one canoe. Now they had lost two. When they discovered their loss the next morning, the men, hoping against hope that they would recover at least one of the dugouts, immediately mounted a search party. However, the same sharp boulders that had torn open the face of one of their paddlers had made quick work of the old waterlogged dugouts. "Rolling over the bowlders [sic] on the rocky bottom, they had at once been riven asunder," Roosevelt wrote. "And the big fragments that were soon found, floating in eddies, or along the shore, showed that it was useless to look farther."

The men had saved their provisions from the same fate by hauling them up to camp the night before, but with only five canoes left, they could no longer carry all of their food and equipment, not to mention their men, down the river. Now, not only could the members of the expedition not turn back, but they could not move forward. They were stranded on the tree-shrouded banks of the River of Doubt.

CHAPTER 16

Danger Afloat, Danger Ashore

S TANDING AT the river's edge, Roosevelt and his men realized that they had very few options left. They could either try to hack their way through the forest on foot—likely losing most if not all of their men in the process—or they could try to build a new canoe. The last option was nearly as dangerous as the first. "That means time and the eating into our limited supply of provisions!" Cherrie scrawled frustratedly in his diary. He knew as well as Roosevelt and Rondon that the expedition could ill afford a delay of even a few days.

In an effort to find out just how dire their circumstances had become, the expedition's officers gathered together to take stock of their rations. When splitting the provisions with Miller and Amilcar before they launched their boats, the River of Doubt party had taken fifty of the ninety food tins that Fiala had packed, as well as the seventy-five United States Army emergency rations he had purchased as a precaution. Each tin box was meant to hold enough food for five men for one day. Concerned that the former president have not just gourmet condiments but also a variety of foods during what was supposed to be an uneventful journey, Fiala had planned seven different meals—one for each day of the week—and had numbered each box, from one to seven, so that Roosevelt would never have to have the same meal twice in a row. The Friday meal, for example, consisted of rice, bread, gingersnaps, dehydrated potatoes and onions, Erbswurst (a type of sausage), condensed milk, bacon, curry and chicken, dates, sugar, coffee, tea, and salt. The Saturday meal was similar, but Fiala had made some strategic changes, such as replacing rice with oatmeal, and potatoes with baked beans. Each tin, which had been lacquered to protect it from rust, also held a yard of muslin, two boxes of matches, and a single cake of soap.

What the officers discovered when they took stock of these provisions now, however, alarmed even Cherrie. "There were sufficient rations for the men to last about thirty-five days," he wrote. "While the rations that had been arranged for the officials of the party would perhaps last fifty days." With grim certainty, the officers calculated that, if the expedition continued to advance at this slow rate, they would be without food of any kind, beyond what they could catch or forage, for the last month of their journey.

As well as worrying about their quickly dwindling rations, the men were reluctant to stay in one spot for too long for another reason: They were not alone. The jungle was, they now knew, inhabited by a group of Indians that had had no contact with the outside world. Rondon believed that the expedition was probably still traveling through Nhambiquara territory, but that was just a hunch. He could not be any more sure of what tribe of Indians they might face than he was of where the river was taking them. No other nonnative had ever been down the River of Doubt, and even the Nhambiquara who lived near its headwaters had not been able to tell Rondon what he might expect from the Indians who lived on its banks.

Although the members of the expedition had yet to see a single human being since they had launched their boats nearly two weeks earlier, they had seen several signs of human life. Not only had they passed an abandoned village and the remains of a broken bridge, but, while crossing an Indian trail, Kermit had stumbled upon a pateran, an arrangement of branches and leaves designed to convey a message. What concerned the men about this pateran was that, unlike the rotting huts and overgrown fields, it was not a remnant of a deserted village. It had clearly been constructed very recently, and, as Roosevelt wrote, "it had some special significance." It might have been simply an Indian path marker, giving directions to a camp or a prime fishing spot, but it just as easily might have been a warning to the members of the expedition. Either way, they were not willing to take any chances. "No one of us ever went ten yards from camp without his rifle," Roosevelt wrote.

* * *

HAVING SPENT the past week fighting their way through a relentless series of rapids, the men would have little opportunity to rest during their forced delay. Construction of the new dugout had to begin immediately. As the rain fell, soaking everything and everyone, the camaradas trudged through the jungle, fanning out in different directions in an intensive search for trees that would be suitable for a canoe. They finally found three that they thought might work, chopped them down, and dragged them back to camp. Roosevelt judged them all to be "splendid looking trees," but Rondon decided to use only one of them. It was a species of Euphorbiacaea, a Para rubber tree, which can grow to be 120 feet tall in its natural habitat. This one was five feet in diameter, and its timber, which the Brazilians called Tatajuba, was yellowish in color.

Under Rondon's direction, the camaradas fell to work. They only had time to build one canoe to replace the two that had been lost, so, if it had any hope of carrying the expedition's cargo, it had to be big. The men measured off twenty-six feet from the tree's base and then began the backbreaking work of hewing it out. Typically in building a dugout canoe, an ax is used to cut a flat plank from the bark and hollow out the trunk until the interior space is a couple of feet deep. The canoe is then filled with leaves and turned upside down, so that a small fire can be lit inside to help waterproof it and smooth out its rough edges. Next, the builders flip the canoe back over and, while the wood is still warm, scrape the interior walls and floor with the curved blade of an adze. Finally, they place crosspieces from wall to wall in the interior to help stretch the canoe.

The members of the expedition allowed themselves only four days to complete the canoe. They worked in shifts, and Rondon never left their side, tirelessly directing the construction and ensuring that every man pulled his weight. The toll on the camaradas was heavy. Their backs ached, their arms quivered with fatigue, and, under constant attack from insects, their hands, faces, and feet became raw and inflamed. Under Rondon's unwavering gaze, however, they never let up or even slowed down. Even after the sun set, Roosevelt watched the camaradas toil by candlelight, stripped to the waist in the hot, still air, some standing inside the canoe, others bent over its thick hull. "The flicker of the lights showed the tropic forest rising in the darkness round about," he wrote. "Olive and copper and ebony, their skins glistened as if oiled, and rippled with the ceaseless play of the thews beneath."

Since witnessing their heroic struggle to bring the expedition's dugout canoes through the rapids, Roosevelt had developed a deep admiration for his team of camaradas. "Looking at the way the work was done, at the good-will, the endurance, and the bull-like strength of the camaradas, and at the intelligence and the unwearied efforts of their commanders," he wrote, "one could not but wonder at the ignorance of those who do not realize the energy and the power that are so often possessed by, and that may be so readily developed in, the men of the tropics."

Only one camarada had turned out to be, in Roosevelt's words, "utterly worthless." Julio de Lima had proved himself to be so lazy and untrustworthy that if Rondon could have sent him back he would have. "When we were able to discover his bad qualities, his cowardice and complete incapacity to follow up the continuous efforts of his fellow companions, we were so far advanced in the river that it was impossible for us to rid ourselves of his presence," Rondon wrote. When they were hiring camaradas in Tapirapoan, Julio had caught their eye because of his strapping physique, good health, and professed enthusiasm for the work. That enthusiasm, however, had evaporated as soon as they reached their first set of rapids, and his strength was useless to them because he would never use it for the good of the expedition unless threatened with punishment or even abandonment. "In the Expedition no one relied upon the assistance of his strength, and least of all, of his will," Rondon wrote. Roosevelt had absolutely no use for Julio, calling him an "inborn, lazy shirk with the heart of a ferocious cur in the body of a bullock." But Rondon was determined to make him work.

Rondon did not tolerate laziness or disobedience from anyone in his regiment. When it came to his soldiers, he had earned a reputation for being implacable. In the wilderness, where his men had to fight daily just to survive, he had no alternative but to guide his regiment with a firm hand. He had, however, learned through painful personal experience the importance of tempering the anger that flared inside of him at the first sign of rebellion.

Twenty years earlier, Rondon had ordered a group of men who had rebelled against his officers to be flogged with bamboo sticks for more than an hour. Such punishment was against the law in Brazil at that time, but it was widely known to be common practice in Mato Grosso. This time, however, it had disastrous results. Under the force of a blow, a bamboo stick had snapped and punctured the lung of one of the soldiers. Horrified, Rondon had quickly ordered an end to the flogging, but there had been nothing that he could do for the wounded man, who eventually died from peritonitis.

Although Rondon deeply regretted the man's death and vowed never again to resort to violence, he did not, and could not, dispense with all forms of punishment. Nor did he rely on the weight of the Brazilian military to enforce his rules or keep his men in check. Even with his thin, five-foot-three-inch frame, he could intimidate the most unruly mob of young men. Six years earlier, while at work extending the telegraph line, Rondon's soldiers had wreaked havoc on a small town, reeling drunkenly in the streets, breaking windows, and starting fights. After receiving only a lackluster response to his order to leave the saloons and assemble before him in the street, Rondon had turned toward the largest tavern in town, dug his spurs into his horse's sides, and charged at full speed through the front doors. As men scrambled to get out of his way, he vaulted a table and bounded out the back door. One of his officers then solemnly announced that Rondon would smash every bottle in town if the saloons did not close. Moments later, the soldiers staggered into the street, swept along by anxious barkeepers.

*   *   *

WHILE RONDON and his camaradas built a new canoe for the expedition, Roosevelt and his son did their best to find food in the eerily quiet forest. Kermit shot an eight-foot-long water snake and a curassow, a large-crested game bird, and he just missed several red howler monkeys, which were frightened away by Rondon's favorite dog, Lobo. Roosevelt, on the other hand, unfailingly returned to camp empty-handed. "I spent the day hunting in the woods, for the most part by the river," he wrote of one such solo hunting trip, "but saw nothing." Few among them would have been surprised by this revelation. Not only were the animals of the rain forest masters of disguise, but Roosevelt, the mighty hunter, was famously myopic. "He was always alone on these excursions," Rondon would later recall, "and most frequently he returned without any game whatever, as being short sighted he did not always succeed in seeing the game from afar, and the latter, in its turn, was scared and fled when it heard his footsteps as he approached it."

Roosevelt's myopia had hampered his hunting and bird-watching ever since he was a small child. "Quite unknown to myself, I was, while a boy, under a hopeless disadvantage in studying nature," he explained in his autobiography. "I was very near-sighted, so that the only things that I could study were those I ran against or stumbled over." Roosevelt got his first gun and his first pair of glasses at about the same time. Unfortunately, the gun came first. Roosevelt could not understand why his friends were consistently spotting and shooting game that he could not even see. It was not until he confessed his difficulties to his father that his myopia was finally diagnosed and he was fitted with a strong pair of lenses. Those glasses, he wrote, "literally opened an entirely new world to me. I had no idea how beautiful the world was until I got those spectacles."

Roosevelt prized his spectacles; he carried eight or ten pairs with him, carefully distributed throughout his luggage, whenever he traveled. In the tropics, however, his nearsightedness proved to be a greater disadvantage than it had been elsewhere. Not only did his glasses constantly fog over in the heavy humidity, it was almost impossible for him to see when it rained, which it did several times a day. While this frustrating and potentially dangerous disability would have kept most men out of the rain forest, Roosevelt refused even to acknowledge that it was a problem. "It was a continual source of amazement to see how skillfully father had discounted this handicap in advance and appeared to be unhampered by it," Kermit wrote.

On March 13, the camaradas worked until nearly midnight, and the next morning, in the middle of a torrential downpour, they finally completed the canoe. It took all twenty-two men to drag the twenty-six-foot-long dugout down the mud-slick bank, but by early afternoon it had begun its maiden voyage on the River of Doubt. The men were proud of their new, although hastily built, dugout, and they were thrilled to be moving again. But the river gave them little opportunity to celebrate. The farther the canoes traveled downstream, the faster the current became, steadily picking up speed as it cut its way down the northern face of the highlands. Worse, large, shifting whirlpools trailed their dugouts like sharks circling a lifeboat.

* * *

IT WAS a measure of how desperate the men had become that, on their first day back on the river, they decided to run every set of rapids they encountered. They could not predict how their new canoe would hold up in the writhing river, and all of their dugouts were piled so high with heavy equipment and men that, in spite of the burity branches lashed to their sides, they sank to within three inches of the water's surface. But the river's myriad dangers paled in comparison with the threat of starving to death in the rain forest. "Of the two hazards," Roosevelt wrote, "we felt it necessary to risk running the rapids."

So strong was their sense of urgency that Rondon was persuaded to abandon the fixed-station survey and resort to a faster, although less accurate method of mapping the river. Instead of waiting for Kermit to land, cut away the vines on the bank, and plant the sighting rod, Rondon and Lyra had to make their measurements based on sightings of the lead canoe as it raced down the river. Not only was this method less dependable, it placed Kermit and his paddlers in even greater danger. They were now obliged to keep Rondon and Lyra in their sights, as well as keep a sharp eye out for rapids and whirlpools.

Within the course of just four hours that day, the men would run six sets of rapids. But while Kermit, in his small canoe, safely skimmed past every whirlpool he encountered, his father's large, lumbering dugout was not as agile, or as fortunate. While running "one set of big ripples," as Roosevelt described it, his canoe was suddenly caught in the powerful, suctioning grip of a vortex. The dugout began to fill with water so fast that Cherrie and Dr. Cajazeira were forced to leap overboard to lighten the load. With strong, swift strokes, the camaradas fought their way out of the whirlpool, but the canoe had come perilously close to being swamped, and all of its cargo, and perhaps even its men, lost.

That night, as they made camp in the darkened forest, the men felt a deep sense of satisfaction and even relief. In just half a day on the river, they had managed to make nearly ten miles of crucial progress. But while their daring had paid off that day, they knew the odds of repeating that success were slim. The more chances they took, the more likely they were to lose everything.

"We had already met with misfortune," Cherrie would later write, "but the following day was to be one of tragedy."

Death in
the Rapids

O N THE MORNING OF March 15, the men awoke with a renewed
determination. They had survived a week-long series of raging
rapids, one following hard on the heels of another, and they had
weathered the loss of two canoes. They had built a new dugout, and
they had driven it straight through six more sets of rapids. They were
wet, hungry, and exhausted, but they were hopeful that they could
survive just about anything the river had in store for them.

Even the river itself seemed to cooperate. When they climbed
aboard their canoes at 7:00 a.m., an unusually early start time for the
expedition, the river was so smooth and unchallenging, though still
swift, that they were free once again to admire the beauty and complexity of the jungle.

This idyllic interlude was heartbreakingly brief. After the expedition had traveled only three miles, the land on either side of the river
began to rise like an emerging mountain chain, and the men quickly
found themselves surrounded by high, boulder-strewn hills. The river
still twisted and turned too tightly for them to be able to see very far
ahead, but they could hear a familiar distant roar.

Like the first set of rapids that they had been forced to portage around two weeks earlier, this wide stretch of white water was split down the center by a small island. Pushing past the island, the river rushed heavily over a low waterfall. Beyond the waterfall, all they could see was, in Rondon's words, "furious bubblings." Although they had successfully passed through half a dozen rapids only the day before, Rondon drew the line here. Even with time slipping away and their rations in short supply, they could not risk running these rapids. They would have to make another portage.

Rondon quickly ordered his three paddlers to pull over to the bank, and he gestured to João and Simplicio, the two camaradas who were in the lead canoe with Kermit and his dog, Trigueiro, to do the same. After their boat had been tethered to a tree, Rondon, Lyra, and their prowman, Joaquim, climbed up the muddy bank and set out to find a route for the expedition's portage. With the easy self-assurance of an experienced commander, Rondon strode into the forest-cloaked hills, confident that his orders were being carried out in full.

* * *

AS RONDON disappeared from sight, Kermit decided to take a chance. Sitting in his cramped dugout as it bumped heavily against the bank, he ordered his paddlers to cross over to the small island that bisected the rapids so that he could see if the right side of the river was more passable than the left. Although the confidence of most of the men in the expedition had been shaken, Kermit's determination to forge ahead was as strong as ever. He had postponed his own life to join this expedition, and he had been frustrated for months by its glacial pace. Young, strong, and skilled at working in the wilderness, he also appeared to be blithely certain of his own ability to survive this journey. It was his aging father's health and safety that concerned him, not his own, and he believed that it was more important to move quickly through the rain forest than to fritter away their time and provisions by being overly cautious.

For Kermit, feeling confident in the wilderness was second nature.

His father had hammered it into him, as well as each of his children, from a very young age. So determined was Roosevelt that his children grow up to be strong, fearless adults that he had said that he would "rather one of them should die than have them grow up weaklings." To ensure that none of them would ever be the kind of weakling he himself had been before he had resolved to "make" his body, Roosevelt had put his children through frequent and, for some of them, terrifying tests of physical endurance and courage. Most of these tests took place during what came to be known in the Roosevelt household as scrambles, long point-to-point walks led by Roosevelt himself. The only rule during these walks was that the participants could go through, over, or under an obstacle, but never around it. Roosevelt and his children, as well as a revolving crowd of cousins and friends, would not turn aside "for anything," Ted Jr. would later write. "If a haystack was in the way we either climbed over it or burrowed through it. If we came to a pond we swam across."

Roosevelt used these scrambles, as well as other, separate excursions, to attack his children's wilderness fears, which he referred to as buck fever—"a state of intense nervous excitement which may be entirely divorced from timidity." Even the most courageous man, he believed, when confronted by real danger in the wilderness—whether it be an angry lion or a roaring river—could suffer from buck fever. "What such a man needs is not courage but nerve control, coolheadedness," he explained. "This he can get only by actual practice."

Roosevelt's children never suffered from a lack of opportunity to master their buck fever. On one occasion, their father found a big hollow tree that had a wide opening twenty feet up—perfect, he thought, for dangling small children in. "With much labor, I got up the tree," Roosevelt proudly wrote to his sister Bamie, "and let each child in turn down the hollow by a rope." His method for teaching his children to swim was not much gentler. He took them to a dock and ordered them to leap into the deep water. His oldest child, Alice, was particularly frightened of diving, but her father was not about to let her off the hook. He would shout, "Dive, Alice! Now, dive!" until, finally, trembling with fear, she would launch her tiny body into the cold, dark water.

Kermit, although he was always a sober little boy and less demonstrative than his siblings, worked as hard as any of the children to please his father and prove himself. There was never any question that he had been paying attention during his childhood scrambles across Oyster Bay. The problem was that Roosevelt's lessons in manliness may have struck too deep a chord in his second son. Kermit had become almost too fearless, and certainly too reckless for even his father's comfort. Although Roosevelt was proud of his son's physical strength and courage, he worried that Kermit's thirst for adventure was ungoverned by the kind of wisdom that comes with age, and untempered by even a small measure of caution.

Roosevelt's letters home from Africa had been filled with stories of Kermit's utter disregard for danger and his own incessant fretting. To his sister Corinne, he had written, "Kermit is a great pleasure to me, and of course often a cause of much concern. Do you remember how timid he used to be? Well, my trouble with him now is that he is altogether too bold, pushing daring into recklessness." Kermit had faced down charging lions, elephants, and rhinoceroses in Africa. He had disappeared into the bush for two months with one of their guides and returned, Roosevelt wrote, "a better hunter than I am." But Roosevelt knew that all of his son's courage and skill could not save him if he continued to act carelessly. "Since I have been out here twelve men have been killed or mauled by Lions," he had written Corinne, "and, naturally, when Kermit shows a reckless indifference to consequences when hunting them, I feel like beating him."

Now, on the River of Doubt, Roosevelt's old fears for his son's safety had returned with a vengeance, and he winced every time Kermit climbed into his dugout to set off ahead of the rest of the expedition. Roosevelt wrote that Kermit was a "great comfort and help" to him on this expedition, but he admitted that he could never completely relax while his son pushed along on the unknown river so far ahead of him. "The fear of some fatal accident befalling him," he wrote, "was always a nightmare to me."

Although Roosevelt had long lectured Kermit about his recklessness, his advice appeared to have had little effect on his son's actions. It certainly did not that afternoon on the River of Doubt, as he ordered his paddlers to carry him to the island that rested in the center of the rapids. Feeling that they had no choice but to obey Kermit's command, João and Simplicio braced their paddles against the bank and shoved off. The three men successfully rode the current downstream and halfway across the river to the island. As soon as they disembarked, however, they realized that Rondon was right: There was no safe channel on either side of the river.

Now they were not only stranded on the island, they were farther down the river than they had been—and closer to the thundering waterfall. Kermit ordered the camaradas to board the dugout and cross back to the left bank. Both João and Simplicio, Roosevelt wrote, were "exceptionally good men in every way," but they balked at this command. Kermit had to repeat his order before they reluctantly dug their paddles into the rushing river.

The three men were on their journey back when their canoe was suddenly struck by one of the shifting whirlpools that they had seen the day before. The vortex spun them around and, as Kermit shouted to his steersman to turn the dugout so that it would take the inevitable blow head-on rather than broadside, forced them over the fall. Incredibly, when they reached the bottom, their small canoe, which Roosevelt complained was "the least seaworthy of all," was still upright. However, it had taken in so much water it could hardly float. Realizing that their only chance for survival was to make it to the shore, João and Simplicio paddled as fast and as hard as they could. They had just pulled themselves to within grasping distance of the bank when another whirlpool sucked them in and spat them back out into the middle of the river.

Fighting to save not just his companions but their crude canoe,

João leapt into the water and desperately grabbed a hawser that had been tied to the bow. Straining against the rope, he tried to drag the dugout back to the bank as he slipped and stumbled over the riverbed. The current, however, was too strong for him. It quickly ripped the hawser out of his hands, flipped the canoe over, and hurled it downstream. The last thing that João saw as the dugout swirled out of sight was Simplicio and Kermit clinging to its splintered, capsized hull.

* * *

FROM THEIR canoe above the rapids, Roosevelt and Cherrie had watched in horror as Kermit, João, and Simplicio struggled to maintain control of their dugout and then disappeared over the waterfall. Shouting to their paddlers to pull over, they had scrambled out of their canoe and raced along the uneven bank until they reached the bottom of a second waterfall. What they saw there would have stopped any father's heart. Kermit's dugout lay among the rocks, as Cherrie would later write, "crushed to splinters."

PART FOUR

Iron Cruelty

Attack

A S HIS FATHER STRAINED desperately to catch a glimpse of him in the roiling river, Kermit fought for his life downstream. When his dugout was swept over the second waterfall, the impact had crushed the boat and hurled Kermit, Simplicio, and Kermit's dog into the water. Kermit was still alive and conscious, but his battle with the river was only beginning. His favorite rifle, the .405 Winchester he had carried in Africa, was knocked from his hands, and the rushing water blinded, choked, and pummeled him. Like a relentless hammer, the torrent drove his broad, hard sun helmet over his face and forced his body down to the jagged riverbed. His waterlogged jacket became an anchor, dragging him to the bottom of the river.

Somewhere in the middle of the raging rapids, Simplicio was also being propelled through layers of white foam and black water. The powerful, rushing water and deadly whirlpools created by the rocky riverbed swept him violently downstream, threatening at any moment to pull him under long enough for his life, in Roosevelt's words, to be "beaten out on the bowlders beneath the racing torrent."

While Kermit and Simplicio struggled in the river, Rondon was walking back along its left bank, unaware of their plight, having found the portage route that he was looking for. As he approached his canoe, preoccupied with his orders for the camaradas, he was suddenly startled by what he saw—or, rather, did not see—in front of him. He had expected to find Kermit's dugout tied to a tree alongside his own. Turning to his pilot, a well-respected camarada named Antonio Correia, Rondon demanded to know what had happened after he left. He listened in astonishment as Antonio told him that Kermit had blatantly disobeyed his command.

Furious, and worried that Kermit had put his boat and its precious provisions at risk, Rondon turned and hurried with Lyra toward the falls. In the distance, the two men caught sight of Kermit's dog, Trigueiro, running toward them. The closer the dog approached, the greater Rondon's concern became and the faster he began to walk, until he and Lyra were practically running along the river's edge. By the time they reached Trigueiro, it was obvious to both men that the dog had been thrown into the river. Trigueiro was soaking wet. More ominously, he was alone.

Rushing past the dog, Rondon and Lyra raced to the bottom of the first waterfall. As they approached the crest of a small hill, they saw a lone figure climbing toward them on the other side. It was Kermit—drenched, battered, and weak with exhaustion, but alive. Rondon's first reaction was overwhelming relief. His relief, however, quickly gave way to anger. Rondon was not accustomed to being disobeyed, even by the son of a former president of the United States. By refusing to listen to him, Kermit had endangered the entire expedition. When Kermit was finally standing before him, Rondon's rage boiled over into sarcasm. "Well," he said caustically, "you have had a splendid bath, eh?"

Standing on the narrow, muddy trail, water running in rivulets down his pants and pooling at his feet, Kermit tried to explain what had happened to him and, he believed, João and Simplicio. After he was driven to the bottom of the river by the rapids, a back current had carried him to a stretch of swift but calm water. "Almost drowned, his breath and strength almost spent," he had spotted an overhanging branch and recognized it as his best and probably last chance for survival. Grabbing the branch, he had hauled himself out of the river. Trigueiro, who had been by Kermit's side throughout the ordeal, scrambled up the bank next to his master as he collapsed on the shore. João and Simplicio, Kermit now told Rondon, must have swum to safety on the other side of the river, but he did not know what had happened to his canoe or its contents.

Accepting Kermit's assumption that everyone was probably safe, Rondon and Lyra focused their attention on the problem of portaging around the second waterfall, which they had not even known existed until they heard Kermit's story, and searching for his canoe and any provisions that might have survived the rapids. As valuable as the canoe itself was the cargo that it had been carrying: essential boat-building tools as well as ten days' worth of rations, the loss of which would be devastating. No sooner had Kermit walked away, however, than João appeared before Rondon and Lyra. As Kermit had guessed, João had emerged from the river on the other side and had somehow managed to make his way back across. But he had not seen Simplicio since the camarada had disappeared over the second waterfall with Kermit.

Rondon ordered an immediate manhunt. It was, he wrote, their "one hope left." After a frantic search, which extended about a mile downstream, however, the men were able to recover nothing more than a battered paddle and a single box of rations. It was clear to them all what had happened. "Unfortunately the moment arrived when it was impossible to deceive ourselves," Rondon wrote. "Simplicio was drowned."

* * *

THAT NIGHT, after the men, now numbering only twenty-one, had finished their portage around the last waterfall, they retired to their tents and hammocks. Hunched over his small table, Roosevelt acknowledged in the article he was writing that his son had had a "very narrow escape." Had they lost Kermit rather than Simplicio that day, he wrote, he did not think he could have borne the pain of bringing "bad tidings to his betrothed and to his mother." Kermit's near-drowning had been a result of the young man's own recklessness, but Roosevelt felt a heavy weight of responsibility for having chosen to descend this dangerous river, and for having brought his son along with him. Although Kermit had joined the expedition in order to protect his father, Roosevelt's mission from this point onward would be to protect Kermit, and to ensure that he made it out of the rain forest alive.

Having faced his own mortality and having caused, albeit indirectly, another man's death, Kermit showed no signs of remorse or even any sense of responsibility when he scribbled a brief account of the day's events in his journal that night. He recorded the fact of Simplicio's death as tersely and unemotionally as he did his own near-drowning. "Simplicio was drowned," he wrote. If he felt sorrow for Simplicio's death, or regret for his own rash decision to cross to the other side of the river when Rondon had warned him not to, he did not admit it in his diary. Nor did he appear to have any desire to change his ways. If Roosevelt had hoped that this tragedy had driven some degree of fear or even caution into his son, he was to be disappointed.

The man who seemed to be most shaken by what had happened that day was Cherrie. Having spent half his life traveling through South American jungles, he understood the gravity of their situation better than did Kermit or Roosevelt, and he was more concerned about surviving the journey than was Rondon. Although he regretted Simplicio's death, he was much more disturbed that they had lost Kermit's dugout and most of its cargo. "The loss of a human life is always a tragedy," he wrote. "But the loss of the canoe and its contents was an even greater tragedy to the remaining members of our party." In his last letter home, which he had written the day before they launched their boats on the river, Cherrie had told his wife, Stella, that he hoped to be back in Vermont in time to help sow the spring crops at Rocky Dell. "We may reach New York by the end of May," he had written. "I hope we shall for I would like very much to be able to help get in the potatoes and other crops." He realized now, however, that if he was ever going to see his family or Rocky Dell again, the expedition could not afford any more losses like those they had suffered that day.

Rondon, although angry that Kermit's disobedience had cost him the life of one of his men, was neither shocked by Simplicio's death nor deterred by it. "Certainly no one commences an enterprise of the kind in which we were engaged, without having previously become acquainted with the idea of the danger which same may offer, and of the innumerable occasions in which one has to face death," he wrote. For Rondon, death was merely one of the many costs of achieving a much larger goal that had already cost the lives of countless of his men: opening the country's interior and integrating the Amazon's native peoples into Brazilian society.

Few Brazilians, including many of Rondon's soldiers, shared his passion for contacting and befriending Indians, or even believed that such a thing was possible. Backed by a number of vocal civilians, his men resented the sacrifices that they were expected to make in the name of their commander's ideals. At one point, a group of rubber plantation owners wrote to the Brazilian newspaper *A Cruz* that Rondon "lets his soldiers die of hunger while distributing food to the savages." In the most remote reaches of the Amazon, however, Rondon was unreachable and unstoppable. He had never allowed his men's suffering or even their deaths to affect his work in the wilderness, and he never would. "Death and dangers, in spite of how much suffering they bring," he wrote, "should not interfere with the expedition's mission."

* * *

THE NEXT morning, March 16, the men awoke ready to face the river once again. While the rain fell heavily in the still-dark forest, they gathered around Rondon to listen to his Orders of the Day. As a representative of the Brazilian government, Rondon "perpetuated the name of the unfortunate Simplicio" by officially naming for him the waterfall that had ended his young life. Simplicio was unmarried, so Rondon and Roosevelt agreed that, if they survived this journey, they would send the money that he would have earned to his mother. Unable to do anything more for the young man who had lost his life for their ambition, they carved a short inscription on one side of their camp marker—"In these rapids died poor Simplicio"—and solemnly walked away.

There was no doubt in anyone's mind that they had another hard and dangerous day ahead of them. The day before, during their desperate search for Simplicio, they had found another series of rapids downstream, even worse than the one that had drowned the camarada. Further complicating the situation was the fact that they now had twenty-one men and only five canoes, and none of the trees near their camp were suitable material for dugouts. Some of the men would have to walk.

At 7:00 a.m., in a blinding rain, Kermit climbed into the expedition's large new canoe and set off ahead of the rest of the boats, just as he had for the past two and a half weeks. After only half an hour on the river, the men reached the rapids that they had known awaited them. As Kermit had already explored the left side of the river in his search for Simplicio, Rondon and Lyra paddled to the right side, where they found a channel that circumvented the worst part of the rapids. Luiz and Antonio Correia, the expedition's two best watermen, were then charged with the job of lowering the empty dugouts by ropes from the right bank. At the same time, the rest of the camaradas would begin cutting a half-mile-long portage road along the left bank for the baggage carry. Having satisfied himself that all of his men were suitably engaged in useful work, Rondon took his favorite dog, Lobo, and set off over a hill just behind their camp in the hope of finding game or, failing that, Brazil nuts.

Although the rest of the men rarely left camp alone, especially after they saw the abandoned Indian village and found the pateran,

Rondon was most at ease when he was on his own. He was, and had always been, a loner. He had found his own way in the world, first as an orphan and then as an outsider at the military academy in Rio de Janeiro. Even after he had married, he had been separated for long periods of time and by hundreds of miles from his wife and children.

Francisca Rondon had suffered as much as any of her husband's soldiers over the past twenty-two years. She had been raised as a sheltered city girl in Rio de Janeiro, the daughter of one of Rondon's professors at the military school, but soon after she married, she had left that life behind, moving to remote Mato Grosso to be closer to Cândido. Since then, she had given birth to seven children, endured isolation and illness—including malaria and yaws, an infectious tropical disease that attacks the skin and bones—and been forced to carry on without her husband for months and even years at a time. She finally taught herself telegraphic code so that she could send brief messages to him while he was in the field. On their ninth wedding anniversary, in February 1901, Rondon had sent her a wistful telegram: "This day brings us sweet remembrances of the past. Let us accept our sad life. Miss you deeply. Embraces. Candido."

In the field, surrounded by hundreds of men, Rondon had found his job as commander to be a lonely and friendless one. But for a handful of close confidants, such as Lyra and Amilcar, Rondon's only companionship had come from his dogs. At times he had as many as twenty dogs in his camp, and he always had a favored pack of three or four that were constantly by his side. They did not complain or mutiny, and they were cheerful, trustworthy, and devoted to their master. There was no question that Rondon cared more for these dogs than he did for his own men, or that he worried about their safety and comfort. He showered them with affection, shared his food with them, and, on one occasion, even halted a march so that they could rest. On another march, he had carried one of his dogs in his arms so that he "would not die of exhaustion." Although he rarely devoted more than a single sentence in his journal to the death of one of his men, Rondon penned heartfelt eulogies to his dogs. After his dog

Vulcão died, for instance, he wrote, "Travel companion who guarded my tent . . . Poor companion! How I feel your death. . . . You who served me so well, without my being able to pay you back for half of your dedication."

Now, contentedly walking through the forest with faithful Lobo at his side, Rondon turned north after cresting the hill behind the expedition's camp and headed back in the direction of the River of Doubt. After following the river about a mile downstream, he came to a point at which a narrow canal split off from the main waterway. Making his way through the tangle of trees and vines along the canal, Rondon suddenly heard the unmistakable quavering whinny of the coatá, or spider monkey, the largest primate in the Amazon rain forest. Taking "a thousand precautions" so that he would not frighten the monkey, Rondon crouched down in the thick vegetation and slowly made his way toward the sound. As he scanned the trees' highest branches, where he knew the coatá lived, he could imagine his men's delight when he walked into camp holding a twenty-pound spider monkey by its long, dark tail.

The forest was typically quiet, and Rondon did his best not to snap branches or rustle leaves as he crept through the underbrush. Excited by the hunt, Lobo sprinted ahead of his master and quickly disappeared from view. Moments later, the silence was rent by a high-pitched yelp.

Certain that Lobo had been attacked by an animal, a jaguar or perhaps a peccary, Rondon braced himself for the worst. Then he heard something even more bone-chilling—the sound of human voices. "These were well known to me," he would later recall. "They were short exclamations, energetic, and repeated in a kind of chorus with a certain cadence peculiar to Indians who when they are ready for the fight commence the attack on the enemy." At that moment, Rondon was the enemy, and he had no protection beyond his rifle and the cover of the rain forest. His only hope was to remain as invisible to the Indians as they were to him.

Suddenly Lobo reappeared, staggering toward his master and giving away Rondon's hiding place. As the dog drew near, Rondon could see two long arrows protruding from his side. In desperation, with the Indians' war cries ringing in his ears, Rondon raised his rifle and fired into the air. The blast shook the leaves around him and put startled animals to flight, but the Indians kept coming. Although Rondon still could not see Lobo's attackers, he could hear them clearly, chattering excitedly to one another from the dense cover of the rain forest. He fired his other barrel, but the war whoops continued. Finally, realizing that he could not defend himself against certain attack, Colonel Rondon turned and fled.

* * *

HE FOUND the rest of the men at the foot of the rapids, where he had established the expedition's next camp earlier that morning. Gathering his officers together, he told them what had happened. Their worst fear had been realized: The Indians that lived on the River of Doubt were no longer ghosts. They were real, and they were prepared to attack.

The others had alarming news of their own. While Rondon was gone, they had lost another canoe. Luiz and Antonio Correia had successfully brought one of the dugouts down the channel, but as they were lowering the large canoe that they had built themselves just a few days earlier, the rope had broken and the canoe had been swept into a colony of boulders. Luiz had almost been swept away with it. The other camaradas had managed to save him, but they had not been able to save the canoe, or the ropes and pulleys that it had carried.

Rondon was deeply concerned about the loss of the new dugout, but the Indians worried him more. Turning to Lyra and Kermit, he asked them to return with him to the scene of the attack. They agreed and, taking Dr. Cajazeira and Antonio Pareci with them, immediately set out to retrace Rondon's steps.

By the time the five men reached the canal, the Indians had vanished. The men discovered a few items that they had left behind, however, including a small basket filled with animal entrails and tied to a long rod. Rondon guessed that the basket had been used for fishing. The Indians, he thought, must have lowered it into the river, waited for fish to swim over to the bait, and then speared them with their arrows. Kneeling down, he placed some gifts—a couple of axes and a few beads—next to the basket, a gesture he hoped would send the message that, not only did he and his men not want to be the Indians' enemies, but they hoped to be their friends.

Scanning the forest, the men found a rough trail that led across the canal and had clearly been the Indians' path of retreat. Then Rondon found another, more grizzly trail: drops of blood smeared on leaves and dripped on branches. He followed the bloody trail for about three hundred yards, until, at its end, he found Lobo. The dog had tried to make his way back to camp but had finally collapsed. The arrows that had killed him still protruded from his small body. One had struck his left leg and torn away the muscle. The other had entered his stomach, just below his heart. That arrow had been launched with such force that it had been driven completely through his body, and its blood-stained tip emerged from the other side. Looking down at Lobo, no one could have any doubt that the Indians' intent had been to kill— and that, had Rondon walked into the ambush first, it would have been his body rather than Lobo's that lay in a pool of blood on the forest floor.

Despite his sorrow and fear, Rondon refused to abandon his principles. "These melancholic reflections," he wrote, "did not divert me away from my habitual norm of conduct regarding the Indians." He had faced hostile Indians before and would likely do so again, and he was more worried about alienating them than dying at their hands.

Rondon had long argued that Indians attacked only when forced to do so. In fact, he claimed that 90 percent of the Indian attacks that took place in Brazil were nothing more than acts of self-defense and retaliation. The idea that Indians might attack the expedition for reasons of fear or self-defense offered little comfort to Roosevelt, who noted wryly, "If you are shot by a man because he is afraid of you it is almost as unpleasant as if he shot you because he disliked you."

Even Rondon was shaken by what he found when he knelt down to get a closer look at the arrows that had impaled Lobo. Since the expedition had passed the abandoned village more than two weeks earlier, Rondon had assumed that the Indians that surrounded them in the rain forest were Nhambiquara, members of the tribe with whom he had made first contact seven years earlier. But as he examined these arrows, he realized that he was wrong. The arrow that had impaled Lobo had a point that was shaped like a barbed lance and was made from bamboo. This, Rondon knew, was not the work of the Nhambiquara. "The river Duvida," he concluded, "was inhabited by a new tribe of Indians with regard to which we possessed no information."

Rondon did not know these Indians, and they did not know him. There was not even the pretense of peace between them and the outside world. Rondon, moreover, could only assume that, whoever these Indians were, they would defend their land as fiercely as the Nhambiquara had defended theirs. The critical difference was that he had been able to retreat after being attacked by the Nhambiquara. Now retreat was impossible. In fact, in order to survive, they would have to go deeper into the territory of this unknown tribe—a land where, they now knew with certainty, they were not welcome.

CHAPTER 19

The Wide Belts

By ROUGHLY TWO MILLION years ago, humans had spread out of Africa and into Europe and Asia. Hundreds of thousands of years later, they migrated to Australia and New Guinea, which were then connected as a single continent. Because they did not yet have boats and could not endure the cruel cold of Siberia, tens of thousands of years more passed before they crossed the Bering Land Bridge and made their way into the Americas. When they finally began to populate North America, however, human beings quickly dispersed throughout the continent and, by crossing the Panamanian Land Bridge, soon reached South America. Some twelve thousand years ago, they entered the Amazon.

In the eyes of the rest of the world, the humans who reached the Amazon Basin virtually disappeared. For thousands of years, there was no further contact with the Amazonians. Whereas most regions of the world continued to change and interact, to form new peoples and nations by fusing races and cultures, the inhabitants of the Amazon remained insular and isolated. Even in 1500, when European explorers began to land on the shores of South America, claiming the land for themselves and their kings and enslaving its aboriginal inhabitants, the continent's vast interior remained untouched and its people unknown and unreachable.

After the Spanish explorer Orellana finally penetrated the Amazon Basin in 1542, he returned with startling tales of dense jungles, deadly poisons, and, most astonishing of all, a tribe of vicious women warriors. The expedition's chronicler, the Dominican friar Gaspar de Carvajal, described the women as going "about naked but with their privy parts covered, with their bows and arrows in their hands, doing as much fighting as ten Indian men." Orellana named these women the Amazons, after the famed women warriors of Greek mythology, who were said to have removed their right breast so that they could more effectively shoot a bow and arrow. It is from the Greek word *a-mazos,* or "no breast," that the word "Amazon" is derived.

After Orellana, few outsiders disturbed the Amazon's native peoples for the next two hundred years. In the mid-eighteenth century, however, things changed dramatically and, for the Amazon's human inhabitants, disastrously. While traveling down the Amazon River from Ecuador, the French naturalist and mathematician Charles-Marie de La Condamine saw natives extracting a milky substance from a tall tree. After the strange liquid, which the Indians called *caoutchouc,* had coagulated, it was used to make everything from boots to bottles. La Condamine saw potential in *caoutchouc* and brought a sample with him back to France. When the strange, pliable substance made its way across the channel, the British soon discovered that it worked extremely well as an eraser, and so began referring to it as "rubber." By the end of the eighteenth century, rubber was well known and widely used throughout Europe and the New World. By the middle of the nineteenth century, the Amazon was exporting more than 150 metric tons of it each year.

La Condamine's discovery meant great wealth for a few South Americans and Europeans, but nothing but sorrow and terror for Amazonian Indians. Settlers who had made their way to the Amazon in the hope of making their fortunes in rubber, quickly became frustrated by the dearth of willing cheap labor and began to organize slaving expeditions. Already laid low by European diseases, many Indian tribes were nearly decimated by these expeditions. Those Indians who survived were perhaps even less fortunate than those who lost their lives. Rubber barons were notorious for treating their slave laborers with exceptional cruelty. Julio César Arana, the son of a Peruvian hatmaker who made millions of dollars harvesting and selling Amazonian rubber in the late nineteenth and early twentieth centuries, ordered his men to go into the rain forest with rifles to "recruit" Indians. The tens of thousands of men, women, and children whom they rounded up were shackled into chain gangs. If they did not make their quotas, Arana's men would burn them alive, hang and quarter them, or shoot off their genitals. During the twelve years that Arana held his reign of terror along the banks of the Rio Putumayo, the native population plummeted from more than fifty thousand to less than eight thousand. Those who survived did so with horribly disabling and disfiguring wounds that became known as "la marca arana," the mark of Arana.

The Indians' only advocates were the missionaries who had already established themselves in the Amazon by the early seventeenth century, searching for souls to save. They made an effort to protect their charges, but they were powerless against wealthy and merciless settlers such as Arana. Their best hope came in offering the Indians as wage laborers instead of slaves. The settlers, however, reverted back to slavery when they found that they could not get as many laborers as they needed and did not have as much control over them as they had had over their slaves. Even the missionaries themselves wanted to force the Indians into reductions, or missions, in which they were made to wear clothing and worship the Christian God.

Before Rondon's Indian Protection Service was established in 1910, and even after, the Indians' best protector was the Amazon itself. So dense and dangerous was the rain forest that few white men were able to venture very far into it, even for the promise of rubber. Despite the intense search for Indians by the men who wanted their labor or their souls, several tribes had not yet had any contact with the outside world by the time Roosevelt reached South America in 1913. Even those who had had some limited contact with outsiders were so isolated by the jungle in which they lived that they did not have even the vaguest understanding of what the rest of the world looked like. "Such isolation makes it well nigh impossible for them to grasp the significance of large communities," George Cherrie observed. "The distant villager is incapable of picturing a much larger group of human beings living together than that in his own tiny settlement. . . . They picture the rest of the world as one of jungles, great rivers, and vast seas; with here and there tiny pools of humanity no larger than their own. Thus it is that they look upon the stranger from afar as a traveller between villages."

* * *

THE MYSTERIOUS Indians who surrounded Roosevelt and his men on the banks of the River of Doubt were so isolated that they had never seen a white man. The intersection of their world and that of Roosevelt and Rondon was not simply a clash of different cultures; it was a collision of the Industrial Age and the Stone Age, the modern world and the ancient. Known by modern anthropologists as the Cinta Larga, which is Portuguese for "wide belt"—a reference to the strips of bark that they wrap around their waists—this tribe had remained shrouded from the rest of the world not just by the impenetrable rain forest but by the very thing that had exposed most Amazonian Indians to settlers and missionaries: a river.

For European explorers, South America's rivers had long been the only highways into the interior. It had been along the Amazon River and some of its thousands of tributaries that they had discovered the rain forest and its occupants, and the Indians had discovered another world beyond their own. Some Amazonian tributaries, however, were so rapids-choked that they were impossible to ascend and too dangerous to descend. The River of Doubt's fierce rapids had dissuaded even the most determined settlers from exploring its course. The same rapids that had already cost the expedition the life of one man and had nearly robbed Roosevelt of his son had kept the Cinta Larga in a time capsule, which had been sealed for millennia.

While the world in which Roosevelt lived had undergone dramatic recent changes, including skyscrapers, automobiles, and even airplanes (Orville and Wilbur Wright had made their first successful flight over Kill Devil Hill eleven years earlier), the Indians in this region were still using the simplest of tools. Their axes were ground and polished stone, and their cutting tools sharp slivers of bamboo. They made their fires by drilling a hard stick of wood into a softer one. The men all carried their hard "drills" with them while they were out hunting so that they could start a fire.

So cut off from the outside world were the Cinta Larga that, when they first saw the expedition, they were not even certain that Roosevelt, Rondon, and their men were human. By this point in their journey, most of the men in the expedition had grown rough beards, which looked strange and animalistic to the Cinta Larga, who, like all native Amazonians, had little facial or body hair. After watching the men from the shadows of the forest, the Cinta Larga mothers warned their children to sleep close to the fire at night so that they would not grow a patchy layer of fur like these strange creatures.

The Cinta Larga must also have been curious about the expedition's canoes. As simple and crudely made as they were, the dugouts represented a level of technological sophistication that was unknown to the Cinta Larga. Although they lived on both sides of the River of Doubt, fishing from it, drinking from it, bathing in it, and traveling long distances along its banks, the Cinta Larga had not yet conceived of boats, even those as simple as the expedition's dugout canoes. The only means they had developed for crossing the river were simple rope-and-plank bridges. Nor, despite their dependence on the river, had they yet developed the means of fishing with a hook and line, relying instead on spears or arrows to kill the fish that were so central to their diet.

*   *   *

DESPITE THESE limitations and, in part, because of their isolation, the Cinta Larga were masters at surviving in the jungle. During their portages, the men of the expedition crashed through the underbrush, scaring off game and announcing their presence to the Indians. Even when they did not have to wrestle with their dugouts, the men found it nearly impossible to fight their way through the jungle. Long vines crisscrossed the forest. Sharp branches caught their loose clothing, snagging and ripping it and holding them hostage while they struggled to set themselves free.

In contrast to Roosevelt and his men, the Cinta Larga moved through the rain forest quickly and silently. They wore no clothing and so were able to slip through the tangle of vegetation unrestrained. The women, who wore their hair long and parted down the middle, had nothing on their bodies but necklaces of black vegetable beads, which they strung around their necks, wrists, waists, and ankles. But for a simple liana covering to protect their penises, the men were similarly naked.

The Cinta Larga were also fast and invisible in the jungle because they had blazed trails that an outsider could not possibly discern or follow. Even if Rondon, in his ardor to make contact with this unknown tribe, had started down the Cinta Larga trail that he had found near Lobo's body, it would have been useless to him. The Cinta Larga's trails zigzagged through the forest, cutting in and out of thickets, crisscrossing the river, and going over rather than around any obstacle they encountered.

The tribe's trails were marked, but ingeniously so. Markers appeared only once every twelve or eighteen feet and were simply small branches that the blazer had half broken and then bent backward. To anyone but a Cinta Larga, these markers were indistinguishable from any of a million other broken and bent branches in the rain forest. A change of direction was indicated by nothing more than a slightly larger broken branch whose bent end vaguely pointed the way. Only the Cinta Larga knew, moreover, that the markers also showed the direction to and from their camp: In a system like that used in modern maritime navigation, markers were placed so that when approaching the tribe's camp they appeared on the left side of the trail, and leading away from camp they appeared on the right.

The Cinta Larga were as skilled at hunting as they were at trailblazing. While the men of the expedition slowly starved, wandering through what seemed to them to be a lush but empty rain forest, the Indians saw, heard, and smelled game everywhere they turned. Their ability to move soundlessly through the forest also helped them to sneak up on their prey as the members of the expedition never could, and their skill with a bow and arrow was uncanny. These Indians were such expert hunters that they were even able to trick their game into coming to them. As Rondon had learned when they lured him with the whinny of the spider monkey, the Cinta Larga were talented mimics and could re-create nearly any animal call. In fact, so familiar were they with these calls that they used them not only to draw game within striking distance but even to express time. When referring to a time before sunrise, for example, they used the cry of the howler monkey.

One of the greatest frustrations that the men of the expedition faced on the River of Doubt was that they were descending a river crowded with fish that they could not catch. Those same fish, however, were easy prey for the Cinta Larga. The Indians made up for their lack of poles, lines, or hooks with the type of fishing basket that Rondon had found. More important, they had *timbó*. This milky liquid, which the Cinta Larga extracted from a vine by pounding it with a rock, stuns—or, depending on the quantity, kills—fish by paralyzing their gills. Used in slow-moving inlets and pools, *timbó* allowed the Indians to spear or scoop up the fish as they floated to the river's surface.

As well as being expert hunters and fishermen, the Cinta Larga had access to crops that Roosevelt and his men did not, and they were willing to consume a larger variety of protein sources. The Indians grew vegetables such as manioc, yams, and sweet potatoes, but even they struggled to do so. Clearing the land in the jungle was grueling work. It often took a man with a stone ax an entire day just to fell a single large tree. Then, while sowing his crops, he had to contend with the long tree roots that lay frustratingly near the surface of the soil. After only three or four years had passed, the cleared land—scorched by the sun, robbed of its nutrients by the growing crops, and deprived of the cyclical nutrient exchange that had sustained it when it supported a forest—would become depleted, and the Indians would be forced to find another patch of land to till.

Each Cinta Larga village, which had one or two large houses that each held three to five families, was almost completely autonomous from the larger tribe, and every one had its own chief. The chief had to exhibit strong leadership qualities, such as taking the initiative in building a house or clearing a garden, but he was not their commander in the traditional sense. The Cinta Larga would not allow their village chief to tell them how to live their lives. Instead, the chief's job was to oversee the tribal ceremonies—an important role, because the Cinta Larga did not have a written language. Their only ceremonial guides were their own memories and the stories that they had heard their parents and grandparents tell.

Not only did the chief not command the village as a whole, he did not have power over any family within it but his own. Each man was the chief of his own family, which consisted of as many wives as he could convince to marry him and as many children as his wives could bear. A Cinta Larga man usually chose a new wife as soon as his first wife began to age. Girls were considered to be ready for marriage when they were between eight and ten years old, and they often married their mother's brother. In such small communities, a young man ready to take his first wife often found that there were no eligible girls left in his village. He was then allowed to take a wife from a man who had three or more, or, failing that, he had to look for a wife in a neighboring village. It was not unusual for villages to trade women. The women, however, usually consented to the switch.

Like women in most early cultures, the Cinta Larga women did not have a voice in tribal or even family decisions. However, the Indian women did have a surprising amount of control over their own lives. For instance, if a Cinta Larga woman was unsatisfied in her marriage, she was free to do something about it. She could dissolve the marriage. She could marry another man. Or she could even stay with her husband and take a lover. In such circumstances, a husband would usually look the other way, unless he became the object of derision within his village.

As important as children were to the future of a village, they were far from coddled, and they were expected to take on the role of an adult by the time they turned twelve years old. Also, although the Indians lived together in one or two large huts, they did not appear to feel any particular responsibility for anyone outside their own immediate family. Each family had its own corner of the hut and its own fire, and when a man had been out hunting and returned with game, his neighbors rarely benefited from his good fortune. The hunter ate first, then his wives, children, and other relatives—in that order.

* * *

ALTHOUGH ROOSEVELT and Rondon did not realize it, the Cinta Larga's strong independence was probably keeping the men of the expedition alive. Because the Indians did not have a traditional chief, they were forced to make all of their decisions by consensus. If it was time to move the village, for instance, they had to agree on the time and location of the move. When it came to dealing with the expedition, the Cinta Larga were divided. Some of them believed that they should remain invisible to the outsider. Others, however, argued that they should attack. These men had invaded their territory, and there was no reason to believe they did not mean the Indians harm. By attacking first, the Cinta Larga would have the upper hand. They would also be able to loot the expedition, which was carrying valuable provisions and tools—especially those made of metal.

War was not a rare event for the Cinta Larga. The most common cause was the death of one of their own, from an earlier attack or even from natural causes. The Cinta Larga believed that death was brought about by witchcraft. If a man became ill and died, the others in his village never blamed their healer, a man who used plants and religion to cure the sick. Instead, they looked around their own village, and if they did not find anyone suspicious, they assumed that someone from another village must have performed the dark magic. The only response was to avenge the death by attacking the offending village.

The Cinta Larga also occasionally went to war if the population of their own village had become so depleted by disease, murder, or both that they needed to steal women and children. Such attacks took place at night. The men would camp near their victims' village, and then, after the sun had set, they would slip inside their communal hut. As the male members of the other village slept in their hammocks, the warriors would club them to death before rounding up as many women and children as they could find.

Although the Cinta Larga rarely wore much adornment, when they went to war they dressed for the part. They would cut their hair very short, place hawk-feather headdresses over their shorn heads, paint their bodies with animal and plant extracts, and hang bead necklaces from their necks. The most important item in the Cinta Larga's war dress, however, was the wide belt for which the Portuguese would later name them. These belts were made from the couratari tree, which was difficult to find. The men were sometimes forced to walk for several days in order to harvest the smooth, mahogany-colored bark of this tree. They wrapped an eight-inch-wide strip around their waists one and a half times and then tied it tightly with a fine liana. The stiff bark, which was a tenth of an inch thick, was uncomfortable and often cut their stomachs and backs, thus exposing them to infection, but the belt was ubiquitous among the warlike Cinta Larga because it covered the abdomen and so was useful as body armor.

Although skilled with both clubs and poison, the Cinta Larga's most lethal weapons were bows and arrows. As Rondon learned when he examined the arrows that had killed Lobo, the Cinta Larga's arrows were exquisitely made and deadly accurate. Made from bamboo, the shaft was adorned with braids of peccary hair and topped with a knife-shaped bamboo tip. The arrows were, on average, five feet long—nearly as tall as the Cinta Larga men, and taller than many of the women—and were adorned with hawk wings or curassow feathers, which stabilized them in flight. The tribesmen made several different types of arrows—for shooting fish, birds, monkeys, large animals, and men—but they used only one type of bow. About six feet long, the bows were made from the trunk of the peach-palm tree and were so stiff and difficult to pull that it is doubtful that any of the men in the expedition could have used a Cinta Larga bow had they found one.

*　*　*

THE MOST striking fact about the Cinta Larga—and one that would have alarmed the men of the expedition had they known it—was that these Indians were cannibals. Unlike the type of cannibalism much of the world had come to know—among desperate explorers, marooned sailors, and victims of famine—the Cinta Larga's consumption of human flesh was born not out of necessity but out of vengeance and an adherence to tribal traditions and ceremony. The tribe had very strict rules for cannibalism. They could eat another man only in celebration of a war victory, and that celebration had to take place in the early evening. The man who had done the killing could not grill the meat or distribute it, and children and adults with small children would not eat it. If they did, the Cinta Larga believed, they would go mad.

The most important rule of cannibalism within the tribe was that one Cinta Larga could not eat another. The tribe drew a clear distinction between its own members and the rest of mankind, which they considered to be "other"—and, thus, edible. An enemy killed during war, therefore, was ritually dismembered and eaten. While still on the battlefield, either in the enemy's village or in the forest, the Cinta Larga would carve up the body just as they would a monkey that they had shot down from the canopy. First they would cut off and discard the man's head and heart. Then they would section off the edible portions: the arms, legs, and a round of flesh over the stomach. They grilled this meat over an open fire and brought it home to their village for their wives to slice and cook with water in a ceramic pan.

If Indians from other tribes were considered "other," then the men of the expedition, who did not even look human to the Cinta Larga, certainly fell into that category. Moreover, should the Indians attack the expedition, Roosevelt would likely be one of their first targets. After watching the expedition for several weeks, the Cinta Larga had surely figured out by now that Roosevelt and Rondon were its commanders. Not only did they give orders and do less physical work than the other men, but the camaradas and even the other officers clearly treated them with deference. Even if the Indians had only recently stumbled upon the expedition, they probably would have aimed for Roosevelt first—simply because of his substantial girth. The Cinta Larga often tossed pieces of a slain enemy into the jungle if they thought that he was too lean. Although Roosevelt had already begun to lose much of his 220 pounds to illness and the intense physical work and meager diet of the past few months, he was still by far the heaviest man in the expedition. If the men were massacred, the former president would make the best ceremonial meal.

Hunger

AFTER A MISERABLE NIGHT OF worry and fear, the men of the Roosevelt-Rondon Scientific Expedition awoke on the morning of March 17 to the dire reality of their situation. They could not get back on the river, but neither could they stay where they were. The loss of the new dugout the day before had left them with only four canoes—three fewer than they had started out with, and far too few to carry twenty-one men and all of their food and equipment. There were no trees suitable for boatbuilding anywhere near their camp. They were quickly running out of rations, and they were surrounded by hostile Indians.

Whatever the cost, they had to keep moving, and most of the men would have to walk. By this point in the expedition, none of them had any illusions about what it meant to walk along the banks of the River of Doubt. So dense was the vegetation along the river's sun-washed shoreline that they would have to laboriously carve a path for each step with a machete. Although the dark interior of the rain forest offered a potentially easier route than the overgrown riverbank, that advantage was outweighed by the risks of dividing the expedition, and would have exposed those on foot to even greater risk of attack.

Moving forward with only four canoes also meant that the men would have to leave behind almost anything that was not essential to their survival. "We left all the baggage we could," Roosevelt wrote. "We were already down as far as comfort would permit; but we now struck off much of the comfort." However, after months of similar cutbacks and the loss of much of their clothing to oxen, ants, and termites, they had so few personal items left that, as Roosevelt put it, "The only way to make a serious diminution was to restrict ourselves to the clothes on our backs."

Early that morning, the expedition set off down the river once again—eight men riding in the canoes and thirteen men walking. For better stability, the four dugouts had been tied together to form two balsas, and the expedition's three best paddlers had been assigned to navigate them. Roosevelt, who had been battling fever, rode in one balsa, and Dr. Cajazeira rode in another, so that he could look after three camaradas whose feet were so swollen with bruises, gashes, and insect bites that they could no longer walk. The remaining nine camaradas, along with Rondon, Lyra, Cherrie, and Kermit, hacked their way with knives and machetes through the underbrush that crowded the banks. Their misery growing with every step, several camaradas wrapped their legs and feet in strips of canvas, but even this measure provided little protection from the sharp branches that sliced open their skin and ripped and unraveled their makeshift shoes.

For the camaradas, the exhausting and painful trek along the riverbank had one benefit: It gave them an opportunity to search for food in the forest. Hunger, and the possibility of starvation, now tormented and frightened the men as much as any other danger they faced. They had already consumed more than a third of their provisions, and they had not traveled even ninety miles down the river. They feared that they had at least five times that distance still to go.

Game was still nearly nonexistent, and they had been unable to catch even a single fish. Because it was the rainy season and the river had flooded its banks, the fish were dispersed over a larger area.

Despite their constant hunger and the expedition's relentless physical demands, the men had no choice but to eat less to conserve their provisions. They limited themselves to only two meals a day. The officers also spread one day's rations out over two days, and felt compelled to share some of what was left with the camaradas, who were in even worse shape than they.

The camaradas had begun to rely more and more heavily on whatever they could scavenge from the rain forest. As they walked along the riverbank, they scanned the jungle for beehives or even milk trees, a relative of the breadfruit tree that, when nicked with an ax, oozes a thick, milky latex that tastes something like cow's milk. Roosevelt had tried the liquid but had complained that, while the "taste was not unpleasant . . . it left a sticky feeling in the mouth"—a fact that reflected the liquid's evolutionary purpose as a chemical defense compound aimed at plant-eating insects. The camaradas eagerly lapped up as much of it as they could find, but the principal item in their diet had become *palmito,* or hearts of palm, the inner core of small palm trees. Although raw *palmito* was bland—Cherrie described it as tasting like celery—and had few nutrients, it filled their stomachs and eased their gnawing hunger.

Even the officers had begun to take an interest in *palmito,* sending two men into the forest each day to search for the vegetable. What they really hoped to find, however, was Brazil nuts. For centuries, Amazon explorers had counted on these high-fat, high-protein nuts to get them through the rain forest. In fact, Brazil nuts had likely saved the lives of Rondon and his men during their 1909 expedition. The almondlike nuts grow in a hard, round, wood-walled shell that holds as many as twenty-four nuts and can reach seven inches in diameter and six pounds in weight. When ripe, these shells crash to the ground like small cannonballs from the branches of the 130-foot-tall Brazil nut tree, sometimes striking gatherers below with stunning force. So hard that they resist the blow of a hammer, Brazil nuts have been known to knock men out cold, even kill them. Roosevelt and his men, however, were in no danger from falling Brazil nuts. Mysteriously, they had found virtually none at all.

As surprising as it was to Roosevelt and the other officers, the inability of the expedition to sustain itself on fruit or nuts from the lush forest around them was not merely a reflection of bad luck, or the time of year in which they made their journey. Like their inability to find game animals, the apparent lack of fruit was also a product of millions of years of evolutionary pressure, which had refined the reproductive methods of the jungle's plants and trees to an extraordinary level of complexity and sophistication.

In temperate forests, with their large stands of similar trees, reproduction can frequently be accomplished in fairly indiscriminate fashion. Given the large number of nearby trees of the same species, pollen can be successfully transferred to other trees of the same species by a wide range of means, from insects to the wind alone, and the dispersal of seeds can be achieved through simple methods. A downy parachute of fluff carries the seed of the cottonwood randomly upon the breeze, and the apple doesn't need to fall far from the tree in order to achieve its reproductive mission.

In the rain forest, by contrast, the requirements for successful reproduction are much more demanding. The wide separation of trees or plants of a single species means that pollinators must be attracted very selectively, and the intense competition for every available food source means that fruits and seeds must evolve highly refined strategies of dispersal if they are to avoid being consumed or destroyed long before they reach their intended destination.

Plants and trees in the rain forest must find ways not only to attract pollinators, but to attract only those that will reliably go on to seek out other members of the same species, even if they are some distance away. For this reason, many plants and trees have "co-evolved," or developed highly specialized relationships, with the insects, birds, or mammals that pollinate them, creating mutual dependencies aimed at providing access for those pollinators—and keeping all others away.

Because it touches nearly every aspect of life in the rain forest, the demands of this reproductive quest were responsible for many of the bright colors and distinctive features that Roosevelt and his men could see, feel, and smell around them. Flowers that attract hummingbirds, for example, are typically red or orange in color so that they can be seen easily in daylight, and have deep throats to make it difficult for other animals to reach their nectar. Flowers that have evolved to attract some beetles smell like urine or rotting meat. Flowers that attract bats tend to be green or cream-colored, because they need to be smelled rather than seen, bloom only at night, and are frequently located on the trunk, rather than the branches of a tree, so that bats may reach them more easily.

These specialized strategies may be combined with symphonic sophistication, as in the case of the giant Victoria *amazonica* or royal water lily, whose flowers bloom, turn white, emit a strong odor, and sharply increase their temperature to attract the scarab beetles that pollinate them. When they arrive, the flower chamber closes around the feeding beetles, imprisoning them so that they become covered with pollen. Approximately twenty-four hours later, the flower changes to a red color that does not attract beetles, cools off, and releases the beetles, which then fly on, carrying the pollen to newly heated, white, fragrant lily flowers farther down the line.

The complex defense mechanisms, timing sequences, and dispersal strategies that characterize pollination in the rain forest are compounded when it comes to the fruits, seeds, and nuts that the expedition had hoped to eat during its journey down the River of Doubt. Given the high cost of producing them, such precious offspring are protected with a striking array of defenses. To ensure that it is not eaten before it is ready for dispersal, most fruit is protected by distasteful or poisonous chemical defense compounds until it is mature—a phenomenon that, in its most basic form, is familiar to every child who has eaten an unripe apple. Fruit that is dispersed when it is eaten, moreover, frequently remains visually inconspicuous—often green—until it has developed fully enough to accomplish its evolutionary purpose. Only then does it transform itself to attract the attention of its intended distributors by turning bright-colored, fragrant, and delicious.

Even when they are mature, fruits and seeds cannot be wasted on just any hungry passerby, and have evolved to narrowly target only specific dispersers. To avoid ground-based predators, and to give access to birds and other preferred dispersers, many fruits and seedpods are produced high in the canopy, where they were out of the expedition's sight. To ensure that fruits are not simply eaten one by one and destroyed, many plants and trees have adapted by "masting," or producing mass fruitings at irregular intervals—a strategy that defeats the development of unwanted predators by alternately starving and overwhelming them.

For Roosevelt and his men, the evolutionary sophistication of pollination and fruit production in the rain forest resulted in a frustrating and confusing inability to glean sustenance from the plants and trees around them. As well as hinging on rainfall or other weather conditions as the men supposed, for example, the abundance or scarcity of the Brazil nuts that they so hoped to find was also the result of a delicately balanced chain of apparently unrelated factors, all of which were necessary for their production, and any one of which could have served as the underlying cause of the men's frustration.

As would-be cultivators of the Brazil nut would later discover to their dismay, the tree's hooded flowers have evolved to require pollination by a small group of large-bodied bees which are strong enough to pry them open. Those bees, in turn, rely for their own reproduction on a certain type of rain forest orchid, whose absence or disruption is devastating to the production of nearby Brazil nut trees. Even when a mature fruit is successfully produced, moreover, the Brazil nut's hard casing is so effective at deterring unwanted predators that it can only be opened and dispersed by the agouti, a small rodent with chisel-like teeth, whose presence also becomes essential to the tree's reproductive process.

Like the men's inability to find game animals, therefore, the difficulty of finding fruit and nuts reflected their own unfamiliarity with the rain forest, and the dizzying complexity of the reproductive systems at work around them. In its intense and remorseless competition for every available nutrient, the Amazon offered little just for the taking. To the extent they were obliged to rely on the jungle for food, the men of the expedition were destined to do without.

* * *

As a result of their restricted rations, the men were beginning to feel the effects of a near-starvation diet. As is common in instances of extreme hunger, they began to obsess about food. When they were not looking at it, they were talking about it, and when they were not talking about it, they were thinking about it. "A curious effect on our having been on short rations for so long showed itself in our conversation in the evenings," Cherrie wrote. "We talked much about the river and its rapids, which were ever present in our thoughts; but we also talked incessantly about food." Like castaways on a desert island, the men discussed in delicious detail what they were going to eat when they got home. "Colonel Roosevelt always wanted a mutton chop 'with a tail to it!' " Cherrie recalled. Kermit was looking forward to a bowl of strawberries and cream, and Cherrie, the Vermonter, dreamed of pancakes and maple syrup.

Although carried out in good spirits, these talks were always darkened by the reality of their situation. When the conversations went on too long, and his longing for not just food but home and Belle became too painful to bear, Kermit often had to get up and walk away. By this point in the expedition, with drowning, disease, Indian attack, and starvation waiting to claim their lives, all of the men understood that they might never again see home. "When food was scarcest and things looked most gloomy the Colonel and I had a great many talks about what we were going to have when we got out," Cherrie wrote. "I don't think either of us expected to come out."

The men feared for their lives, but they had not yet lost hope, and even small victories helped to revive their spirits. On March 16, Cherrie had written in his diary that it was "very doubtful if all our party ever reaches Manaos." The very next day, however, he had to admit that there had been a "rift in the clouds of our misfortune." At the foot of a second series of rapids, the men found a deep, seventy-foot-wide tributary, the largest they had yet come across. The discovery of this river was cause for celebration. Not only did it banish any lingering thoughts that the River of Doubt might be simply an affluent of the Gy-Paraná, as Lyra had argued—the Gy-Paraná certainly did not have any tributaries of this size—but it convinced even Roosevelt that the river they were descending was one of great importance. "Up to this point it was still possible to give way to the existing doubts in the mind of Mr. Roosevelt and of some of the other members of the Expedition, relative to the importance of the river," Rondon wrote. "But now there was no motive whatever for hesitation." Thrilled that the River of Doubt was going to have a prominent place on the map of South America, Rondon, perhaps in a gesture of forgiveness toward the impulsive young American who had cost him the life of one of his men, decided that he would name this tributary, the river's largest, the Rio Kermit.

As momentous as the discovery of the Rio Kermit was, the men were made much happier by the good fortune they enjoyed that night, as they made camp at the mouth of the tributary. Not only did they find and recover two of the boxes of provisions that had been lost when Simplicio drowned, but, to everyone's great surprise and joy, Lyra caught two fat fish. Few of the men could imagine a happier sight than the lieutenant holding aloft two large, deep-bodied, delicious-tasting pacu, the first fish he or any of the men had been able to catch on the River of Doubt. Even better, Antonio Pareci, one of their most experienced paddlers, assured them that pacu never traveled up heavy rapids. He was certain that, if there were more rapids to come, they would be small ones that the pacu could jump and would, therefore, certainly not necessitate a portage.

The good mood carried over into the next morning, when, during his usual recitation of the Orders of the Day, Rondon officially renamed the River of Doubt. With all of the flourish that he could manage in their tiny, ramshackle camp, the Brazilian colonel formally announced to the small band of dirty and exhausted men standing before him—in his words, "the Brazilian and American Commissions"—that "from that day onward the river which we had since 1909 called 'Duvida' would henceforth be known as the 'Roosevelt.' "

Although Roosevelt knew that the Brazilian government had planned to name the river in his honor if it proved to be a large and important one, he was surprised that they had carried through with the idea. "I had urged, and Kermit had urged, as strongly as possible, that the name be kept as Rio da Dúvida," he wrote. "We felt that the 'River of Doubt' was an unusually good name." Roosevelt also realized, however, that this was a generous sentiment on the part of the Brazilians and an occasion of rare good cheer for the members of the expedition. Had he protested the river's new name, the moment would have been ruined.

The men's happiness and the spontaneous display of good will that followed the renaming ceremony proved Roosevelt right. After he had finished his proclamation, Rondon led all of the men in a hearty cheer for the United States, for Roosevelt, and for Kermit. "The camaradas," Roosevelt wrote, "cheered with a will." Touched by the sentiment and by the simple but well-intentioned ceremony, Roosevelt responded with three cheers for Brazil, and then another round for Colonel Rondon, Lyra, and Dr. Cajazeira, and yet another for the camaradas. Realizing that everyone had then been cheered except for Cherrie, Lyra proposed three cheers for the American naturalist. All of the men were "in high good humor" by the time the meeting broke up and they prepared to resume their journey, Roosevelt wrote.

* * *

THE MEN began that day, March 18, with a renewed sense of their common cause and hope for their own lives. Setting off as a divided expedition, the thirteen men on foot were thrilled when they found a narrow path that ran along the river's edge. The trail made their journey faster and easier and, for the barefoot camaradas, took away much of the danger of stepping on a snake. It quickly became obvious, however, that the well-worn route was not a game trail but an Indian path.

The men felt, saw, and heard the Indians' presence everywhere they turned. The dogs were on edge. Running ahead of the rest of the expedition, they would stop short and bark excitedly into the forest, their attention caught by some distinctive human scent that the men could not detect. Increasingly bold, the Indians did not bother to hide their presence from the members of the expedition. They left fresh footprints in the mud, and they let themselves be heard. As the men walked between the river and the jungle, Indian voices broke through the heavy leaves, clear and guttural, and all the more terrifying for being disembodied.

The Indians had decided to let the members of the expedition know that they were watching them, but they carefully followed the protocol of survival in the rain forest, and remained invisible themselves. Rounding a bend, the men again suddenly found themselves confronting a fishing village—this time bearing clear signs that it had been abandoned only hours or even minutes before their arrival. The village consisted of three huts, whose arrangement was indicative of the Indians' warlike life-style. Each of the huts, which were low, oblong, and covered entirely in palm leaves, had only one small opening, which was artfully hidden underneath the roof's leaves. Not only were the huts' entrances concealed, but so, from each angle, was one of the huts. Two of the huts had been built side by side, and the third had been tucked in between the other two perpendicularly. "In this way if they were to be attacked from one side or another," Rondon explained, "one at least would be covered by the other two, and . . . being invisible to the assailants, could serve as a refuge for the women and children."

Before leaving the village, Rondon insisted on once again offering the Indians a sign of the expedition's friendly intentions. The best way to do that, he knew, was through gifts. While the Cinta Larga likely watched from the forest, the men tied an ax, a knife, and some strings of beads to a pole. The offering of such gifts was a calculated gamble. They might have bolstered the position of the Cinta Larga who had been arguing against attacking the expedition. On the other hand, they could have been a tempting reminder of the provisions that the expedition was carrying—food and useful equipment that, if the Indians attacked, could be theirs in its entirety rather than doled out as token gifts. "There is no doubt that there are many Indians on all sides about us," Cherrie wrote in his journal that night. "If they are to prove friendly or hostile remains to be seen."

Although he was eager to make contact with this unknown tribe, Rondon understood the extreme danger that he and his men were in, and had long since posted sentinels to watch over the members of the expedition while they slept, but he knew that a few frightened men were little protection against a silent band of Indians armed with clubs and poisonous arrows. One night, Cherrie, who, after years in the wilderness, had trained himself to be a light sleeper, watched as Rondon climbed out of his hammock at 2:00 a.m. With his military khakis pulled over his sinewy frame, the Brazilian officer stepped out of their tent and disappeared into the black forest, prepared to protect his men against an attack if he could, but unwilling to fire a single shot in their defense.

*   *   *

RONDON'S CONCERN about the Indians did not mean that he agreed with the expedition's forced march through the rain forest. He had faced unknown, unpredictable Indian tribes before, and if he was killed with an arrow or the entire expedition was massacred, he accepted that fate as the price of completing the work to which he had devoted his life. Roosevelt, on the other hand, was more determined than ever to finish their journey as quickly as possible, and was willing to make whatever sacrifices were necessary to minimize the dangers to the men, especially to Kermit.

Under the strain of their diametrically opposed ambitions, Rondon and Roosevelt's relationship began to fray. A couple of hours after they had passed the Indian village, the men found another tributary, this one broad and shallow with a small green-and-white waterfall that splashed into the River of Doubt from its right bank. While Roosevelt and the rest of the men sat down near the fall to rest for a moment and admire its beauty, Lyra and Rondon measured the tributary and made plans to study it more carefully. Roosevelt, however, insisted that the expedition keep moving. Frustrated that once again he was unable to do what he had come to do—not just map the river but survey the surrounding region—Rondon bowed to Roosevelt's wishes but later complained that he "could only make a small reconnaissance of this new tributary, along its bank, as it was necessary to attend to the wish of the chief of the American commission relative to accelerating our voyage."

The men made camp soon afterward at the foot of a short stretch of rapids. It was here, in the woods surrounding a large bay, that they finally found the right kind of trees for boat building. They would be taking a chance in stopping for several days to carve new dugouts while they were still so close to the Indian village, but if they ever hoped to make it home, they could not continue at such a slow pace and with a divided expedition. Nor did they know when they would again find suitable trees. They had not chosen well when they built their first dugout, and it had cost them dearly. Instead of looking for a type of wood that would be buoyant in the river, they had selected the tree for its size. Like many rain forest trees that have adapted to protect themselves from insect predators, however, the tree they chose was extremely hard and heavy, making it useless for boat building.

The Aripuanã's timber, as Cherrie would later write, "proved to be so dense and heavy that a chip thrown into the water sank like lead. This lack of buoyancy was one of the chief reasons why we had lost our new canoe."

The men had learned their lesson. The trees that they found near the new tributary were araputanga, a species of mahogany that is resistant to rot, easy to carve, and nearly as light as cork. But when work on the new dugouts began early the next day, the camaradas did not get off to an auspicious start. The first araputanga tree that they chose was very close to camp, and suddenly collapsed in the wrong direction. By the time the tree hit the ground, it had knocked over a series of other, smaller trees, which in turn crashed into Franca's makeshift kitchen. "Hard-working, willing, and tough though the camaradas were," Roosevelt wrote, "they naturally did not have the skill of northern lumberjacks."

As the camaradas began the boatbuilding process all over again, the officers made a sickening discovery: Fifteen boxes of their emergency rations had disappeared. It was possible that several men had been involved in the theft, but one camarada's name leapt to all of their minds as the principal suspect: Julio de Lima. Of the entire expedition, Julio was the only man who, in Roosevelt's words, "had kept in full flesh and bodily vigor." He could no longer be trusted even to go out into the forest to gather nuts or cut down palms. Instead of bringing the food back to the camp to be divided equally among all the men, he would devour everything he found. Because they could not prove their suspicions, however, the officers could do nothing but watch Julio even more closely than in the past.

The very next day, Roosevelt made an even more frustrating discovery when he learned that Rondon had been slowing the boat building in order to buy time for his survey of the river. Anxious to resume their journey, the Americans had done everything they could to speed up the work, including helping to carve out the dugouts. On the morning of the 21st, both Kermit and Cherrie rushed back to camp from separate hunting trips expecting the canoes to be finished and the expedition to be ready to start back down the river. They were surprised and bewildered when Rondon told them that they still had some work to do and that they would have to spend yet another day at that campsite. Under intense questioning by Roosevelt and Kermit, Rondon finally admitted that he had ordered the camaradas to work slowly so that Lyra would have one more day to establish the latitude of the new tributary that they had found a few days earlier. The Americans were furious, but the damage had been done, and they had no choice now but to wait for the dugouts to be finished.

The tension between the Brazilian and American commanders only heightened after the men finally launched their six canoes at 8:30 a.m. the following day. After traveling only six miles, the men reached a series of rapids. Everyone wearily disembarked, pulled all the provisions out of the canoes, and watched as the expedition's three best paddlers successfully ran them through the falls. It took them only an hour to get around these rapids, but the next set they hit was so long and steep that they spent six hours carrying their baggage around them and lowering their empty canoes down by ropes. The day was lost again to the river.

After the men had set up camp at the foot of these falls, Roosevelt asked Rondon to step into his tent. Having taken a subsidiary role in the commanding of the expedition up until this point, Roosevelt decided that he could no longer simply watch over Rondon's shoulder while the expedition slowly stumbled through the rain forest. His son's life was at stake. With the theft of the emergency rations, the men were in even greater danger of starvation, and, as they had discovered during their six-hour portage that afternoon, they were still in Indian territory. They had found another empty village, and, the night before, Kermit had noted in his journal that he had seen several "bark stripped trees"—likely couratari trees, the type of trees that, unknown to anyone in the expedition, the Cinta Larga stripped in order to make their distinctive wide belts.

"Mr. Roosevelt asked me for a chat as he wished to give me his opinion as to how we should conduct the work of the Expedition,"

Rondon would later write of his private discussion with his co-commander. "His view was that the chiefs of undertakings of certain importance, should not occupy themselves with the details of the work to be carried out." Roosevelt explained to Rondon that he believed that their duty lay in recording the most basic information about the river, such as its longitude, and then simply surviving the journey so that they could share with the world what they had found. After that, they should step aside and let those who would follow in their footsteps worry about the minutiae.

The point of Roosevelt's talk with Rondon was that he wanted the Brazilian colonel to abandon the fixed-station survey for good. The principal motive behind his request, he admitted, was his son's safety. "Kermit was extraordinarily lucky to escape alive from the accident in which Simplicio perished," he told Rondon. "I cannot accept seeing my son's life threatened at every moment by the presence of Indians, more than that of any other member since his canoe goes at the head of the expedition."

Rondon had no choice but to acquiesce. "Mr. Kermit will not go farther ahead," he told Roosevelt, and he agreed to revert to the faster method of survey. He was not happy about it, however. "The topographical survey proceeded without our being able to obtain all the benefit of the technical resources which we had at our disposal," he later wrote. Roosevelt's demands would prevent him from carrying out "a sufficiently exact and correct work." Rondon would do what it took to please Roosevelt this time, but he would not—and felt that he could not—abandon his mission. He would not sacrifice his expedition even to save lives.

The Myth of "Beneficent Nature"

A T 7:00 A.M. ON MARCH 23, the men carefully climbed into their dugouts under the cloak of a white mist. "The day was overcast and the air was heavy with vapor," Roosevelt would recall. "Ahead of us the shrouded river stretched between dim walls of forest, half-seen in the mist." The landscape ahead, behind, and on either side of them was so obscured that it must have seemed as if anything could rise out of that fog, from a band of Indians to a brutal series of rapids. As the sun rose, it slowly began to burn off the vapor, "and loomed through it in a red splendor that changed first to gold and then to molten white," Roosevelt wrote. "In the dazzling light, under the brilliant blue of the sky, every detail of the magnificent forest was vivid to the eye: the great trees, the network of bush ropes, the caverns of greenery, where thick-leaved vines covered all things else."

As the air cleared, a dispiriting sight materialized in front of the men: a quartzite canyon that spanned the river from bank to bank and squeezed the water once again into a foaming torrent. "On all sides could be seen huge boulders hurled one over the other by the tearing force of the current," Rondon wrote. After all that they had endured during more than three weeks on the river, none of the men even bothered to argue that they might be able to run these rapids. They simply stopped their canoes and unloaded them in preparation for what they knew would be a long portage. While the camaradas began carrying the expedition's baggage to the foot of the falls, Rondon searched along the left bank for a channel through which they could pass the empty canoes.

The Brazilian colonel did not find a channel, but he did find Indian huts. Immediately alerting the rest of the expedition, he ordered everyone to move to the opposite side of the river. As well as keeping the width of the river between them and the huts, and possibly the Indians themselves, the move had the advantage of putting them in the path of a quiet canal that ran along the right bank. It was an uneventful portage, but not an easy one, and by the time they finished, it was already 4:00 p.m. Most days, the men would have stopped there for the night, but even at that late hour, they felt compelled to push on. They no longer had the luxury of traveling when they wanted to, or even when it was safest. "Our position," Cherrie wrote in his diary that night, "everyday grows more serious."

* * *

As they moved through the silent forest, the men's only constant companions were the insects that thickened the air around them. Sweat bees tickled their mouths and eyes, piums hovered over them in thick clouds, and ants and termites regularly raided their camp and devoured their few belongings. Worse even than the insects that fed on their hammocks and undershirts were those that wanted to feed on the men themselves. The barefoot camaradas were vulnerable to intestinal worms, which usually enter the body through the soles of the feet, and all of the men had to watch out for grubs and botflies. As Rondon had learned during earlier expeditions, flies, with their long, sharp ovipositors, or egg-laying organs, could easily deposit grubs into human flesh, even through clothing.

Botflies were, if possible, even more loathsome than grubs. As big as a bumblebee, a botfly can snatch a mosquito out of the air as it is flying by and paste its eggs onto the mosquito's abdomen. The mosquito then rubs the botfly's eggs onto a human being as it extracts his blood. As soon as the eggs hatch on the warm, wet skin, the new maggots begin to burrow into their host. A botfly maggot can be removed either by smearing petroleum jelly over its breathing tube, which discreetly protrudes from the surface of the skin, and then squeezing the maggot out after it dies, or by taping a piece of meat over the wound and waiting for it to wriggle out into its new home.

The real menace, however, came from a long-limbed, long-mouthed insect that is less than a quarter-inch long and weighs as little as a grape seed: the mosquito. By the time Roosevelt set sail for South America, it was well known that mosquitos transmit a variety of lethal diseases, including yellow fever, dengue, encephalitis, filariasis—which causes elephantiasis—and, perhaps most infamously, malaria.

Although the risk of contracting one of these diseases while in the Amazon was great, not every mosquito the men saw was a danger to them. Of the roughly twenty-five hundred different species of mosquito, very few actually feed on human blood, and of the species that do, only the females, who need the blood to help their eggs mature, practice what is known as "vampirism." Different genera, moreover, specialize in different diseases. The genus *Aedes* carries yellow fever, dengue, and encephalitis. *Culex* is also a carrier of encephalitis but spreads filariasis as well. Only one genus, however—*Anopheles*—is known to transmit malaria.

When they were moving swiftly down the river, the men were notably unmolested by mosquitoes. In camp or in the forest during a portage, however, they not only saw mosquitoes, they could hear them. By beating their wings at a frequency of a thousand times per second, the females produce a distinctive high-pitched whine that attracts males for copulation. The best time for copulation is right before a blood meal.

Once she has found her victim, a female mosquito needs just ninety seconds to extract two or three times her weight in blood. She keeps the blood flowing by injecting a chemical that inhibits coagulation. Mosquitoes transmit this chemical through their saliva—along with any diseases that they are carrying. When the mosquito flies off, she is almost staggering under the weight of her meal, and is so slow that she is extremely vulnerable to being swatted. The man she has just injected with malaria-tainted saliva, however, is also in danger. He will certainly experience pain and discomfort; he may become too ill to walk; and if he is very unlucky or far from help, he could be dead within a month.

Malaria was the danger that Rondon's telegraph line soldiers feared most. According to one estimate, at that time 80 to 90 percent of the people working in the Amazon had contracted malaria. Rondon was used to operating with only 75 percent of his soldiers— the other 25 percent being incapacitated by the disease. Just four years earlier, construction of the telegraph line had been forced to halt for an entire year because so many soldiers had been laid low by malaria. Even Rondon himself, who at times seemed almost immortal, had been stricken.

Having seen countless cases of malaria, Dr. Cajazeira did everything he could to protect Roosevelt, Rondon, and their men from the potentially deadly disease. He had only one effective drug in his medicine bag, however: quinine. Made from the bark of the flowering cinchona tree, qurinine was introduced to Europe in the 1630s by Jesuit missionaries who had been working in South America. The alkaloid, which became known as "Jesuit powder," was quickly adopted in the Old World, and nearly three hundred years later, when Cajazeira was administering it on the banks of the River of Doubt, it was still the best, and only, treatment for malaria.

The Brazilian doctor made sure that each of the men under his charge received half a gram of quinine each day and a double dose every third or fourth day, but neither the drug's potency nor the doctor's devotion to his patients was enough. The men kept getting sick.

To be truly effective as a prophylactic, quinine would have to be administered more frequently than the members of the expedition were taking it. Dr. Cajazeira could not increase the frequency, however, because of the drug's toxic side effects, the most common being a maddening, and disabling, ringing of the ears. In extreme cases, quinine even caused deafness.

The first sign of malaria—a deep, spreading chill—begins to surface a week to two weeks after the disease takes hold. The chill quickly turns into a cold so penetrating that the body begins to shake violently and uncontrollably, in a desperate effort to warm itself. Careening from one extreme to the other, a malarial victim soon trades his chills for a raging fever that can reach 106 degrees. Instead of shaking, the patient now sweats so profusely that his clothing and bedsheets are constantly drenched. This sweat, the mirror twin of shaking, is the body's attempt to cool itself.

Kermit was well acquainted with malaria's most insidious quality: It returns to torment its victim, again, and again, for months and even years to come. Since contracting the disease as a child, Kermit had regularly suffered from recurrences of malaria that would drive his temperature up to 103 degrees and cause his teeth to chatter and his hands to tremble so violently that he felt he could not appear in public. Moving to South America might have been beneficial to his career, but it had been hard on his health. He had had several attacks while building railroads and bridges, and since setting off on this expedition with his father, he had fought off a near-constant fever.

Roosevelt too had fallen victim to malaria—as well as dysentery. Until the expedition reached the river, Dr. Cajazeira wrote, Roosevelt had "enjoyed the most perfect health." After the men had launched their dugout canoes, however, the doctor had watched with deepening concern as the former president's health began to decline.

The River of Doubt, moreover, was one of the worst places on earth to be sick. Unless they were too weak even to walk, the men had no choice but to work in order to keep the expedition moving. Shaking and sweating, they carried baggage, lowered canoes through rapids, and cut away underbrush to set up camp. The alternating intense heat and pounding rains added to their misery, as did their festering wounds, which made them even more susceptible to disease. From the insects that fed from their bloodstreams to the parasites that teemed in their food, the rain forest was filled with creatures that had evolved to exploit every weakness or vulnerability that the men might suffer. "The very pathetic myth of 'beneficent nature,' " Roosevelt wrote, "could not deceive even the least wise being if he once saw for himself the iron cruelty of life in the tropics."

*   *   *

THE ACCUMULATION of disease, hunger, exhaustion, and fear had begun to wear the men down, and their true selves were starting to show through. "There is a universal saying to the effect that it is when men are off in the wilds that they show themselves as they really are," Kermit wrote. "As in the case with the majority of proverbs there is much truth in it, for without the minor comforts of life to smooth things down, and with even the elemental necessities more or less problematical, the inner man has an unusual opportunity of showing himself—and he is not always attractive. A man may be a pleasant companion when you always meet him clad in dry clothes, and certain of substantial meals at regulated intervals, but the same cheery individual may seem a very different person when you are both on half rations, eaten cold, and have been drenched for three days—sleeping from utter exhaustion, cramped and wet."

According to Kermit, Roosevelt had always held his children "responsible to the law of the jungle." He never tolerated greed or sloth, especially during camping trips, when, even only a few miles from home, the children's courage, patience, and magnanimity could be tested to their limits. "Not even the smallest child was allowed to show a disposition to grab, or select his pieces of chicken," Kermit recalled. "We were taught that that was an unpardonable offense out camping, and might cause the culprit to be left behind next time." Roosevelt had witnessed this low threshold for discomfort in some of his closest friends, and he believed that it showed a shallowness of character that he was determined never to see in his own children.

Roosevelt was proud of his son on this expedition, as he had been proud of him in Africa. Not only did Kermit never fight for the best piece of meat, but the few times that the expedition had meat, he was often the man who had brought it into camp. Kermit also worked as hard as any of the camaradas, and harder than many. He had spent so much time in the river, struggling to bring the dugouts through rapids or free them from the grip of the racing current and immovable boulders, that his shoes had begun to rot right off his feet.

Nearly every time Kermit was in the water, Lyra was right by his side. "Their clothes were never dry," Roosevelt wrote of his son and his co-commander's right-hand man. "Their shoes were rotten. The bruises on their feet and legs had become sores. On their bodies some of the insect bites had become festering wounds." Over the past month, Kermit and Lyra had become a consistently strong team, and the rest of the expedition had come to rely on the two men to get them through tough rapids by lowering the empty dugouts down by rope or coaching the camaradas as they ran them straight over the falls. While working together day after day, Kermit and Lyra had formed a strong bond of trust and friendship—a bond that was certainly stronger than Roosevelt and Rondon's.

As tense as the relationship between the two commanders had become, however, they had great respect for each other's previous accomplishments, as well as for each other's work ethic while on the expedition. Although he was frustrated by his inability to survey the region carefully, no one tried harder than Rondon to keep the expedition on track. Roosevelt worked equally hard, both for the expedition and to satisfy his obligations back home. "He wrote every day, never neglecting his literary work, even when heroic effort was required, in the days after he had been weakened by fever," Rondon marveled. "As soon as we were camped for the night and the tents were erected he would begin writing, even while the meal was being prepared. Sometimes he would continue writing until 9 o'clock."

In spite of his privileged background, Roosevelt helped the other men however he could. Cherrie would call Roosevelt "the best camp companion I have ever had." "There was no camp duty that the Colonel shirked," Cherrie wrote. "He stood ready and willing to do his share." So willing was Roosevelt to help that he even washed his naturalist's clothes one day. Cherrie had just taken a small bundle of clothing down to the river's edge to wash when Roosevelt appeared and told him that Kermit needed his help in getting the dugouts through some rapids. Cherrie began to roll up his clothes to tuck between some stones until his return, but Roosevelt stopped him. "Never mind those things," he said, to Cherrie's great astonishment. "I'll take care of them." "That evening when Kermit and I returned to camp we found the washing had been done and hung up to dry," Cherrie later wrote. "It is the only time I have ever had my clothes washed by an ex-President of the United States!"

Since they had begun their expedition, Cherrie's admiration for Roosevelt had grown, as had his affection. The long journey had given the two men plenty of time for drawn-out conversations on everything from the Civil War to specimen collecting. Roosevelt had never lost his fascination with natural history and his admiration for the life of a field naturalist. While on the River of Doubt, he intended to learn as much as he could from Cherrie, a man who was as knowledgeable as any other living naturalist when it came to the wildlife, especially the bird life, of the Amazon. "Day after day the Colonel would ply me with questions regarding the birds and other animals that were being collected and preserved," Cherrie would later recall. "And he wanted to know all about them; their technical relations to one another, their geographical distribution, their food, their voices, their songs and calls, and their habits—especially the last. In short he wanted to know their life histories from 'a' to 'z.' "

These long discussions between Roosevelt and Cherrie, which took place in their canoe and around the campfire, gave Cherrie an opportunity to know Theodore Roosevelt as few men ever had. And Roosevelt, in turn, came to know his taciturn naturalist. "We talked together often, and of many things, for our views of life, and of a man's duty to his wife and children, to other men, and to women, and to the state in peace and war, were in all essentials the same," Roosevelt wrote.

These similarities were surprising given that the two men had come from such different backgrounds. Roosevelt's father was a wealthy man, able to send his son to the best schools and ensure his comfort no matter what career he chose to pursue. Cherrie, on the other hand, had had no one to rely on but himself. He had gone to work at a wool mill in Iowa when he was just twelve years old, putting in fourteen-hour days and making three dollars for a six-day work week. Three years later, driven by his own ambition, he entered Iowa State College. While Roosevelt played the campus dandy at Harvard, Cherrie worked his way through college by running the campus's steam pump at night. He tried to study while stoking the pump, but more than once he fell asleep and woke to find that the steam had fallen and the pump, which fed water to the entire campus, had come to a shuddering halt.

After graduation, Roosevelt stepped into the rough-and-tumble but exciting world of New York politics. Cherrie took a bland but steady job as an engineer, but after just two years, he made his escape. Cherrie's life as an ornithologist had led not only to quietly collecting specimens in the Amazon—a dangerous enough activity in its own right—but also to entanglements with various South American insurrections. He had spent the better part of two and a half years as a gunrunner for one revolutionary chief, and had languished in a South American prison for three months, each day expecting to be hauled outside and shot. In spite of all he had endured in South America, however, he had never managed to stay away for long.

*　*　*

ROOSEVELT COULD understand the continent's appeal to his naturalist. He himself had begun to develop a deep-seated admiration for South Americans, especially the expedition's own camaradas. The former president, who had himself once believed that the white race was superior to others, had been deeply impressed by the camaradas' endurance and good cheer on this dangerous and dispiriting journey. "They say that the Brazilians are indolent!" he told Rondon one day. "Well, my dear Colonel, a country that has men like these has assured a great future for itself, and will certainly carry out the biggest undertakings in the world."

One camarada stood out above the rest, impressing everyone in the expedition with his hardy health, great discipline, and strength of character. His name was Paixão—Paishon—and he, like Lyra and Amilcar, was a veteran of Rondon's telegraph line expeditions. He was a sergeant in Brazil's Fifth Battalion of Engineers, and Rondon had made him the commander of a military post near the Juruena River. A few years earlier, Paishon had received a visit from a band of Nhambiquara Indians, and even they had been impressed with him. "He acquitted himself so well on this occasion," Rondon proudly wrote, "that in a very short space of time, he succeeded in conquering the confidence of these Indians and acquiring great prestige among them."

When Paishon accepted Rondon's invitation to join the expedition, Rondon had placed him in charge of the other camaradas, who came to admire the burly black man even though he was a stern disciplinarian. Like Rondon, Paishon expected his men to work as hard as he did. In fact, since the expedition had begun, he had worked so hard that he had torn his one pair of pants to shreds. He walked around with them literally hanging off of him in tatters until Roosevelt gave him one of his own pairs.

The only man who had not earned Roosevelt's admiration, or that of any other man in the expedition, was Julio. He shamelessly begged for special favors, lobbying to get extra food or, futilely, demanding that Kermit give him some of the tobacco that he willingly shared with the men who worked well and hard, something Julio had never done. "Nothing could make him do his share," Roosevelt grumbled. The only incentive that seemed to work with the muscular Brazilian was when Lyra finally resorted to threatening to leave him in the jungle if he did not pull his own weight.

One night, Paishon discovered Julio stealing from the expedition's limited store of rations. Shocked and enraged, the senior camarada raised his powerful fist and struck Julio in the mouth. Julio immediately ran to Roosevelt and Rondon, unashamed of his own, much more serious crime. "Julio came crying to us, his face working with fear and malignant hatred," Roosevelt wrote. Although it was immediately clear to both commanders who was at fault, they agreed to investigate the matter. It did not take long for them to conclude that Julio was thoroughly guilty and that, in Roosevelt's words, he had "gotten off uncommonly lightly."

No one had trusted Julio before this incident, but the gravity of his crime and the depth of his betrayal were breathtaking. Had the expedition's American commander had his way, Julio would likely have been shot on the spot. "On such an expedition the theft of food comes next to murder as a crime," Roosevelt wrote bluntly, "and should by rights be punished as such."

CHAPTER 22

"I Will Stop Here"

O VER THE NEXT FOUR days, the expedition advanced less than four miles. All day on March 23, the men had been haunted by a distant roar that was as ominous as the sight of a still-smoldering fire in an empty Indian village. The sound disappeared on the 24th, and they were tempted to tell themselves that they had been hearing things, and that they were not really headed straight into a savage series of rapids. However, Antonio Correia, the expedition's best paddler, warned them that not only were more rapids awaiting them downstream, but they would be worse than any they had encountered for many days. "I was brought up in the water," he said, "and I know it like a fish, and all its sounds."

In fact, Antonio had underestimated the gravity of their situation. The rapids ahead of them were worse than any they had yet seen on the River of Doubt. On the 24th, the men reached the first set of rapids after less than thirty minutes on the river. After that, they rarely had more than fifteen minutes of smooth water between rapids for the next two days. They spent far more time carrying their cargo and canoes than the dugouts carried them. Every hour of the day, moreover, a low range of hills along the horizon cast its dark and foreboding shadow over them, threatening more heartbreak ahead. The range, Cherrie lamented in his diary, "probably means many more rapids before we will have passed it!"

The skies had been clear for the past five days, and, without the rain, the river had begun to fall, exposing debris that had previously been covered by the high water and sharpening the boulder-strewn rapids. The men spent the entire day on March 26 circumventing a single set of rapids. Lyra directed Antonio and Luiz Correia and one other paddler as they guided the dugouts down one side of the river. The rest of the men carried the cargo and set up camp at the foot of the rapids, surrounded by vines that, in Roosevelt's words, were "as big as cables [and] bore clusters of fragrant flowers."

In spite of the hope that Lyra's pacu had brought the members of the expedition a week earlier, their food situation had become increasingly desperate. Any food they captured or found now was cause for celebration. In their writings, Roosevelt, Rondon, Kermit, and Cherrie all made special note of the meal that they had on March 26, which seemed to them to be a veritable feast. On that day, the men found *palmito*, honey, wild fruit, and even some small knobby-shelled coconuts in the jungle near their camp. One of the camaradas also caught two big piranha, and, best of all, they discovered about a bushel's worth of Brazil nuts. "This is a very important find," Cherrie wrote in his diary that night. "For we may need them very much if our provisions give out."

Increasingly, it appeared to all of the officers that their provisions would indeed run out. They had already eaten half their rations, and they had traveled little more than a hundred miles. Rondon's meticulous charting—including the measurements Lyra had taken while Rondon purposely slowed the boat building—told them that they probably had three or four times that distance yet to go. They were traveling so slowly, and consuming their rations so quickly, that Cherrie estimated they did not have enough food left to last them more than twenty-five days.

*   *   *

ON THE day after the men's wilderness "feast," they had paddled less than two miles when they reached the steep hills that they had seen from afar several days earlier. The hills were "beautiful to look upon, clad as they were in dense, tall, tropical forest," Roosevelt wrote, "but ominous of new rapids." Those new rapids appeared just minutes later, and the men were forced once again to pull over in preparation for a long portage. They decided to carry their baggage and risk running the empty dugouts through the rapids, in an attempt to save time and avoid the onerous work of hauling the boats through the forest.

All of the cargo had been transferred to the foot of the rapids, and most of the dugouts had been successfully run through, when their tightly choreographed portage suddenly unraveled. Cherrie had wandered away from the rest of the men and was watching from the foot of the rapids as the three paddlers struggled with Roosevelt's balsa, the expedition's largest. They were trying to guide it through the same channel that they had used for the other dugouts, but the channel was too narrow for the large balsa, and it made a treacherously sharp turn right near the rocky shore. "In trying to make the turn," Cherrie would later write in his diary, "the inside boat caught on the rocks and also against some bejucas [vines] and tree trunks. In the twinkling of an eye the current had wrenched the outer boat loose, driven it under the prow of the inside boat that was thrown on its side, both filled with water and sank."

The two boats were pinned against a grouping of boulders, the racing current, and each other, and the three camaradas alone could never have moved them. The power of the current was such that it might eventually dislodge the canoes, but if that happened, they would be catapulted downstream, where they would be smashed to pieces on the jutting rocks. Cherrie heard the camaradas yelling for help and rushed to their side to lend his strength. He quickly realized, however, that they would need every member of the expedition if they

From a bridge that Rondon's men had built, the
Roosevelt-Rondon Scientific Expedition launched its
seven dugout canoes down the unmapped River of
Doubt on February 27, 1914. Even Rondon, directing
the loading of the dugouts, had no knowledge of the
mysterious river beyond the first bend.

Roosevelt (in sun helmet) and Cherrie (stepping into their shared canoe) were
given the expedition's largest and most reliable dugout; but none of the boats,
which Rondon had bought from the Nhambiquara at the river's edge, were fit for
travel on a rapids-choked tributary of the Amazon. "One was small, one was
cranky, and two were old, waterlogged, and leaky," Roosevelt wrote. "The other
three were good."

Shouting a final "Good luck!" Miller, who had been relegated to a different journey, took this photograph as the expedition disappeared down the River of Doubt. "For several minutes we stood upon the fragile structure that bridged the unexplored river and stared at the dark forest that shut our erstwhile leader and his Brazilian companions from view," Miller wrote. "And then, filled with misgivings as to whether or not we should ever see them again, we turned our thoughts to the task before us."

Despite the burity branches that they had lashed to the sides of their dugouts for buoyancy, the men sat at most just a few inches above the river's dark surface, uncomfortably close to the piranhas that they feared but could not catch.

The expedition's camaradas outnumbered officers like Cherrie (seated second from left) nearly three to one and could mutiny as easily as sailors at sea. Roosevelt traveled with the best and worst of the camaradas— two men whom he would grow to admire greatly and a third who would prove to be not only a coward and a thief but a murderer.

Although Roosevelt (left) and Rondon (right) had great respect for each other, their relationship suffered under the strain of the expedition's dire circumstances, Roosevelt's demand that they push ahead quickly, and Rondon's determination to survey the river at any cost.

While on the river, Kermit grew a beard and eventually, Roosevelt wrote, began dressing "substantially like the camaradas themselves." Having joined the expedition to protect his father, Kermit worked as hard as any of the camaradas and harder than most, spending such long hours in the river that his shoes literally rotted off his feet.

To shield himself from the onslaught of biting, stinging insects while he worked on his *Scribner's* articles each night, Roosevelt pulled long, fringed gauntlets over his hands and arms and draped his sun helmet in mosquito netting.

Lobo, Rondon's dog and his closest companion on the River of Doubt, was killed by poisonous arrows in an attack by Indians who shadowed the expedition throughout its journey.

Able to span the water with his rifle, Cherrie marveled at how the River of Doubt could contract from a hundred yards across to less than two yards in a single mile. "No canoe could ever live through such whirlpools," he wrote.

To the men of the expedition, few sounds were more frightening than the thunderous roar of rapids. Kermit barely escaped with his life from a stretch of churning water that drowned one of his paddlers.

After losing two dugouts to the rapids, the camaradas worked all day and well into the night, laboring even by candlelight to carve a new dugout. "The flicker of the lights showed the tropic forest rising in the darkness round about," Roosevelt wrote. "Olive and copper and ebony, their skins glistened as if oiled, and rippled with the ceaseless play of the thews beneath."

When forced to portage, the camaradas hacked a narrow path through the jungle and then, harnessing themselves to a drag rope, lined up like draft horses to pull their massive dugouts over a crude skidway.

Despite the risk of whirlpools and flesh-eating fish, the members of the expedition were compelled by heat, fatigue, and filth to swim and bathe in the river. Floating in the shallow water with Cherrie, the 220-pound former president looked to Rondon "like some sort of a great, fat fish."

It did not take long for the men to realize that, on the River of Doubt, mountains meant rapids. "In the valley below we could see the [river] rushing like an arrow of light straight away toward the distant hills, there to disappear into the somber forest," Cherrie wrote. "It was a beautiful view but it filled everyone with dread."

While still weeks from rescue, an injured Roosevelt became so ill with malaria and a bacterial infection that he could no longer even sit up in his dugout canoe, but was forced to lie on a bed of jagged food canisters under a makeshift canvas tent.

Having lost three of their fellow paddlers and porters to drowning, murder, and abandonment in the jungle, the thirteen surviving camaradas solemnly posed by a plaque that commemorated the official renaming of the River of Doubt.

Although ill and considerably aged, Roosevelt returned to New York triumphant on May 19, 1914. Thousands of people in his hometown of Oyster Bay turned out to welcome their local hero (seated in the car at center) home from the Amazon.

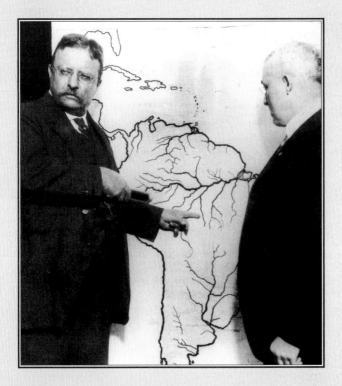

Outraged that his expedition's achievement had been met with skepticism, Roosevelt presented his case to the world's preeminent geographic institutions, ultimately convincing even his most vocal detractors that he had indeed placed on the map of South America a nearly thousand-mile-long tributary of the Amazon River.

ever hoped to free the dugouts. Pulling himself out of the water, he ran to where the rest of the men were waiting, and sounded the alarm.

Terrified of losing two more canoes, the men all ran to help. Roosevelt was the first man in. "His rushing into the water to assist was entirely characteristic of him," Cherrie would later write. "And he did this after many days of suffering from fever which had weakened his vitality. He could not stand idly watching others at a time when action was required." Yet even Cherrie did not understand how great a risk Roosevelt was taking each time he dived into the roiling river.

For the past twelve years, Roosevelt had had only one strong leg—his right. After a trolley-car accident in 1902 had nearly crushed his left leg, he had been told that even the slightest injury to that leg could be dangerous, costing him part of the leg or, if left untreated, possibly even his life. Six years later, while he was riding his horse around Oyster Bay, a branch had hit him on the shin. Even that slight rap had caused an inflammation that, Roosevelt wrote, "had grown so serious . . . that Doctor Rixey had to hastily take it in hand." For a while, the White House doctor had thought that he might have to operate on Roosevelt's leg, but he had been able to check the inflammation before it advanced that far.

On the River of Doubt, Dr. Cajazeira did not have anything close to the medical resources that Dr. Rixey had had access to in the White House. If Roosevelt reinjured his left leg, Cajazeira might be forced to attempt an operation in the rain forest that Rixey had been loath to perform in one of the best hospitals in the United States. If Roosevelt hurt his right leg, he would find himself all but paralyzed on an expedition that demanded long hikes over difficult terrain and through dense forest. Both of his legs would be uniquely vulnerable to injury and infection in the steaming jungle.

Although the water level had fallen over the past few days, it was still deep enough to reach up to the men's armpits as they strove to reach the swamped canoes, slipping over moss-wrapped rocks and stumbling on the river's sharply uneven bed. When they reached the balsa, they used axes to cut away the ropes that had bound it. Kermit and six other men stripped down to the skin and swam to an island in the small series of falls just above the trapped canoes, from where they lowered a rope. Roosevelt and the rest of the men used all the strength they had left to wrench the canoes free and secure them to the rope, so that Kermit and his team could drag them up to the island.

As the river roared darkly around him, making it almost impossible to keep his balance, Roosevelt suddenly slipped, striking his right shin against the sharp edge of a rock. Blood spun out of the wound like an unraveling spool of thread, mixing with the muddy water and disappearing downstream. Roosevelt immediately realized the gravity of this seemingly minor injury as he pulled himself out of the river and quietly limped back to camp, blood beginning to mat the hairs on his leg under his one remaining pair of pants.

For Roosevelt, in a dripping rain forest where every muddy step throbbed with bacteria, parasites, and disease-carrying insects, this injury was potentially fatal. "From that time on," Cherrie wrote, "he was a very sick man."

* * *

WHEN THE men had finally rescued the sunken dugouts and were ready to start back down the river, they were buffeted by a rainstorm. For the next three or four hours, the rain fell in such heavy sheets that the men could not even see across the river. It was 4:00 p.m. before it slowed enough for them to resume their journey. Just ten minutes later, however, they reached another sinister-looking series of rapids, and were left with no choice but to make camp in the rain. Trying to help a limping, quickly weakening Roosevelt, while fumbling with their waterlogged dugouts, rain-drenched bags, and the officers' two slick tents, the men moved as fast as they could, but they could not protect themselves, or their injured commander, from the deluge. "Practically everything we had was soaked," Cherrie wrote. "And our camp was a dreary one."

On the morning of the 28th, the men left camp early, but they were on the river for less than a mile when they were stopped by the rapids that they had seen the day before. While Rondon, Lyra, Kermit, and Antonio Correia hiked ahead to find out just what awaited them downstream, Cherrie and Dr. Cajazeira watched over Roosevelt. But even their careful attention could not halt the consequences of his injury. Although only one night had passed since he had crushed his leg, an infection had already begun to bubble in the wound, and his temperature had spiked in a sudden attack of malaria. The result was a transformation as startling as it was ominous. After only a few hours away from camp, Kermit returned to find that his father's condition had worsened dramatically, changing the ex-president from an injured but able man to an invalid scarcely able to rise from his cot.

As Roosevelt's conditioned swiftly deteriorated, so did the expedition's. After fighting their way along the river's edge for about a mile of what Kermit termed "miserable going," the men who were scouting ahead of the expedition came to a gorge that was so tall and steep that the sheer cliffs that bordered the river seemed to lunge toward each other, squeezing the water through a narrow passage. Within this gorge, which was more than a mile long, the men found a series of six waterfalls, each larger and more treacherous than the last. The final fall was more than thirty feet high.

It was immediately apparent that the expedition's awkward dugout canoes could never survive these falls, even empty. The only way around them would be for the camaradas to build a corduroy road and portage everything, from cargo to canoes. When the four men studied the surrounding land, however, they discovered that it would be almost impossible to carry even their baggage around the falls, much less haul the massive dugouts. The gorge, Rondon realized, had been carved from hornfels, a hard, fine-grained, and slippery stone. There was no way, he told the men who were standing dejectedly at his side, that they could carry the canoes over the steep, jagged, and rocky pass.

When they returned to camp, Rondon assembled the weary and

frightened men in front of him and explained the situation in blunt, unemotional terms. Cherrie wrote that he would never forget the expression on Rondon's face as he delivered the crushing news: "We shall have to abandon our canoes and every man fight for himself through the forest." Cherrie was as incredulous as the camaradas. "To all of us his report was practically a sentence of death," the naturalist wrote.

Unless they stayed close to the river's steep and heavily forested edge, they would not be able to find their way out of the jungle. The thought of losing their way terrified even the most hardened and experienced men among them. In the mid-twentieth century, the Polish explorer and writer Arkady Fiedler wrote of the dangers of becoming lost in the Amazon. "Many cases have been known of travelers and explorers returning from its green labyrinth to become chronic patients of sanatoria, or even not returning at all," he wrote. "They have simply disappeared in the forest like stones in water. The jungle is jealous and voracious. . . . Of all the possible deaths man can die in the jungle, the most dreaded is that which results from being lost."

Cherrie and Kermit's greatest concern, however, was for Roosevelt. As devastating as it was for the other men, the idea of abandoning the canoes meant certain death for Roosevelt, and he knew it. Cherrie wrote that, although Roosevelt did not "utter a word of complaint" when he heard Rondon's decision, "the effect of Rondon's report on him, with his feeling of keen responsibility to us all," immediately caused Cherrie to fear what the ex-president might do in response.

* * *

ONE OF Roosevelt's most entrenched beliefs, as a cowboy, a hunter, a soldier, and an explorer, was that the health of one man should never endanger the lives of the rest of the men in his expedition. Roosevelt had unflinchingly cast off even good friends like Father Zahm when it became clear that they could no longer pull their own weight or were simply not healthy enough to endure the physical demands of the journey. "No man has any business to go on such a trip as ours unless he will refuse to jeopardize the welfare of his associates by any delay caused by a weakness or ailment of his," he wrote. "It is his duty to go forward, if necessary on all fours, until he drops."

Roosevelt had always applied this wilderness law more strictly to himself than to anyone else. When he was a rancher in the Dakota Territories, he had had several painful accidents, once smashing his rib on a stone when he was bucked off his horse, and another time cracking the point of his shoulder when a "big, sulky" horse named Ben Butler flipped over backward while Roosevelt was still riding him. Every time he had been hurt, Roosevelt had forced himself to go on. "We were hundreds of miles from a doctor, and each time, as I was on the round-up, I had to get through my work for the next few weeks as best I could, until the injury healed of itself," he had written.

Roosevelt had even held himself to these unyielding standards after Schrank, the would-be assassin, shot him in Milwaukee. Few men would have even considered giving a speech with a bullet in their chest. Roosevelt had insisted on it. This was an approach to life, and death, that he had developed many years earlier, when living with cowboys and soldiers. "Both the men of my regiment and the friends I had made in the old days in the West were themselves a little puzzled at the interest shown in my making my speech after being shot," he wrote. "This was what they expected, what they accepted as the right thing for a man to do under the circumstances, a thing the nonperformance of which would have been discreditable rather than the performance being creditable."

Roosevelt had never allowed himself to fear death, famously writing, "Only those are fit to live who do not fear to die." From a very young age, he had been prepared to die in order to live the life he wanted. When a doctor at Harvard told him that his heart was weak and would not hold out for more than a few years unless he lived quietly, he had replied that he preferred an early death to a sedentary life. After the Spanish-American War, he had written his friend Henry

Cabot Lodge that, although he was then only thirty-nine years old, he was "quite content to go now. . . . I am more than satisfied even though I die of yellow fever tomorrow."

Driven in part by his father's decision to pay another man to fight for him in the Civil War, Roosevelt had a passion for military combat that, to a large degree, had shaped his adult life. "I had always felt that if there were a serious war I wished to be in a position to explain to my children why I did take part in it, and not why I did not take part in it," he had written in his autobiography just months before heading to South America. Many of Roosevelt's friends, however, suspected that he wanted not only to fight in a war, but to die in one. "The truth is, he believes in war and wishes to be a Napoleon and to die on the battle field," former President William Howard Taft had written of his estranged friend. "He has the spirit of the old berserkers."

There was no question that Roosevelt considered the descent of the River of Doubt to be a great cause—a cause that was, like war, worth dying for. To John Barrett, the former director general of the Pan-American Union, he wrote, "If I had to die anywhere, why not die in helping to open up to the knowledge of the world a great unknown land and so aid humanity in general and the people of Brazil in particular?" Roosevelt had also terrorized Henry Fairfield Osborn, the president of the American Museum of Natural History, under whose auspices he was traveling, with his assurances that, if necessary, he was "quite ready" to leave his bones in South America.

So determined was Roosevelt not to endanger the life of anyone else in his expedition that he had made a secret provision for a quick death in the Amazon, should it become necessary. Before he even left New York, he had packed in his personal baggage, tucked in among his extra socks and eight pairs of eyeglasses, a small vial that contained a lethal dose of morphine. "I have always made it a practice on such trips to take a bottle of morphine with me. Because one never knows what is going to happen," he told the journalist Oscar Davis. "I always meant that, if at any time death became inevitable, I would have it over with at once, without going through a long-drawn-out agony from which death was the only relief."

Now, on the River of Doubt, that vial of morphine represented his only chance to avoid becoming a burden to the other men in the expedition, especially his own son. He knew that he could not possibly make it through the dense jungle on his own, and that Kermit and the other men would try to carry him. Simply carrying the provisions that they would need to stay alive would take more strength than they had. Roosevelt refused to slow down the expedition when each man was fighting for his own life. For him, this was not about suicide, it was about doing the right thing.

That night, after the rest of the men had retired to their hammocks, caught up in their own worries about what lay ahead of them, Cherrie and Kermit agreed to take turns keeping watch over Roosevelt, whose condition had continued to worsen. Both men realized that it would be a long, difficult night, but neither of them was prepared for the decision that Roosevelt would make by morning.

Just before dawn, Cherrie was awakened by the sound of Roosevelt's weak voice calling for him: "Cherrie! Cherrie!" The naturalist sprang from his hammock and stood with Kermit before Roosevelt. Lying on his small, rusted cot, the injured ex-president talked about the dangers that they faced with or without their canoes. Then, without a trace of self-pity or fear, Roosevelt informed his friend and his son of the conclusions he had reached. "Boys, I realize that some of us are not going to finish this journey. Cherrie, I want you and Kermit to go on. You can get out. I will stop here."

PART FIVE

Despair

CHAPTER 23

Missing

THOUSANDS OF MILES AWAY, in New York City, Roosevelt's family and friends had begun to fear the worst. They had been prepared to lose contact with Roosevelt for several weeks, perhaps even months. They were not prepared, however, for the news that they had received on March 23, when the *New York Times* announced that Roosevelt had "lost everything" in the rapids of the River of Doubt and that his whereabouts were unknown. Accompanying the article was a large but strikingly incomplete map of Mato Grosso, Brazil, the region through which Roosevelt was known to be traveling, and a picture of the former president framed in a circle in the left-hand corner. A series of fourteen headlines filled much of the far right-hand column, spilling down the page in a cascade of speculation and fragments of information. "May Be on Unknown River," one headline read. "District Never Explored," "Party Had Been Divided," "No Word Yet to Family."

The article had been sparked by a telegram that Anthony Fiala, the expedition's outfitter, had sent to the newspaper the day before from Santarém, Brazil, a relatively large town on the Amazon River to which he had made his way after successfully descending the Papagaio River. The telegram was only two sentences long, but it was notable both for its brief but startling description of a disaster in the rapids, and its omission of any news about Theodore Roosevelt. "We have lost everything in the rapids," Fiala had written. "Telephone my wife of my safety." At that time, no one outside of the expedition, including even Fiala's wife, knew that Fiala had been bumped from the descent of the River of Doubt and relegated to a different journey. They assumed that the quartermaster was still with the expedition he had outfitted and that, because he had lost everything, so had Roosevelt.

The newspaper did its best to reassure its readers that Roosevelt was "probably safe." The fact that Fiala had not mentioned Roosevelt, the article argued, was a good sign rather than a bad one. "Mr. Fiala's silence on the subject indicates that the Colonel is safe," the article read. "The understanding with Mr. Fiala was that any personal injury to the Colonel was to be cabled immediately and fully." This argument, however, must have been cold comfort to Edith Roosevelt and her children. The absence of any word on Roosevelt's condition was conspicuous and alarming. Why had Fiala not mentioned the former president's safety when he telegrammed his own, and if he had been in a position to send a telegram to New York, why hadn't Roosevelt?

Since her return from South America in December and Margaret's death just a few weeks later, Edith had tried to find distractions that would keep her too busy to worry about her husband and son, but she was struggling. Earlier in the year, she had moved into a hotel in New York City so that she could be near her daughter, Ethel, during the final months of Ethel's first pregnancy. After the baby was born on March 7, Edith had stayed in the city for another week to help her daughter. She had then traveled to Groton, the prestigious boarding school in northern Massachusetts, which all of the Roosevelt boys had attended, to witness her youngest son, Quentin's confirmation. Ten days later, on March 25, she had finally returned to Sagamore Hill, her peaceful but conspicuously empty home on Oyster Bay.

Edith had been at Groton when Fiala's telegram reached the *New York Times*. By then, she had not heard from her husband in nearly a month, and she had no idea where he was or even if he was still alive. Representatives of the American Museum of Natural History, presumably at the urging of Henry Fairfield Osborn, had sent a cable to the American Consul in Para, Brazil, the same night the article had appeared. "Can you obtain any information concerning the Roosevelt party?" the telegram read. "Advise by telegraph at earliest possibility. All expenses guaranteed." The next day, Fiala, still in Santarém, had sent another, longer telegram to the *New York Times*. To everyone's great relief, he explained that, "as part of the expedition plan," he had left Roosevelt's party at Utiariry to descend the Papagaio River. "The Roosevelt party is in good health, exploring the Duvida River," he assured the newspaper.

It must have been clear to Edith, however, that Fiala had no more ability to know whether the Roosevelt party was in good health or bad than she did. The story of his own disaster on a much less dangerous river did not ease her mind, nor did the April release of the first articles in the series that Roosevelt was writing for *Scribner's*. Filled with stories of man-eating fish and warlike Indians, these articles only served to feed Edith's fears and multiply in her mind the dangers that her husband and son were facing.

While Edith had spent much of her life worrying about her husband, Theodore had roamed the world in search of adventure and achievement, never showing much concern about leaving his family. After his first wife's death, he had left his infant daughter in his sister Bamie's care and fled to the Dakota Territories. At the start of the Spanish-American War, he had been desperate to get to the front even though Edith, who was struggling to recover from surgery that had probably saved her life, had asked him not to enlist. When he got his wish and was able to make his way to the heart of the war, Roosevelt had sent a letter home to his wife and children bluntly stating that he probably had a two-in-three chance of survival and asking Edith to give his sword and revolver to Theodore Jr. and Kermit, who were then only ten and eight years old, if he did not make it home alive. Edith had read the letter aloud to her two oldest boys, who buried their heads in her lap and sobbed.

After leaving the White House, Roosevelt had increasingly begun to bring his children, at least his sons, with him when he traveled. Kermit had been a restless eighteen-year-old college student when his father had invited him on his African safari, and he had savored every moment. The Amazon expedition, however, had come when Kermit—twenty-four years old, just beginning to make his own way in the world, and in love—wanted to be almost anywhere in the world but on a remote river in the rain forest. Kermit had succeeded in convincing his father that, as Roosevelt had written to Ethel, "his feelings would really have been hurt if I had not let him come on this trip," but Roosevelt understood how difficult it was for his son to be apart from his fiancée so soon after their engagement and while plans for their wedding were taking shape without him. The fact that Kermit had put his wedding, and his life, on hold for this expedition had weighed heavily on Roosevelt from the beginning of their journey. "I wish he would have gone straight to Belle," he had written Ethel.

* * *

ALTHOUGH SHE missed Kermit, Belle, for her part, had not been suffering during the months of the expedition as her fiancé and her mother-in-law had. As Kermit fought for his own and his father's survival on the River of Doubt, Belle happily settled into her new role as the fiancée of a Roosevelt while continuing to live the life of a trans-Atlantic aristocrat. From her hotel in Madrid, she traveled to New York, made trips into neighboring France, and, while there, occasionally crossed the English Channel. In London, she had even been presented to the Court of Saint James.

In January, with a brief cable to their friends back in Richmond, Virginia, Belle's parents had announced their daughter's engagement to Theodore Roosevelt's son, and the newspapers had quickly picked up the story. A few days after Fiala's disturbing telegram had appeared in the *New York Times,* Belle and her mother had been spotted in Paris happily shopping for her trousseau. When a correspondent for the *Washington Post* inquired, Belle "smilingly admitted the nature of her errand." Less than two weeks later, she was back in New York, attending the opera with her anxious future mother-in-law.

While Belle charmed Europe, Kermit missed her deeply, almost obsessively. Although she had shown a flirtatious interest in him throughout their long-distance courtship, Belle had never seemed to yearn for Kermit with the intensity that he had for her. When he complained that he had not heard from her in far too long, she had insisted that she had written to him, although always in a rush. "I have sent you quite a lot of letters in the last few months—all very hasty, and untidy, and incoherent," she had written teasingly. "I can't imagine why you haven't received them. However, if not writing will bring you to Spain I think I shall cease entirely!"

During the expedition, Kermit's longing for Belle had only deepened. On the overland journey, he used to break away from the rest of the expedition to go hunting with his big white mule and his beloved dog, Trigueiro. He particularly loved the vast, empty deserts of the Brazilian Highlands, where he could wander alone, dreaming of Belle. "The desert has always been a very good friend of mine," he had once tried to explain to her.

Belle could have had no doubt as to the intensity of Kermit's feelings for her, for he had written to her until he had finally run out of stationery as he made his way across the highlands to the River of Doubt, and he had never failed to tell her how much he ached for her. "You must be getting very tired of hearing me say how lonely I am for you," he had written in late January. "But it's what I am all the whole time, and I can't keep it out of my letters. Oh, Belle dearest dearest one it just seems too good to believe that we'll ever be together."

Reading Kermit's letters, it is difficult to remember that he barely knew Belle. Not only were the two young expatriates separated by thousands of miles, but they were fundamentally different people. Kermit's and Belle's childhoods, and the expectations placed upon them by their parents, could not have been more different. They both came from wealthy, well-known families, but Belle had been raised in the rarefied world of high society, whereas Kermit, although the son of a president, had spent most of his childhood tearing through the woods of Oyster Bay. Even Roosevelt's sister Bamie had commented that she "never knew of such a badly brought up family." Instead of stressing things like table manners—he himself was a notoriously sloppy eater—Roosevelt had expected his sons to know how to shoot a gun, skin a rabbit, and chop down a tree. Even when his family lived in the White House, he had winked at his children's mischievous, even mildly destructive, adventures. Kermit, who had been twelve years old when his father became president, had regularly brought his kangaroo rat with him in his pocket to breakfast, and his younger brother Archie had used the passenger elevator to transport his pony to the second floor. "The house became one general playground for [Roosevelt's children] and their associates," Irwin Hoover, a longtime White House employee, once wrote. "Nothing was too sacred to be used for their amusement, and no place too good for a playroom. The children seemed to be encouraged in these ideas by their elders, and it was a brave man indeed who would dare say no or suggest putting a stop to those escapades."

The Roosevelt men were rough around the edges, but they were also vulnerable to what Roosevelt's older daughter, Alice, characterized as a "melancholic streak" that, she believed, ran in the family. Of all Roosevelt's sons, Kermit was perhaps at greatest risk of falling prey to this family melancholy. Although he was smart and strong, he did not have his father's ability to forge his own happiness.

Even Edith, Kermit's greatest admirer, acknowledged that there was a dark side to her blond son. In a letter that she had written to Roosevelt's sister Bamie just months earlier, she had referred to Kermit as the "one with the white head and the black heart." Her second son, she had once explained, had always been "odd and independent" and had seemed to prefer his own company to any other, with the occasional exception of his mother's. "He never need retire to a cloister for a life of abstraction from outside interests," Edith had once written to her sister, Emily. "I believe I am the only person he really cares for." While at Groton, Kermit had also begun to drink— heavily enough at times for even the rector, Endicott Peabody, to notice. When Peabody confronted Kermit, the young man had become so angry that he had thought that he and the rector were "going to come to blows."

* * *

KERMIT'S BROODING temperament and early taste for alcohol were character traits that Roosevelt had seen in his only brother, Elliott, who had died at the age of thirty-four from complications related to alcoholism and morphine addiction. In childhood, Elliott had been as charming and lighthearted as his older brother had been awkward and serious. He had been the stronger, taller, more athletic of the two Roosevelt boys, but as he had approached adolescence, Elliott had begun to lose his footing, developing, as one biographer put it, "an inclination toward poetic introspection" and a desire for solitude that was hauntingly similar to that of his future nephew.

When their father died in 1878, Theodore, who had been at Harvard and had not witnessed the horrible ravages brought on by the final stages of cancer, was devastated. Elliott, who had been at their father's side throughout his illness, nearly lost his mind. "Elliott gave unstintedly a devotion which was so tender that it was more like that of a woman," their sister Corrine recalled, "and his young strength was poured out to help his father's condition." Theodore Sr.'s final days stayed with Elliott for the rest of his short life. "He was so mad with pain," he would later remember with horror, "that beyond groans and horrible writhes and twists he could do nothing. Oh my God my Father what agonies you suffered."

Four years later, Elliott fell in love with a young society beauty named Anna Hall, who, like Belle Willard, came from a wealthy, well-connected family. Just as Belle now seemed to Kermit almost untouchable in her perfection, so did Elliott romanticize and idealize Anna.

"She seems to me so pure and so high and ideal that in my roughness and unworthiness I do not see how I can make her happy," he wrote.

In December 1883, Elliott and Anna married. Two months later, Theodore lost his young wife, Alice, to Bright's disease. Theodore survived the tragedy but Elliott, who seemingly had everything he could hope for, slowly unraveled. He and Anna had three children—among them Eleanor, who grew up to marry her distant cousin Franklin Delano Roosevelt—but their marriage was a travesty. As the years passed, Elliott sank progressively deeper into alcoholism, morphine addiction, and a series of scandalous affairs that humiliated his proud wife and alienated his puritanical brother.

In the end, Theodore simply gave up on Elliott. He finally had his brother admitted to an asylum in Paris and declared incompetent and insane. The next year, Anna died of diphtheria at the age of twenty-nine, refusing to see her husband even on her deathbed. Had Elliott been a stronger man, the sorrow and shame surrounding his wife's early death might have turned his life around. But he was not, and it did not. Two years later, Theodore wrote to Bamie that he wished their sister, Corrine, "could get a little of my hard heart about Elliott. . . . He can't be helped, and he must simply be let go his own gait. He is now laid up from a serious fall; while drunk he drove into a lamp post and went out on his head. Poor fellow! If only he could have died instead of Anna!" Elliott did die less than a month later, leaving nine-year-old Eleanor and her two siblings orphans.

For Roosevelt, Elliott's death transported him back in time, to twenty years earlier, when his brother was still a handsome, charming boy with a bright smile and a promising future. "I only need have pleasant thoughts of Elliott now," he wrote his sister Corinne. "He is just the gallant, generous, manly, loyal young man whom everyone loved." When Roosevelt saw his brother's body, he was "more overcome than I have ever seen him," Corinne later recalled. He "cried like a little boy for a long time."

*   *   *

THROUGHOUT KERMIT'S adolescence and young adult life, Roosevelt had gone to great lengths to keep his son focused and industriously occupied. When Kermit was at Groton, his father, who was then president, always found time to monitor his schoolwork closely. In an attempt to encourage his son in any interest that he himself viewed as positive and worthwhile, Roosevelt had even rescued Edwin Arlington Robinson, the down-and-out American poet to whom Kermit had become devoted while at Groton. After leaving Harvard, Robinson had fallen into obscurity, misery, and alcoholism. Kermit had sent one of Robinson's works to the White House and asked his father if he could help the poet. Although Roosevelt admitted that he did not think he truly understood Robinson's poetry, he not only gave him a position as a special agent in the New York Treasury, but he reviewed *The Children of the Night* for *Outlook* magazine, thus bringing his writing to a much wider audience than it had ever had. "I do not like to think of where I should be now if it had not been for your astonishing father," Robinson later wrote to Kermit. "He fished me out of hell by the hair of the head."

Determined to keep his son from descending into the blackness that had swallowed Elliott and had nearly destroyed Robinson, Roosevelt had taken Kermit along on his most challenging adventures and had always given him a mission, something to work toward, something to give him a sense of direction and accomplishment. Besides encouraging Kermit in his schoolwork and literary interests, Roosevelt had exposed him to the physical challenges that had toughened his own body and mind. While Kermit was at Groton, Roosevelt had sent him to South Dakota one summer to work in the Badlands that had been his own salvation after Alice's death. Africa, too, had been a constant physical challenge, and Roosevelt had watched with soaring pride as his son thrived on the difficult work.

"We worked hard; Kermit of course worked hardest, for he is really a first-class walker and runner," Roosevelt had written proudly from the Sudan to Kermit's brother Archie. "Kermit has really become not only an excellent hunter but also a responsible and trustworthy man, fit to lead."

* * *

STANDING NEXT to Roosevelt's prone, sweat-soaked figure in their dim tent beside the River of Doubt, Kermit met his father's decision to take his own life with the same quiet strength and determination that the elder Roosevelt had so carefully cultivated and admired in him. This time, however, the result would be different. For the first time in his life, Kermit simply refused to honor his father's wishes. Whatever it took, whatever the cost, he would not leave without Roosevelt.

In the fraction of a second that passed between Roosevelt's grim declaration and Kermit's reaction, father and son reversed the roles that had defined their relationship, and which neither of them had ever questioned. Over nearly a quarter-century, through lectures, letters, camping trips, grand adventures, and strong example, Roosevelt had molded Kermit in his own image, creating a young man who, given a goal, would fight with everything he had to achieve it. But, although Roosevelt was proud of his son's growing independence, he had always remained the patriarch, continuing to make the final decisions. On this night, Kermit not only refused to do what his father asked of him but demanded that Roosevelt step back and let his son determine his, and the entire expedition's, course of action.

Recognizing the resolve on his son's face, Roosevelt realized that if he wanted to save Kermit's life he would have to allow his son to save him. "It came to me, and I saw that if I did end it, that would only make it more sure that Kermit would not get out," Roosevelt would later confide to a friend. "For I knew he would not abandon me, but would insist on bringing my body out, too. That, of course, would have been impossible. I knew his determination. So there was only one thing for me to do, and that was to come out myself."

CHAPTER 24

The Worst in a Man

THEODORE ROOSEVELT HAD DECIDED to live. In the past, that would have been enough. On the River of Doubt, however, his decision would save him only from himself. He was still perilously ill, and he and his men still faced a deep, rocky gorge, an impassable series of rapids, and a commander who believed that their only hope lay in abandoning their canoes and striking out into the pathless jungle. With the growing infection in his leg and his raging fever, Roosevelt knew that he would never be able to survive a forced march through the rain forest, no matter how determined he was to do so.

Although his will was strong, his body was not. For the first time in his adult life, Roosevelt would have to rely on someone else's physical strength to pull him through. He would have to rely on his son. Kermit had been battling malaria almost since the expedition began, but he was still strong, and he had the endless endurance of youth.

Having inherited his father's unshakable confidence, Kermit was certain that he could get the expedition's dugouts through the canyon. The problem was convincing the other men. "Kermit," Roosevelt would later write, "was the only man who believed we could get the canoes down at all." The young man's conviction, however, quickly swayed not just Cherrie but also, even more important, Lyra. The Brazilian navigator had been Rondon's right-hand man for much of his life, but he had spent the past month working side by side with Kermit as they struggled to get past one series of rapids after another. Lyra had come to respect Kermit's energy, courage, and, more to the point, considerable dexterity with ropes, a skill that he had gained while helping to build bridges in other corners of Brazil. Rondon still believed that the effort was a lost cause, but, when confronted by these three determined men, he agreed to do what he could to help.

Kermit's plan was to lower the empty dugouts down the falls with ropes while the camaradas carried the baggage over the steep canyon cliffs. In order to make the plan even feasible, the men first had to whittle down their cargo yet again. This purge—the fourth since their expedition had begun—was particularly difficult because there was little left that they could afford to lose. Nonetheless, the men examined their baggage with misers' eyes, cutting down "everything except the food," Kermit wrote in his diary.

Roosevelt kept only two small bags. One was his cartridge bag, which, along with his cartridges, held the head net and gauntlets that he used to protect himself while he wrote. The other bag, a duffel, contained his cot, a blanket, and a mosquito net, as well as a meager set of personal items: a single pair of pajamas, one extra pair of underwear, a pair of socks, six handkerchiefs, his wash kit, his pocket medicine case, some gun grease, adhesive plaster, a bottle of fly dope, needles and thread, his spare eyeglasses, his wallet, and a letter of credit, which would be essential should the expedition reach Manáos. He gave the shoes that he had been wearing to Kermit, whose own shoes had finally disintegrated, and pulled on his only spare pair.

With the expedition's supplies cut down to the barest necessities, Lyra and Kermit climbed to the top of the gorge and prepared to lower the dugout canoes. Although they had used this method to hoist their boats over falls in the past, they had never before been forced to work in such extreme circumstances. The canyon walls were so steep—an almost vertical line from ridge to river—that at times the men had to cling to narrow, crumbling rock shelves while they struggled with the rough ropes and their massive cargo. "The work was not only difficult and laborious in the extreme, but hazardous," Roosevelt later recalled. The chances that the dugouts would not survive the ordeal, moreover, were very high. The men understood that, even if the plan worked, they might still end up spending several days at the other end of the gorge building new canoes.

The canyon walls were also far too steep for a cargo carry. Instead of walking along the river, as they had in the past, the camaradas would have to hike some distance away and then carve a trail more than 350 feet up the side and over the top of the densely forested mountain. While Kermit and Lyra struggled with the canoes, Rondon and a team of camaradas began to scout out a path. At the summit, Rondon stopped and ordered his men to cut down a few trees so that he could have an unimpeded view of the horizon. What he, and later Cherrie, saw from that mountaintop only made their situation seem even more hopeless than they already believed it to be. "In the valley below we could see the Rio Roosevelt rushing like an arrow of light straight away toward the distant hills, there to disappear into the somber forest," Cherrie wrote. "It was a beautiful view but it filled everyone with dread. We had learned that wherever the river entered among the hills it meant rapids and cataracts and our strength and courage alike were almost exhausted. We again discussed the possibility of having to abandon our canoes but dreaded to think what our fate would be should we be forced to do so."

It took four days, but the expedition's men, baggage, and canoes finally emerged from the northern end of the canyon on April 1. Although this extraordinary achievement had likely saved their lives, there were no celebrations in the camp that night. The men were too exhausted and sick, and they had not escaped from the canyon unscathed. On the third day of the portage, Kermit and Lyra, in spite of all that they had done to protect their precious cargo, had watched helplessly as one of their dugouts had slipped from its rope and was smashed among the rocks on the river's bottom.

To add to the men's unhappiness on their first night beyond the gorge, the heavens opened, and they were swept up in a rainstorm that was so punishing that even Rondon referred to it as "tempestuous." It rained so hard that the canvas awnings that the men had rigged up collapsed under the weight of the water, and they feared that their remaining five canoes would be swamped. The storm even drove rain under the officers' tent, drenching Roosevelt as he lay on his cot, his fever raging.

The men began the next day, April 2, more exhausted than they had ever been, following four days of a perilous portage and a terrible night's sleep. Although they looked forward to their return to the river, it brought with it little opportunity for rest. With only five canoes, everyone but Roosevelt and the paddlers had to walk. After less than two miles, moreover, the expedition reached yet another steep-sided canyon. "Instead of getting out of the hills at once as we hoped to do," Cherrie despaired, "we are deeper in among them!"

By that point, the men had been fighting rapids for a month straight since they had heard the river's first roar on March 2. During that month, they had made only sixty-eight miles and descended nearly five hundred feet. Worse than this portage, or even the last, was the probability that countless more awaited them downstream. "No one can tell how many times the task will have to be repeated, or when it will end, or whether the food will hold out," Roosevelt wrote. "Every hour of work in the rapids is fraught with the possibility of the gravest disaster, and yet it is imperatively necessary to attempt it; . . . failure to get through means death by disease or starvation."

* * *

THE BRUTAL job of getting through and around the rapids had begun to destroy what remained not only of the camaradas' health but also of their hope. Each new series of rapids reminded them of their drowned companion, Simplicio, and each portage held the threat of snake or Indian attack and the promise of heartbreaking toil. So dejected were the camaradas that they began asking the officers if they really believed that they would ever get out of the jungle alive. The officers were as frightened and unsure as their men, but felt obliged to put on a brave face. "We had to cheer them up as best we could," Roosevelt wrote.

From the beginning of the expedition, Roosevelt had worried about the camaradas, and done what he could to bolster their spirits. "In the weeks of trying hardships when the fates seemed all against us, despite the fever and dysentery that were sapping his strength, he never failed, day after day, to make inquiry about his camp companions including the canoemen and camp helpers," Cherrie wrote of Roosevelt. Early on, Roosevelt had begun giving the camaradas chocolate bars at noon from his meager supply. The men treasured this treat so much that, instead of immediately devouring it, they would hoard it until 3:00 p.m., when they would make it into a mid-afternoon meal. "It was a strange form of food for the Brazilian interior, and was especially enjoyed by the laborers," Rondon wrote. "Those little daily acts of thoughtfulness were much appreciated and the men soon loved him."

Now that their food supplies were so low and their chances for survival worsening, the ailing Roosevelt did more than give the camaradas chocolate. He began to give them his own share of rations. When Kermit and Cherrie realized what he was doing and protested, Roosevelt simply replied, "I can't do anything to help and they need the food." "We had to watch him constantly," Cherrie wrote. It "reached the point where if he didn't eat all of his share either Kermit or I would take what was left and guard it until a later meal. We had so very little that every mouthful counted."

By this point in the expedition, many of the camaradas had become visibly depressed, and the officers worried about their sullen attitudes and deteriorating morale. "A sense of gloom pervaded the camp," Cherrie wrote. On March 30, Kermit had written in his diary that the men were "very disheartened." Rondon insisted that they were still in good spirits, but even he had to admit that the rapids were causing "considerable suffering to our men" and that, with very few exceptions, they had "broken down."

The officers knew that frightened and unhappy men were not only hard to motivate but potentially dangerous. Outnumbering the officers by more than two to one, and with no possibility of outside interference, the camaradas could easily wrest control of the expedition from their commanders. Rondon had fought against mutiny and its precursors—fear and frustration—his entire career. He knew its signs, and he knew that this expedition had all the right ingredients for it.

Cherrie too had had enough experience with disgruntled camaradas to be wary of them. During an earlier expedition, a man he had dismissed from his team of guides had tried to kill him. In an exchange of gunfire, Cherrie had ended up killing the man instead, but not before being seriously wounded. He had nearly bled to death trying to get to help, and he would never again have complete use of one of his arms.

The officers on the River of Doubt were fortunate. With very few exceptions, their camaradas were good, decent, and trustworthy men. As the weeks had passed, however, and their situation had steadily worsened, they had grown increasingly desperate. "Under such conditions," Roosevelt wrote, "whatever is evil in men's natures comes to the front."

*   *   *

THE MEN awoke on the morning of April 3 with little hope for an easy or successful day. Their plan for getting the dugouts through the second gorge consisted of three distinct, and progressively more grueling, stages. The first stage involved running the empty boats down the river as far as they could safely take them. When the river became too rough, they would lower the canoes over the rapids by ropes. Then, at the point at which the ground began to level, they would slash a trail through the forest, chop down trees for a corduroy road, and haul the dugouts along the bank to the mouth of the gorge.

Disaster struck almost immediately, during the first and easiest stage of the plan. While Antonio Correia and another camarada were steering one of the canoes down the river, they suddenly lost control and found themselves being swept toward the rapids. They desperately grasped at the branches and vines that looped over the bank, but the current was too strong, and the branches simply snapped in their hands. Realizing that they were about to be hurled into the rapids, the two men finally dived into the rushing river and watched as the dugout was, in Cherrie's words, "whirled out of their hands to be crushed to splinters in the whirlpools and rapids below." Their expedition was left once again with only four dugouts, two of which they had built themselves.

Adding to the men's already overwhelming feeling of isolation and vulnerability, the work of pushing past the rapids obliged them to be scattered from one end of the canyon to the other. While Lyra and his men were at the river's edge, cutting away undergrowth so that the canoes could be let down the falls, Rondon had assembled a team to carve a trail along the face of the cliff to the foot of the rapids. The rest of the camaradas, under Paishon's direction, were carrying the baggage to an intermediate station above the falls, where Kermit and Cherrie were waiting to assemble the supplies.

Only one man, a trusted and valued camarada named Pedrinho, remained behind at the previous night's camp in order to guard the cargo as it was slowly carted off. Early that morning, as the camaradas filed by in their dirty, tattered clothes, picking up boxes and hefting them onto their tired shoulders, Pedrinho noticed some suspicious activity. Stepping forward, he surprised Julio de Lima as the muscular camarada was once again slipping some food out of one of the ration tins. This time, he was taking dried meat, a particularly rare and treasured commodity, and Pedrinho immediately reported the theft to Paishon.

Paishon was enraged to hear that the camarada had been caught stealing food once again. As serious as the theft was, however, there were few available options for punishment beyond a harsh rebuke. They had too much work to do to sacrifice one of the expedition's healthiest men to any sort of imprisonment. Soon after the theft, both Paishon and Julio returned to their places in the line of baggage carriers, and Pedrinho resumed his duties as camp guard.

It was not long before Julio raised Paishon's ire again. As the other men hauled their heavy loads up the steep hillside, Paishon reprimanded Julio for not pulling his weight. At the intermediate station, Kermit and Cherrie were waiting with the ailing Roosevelt, and all three men were attempting to distract themselves by reading, when Julio appeared, groaning under the weight of his load and muttering to himself as he shuffled forward. When he heard Julio approach, Cherrie looked up and joked to Roosevelt and Kermit, "One would know who that was by the groans." The two Roosevelts both gave a short laugh of acknowledgment and returned to their books.

After Julio had set down his cargo, Cherrie happened to look up and see the camarada walk over to a group of rifles, which were leaning against a tree, and pick up a carbine. The camaradas often carried rifles with them in case they saw game, so Cherrie did not give much thought to Julio's action, other than to remark to Kermit and Roosevelt that Julio must have seen a monkey or bird near the trail.

Only a few minutes after Julio had disappeared, the three Americans heard the unmistakable crack of the carbine going off. "I wonder what he has shot at?" Roosevelt said, rousing himself from his illness. He, Kermit, and Cherrie began to speculate, hoping that, if Julio's shot had found its mark, whatever he hit would be fit for dinner. No sooner had they started savoring the prospect of a good meal, however, than they saw three camaradas running toward them up the trail.

The men's voices reached them in a breathless panic. "*Julio mato Paishon!*" they shouted in Portuguese. "Julio has killed Paishon!"

CHAPTER 25

"He Who Kills Must Die"

As news of the murder spread across the stone canyon, the members of the expedition froze in fearful expectation, their ears primed to hear another rifle shot ring through the trees. No one believed that Paishon was Julio's only target. They were certain that the volatile camarada had snapped under the pressures and hardships of the expedition and gone on a killing spree. "We all felt that Julio had run amuck and had probably determined to kill as many of us as he could," Cherrie wrote. Several minutes passed, however, and the men heard nothing more. The forest's heavy silence in the wake of the single shot was more sinister than a fusillade, threatening to break at any moment, and from any direction.

At the intermediate station, the Americans realized that the silence might mean that Julio was making his way back to the last camp, and his next victim: Pedrinho. The guard who had caught Julio stealing food earlier in the day was not only unaware of the murder, but also alone and unarmed. Roosevelt's health had continued to deteriorate since his accident a week earlier, but, despite his physical frailty, the murder of one innocent man and the imminent threat to another triggered in him a lifelong instinct for action. To Kermit and Cherrie's dismay, Roosevelt suddenly pulled himself to his feet and lunged for the same group of rifles from which Julio had taken his murder weapon just minutes earlier. Ordering his son and the naturalist to guard the canoes and supplies, he set off to warn Pedrinho, a rifle clenched in his hand. "Before we could stop him he had started down the path where Julio had disappeared," Cherrie wrote. "Without hesitation he himself chose to go back over a trail on which the murderer might be concealed."

Roosevelt—followed closely by Dr. Cajazeira, who had raced after him with a revolver at his side—did not get very far before he found Paishon. The young man lay facedown near an abandoned pile of baggage, his lifeless body crumpled and still, a pool of blood slowly spreading beneath him. Julio had shot Paishon straight through the heart, and he had dropped dead on the spot, pitching forward until he slammed into the soft forest floor like a felled tree. "The murderer," Roosevelt determined, "had stood to one side of the path and killed his victim, when a dozen paces off, with deliberate and malignant purpose."

Now that he had seen with his own eyes what Julio was capable of, Roosevelt's concern for Pedrinho and sense of urgency redoubled. Struggling on with his infected leg, he pushed past Paishon's body and continued to make his way to the last camp, searching for any signs of Julio. When they finally reached the camp, Cajazeira swiftly and silently stepped in front of Roosevelt. "My eyes are better than yours, colonel," he said. "If he is in sight I'll point him out to you, as you have the rifle." Julio, however, was nowhere to be seen. Pedrinho was unharmed, but the murderer had disappeared. They realized that he must be hiding somewhere in the forest, probably not far from where he had shot Paishon.

By that time, the other officers had reached the scene of the murder. After Roosevelt left, Kermit and Cherrie had waited at the intermediate station until they found two camaradas who could be trusted to guard the canoes and supplies. It had taken Lyra and Rondon nearly half an hour just to get word of Paishon's death and to make their way back to the muddy stretch of trail between the station and the last camp. Lyra, who was still struggling to lower the canoes over the falls, had heard about the tragedy first and had sent a cama-rada to tell Rondon. After instructing his men to continue their work cutting a path along the cliff face, the Brazilian commander had left immediately. The four men finally met on the forest trail, gathering around Paishon's body.

Rondon had seen many dead men during the quarter-century that he had spent in the Amazon. He had watched them in their death throes, unable to help as they writhed in agony with a poisoned arrow in their chest, burned with fever until they fell into a disease-induced coma, or withered away from starvation. But he had never before seen one of his own men kill another out of pure hatred. When he looked down at Paishon, he saw senseless death, a wasted life, a sacrifice that had gained nothing for the telegraph commission's greater mission, or even for this single expedition. The murder sparked a deep-seated out-rage in Rondon. Despite his great discipline, the Brazilian colonel was, Kermit would later write in his diary, "in a blind rage to kill" Julio.

As Rondon would later describe the strange events of that day, however, it was his hot-blooded American co-commander, not he, who demanded an eye for an eye. After finding Paishon, the four offi-cers walked back to camp looking for Roosevelt. "When I met him," Rondon later recalled, "he was very pent up." "Julio has to be tracked, arrested and killed," Roosevelt barked when he saw Rondon. "In Brazil, that is impossible," Rondon answered. "When someone com-mits a crime, he is tried, not murdered." Roosevelt was not convinced. "He who kills must die," he said. "That's the way it is in my country."

If they found Julio, Rondon argued, they should apply the laws of the Brazilian government, not wilderness justice. Rondon believed, his faithful friend and soldier Amilcar would later explain, "that the evil doer should be taken in and fed, demanding that he would work in re-turn for the food he was entitled to, although he would still be a prisoner, awaiting contact with the civilized world in order to eventually be duly tried." Ever the pragmatist, however, Roosevelt thought that it would be folly to subject themselves to a dangerous man and to ask their camaradas to share their scarce rations with a thief and murderer.

As they argued, Roosevelt and Rondon were literally handed a quick if temporary resolution to their situation—in the form of the .44-caliber Winchester rifle that Julio had used to kill Paishon. Although Rondon had doubted that Julio could be found in the tangle of trees and vines that flanked the trail, he had sent two men, Antonio Correia and Antonio Pareci, to search for him. The two camaradas found the spot at which Julio had fled into the jungle, and quickly disappeared from sight. Moments later, the officers heard a cry of surprise, and Antonio Correia stepped back onto the trail holding the murder weapon in his dirt-streaked hands.

Julio, they realized with great relief, had lost his rifle as he fought his way through the thick vegetation. "Perhaps hearing someone coming along the path, he fled in panic terror into the wilderness," Roosevelt speculated. "A tree had knocked the carbine from his hand." Broken branches and matted leaves told them that Julio had doubled back to retrieve the rifle but then must have been frightened away by the voices of the other men as they discovered Paishon's body. "His murderous hatred had once again given way to his innate cowardice," Roosevelt wrote with contempt.

Now that they knew Julio was unarmed, Roosevelt and Rondon's desperation to find him—whether to kill him or to imprison him—was defused, at least for the moment, and they could finally turn their thoughts to Paishon. Someone had laid a handkerchief over the dead camarada's face, but it was still hard for them to believe that, as Roosevelt wrote, "the poor body which but half an hour before had been so full of vigorous life" would never move again. When they had lost Simplicio more than two weeks earlier, the men had been deeply saddened, but Paishon's death was an even greater blow. They had never found Simplicio's body, and somehow that had made his death seem less real, less immediate. The sight of Paishon's broken body, however, would stay with them, a painful reminder of the violence and tragedy that they had witnessed that day.

All that the men could do for Paishon now was give him as digni-fied a burial as they could manage. Rondon announced that he would name the falls and the mountains that surrounded them Paishon, as they had had "the bad destiny of being [the] indirect cause and the-ater" of the young man's murder. He decided to bury his camarada where he had died, "with his head towards the mountain and his feet towards the river."

The principal obstacle to Rondon's plan was that, having already abandoned most of their tools, the men did not have any shovels with which to dig a grave. While the officers stood watching, their hats re-moved, the camaradas used knives, axes, and their own hands to claw back the wet earth. When they finished, Roosevelt and Rondon "rev-erently and carefully" picked up Paishon's shoulders while Lyra, Kermit, Cherrie, and Dr. Cajazeira supported his back and legs. Together they laid the blood-soaked body in its shallow grave, heaped a low mound over it, placed a rude cross at the head, and fired a vol-ley in Paishon's honor. "Then we left him forever," Roosevelt wrote, "under the great trees beside the lonely river."

* * *

ALTHOUGH FINDING Julio's gun had eased their minds, it did not ensure their safety. With nowhere to go and nothing to lose, Julio would likely try to steal another gun or, at the very least, provisions from the expedition. If he was still feeling angry and vindictive, he could damage their dugout canoes or even try to kill them by pushing boulders over the cliff's edge while they were working on or near the river. Until they passed these rapids, moreover, the men would still be scattered across the gorge. In an effort to protect themselves and their cargo and canoes, they posted guards wherever they could. One man was stationed at each of the two camps, and another was assigned to follow the camaradas as they completed the baggage carry. Cherrie himself guarded Lyra, Kermit, and their men as they lowered the rest of the canoes over the falls.

Despite a determined struggle, the men were able to move only part of their baggage and two of their four canoes to the bottom of the falls before darkness fell. Since they could not risk losing any of their dugouts or even the smallest box of provisions, they would have to divide the party overnight, the first time they had had to do so since their expedition had begun. Some of the men slept at the head of the rapids that night, while the rest swung their hammocks between a clutch of trees that had somehow grown up among the boulders that littered a narrow strip of land at the bottom of the cliff.

That night, as they helped Roosevelt struggle to reach the new camp, the men were struck anew by how sick he was. With the excitement and outrage of the murder circulating in his veins, the former president's urgent determination to take action had temporarily prevailed over the effects of his illness. As his chest heaved with each step up the steep side of the gorge to the new camp, however, it was painfully apparent to them all that he had lost the vitality that had awed them at the outset of their overland journey not even three months earlier. "At 5:30 p.m. Mr. Roosevelt arrived breathless with the great effort which he had made to climb up the slopes of the rocky mountain," Rondon noted. "That violent exercise was too excessive for his state of health and made him suffer very much."

Roosevelt's heart worried them now as much as his infected leg. For the past few days, the man who had torn through every backwoods he could find, from Oyster Bay to Maine to Washington, D.C.'s wild Rock Creek Park, could hobble only a few steps before becoming utterly exhausted. A few days earlier, on a downhill walk with Roosevelt from one camp to the next, Cherrie had been shocked by his friend's rapid and severe decline. "As he and I went down the trail to our camp at the foot of the rapids, his heart was so affected that frequently he had to sit down and rest," Cherrie wrote. "He was evidently in great pain because three or four times he threw himself on the ground and begged me to go on."

Kermit was acutely aware of his father's serious condition, writing in his diary the day before the murder that he "worried a lot about F's [Father's] heart." His concern was rivaled by Cherrie's. The respect that the American naturalist had long held for Roosevelt had deepened over the past few months into a brotherly affection, and he was as determined to bring him out of the Amazon alive as he was to get himself out. With each passing day, however, that goal seemed increasingly unreachable. "There were a good many days, a good many mornings when I looked at Colonel Roosevelt and said to myself, he won't be with us tonight," Cherrie wrote. "And I would say the same thing in the evening, he can't possibly live until morning."

It was Roosevelt's earlier, although aborted, decision to take his own life as much as his rapidly deteriorating health that kept Cherrie awake at night. Cherrie had already lived through a friend's suicide, and he would never forget it, or his role in it. While on an earlier expedition, one of his campmates had approached him looking pale and drawn but, the naturalist recalled, "with the fire of decision burning in his eyes." "Cherrie, lend me your revolver," the man had said. "What are you going to do with it?" Cherrie had asked. The answer had been quick and blunt: "Shoot myself." "I thought: is he desperate?" Cherrie later wrote. "Hysterical? Ill? Temporarily demented? I talked with him for a few moments; not going into details, but probing the soundness of his state of mind. Then I took the gun from its holster and handed it over. He killed himself that day."

Kermit and Cherrie were not the only members of the expedition to worry about Roosevelt. Dr. Cajazeira, although he had his hands full administering prophylactics and treating all of the expedition's nineteen men (including himself) for a wide variety of ailments, had begun to spend most of his days and nights hovering over his American commander. So closely did he watch Roosevelt that, in his official report, he dedicated an entire chapter to "Colonel Roosevelt's Health Status." On the afternoon of April 4, as the rest of the men tried to finish bringing down the last two canoes and the remainder of the provisions, Cajazeira and Roosevelt stayed behind at the camp. At about 2:30 p.m., while the two men were talking quietly, the doctor suddenly noticed that all of the color had drained from his patient's face and that he had begun to shiver uncontrollably. Cajazeira took Roosevelt's temperature and found that it was rising rapidly. Covering him as well as he could, he gave him another half-gram of quinine to swallow, "since by that time we were already deprived of almost everything including medications," he wrote in frustration.

Cajazeira wanted to move Roosevelt to a better camp than the makeshift one that they had set up amid the boulders the night before. He waited impatiently until the men finally finished the portage and, at 5:00 p.m., reloaded the canoes—with Roosevelt, Rondon, and Cajazeira riding in the largest—and were ready to set off downriver in search of a new campsite for the night.

As an added precaution, in case Julio was still lurking about, the men decided to cross the river to the right bank. They had no sooner launched their four dugouts, however, than it began to rain. The downpour was the hardest they had had in several days, and it flooded forest and river, "drenching most of us to the skin," Cherrie wrote in his diary that night. Cajazeira wrapped Roosevelt in his waterproof poncho, but the men had no way to fit their rough canoes with awnings. By the time they crossed the river and found another camp-site, half an hour later, Roosevelt's temperature had skyrocketed to 103 degrees, and he was, in Cajazeira's words, "restless and deliri-ous."

Roosevelt's condition continued to deteriorate at such a fast rate that Cajazeira began to inject quinine directly into his abdomen. Every six hours, the doctor would open his wooden medical box, which was covered with a spotted animal skin and swung on a heavy hinge, pull out his silver syringe, and give his patient another half-gram injection. Despite all his efforts, however, Roosevelt's fever stub-bornly refused to abate, his temperature falling by "only a few fractions of a degree," Cajazeira noted with dismay.

That night, while the camaradas lay wound up in their cocoon-like hammocks under dripping palm leaves and a black sky, the officers took turns watching over Roosevelt in their tiny, thin-walled tent. As his temperature once again began to rise sharply, Roosevelt fell into a trancelike state, and he began to recite over and over the opening lines to Samuel Taylor Coleridge's rhythmic poem "Kubla Khan": "In Xanadu did Kubla Khan a stately pleasure-dome decree. In Xanadu did Kubla Khan a stately pleasure-dome decree. In Xanadu . . ."

* * *

As the night wore on, Roosevelt slipped in and out of consciousness. One moment he was looking directly at Kermit and asking him if he thought that Cherrie had eaten enough to keep going, and the next he had forgotten his son's presence entirely and was feverishly murmuring to himself, "I can't work now, so I don't need much food, but he and Cherrie have worked all day with the canoes, they must have part of mine." While Kermit tried to calm and reassure his father, he felt a soft tap on his shoulder and turned to find Cajazeira, who had pulled himself out of a deep sleep to relieve the young man.

At about 2:00 a.m., Rondon, in turn, relieved Cajazeira, taking his place next to Roosevelt's sagging cot. Although still determined to fight to the last for Kermit's sake, Roosevelt, in his few lucid moments that night, realized that he was so sick he might not be able to keep the promise he had made to himself and his son. He wanted one thing from Rondon now: reassurance that, if he fell into a coma, his co-commander would do the right thing and keep going. Glassy-eyed and bathed in sweat, Roosevelt turned to Rondon and said, "The expedition must not stop. . . . Go, and leave me here."

It wasn't until the sun had begun to wash over the treetops, turning them from black to gold to green, that Roosevelt's fever finally broke. The men's relief was heavy and universal, but not complete. Roosevelt had come so close to death that night that no one was willing to take any chances with his health. Rondon immediately ordered the camaradas to prepare to find yet another new campsite. They had run into more rapids at the end of the previous day and would probably spend most of this day trying to get around them, but Rondon pronounced last night's camp too wet and muddy for Roosevelt and insisted that they move.

As it turned out, the best spot they found for a new campsite required a walk of half a mile. Although he was much improved from the night before, Roosevelt was still very weak, and his fever hovered around 101 degrees. Cajazeira planned to have some of the camaradas carry him to the next camp on his cot, but Roosevelt refused to be carted through the forest like a king—or an invalid. "As soon as Colonel Roosevelt learned of our decision, he opposed it strongly, finally stating that he did not want to become a heavy burden on the expedition," Cajazeira wrote. Helped along on quivering legs, Roosevelt slowly made his way to the next camp—Kermit, Cherrie, Cajazeira, and Rondon at his side with his cot and collapsible chair. "From time to time, when he became very tired, he would rest either on his bed or chair," Cajazeira would later recall. "And so he bravely made the journey."

While Kermit obsessed over his father's health, his emotions rising and falling with each rally and relapse, the younger Roosevelt steadfastly ignored his own. He was suffering from a renewed attack of malaria, but he refused to admit how sick he was, continuing to work as though his hands weren't trembling, his body wasn't smoldering, and his head wasn't reeling. "I have fever," he admitted in his diary, "but not very bad."

So determined was Kermit to soldier on that he did not allow himself a moment of rest. He spent the morning helping the camaradas get the dugouts through the rapids. Later, when Antonio Pareci rushed into camp shouting excitedly that there were monkeys nearby, Kermit and Cherrie were the first to grab their rifles and race after him. They quickly spotted the animals—large woolly monkeys that were swinging through the treetops "with surprising speed," Cherrie wrote. Notwithstanding the monkeys' distance and agility, however, together Cherrie and Kermit were able to bring down three of them. Kermit also caught a side-neck turtle, which has an unusually long neck that folds sideways under its shell rather than pulling straight back, and he brought it back to the camp for Franca to boil into soup.

Despite his fever, Kermit even joined Rondon and Lyra as they hiked downstream to try to find out what awaited the expedition. What they saw was worth the difficult trip. "I found," Kermit reported, "that after these rapids we're out of the hills." The men had allowed themselves to believe that prediction in the past, only to be bitterly disappointed when new mountains, and new rapids, had risen up behind a sharp bend in the river, but whether Kermit was right or not, the hopeful news was welcome. "The fresh meat we all craved gave us renewed strength and energy," Cherrie would later write, "and the fact that the mountains that had for so long hemmed us in seemed at last to be falling away from the river brought us new courage."

The next day, April 6, had a promising start as well. The men were finally beginning to feel as if they could predict, if not control, the dangers they might face downriver. To their delight, the hills began to drop away, just as Kermit had said they would, and the river slowly widened into a spacious bay. "For the most part our course was over the scarcely rippling surface of a broad quiet stream," Cherrie wrote in his diary.

The expedition was finally leaving Paishon's sorrowful canyon. As the land leveled and the waters smoothed, the men were able to step back into their canoes and ride for the first time in a long time. The low, heavily forested terrain on either side of them melted into an impressionistic wash of green and brown as Rondon and Lyra rode the racing current. Unencumbered by cataracts or whirlpools, they were finally free to turn their full attention to their survey, cleaning their instruments, taking measurements, and making notes on the river's gently winding course. As they bent over their work, the two men were startled by a man's voice calling to them from the left bank.

The cry—"Senhor Coronel!"—hung, heavy with desperation, in the thick, wet air. Rondon looked up to find a dark figure clinging to a broad tree branch that leaned far out over the river. After a moment of startled confusion, he finally recognized the powerful physique. It was Julio.

CHAPTER 26

Judgment

EVEN RONDON WAS SHOCKED by how pathetic Julio looked, crouching in the gnarled tree like a frightened animal, "imploring for mercy and asking us to receive him on board." Three nights alone in the jungle would have taken their toll on any of the men, but they had been especially excruciating for Julio. By now, the members of the expedition knew that, second only to wrath, fear was the muscular young Brazilian's most powerful emotion. He was, Roosevelt wrote, "an arrant craven at heart, a strange mixture of ferocity and cowardice."

If Julio had expected Rondon to brim with compassion and mercy at the sight of him, he did not know his commander. "It is not possible for me to stop the canoe now, and to interrupt the survey," he called coldly to the desperate man. "Besides, it is best to wait for Mr. Roosevelt." Having said all that he had to say, Rondon returned his attention to his survey charts, and Julio watched in horror as the river swiftly carried his commander's canoe downstream.

The reaction Julio received from the men in the three dugouts that followed gave him less hope than even his encounter with Rondon.

They refused to look at the murderer, much less help him, passing by his tree in stony silence. Although they felt that Julio deserved a harsh punishment for the crime he had committed, they shuddered to imagine his fate. "Surely that murderer was in a living hell," Roosevelt wrote, "as, with fever and famine leering at him from the shadows, he made his way through the empty desolation of the wilderness."

Seated in different dugouts and separated by several yards on a fast-moving river, Roosevelt and Rondon were unable to discuss Julio's reappearance until they reached the next camp. Some seven miles after they passed Julio, the men came upon a large tributary that entered the River of Doubt from the right-hand side, and decided to camp in the protected corner of land formed by the two rivers.

Roosevelt knew that his co-commander would want to survey the new river, and Rondon knew that Roosevelt would object to the delay that such a survey would necessitate. That night, after the camaradas had cleared a spot for the campsite and set up the officers' single tent, Rondon sat down with the ailing ex-president and told him that he wanted the expedition to pause in order to send some men back to look for Julio. Both Roosevelt's and Kermit's temperatures had risen again during the day, and they were feeling feverish and weak. But they remembered how Rondon had slowed the boat building a few weeks earlier so that Lyra could determine the latitude, and neither of them believed his story now. "Rondon," Kermit wrote in his diary that night, "vacillated about Julio with 100 lies. He wants to wait to take the latitude but F[ather] won't let him."

The next morning, with Lyra by his side, Rondon took up his case again, never mentioning the survey, and focusing all of his arguments on the question of locating Julio. He argued that it was "the duty of a Brazilian officer and of a man" to do all that he could to find Julio and bring him back to civilization so that he could be tried for murder. Brazil did not have capital punishment, but even if it had, a government-orchestrated execution would be infinitely more merciful than the horrors Julio faced alone in the jungle. Even knowing all of this, the American officers did not want to take Julio back, and they were outraged by Rondon's suggestion that they lose an entire day of travel to search for him. "What was our astonishment to hear Col. Rondon announce that he intended remaining in the camp for the day!" Cherrie railed in his diary. "And that he intended to send a couple of men back to look for the murderer Julio! . . . This resolution on Col. Rondon's part is almost inexplicable in the face of facts regarding our own position. Our food supply is growing alarmingly less. . . . Furthermore our four canoes are already loaded to the limits. . . . From our point of view this delay and the trying to carry a prisoner places in jeporday [sic] the lives of every member of the party."

Laced with suspicions of ulterior motives, and fueled by the expedition's desperate circumstances, the argument that ensued between the Brazilian and the American officers over Julio was so heated that it fractured the bond, born of a shared sorrow and renewed sense of common purpose, that had formed among all of the men after Paishon's murder. When he and Roosevelt locked horns over the murderer's fate, Rondon would later write, "the clash was tremendous."

Roosevelt regretted that they "could not legally put [Julio] to death" themselves, but, as Rondon had made it clear that that was not an option in his country and under his watch, Roosevelt insisted that the only thing left to do was to abandon the camarada to his fate. "If we brought the murderer in he would have to be guarded night and day on an expedition where there were always loaded firearms about, and where there would continually be opportunity and temptation for him to make an effort to seize food and a weapon and escape, perhaps murdering some other good man," he argued. "Whether the murderer lived or died in the wilderness was of no moment compared with the duty of doing everything to secure the safety of the rest of the party." The idea of wasting any more time, energy, or provisions searching for a murderer seemed almost criminal to Roosevelt. Finally, boiling with anger, frustration, and fever, he shouted at Rondon, "The expedition is endangered!"

However, Roosevelt knew that this was not his decision to make. "He, Colonel Rondon, was the superior officer of both the murderer and of all the other enlisted men and army officers on the expedition, and in return was responsible for his actions to his own governmental superiors and to the laws of Brazil," Roosevelt wrote. "In view of this responsibility he must act as his sense of duty bade him." As soon as his co-commander stepped aside, Rondon ordered two camaradas, Antonio Pareci and Luiz Correia, to hike back up the river and look for Julio.

As the Americans had bitterly predicted, Rondon and Lyra spent that day, April 7, surveying the new tributary and determining the latitude of the Rio Roosevelt. "To take the greatest advantage possible of the stoppage which had been imposed upon us," Rondon would later write, "Lieut. Lyra and I occupied ourselves with the measurement of the rivers and the necessary astronomical observations for the calculation of the geographical coordinates of our position." When Roosevelt suggested that they also use the time to hike ahead to see what the expedition would face downriver, Rondon dismissed the idea as an unnecessary effort. Cherrie, who had become deeply frustrated with his Brazilian commander, an emotion expressed almost nightly in his diary, was once again outraged. "Today Col. Rondon did not even think it necessary to 'explore' ahead the rapids whose roar we hear!" he wrote in the simple paper-and-cardboard notebook that he used as a journal. "And only after Kermit and Col. Roosevelt had protested was Antonio Correia sent ahead to make an examination."

When the camarada returned later in the day, it was with a grim report. Although they had had smooth water and level land the previous day—traveling twenty-two miles, the greatest distance the expedition had yet to make in a single day on the River of Doubt—they would face another difficult series of rapids and falls soon after they launched their boats again the next morning. "It may well be that we are 'up against it' again and good and hard," Cherrie wrote in his diary.

However, as well as bringing bad news back with him, Antonio Correia also returned with dinner: a particularly large Amazonian catfish called a pirarara. The men were thrilled, because the beautiful pirarara, which flashed a bright-orange tail and bore a massive, bony head, was not only huge, measuring three and a half feet long, but was, in Cherrie's words, a "very good flavored fish." When they began to clean the catfish, however, the men were in for a surprise: Slicing open its belly, they found the head and arm of a monkey. "We Americans were astounded at the idea of a catfish making prey of a monkey," Roosevelt wrote, speculating that the monkey had probably been "seized while drinking from the end of a branch; and once engulfed in that yawning cavern there was no escape."

Although the pirarara was a powerful fish, it is more likely that it had taken advantage of a rare opportunity and devoured an already dead monkey that had fallen into the river than that it had caught the animal alive. The idea of a fish catching its lunch on the banks of the river rather than inside it, however, was not beyond the realm of possibility in the Amazon, as the high-jumping arawana, or water monkey, proved.

For the Brazilians, such fish were fairly common and of little interest compared with another, even larger fish, the piraíba, which, they told their American companions, preys on men. The piraíba, which has been known to grow to nine feet in length and weigh more than three hundred pounds, is a bottom dweller, rising up from the murky depths to surprise its prey. Cajazeira himself had examined a piraíba that had been killed by two machete-wielding fishermen after, they claimed, the fish had lunged at them with open mouth and attempted to attack them. He told the men of the expedition that, because of its ability to wage a sneak attack, swimmers feared the catfish even more than caimans, which they could usually see and so had a better chance of avoiding. Rondon agreed with the doctor, adding that, in many of the villages he had visited along the banks of the lower Madeira River, the people had gone so far as to build stockades in the water just so they could have a place to bathe and swim without fear of an attack from piraíba.

Night had fallen by the time Antonio Pareci and Luiz Correia returned from their search for Julio. As they stumbled into camp, it was immediately apparent to every man in the expedition that they were not only exhausted and hungry, but alone. Although they had spent all day looking for the fallen camarada—calling his name, firing their rifles, and building fires in the hope that the smoke would help him find his way to their little makeshift camp—they never even caught sight of him.

*   *   *

THE MEN concluded that Julio must have decided to try his luck with the Indians who had attacked Rondon and Lobo. "It was questionable whether or not he would live to reach the Indian villages," Roosevelt wrote, "which were probably his goal." Julio may have been better off trying to survive another night in the jungle alone than turning to the Cinta Larga for help. Like any inhabitant of the rain forest, the Cinta Larga did not coddle the weak or the vulnerable. Physical strength and self-sufficiency were prerequisites to surviving in their world. Julio's presence, moreover, would have posed an unacceptable risk to the Indians. The simple fact that he would have had to walk into one of their villages or hunting camps as an unannounced stranger would have placed him in grave danger.

According to one account, many years later, one of the first outsiders known to seek help from the Cinta Larga was an English engineer who had become lost in the jungle and had stumbled upon a Cinta Larga village when he was on the verge of starvation. Having nothing else to offer as a gift, he gave the Indians his only possession: his knife. The Cinta Larga took the knife and, in return, gave the man food. After watching him eat his fill, one of the Indians walked up behind him and slit his throat, killing him with the very knife he had given them.

CHAPTER 27

The Cauldron

EVEN AS THEY SPECULATED about Julio's fate, the nineteen remaining members of the expedition knew that they were not much better off than he was. They had a handful of advantages—ranging from weapons to supplies to sheer numbers—over the man that they had just abandoned to the jungle. Each of those resources, however, had proved to be far less valuable than they might have imagined before reaching the rain forest.

Their rifles, which they had assumed they could rely on to supplement their rations, had never fulfilled their promise. In a rare moment of foresight during the pre-journey planning in New York, Fiala had hired a company to pack the expedition's ammunition in zinc cases, a hundred rounds to a case, to protect it from the corrosive effects of the jungle's heavy humidity. Even an endless supply of bullets, however, would have done them little good, since they could find no game to hunt. The best shot that any of them had taken on the banks of the River of Doubt had been Julio's deadly accurate bead on Paishon.

So awkward and heavy were the expedition's dugout canoes that they were only slightly preferable to having no boats at all. Any hope that the men had found in the leveling landscape and smooth waters they had encountered upon leaving Paishon Canyon on April 6 was lost when they launched their boats again on the 8th. They encountered so many rapids that day that they made only three miles. The following day was even worse, allowing the expedition only fifteen minutes of quiet water between sets of rapids. "On the 10th," Roosevelt wrote wearily through the fog of his illness, "we repeated the proceedings: a short quick run; a few hundred meters' portage, occupying, however, at least a couple of hours; again a few minutes' run; again other rapids."

The rapids of the River of Doubt had destroyed six of their canoes in less than a month's time. The problem, Roosevelt realized, was as much the boats that they were riding in as the river that they were descending. "How I longed for a big Maine birch-bark, such as that in which I once went down the Mattawamkeag at high water! It would have slipped down these rapids as a girl trips through a country dance," he wrote. "But our loaded dugouts would have shoved their noses under every curl."

As for their provisions, the men were now eating barely enough to stay alive, much less to fuel the hard work that they had to do in order to get through and around the rapids. "My supper . . . consisted of one soda cracker and a small 'portion' of fish with a cup of coffee," Cherrie wrote in his diary. "Not a very hearty meal for a full grown man!" The officers did their best to supplement the camaradas' diet with food from their own ration tins, but they had too little to spare, and the delicacies that Fiala had packed simply stirred the appetites of the rugged paddlers and porters.

Cherrie suspected that this near-starvation diet was at the root of many of their maladies. "The lack of sufficient food is one potent reason why we are all physically below normal," he wrote. Cherrie and Lyra had been battling dysentery for weeks, and two of the camaradas were so ill that the others feared for their lives. "A long further delay, accompanied by wearing labor, would have almost certainly meant that the weakest among our party would have begun to die," Roosevelt wrote.

Roosevelt himself was at the top of that list, but his son was not far behind. Although Kermit rarely mentioned his malaria in his journal, Cherrie wrote that Kermit's fever was so bad that he was "scarce able to stand." Deeply concerned, Dr. Cajazeira began to inject quinine directly into Kermit's arms, but his fever continued unabated.

Kermit was so sick that he did not even notice when his dog, Trigueiro, leapt out of his dugout just as the paddlers pushed off from the bank. Trigueiro had been given to Kermit as a gift early in the expedition and had quickly become his closest companion. Kermit had even written about his dog in his letters to Belle, recounting their long solitary walks across the *chapadão* and how Trigueiro would wish him good night at the end of the day by thrusting his muzzle into his master's hand as it hung over the side of his hammock.

Despite Kermit's affection for Trigueiro, nothing could be done to retrieve him until the expedition found a place to camp for the night.

The men had traveled roughly two hundred miles by that point, but they still had at least two hundred more to go until they reached the fork in the river where, they hoped, Lieutenant Pyrineus would be waiting for them. Rondon's early decision to send Pyrineus up the Aripuanã to meet their expedition with new provisions had proved prescient and, if all went according to plan, could save their lives. After all that had happened to them, however, they could not feel confident that, if they did make it to the agreed-upon rendezvous point, Pyrineus and his party would be there waiting for them. The Brazilian lieutenant faced a difficult voyage of his own, and there were no guarantees that he and his men had reached their destination.

* * *

THE POSSIBILITY that they might not return home alive, once a remote and abstract idea, had become a corrosive, everyday burden for the members of the expedition. As the journey wore on, the

Amazonian jungle, which had never seemed welcoming, had begun to feel not just dark and dangerous but inescapably oppressive. It was a sensation that most outsiders who plunged into that dense, inscrutable wilderness experienced, and it left behind an indelible, almost violent impression. The Polish explorer and writer Arkady Fiedler wrote that, after he and his companions had spent months in the Amazon rain forest, "something began to go wrong in us. Coming daily into such close contact with the virgin forest we found, as so many other white men had found before us, that its grotesque forms and brilliant colours got on our nerves like a nightmare. It was stifling us; the whole exotic jungle became one gigantic cauldron of hatred and brutality."

For outsiders who are forced to spend lengthy periods in the rain forest, one of its most oppressive and frequently mentioned features is its relentless monotony. Although their boats were passing through a world of infinite variety, to the members of the expedition everything had begun to look simply green. The creatures of the Amazon had become such masters of disguise that all that the men could see on either side of the river was verdant leaves and heavy vines. H. M. Tomlinson, an Englishman who had traveled along two thousand miles of Amazonian rivers just a few years before Roosevelt's expedition, tried to explain this overwhelming sense of sameness by comparing the rain forest to the soaring sky and the endless sea. "The forest of the Amazons is not merely trees and shrubs. It is not land. It is another element," he wrote. "Its inhabitants are arborean; they have been fashioned for life in that medium as fishes to the sea and birds to the air. Its green apparition is persistent, as the sky is and the ocean. In months of travel it is the horizon which the traveler cannot reach."

The camaradas were deeply affected by the forest's stifling monotony, the river's myriad dangers, and their own dark fears, and the American officers charted their emotional decline with growing alarm. Cherrie discovered that a box of shells for his rifle had been stolen by some of the camaradas, who, he wrote in his diary, "doubtless thought the cans contained meat." As the expedition already had little ammunition to spare, the theft was a serious one. "My gun is thus rendered of little value for obtaining meat for our party," Cherrie wrote. Even more damaging than the loss of the shells was the blow to the trust between the officers and the camaradas. No one could blame Julio this time.

Rondon was willing to admit that physically his men were worn thin, but he continued to insist that mentally and emotionally they were as strong as ever. "No sign of mental depression was manifested in them and nothing could make us foresee the possibility of their losing determination to face and conquer new obstacles and resist the shock of the greatest misadventures and sufferings," he wrote forcefully. But Rondon was attributing to his men his own extraordinary fortitude, and expecting them to share his unshakable confidence that what they were doing was worth any sacrifice.

The rain forest did not depress Rondon because it was the only home he knew—more familiar to him even than his own wife and children. For the fever-wracked Roosevelt, however, it was nothing of the kind. Rather, the expedition was becoming an ordeal of inhuman proportions, testing his strength and resolve as nothing he had encountered in a lifetime of self-imposed physical challenges. When he wasn't too sick to sit up, Roosevelt sought comfort and distraction in the world that he knew best: his library. For his trip to Africa, he had spent months choosing the books that he would take with him, ordering special volumes that had been beautifully bound in pigskin, with type reduced to the smallest legible size, so that the books would be as light as possible. Roosevelt, Kermit wrote, "read so rapidly that he had to plan very carefully in order to have enough books to last him through a trip."

He had not had that luxury when preparing for his South American journey, however. "The plans for the Brazilian expedition came into being so unexpectedly that he could not choose his library with the usual care," Kermit noted. Among the books that had made it onto the dugout canoes for their river journey were Thomas More's *Utopia*, the plays of Sophocles, the last two volumes of Edward Gibbon's *Decline and Fall of the Roman Empire,* and Marcus Aurelius and Epictetus. "These and many others comforted me much," Roosevelt wrote, "as I read them in head-net and gauntlets, sitting on a log."

By this point in the expedition, Roosevelt had already read and discarded every book in his small traveling library and was desperate for new reading material. He finally resorted to reading Kermit's *Oxford Book of English Verse,* even though he was unimpressed by it. "The choice from Longfellow's poems appealed to him as particularly poor," Kermit recalled, "and I think that it was for this reason that he disapproved of the whole collection." After tearing through the book of English verse as he lay burning with fever, Roosevelt turned, with great reluctance, to the book of French verse, which he considered to be better than nothing, but just barely. "For French verse father had never cared. He said it didn't sing sufficiently. 'The Song of Roland' was the one exception he granted," Kermit wrote. "It was, therefore, a still greater proof of distress when he borrowed the Oxford book of French verse." Roosevelt read the book, but he complained so bitterly about it that his Francophile son finally threatened to take it away if he did not stop attacking his favorite works.

Kermit too found in his few remaining books some measure of escape from the monotony of the rain forest, but not from its dangers. On April 11, he finished reading *A Retirada da Laguna* by the Brazilian novelist Visconde de Taunay. The book revolved around Taunay's impressions of the War of the Triple Alliance, the five-year conflict that had devastated Paraguay and orphaned Rondon. Every time Kermit picked up the book, rather than being spirited away to some other world, he was reminded, in vivid, nightmarish detail, of the ravages of starvation and the consequences of stumbling into the unknown. The book was, he wrote in his diary that night, "a wonderful account but not cheering to read with our own provisions so low, and no knowledge of what's ahead of us."

More effective than books for Kermit, although in even shorter supply, was a bottle of Scotch that he and Cherrie shared when, in Cherrie's words, they "felt the need of spiritual help." The two men had actually started out with three bottles, but since they had taken "quite generous drinks," the first bottle had quickly disappeared. They were more conservative with the second bottle, but soon it too was gone. With only one bottle left and a seemingly endless river before them, Kermit and Cherrie treated the whiskey they had left with great care. "When we got the third bottle out on the first night," Cherrie would later recall, "we held it up and took a pencil and marked off: this is the 10th, the 11th, the 12th, 13th, 14th, 15th,—marked off the amount we could take from that. . . . You can imagine the marks were close together on the bottle."

* * *

LIKE KERMIT with his books, Cherrie enjoyed his whiskey but found little relaxation in it. With each passing day, the naturalist grew increasingly worried about the expedition, and he bristled at every decision that seemed to him to endanger it further. He continued to blame Rondon for most of the expedition's woes, venting his fury in the pages of his journal at night. But even Cherrie's friends were not exempt from his criticism. On April 11, the day after Trigueiro had leapt from Kermit's canoe and disappeared into the jungle, Cherrie was appalled to learn that the expedition was stopping so that they could send two men back up the river to search for Kermit's dog. "Personally I feel this was a great mistake on Col. Roosevelt's and Kermit's part, when we are so anxious to get ahead," Cherrie wrote. His disapproval only deepened as the day wore on and the men did not return. Finally, at almost 5:00 p.m., the camaradas stepped into camp with Trigueiro at their side.

An entire day had been lost to searching for Kermit's pet. The camaradas must have wondered what kind of people go to such lengths to rescue a dog but intentionally abandon a man to certain death in the wilderness. Cherrie simply thought that it was a waste of precious time and, more important, that it sent the wrong message to Rondon about their willingness to linger in the rain forest. "A precedence is established of which our companions will doubtless avail themselves when again they may wish to stop for a day or part of a day!" he complained in his diary.

By the end of the day, however, the delay had also yielded a piece of exceptionally good news. While waiting for the two searchers to return with Trigueiro, Luiz Correia had taken one of the dugout canoes and gone fishing along the opposite side of the river from the expedition's campsite. "As he worked his way along the shore," Cherrie wrote excitedly, "[he] found a place where a bejuca had been cut off with a knife or an ax!"

Not only did the use of a metal tool indicate that a rubber-tapper rather than an Indian had cut the vine, but it was obvious to Correia that whoever had done the cutting had been sitting or standing in a canoe rather than on the riverbank. Having gone this long without seeing anyone else on the river, the members of the expedition knew that the Indians who lived along its banks were not, as Cherrie put it, "canoe Indians"—making it all but certain that rubber-tappers had reached this far up the river in boats.

This was the first mark of the outside world that the men had seen since they had launched their dugouts on the River of Doubt a month and a half earlier. It was a sign of hope—a sign that salvation lay within reach.

PART SIX

Deliverance

The Rubber Men

IF THE DISCOVERY OF a knife-cut vine offered the men the first tangible sign that they might yet emerge from the rain forest alive, it did not provide any immediate relief. On the contrary, it raised the possibility of a new danger associated with the region that they were approaching—a no-man's-land between unmapped jungle and the Amazon's rough pioneer civilization.

The penetration of outside pioneers into the Amazon had been far from organized or peaceful, centering on rough, impoverished rubber-tappers, or *seringueiros*. Those tappers who had reached this far up the River of Doubt were likely alone, afraid, and in dangerous straits themselves. In approaching their huts from upriver, moreover, the members of the expedition were crossing the frontier from the wrong direction. The only humans the settlers expected to see coming from the river's headwaters were hostile Indians, and they would do whatever they felt was necessary to defend themselves.

Seringueiros were, by default, the true settlers of Brazil's interior. When Henry Ford had introduced the Model T in 1908, the Amazon had been the world's sole source of rubber. The wild popularity of these automobiles, and the seemingly insatiable demand for rubber that accompanied them, had ignited a frenzy in South America that rivaled the California gold rush. In *The Sea and the Jungle,* H. M. Tomlinson complained that the only thing Brazilians saw in their rich rain forests in 1910 was rubber. "It is blasphemous that in such a potentially opulent land the juice of one of its wild trees should be dwelt upon . . . as though it were the sole act of Providence," he wrote. "The passengers on the river boats are rubber men, and the cargoes are rubber. All the talk is of rubber." Two years before Roosevelt had set sail for South America, his friend the great American naturalist John Muir had been similarly astonished by the rubber lust that he had witnessed as he traveled through the Amazon. "Into this rubbery wilderness thousands of men, young and old, rush for fortunes," he marveled, "half crazy, half merry, daring fevers, debilitating heat, and dangers of every sort."

By the time Roosevelt reached the Amazon, the dangers were still there but the promise of riches had all but disappeared. The bottom had dropped out of the South American rubber boom in 1912, when the Amazon lost its lock on the market. Thirty-six years earlier, an Englishman named Henry Wickham had smuggled *Hevea brasiliensis* seeds, the most popular species of Amazonian rubber tree, out of Brazil. Those seeds had then been cultivated at Kew Gardens, and the British had eventually planted their predecessors in tropical Malaysia. There, far from their natural enemies, the trees could be planted in neat rows with no fear that a blight would destroy the entire crop, as it likely would have done in South America. Labor in Malaysia was also not only cheap but readily available, and much more easily controlled. So successful had been the transfer of rubber trees to the Far East that by 1913 Malaya and Ceylon were producing as much rubber as the Amazon.

Because of the cost in time-consuming experimentation and the difficulty of finding reliable labor, very little effort had been made even to try to cultivate rubber trees in South America. Brazilian tappers, therefore, had to live where the trees did. In order to find untapped trees and claim a small slice of land as their own, they had to keep moving deeper into unexplored territory. By the time Roosevelt's expedition descended the River of Doubt, the *seringueiros* had become the point of intersection between the Amazonian wilderness and the outside world.

Settling the Amazon, however, was even more perilous than settling the American West. Not only was it a difficult, lonely life, but it was an almost impossible job. A man could do little more than clear a pocket of land just large enough to hold his own small hut and a subsistence garden. The death rate was dismally high. Many of the dangers that the members of the expedition had faced since setting off on their river journey were a part of the *seringueiros'* daily existence. Not surprisingly, the life of the *seringueiro* appealed to only the most desperate of men. "Such a man," Roosevelt wrote, "the real pioneer, must have no strong desire for social life and no need, probably no knowledge, of any luxury, or of any social comfort save of the most elementary kind." He must also be willing to spend most of every day alone in the jungle.

The *seringueiro*'s day started before the sun rose, when he stumbled through the black forest carrying a curved knife and wearing the kind of headlamp that miners rely on as they descend into the bowels of the earth. As the tapper pushed through the dense vegetation, he could see only a few feet in front of him. Everything beyond, beside, or behind the arc of his headlamp was cloaked in absolute darkness. Even in the full light of day, the trails that he had blazed to his rubber trees were difficult to discern. In the predawn hours, with nothing but the thin, trembling light of his headlamp to illuminate the forest, they were all but invisible—as were the dangers that waited on branches, under fallen logs, and in the very air.

By 10:00 a.m., a typical tapper had visited between 150 and 180 trees, attaching small zinc bowls to the trees to capture the latex as it oozed out of the incision. He then had to retrace his steps in the afternoon, making his way through the steaming jungle to each tree so that he could collect the latex. When he returned home in the evening, more hot, miserable work awaited him. Hunched over a heavy, oily smoke that rolled from a palm-nut fire, he poured the latex onto a rough wooden spit that he turned over and over until it slowly coagulated in thin, even layers. It could take weeks of this relentless work to produce a single ball of rubber that was heavy enough—between 60 and 150 pounds—to be sold.

As difficult for the *seringueiros* as their hardscrabble existence was the knowledge that what little they had managed to build could be taken away from them at a moment's notice. They did not have anything other than squatter's rights to the land on which they lived and worked, and so were constantly vulnerable to the threat of a wealthier, savvier man sweeping into their territory brandishing a title to all that they had thought they owned. The *seringueiros* themselves, of course, thought nothing of taking land from the Indians who had lived on it for millennia. Besides Rondon, few Brazilians at that time believed that the Amazonian Indians had any rights at all, certainly not to something as valuable as land.

* * *

THE MEN'S jubilation at discovering the cut vine on April 11 turned into tense anticipation as days passed with no other signs of the *seringueiros,* and the expedition encountered one series of rapids after another—the kind of rapids that they had dared to hope were behind them. Then, on April 15, good fortune returned in what was, in Roosevelt's words, a "red-letter day." After launching their boats that morning and traveling for two and a half hours, the men spotted a rough plank affixed to a stake on the left bank of the river. Dizzy with excitement, they quickly pulled their dugouts over to investigate. They soon discovered that there were actually two markers, one on each side of the river, and burned into them both were the initials "J.A."

An hour later, they saw a house. It was a very simple house, made of palm thatch with a smaller hut next to it for rubber smoking, but there was no confusing it with the Indian huts that they had seen upriver. It was, in the eyes of the men, a herald of the outside world. "Shouts of exaltation went up from our canoes as this frail outpost of civilization met our eyes," Cherrie wrote.

The house belonged to a *seringueiro* named Joaquim Antonio, the tapper whose markers they had seen on the riverbank, and the belongings inside indicated that he had a wife and child. Much to the dismay of the members of the expedition, however, the house was deserted. Not only were the men eager to meet a rubber-tapper, but the sight of food stored inside was excruciating, because, without Antonio's permission, Rondon would not let them take even a single yam. "So none of the provisions were touched," Cherrie wrote, "although we were sadly in need of some things for our camaradas."

Little more than a mile downstream, a single small canoe appeared in front of them, carried along by the swift current like a fallen tree branch. The sight sent a rush of excitement through the four-dugout flotilla, but it was not excitement that burned in the chest of the *seringueiro* in the canoe. Looking up to find a line of dugout canoes coming toward him from the direction of the river's mysterious headwaters, Raymundo José Marques, an old black man who lived alone on the banks of the River of Doubt, turned his boat and paddled quickly toward the shore.

When Rondon saw Marques, he jumped out of his seat, snatched the cap off of his head, and began waving it like a flag, shouting to the *seringueiro* that there was nothing to fear—they were not Indians. Fortunately for the expedition, Marques did not disappear into the jungle as soon as he reached the bank. Instead, he stood at the river's edge and listened to Rondon. After a few minutes, he climbed back into his canoe and slowly paddled over to the strange flotilla. Upon reaching it, he tried to explain to Rondon the terror that had driven him ashore. "It was quite impossible for him to expect the arrival of civilized people descending the river from its source," Rondon later wrote.

Marques's description of the members of the expedition as "civilized people" only underscored how far the men still were from a settled area. To anyone who had not spent years in the wilderness, the men would have looked almost inhuman. After weeks of surviving on little more than a few bites of fish and a single biscuit each night, they were gaunt and hollow-cheeked. The clothes on their backs—the only clothing they had left—were in tatters, and wherever their skin appeared, it was bruised, cut, sunburned, and peppered with insect bites. They were filthy and wild-eyed from disease and fear, and their American commander was barely clinging to life.

*   *   *

BY THIS point, Roosevelt was so sick that he could no longer even sit up in his canoe. Neither, however, could he lie down. Each of the four dugouts was packed with men and supplies, and there was not an empty space in any of them. The former president had been reduced to painfully balancing on a row of hard-edged metal food canisters that had been covered with a mud-encrusted canvas sheet. The canvas would have been put to better use as a tent to shield Roosevelt from the tropical sun, but the camaradas had no way to rig it up in the tiny dugout. The best they could do was to place his heavy but crumbling pith helmet over his face, trading the glaring sun for suffocating black heat.

Not only was Roosevelt's pain intense, but he and the doctor both knew that if they did not reach help soon he would die. In the weeks since Roosevelt had injured his leg while trying to help free the trapped canoes, he had developed a potentially deadly bacterial infection, which thrives in a wet, warm environment. There was no more perfectly engineered growth medium for this infection than the rain forest.

When Roosevelt had sliced his leg open on the river boulder, the defensive barrier that the skin forms against outside bacteria had been broken, and there was little that Cajazeira could do to shore it up. The infection had spread rapidly, and by early April, Roosevelt was in grave danger. The skin around his wound had become red, swollen, hot, and hard, and a deep, pus-filled abscess had formed on the soft inner portion of his lower thigh. His blood pressure had dropped, and his heart rate had risen. As his temperature soared and he lay on his cot sweating and shaking, it was at times difficult to tell if he was suffering from another attack of malaria or enduring the agonies of his infection.

Cajazeira hovered over Roosevelt as though he were his mother, taking his temperature, cleaning and bandaging his wound, and injecting him with quinine. But the doctor had almost nothing with which to fight the growing infection. "We administered the palliative medication employed in these cases," he wrote. "Nevertheless, day by day his condition worsened and we started to become seriously concerned." If left untreated or treated inadequately, the infection could lead to blood poisoning and, ultimately, death. The best defense would have been an antibiotic, but even penicillin, one of the first antibiotics, would not be discovered for another fourteen years, and would not be widely prescribed until World War II.

Cajazeira wanted to operate on Roosevelt's leg, but Roosevelt was reluctant to undergo surgery. The Rough Rider was less concerned that the doctor would not be able to give him anesthesia of any kind (he had refused anesthetic during the operation on his left leg twelve years earlier) than that the operation would be performed in an environment teeming with bacteria and disease-carrying insects. "As was only natural, Colonel Roosevelt asked us to postpone surgery, hoping he would be cured without the need for such intervention," Cajazeira wrote. "We agreed, clearly explaining, however, that we did not believe in such an outcome."

* * *

So sick was the former president that, when Raymundo José Marques paddled over to the expedition, Roosevelt could not lift himself out of his canoe to meet him. His condition, however, did not diminish the old *seringueiro*'s awe when he learned that the ragged and stricken man he saw lying in the roughest sort of dugout canoe had once been the president of the United States. Astonished, Marques said to Rondon, "But is he really a President?" Rondon explained that Roosevelt was not president any longer but had once been. "Ah," Marques replied. "He who has once been a king has always the right of majesty."

Marques, who was among the poorest of the river's rubber-tappers, had no food that he could share with the starving men, but he did give them some valuable advice: Upon approaching a settler, he instructed them, they should signal their peaceful intent by firing one of their guns three times in a row and then blowing on a bamboo horn that he would give them as a gift.

The *seringueiros* who lived along the River of Doubt had had little more interaction with the local Indians than had the members of the expedition, but their fear was not theoretical. Most of the time the Cinta Larga remained invisible, revealing themselves to the settlers only in brief glimpses in scattered locations. They had, however, appeared to the tappers who lived along this stretch of the river on one occasion, and the result had been disastrous. A frightened *seringueiro* named Manoel Vieira who lived in a hut just below Marques's had met some approaching Indians with a rain of gunfire. Soon after, the Indians had responded in kind, riddling Vieira with poisonous arrows. "After this fact no other of such gravity had occurred," Rondon wrote, "but the rubber tappers did not deceive themselves with regard to the tranquility which they were enjoying. . . . The panic caused by our arrival clearly shows the degree of nervous tension in which those people live, constantly tormented by the expectation of seeing the warlike Indians springing forth from the wilderness."

As they continued down the river, the men were as agitated and high-strung as the settlers they expected to see at any moment. The rain began again, filling the bottoms of their dugouts with muddy water and drenching Roosevelt. Suddenly, out of the monotony of the river's sounds—the water sloshing against the side of his canoe, the occasional grunts of his men as they dug their paddles into the black river—a roar of elation erupted all around him. The men had spotted another house along the riverbank, and this time someone was home.

From their canoes, the men could see smoke billowing from the chimney and two small children playing outside. Before Rondon could snatch up his rifle and bamboo horn, the children had looked up from their games, noticed the expedition coming toward them, and disappeared into their house. A moment later, they reappeared with their mother at their side. Seeing his opportunity and hoping to reassure the woman before she panicked, Rondon fired three shots into the air and blew heavily into the old *seringueiro*'s horn. "Unfortunately," he wrote, "this precaution did not have the desired effect."

So deep-seated was the *seringueiros'* fear of the Cinta Larga that, when the mother of the two children looked at the expedition's weak and exhausted men, she not only saw fierce Indians in their place in the canoes, but believed she heard their war whoops echoing through the forest. Terrified, she scooped her children up into her arms and fled downriver, desperately trying to reach her neighbor's house, where she knew she would find her husband. Driven by fear and blinded by the rain, she stumbled along a rough dirt path that skirted the river's edge until she tripped and fell into a stream that bisected it. The men watched helplessly from their canoes, their efforts to reassure her only heightening her distress. "She succeeded in getting up with her clothes drenched," Rondon wrote, "and continued her wild race until she arrived at the house of a neighbour where she fainted."

As soon as she could talk, the woman told her husband, a rubber-tapper named Honorato, that their house was under attack by Indians. Believing that the confrontation that he had long feared had finally happened, Honorato wasted no time. He and three of his neighbors armed themselves, climbed into a canoe, and made their way upstream, prepared for a bloody battle. As they neared the house, the rain was still coming down and the sun had begun to set, but Honorato could see the fire that his wife had built in preparation for their evening meal, and he could see men standing just outside his door. He and the other men in his canoe silently pulled through the dark water until they reached the bank. Climbing through the soup of mud and half-decomposed leaves under their feet, they sought cover in the thick woods, where they could wait unseen until the moment was right to attack.

As the light of the fire flickered over the faces of the men who had invaded his home, however, Honorato began to realize that something was not right—these men were not Indians. This realization, and Honorato's willingness to step forward and investigate rather than take cover and shoot, very likely saved the lives of many of the men in the expedition that night. Stepping inside, Honorato found Theodore Roosevelt and Brazil's greatest explorer resting in his home while a group of starving and exhausted men made dinner over his wife's fire.

Although their first meeting had nearly ended in tragedy, the Honoratos and their neighbors proved to be extremely valuable to the men of the expedition. They were, Roosevelt wrote, "most hospitable" to their unexpected guests, and, as Raymundo Marques had promised, they agreed to sell the expedition provisions and two large canoes, and they helped them hire a guide. Honorato also explained to the men exactly where they were. The River of Doubt, the western branch of the Aripuanã, was known to the *seringueiros* as the Castanha—ironically, the Portuguese word for Brazil nut, the nuts that the men had searched so desperately for upriver. Even at this point, however, the river was not known to anyone but the settlers and Indians who lived on it. "It was astonishing," Roosevelt wrote, "when we were on a river of about the size of the upper Rhine or Elbe, to realize that no geographer had any idea of its existence. But, after all, no civilized man of any grade had ever been on it."

The Honoratos invited the men to spend the night at their home. It seemed, as Antonio Correia said to Kermit, "like a dream to be in a house again, and hear the voices of men and women, instead of being among those mountains and rapids." The reminder of all that they had missed over the past two months, and were missing still, was painful. Even the sight of a brood of chicks, hopping around the Honoratos' simple hut and pecking at the forest floor, stirred Cherrie to the core. "How nice it was to see them!" he wrote in his diary. "How it made me think of home."

Sitting outside after the first real meal that they had had in weeks, Cherrie and Kermit shared the scotch they had been saving to celebrate the first signs of deliverance from their river journey. As the alcohol slipped down their throats and filled their chests with a warm flush, they looked up into the dark Southern sky and saw the familiar outline of the Big Dipper suspended among the other stars. "Upside down to be sure, but how good it looks," Cherrie wrote.

* * *

WHILE THE men celebrated their warm reception by the rubber men, and savored the prospect of returning to their loved ones in the outside world, they understood only part of the good fortune that had brought them down the River of Doubt alive. As significant as their own efforts had been in triumphing over the churning river, and the unforgiving rain forest that surrounded it, the men remained unaware of the single most important factor in their survival: the decision of the Cinta Larga to let them go.

From the moment they had begun their river journey, their presence had been the subject of ongoing discussion and debate within the clannish communities of Cinta Larga that lined the River of Doubt, provoking a range of reactions from curiosity to fear to covetous fascination with their strange tools and clothing. The ability of Cinta Larga tribesmen to destroy the expedition and all its members was never in doubt. Despite their simplicity, the Indians' weapons were marvels of efficient lethality, refined over thousands of years of experience to kill silently and swiftly. If their poisoned arrows were not enough to dispense with Roosevelt and his men, every Cinta Larga warrior had a lifetime of practice with the war clubs that were carefully designed to dispatch any survivors with a single, savage blow.

The men of the expedition were armed with modern firearms, to be sure, but in the dark jungle at night, when the Cinta Larga preferred to surprise their enemies, there was little chance that Roosevelt or his men would ever have seen their attackers. From the moment they launched their boats on the River of Doubt, the expedition had repeatedly encountered signs of the Indians' presence—passing through their villages, discovering their trail markings, examining their arrows, even hearing their voices. But not once had they so much as glimpsed a single tribesman.

Like the other inhabitants of their rain forest, the Cinta Larga had worked for countless generations to perfect the art of disappearing in the riot of nature that surrounded them. For each member of the tribe, just like every other creature in the jungle, the advantage of concealment was a critical tool of survival that was painstakingly conserved and surrendered only when the payoff was large and certain. In a world of unpredictable, resourceful enemies, invisibility was not merely advantageous, but a matter of life and death. A single unguarded moment could be fatal, and the only look that an enemy was likely to get of a Cinta Larga warrior was a colorful flash of feathers and war paint before a swift and violent death.

The same preoccupation with concealment that made the Cinta Larga so terrifyingly invisible to the expedition, however, also reflected the underlying conservatism that all rain forest inhabitants must exhibit when confronted by new or unfamiliar events. The survival instincts of virtually all jungle creatures favor flight or concealment over attack, and the Cinta Larga were no exception. Weighed against the uncertain benefits of any confrontation with the expedition, the risks of undertaking such an action and exposing themselves and their villages to potential danger were great. This was especially true because the expedition appeared to be moving steadily through their territory, without posing any specific threat. It seems likely that the benign character of the expedition was also reinforced by Rondon's repeated attempts to reassure the Indians of his friendly intentions by leaving gifts for them at every opportunity.

From the start of the expedition's journey down the River of Doubt, these conflicting factors had produced a deep division of opinion between those Indian elders who wanted to kill the members of the expedition, and those who favored waiting to see if they would pass peacefully out of the Cinta Larga's territory without provoking a confrontation. Given the tribe's tradition that all decisions of war be made by consensus, the very existence of this debate became the thin thread on which the lives of Roosevelt and his men would ultimately hang.

As the men of the expedition looked up at the clear black sky above the River of Doubt, and marveled at the brilliant stars which pointed their way home, they neither knew nor likely even suspected who was actually responsible for their safe passage out of the jungle. In the dark, liana-draped trees that towered on all sides around the tiny wooden shack in which the men fell off to sleep, the warriors of the Cinta Larga—with painted bodies, hard bark belts, and poison-tipped arrows—slipped away as silently and invisibly as they had come. Obeying the timeless calculus of survival in the rain forest, they disappeared on swift bare feet into endless dark halls of leaf and vine. For their own reasons, and on their own terms, they would let these enemies live.

CHAPTER 29

A Pair of Flags

ACCORDING TO THE EXPEDITION'S *seringuero* hosts, it would take another fifteen days for the men to reach the confluence of the River of Doubt and the Aripuanã, where the men hoped that Lieutenant Pyrineus would be waiting. After they had spent a month and a half alone on the most treacherous and least known stretch of the river, another two weeks traveling through *seringueiro* territory might have seemed like a frustrating but relatively easy journey. If they could not catch food, they would be able to buy it, and if they lost another canoe, they could purchase one from a rubber-tapper. What they would not find, however, was a hospital, and fifteen days was a long time to keep alive a man as sick as Theodore Roosevelt.

In fact, none of the men—with the notable exception of the seemingly invincible Rondon—was healthy. Cherrie and Lyra had battled nearly constant dysentery. Kermit had fought repeated attacks of malaria. Half of the camaradas were so sick with fever that they could no longer work. Even those who were still on their feet, Kermit noted in his diary, were "working poorly and lifelessly."

Only a few of the men had "retained their original physical and moral strength," Roosevelt wrote. Fear, disease, and hunger had driven them to do things that they never would have done under any other circumstances. They had agreed to abandon one of their own to almost certain death in the jungle. They had stolen food from their fellow camaradas. They had scoured the forest in search of anything that might be even remotely edible. Just two days earlier, several of the camaradas had devoured some unidentified nuts that they had found while they were hunting and had become dangerously ill.

As sick as his men were, even Roosevelt himself had to admit that he was "in worse shape" than anyone else in the expedition. He continued to fight for his life for his son's sake, but he had no illusions about the gravity of his condition, and he had never faltered in his resolve that not a single life in the expedition be risked in an effort to save his own. "If I am to go, it's all right," he told Cajazeira. "You see that the others don't stop for me. . . . I've the shortest span of life ahead of any in the party. If anyone is to die here, I must be the one."

Roosevelt's condition had become so alarming and his pain had become so unbearable that, on April 16, he finally agreed to allow Cajazeira, the man he trusted most on this expedition after Cherrie and his own son, to operate on his leg. The operating-room floor was nothing more than the muddy soil of the riverbank. Using only the simplest of surgical tools and no anesthetic, Cajazeira sliced deep into his patient's leg, releasing a mottled mixture of blood and foul-smelling pus that had collected in the abscess. As the doctor worked to insert a drainage tube, swatting away the legions of piums and borrachudo flies that had been attracted to the stench, Roosevelt did not cry out in pain or utter a word of complaint. "Father's courage was an inspiration never to be forgotten by any of us," Kermit would later write.

* * *

WITH EACH passing day, the expedition's situation improved just enough to keep the men's spirits buoyed and their determination strong. They also had the good fortune of meeting a *seringueiro* named Barboso, a simple man with a "dusky cigar-smoking wife and his many children," who awed the men of the expedition with his generosity. Refusing any payment, despite his own conspicuous poverty, Barboso gave the men a duck, a chicken, manioc, and six pounds of rice. He also lent them a boat—doubtless one of his most valuable possessions—and accepted in return one of the poorly constructed dugouts they had made themselves. Two days later, the expedition was able to gain another boat by trading two more of its dugouts to *seringueiros* it met along the river.

With a local rubber-tapper to guide them, new canoes to carry them, and plenty of food to sustain them, what the men needed most now was speed. Although the operation to lance Roosevelt's abscess had been successful, easing some of his pain as well as Cajazeira's concern, the former president was still dangerously ill. The bacterial infection had continued to spread, and he had developed another abscess, this one on his right buttock. "We did what was reasonable in such an emergency to prevent another abscess," Cajazeira wrote, "but to no avail."

Roosevelt's familiar fat-cheeked face and barrel-chested physique looked deflated, as if the journey had stripped not just strength from his body but years from his life. After months of deprivation and starvation, when the men had finally reached a place where they could eat all that they wanted, Roosevelt had little interest in eating anything at all. "He eats very little," Cherrie fretted in his diary. "He is so thin that his clothes hang like bags on him." In just three months, Roosevelt had lost fifty-five pounds—one-quarter of his original body weight.

In stark contrast to their American commander, the men of the expedition had difficulty restraining themselves when offered food of any size, shape, or origin. They rejoiced when they found a broken-down river store, even though its shelves were nearly empty and what little was there had been carted in nearly a year before. At exorbitant cost, the men bought and feasted on such luxuries as sugar and condensed milk. Several of the camaradas drank entire cans of condensed milk in long, sticky swallows. "In this land of plenty the camaradas over-ate," Roosevelt wrote, "and sickness was as rife among them as ever."

The only food that interested Roosevelt was some eggs that he found and ate raw in a dingy little shack where the men stopped for the night on April 23. "Our stopping place filth[y], wet, and dark," Cherrie wrote in disgust. "Pigs, chickens, and dogs contend for a place." But spending the night with the animals was better than sleeping in another downpour, and it was worth any price to see Roosevelt eat something, anything. After months of worrying about his father, Kermit was now obsessed with the thought that, after all they had been through, he might not be able to bring him home alive.

Concern over Roosevelt's condition increased the next day, when the expedition had to halt because of a long and treacherous series of waterfalls. These falls, known to the *seringueiros* as Carupanan, began with half a dozen rapids. Their guide could not help them here, and the men knew that if they were forced to stumble slowly and blindly through these rapids, as they had done dozens of times before, it would take them at least two weeks to push past Carupanan.

It was painfully apparent to his men that Roosevelt would not survive such a long and harrowing ordeal. Men much younger and stronger than he had died attempting to cross the Carupanan falls, and their buried remains still lay at the edge of the rapids, a sobering reminder that the expedition was not yet beyond the grasp of the River of Doubt. The men of the expedition, however, like the men who had come before them, had no choice but to take their chances in the falls. Ahead of them lay either death or deliverance.

*   *   *

AT THE top of the rapids, the men found a store that was owned by José Caripe, a man who, in Cherrie's words, reigned as "the 'king' of the rubber gatherers" on the River of Doubt. Caripe had begun his career as a lowly *seringueiro* but was now, through hard work and, presumably, hard dealings, a *patrão,* or boss. Most of the tappers along this stretch of the river worked for him, giving him rubber in exchange for tools and provisions from his store.

Caripe was exactly what the expedition needed. Roosevelt immediately recognized the Brazilian as his kind of man, describing him as "cool, fearless, and brawny as a bull." Not only was he a self-made man—working his way up from extreme poverty to relative power and wealth—but he had faced down the dangers of the jungle with courage and even bravado, proving himself to be almost Rondon-like in his invincibility, if not in his interests or motivations.

When he heard that the expedition was about to pass through Carupanan, and he saw the condition that Roosevelt was in, Caripe proposed that he himself should guide the men to the foot of the falls. They gratefully accepted his offer and were thrilled when he also gave them one of his own well-made boats in exchange for the last of their dugout canoes. With Caripe's guidance and the use of their three new lightweight boats, it took the men only a day and a half to pass through the series of rapids. Along those stretches of the river that were at all navigable, Caripe effortlessly guided them to the safest channels. Where the rapids were impassable, he showed them trails that had already been cut through the heavy jungle.

The Carupanan falls demanded several difficult portages, and it nearly claimed one of their new canoes, but in the end, the men lost only one member of their expedition: Kermit's dog, Trigueiro, who wandered off into the jungle while his master was busy preparing to run the boats through a set of rapids. It was a loss that, for Kermit, was particularly painful so close to the end of the journey. But in what had become an all-out race against time, nothing mattered now but getting Roosevelt to Manáos, where, his son desperately hoped, the ex-president's life might yet be saved.

* * *

ON THE afternoon of April 26, the expedition passed through a stretch of the forest that had been partially submerged. The dark, murky river, which was still swollen from the rainy season downpours, swirled around the thick tree trunks and swallowed whole the small islands that held them aloft.

Looking into the distance, the men suddenly saw a row of neat tents lined up along one of the banks. Standing among those tents were Lieutenant Pyrineus and the six men of his relief party, who had established their tiny camp at the confluence of the two branches of the Aripuanã six weeks earlier. Since that time, their fears had risen like the waters of the swollen river as day after day, and then week after week, had passed with no sign of their colonel and his expedition.

When the men on the river and the men on the shore finally spotted one another, shouts of joy rang through the forest, and rifle reports shook the leaves of the sunken trees. Lying under his makeshift tent, Roosevelt pulled himself up with quivering arms to witness his own rescue. What he saw before him were two flags outlined against a sharp blue sky. First, the green, gold, and blue of Rondon's beloved Republic of Brazil. Then, fluttering beside them, the stars and stripes that had for so long driven and defined Roosevelt's own life, and whose promise stirred him still.

Epilogue

O N THE AFTERNOON OF MAY 19, 1914, just three weeks after his expedition's emotional reunion with Lieutenant Pyrineus on the banks of the River of Doubt, Roosevelt triumphantly entered New York Harbor on the steamship *Aidan,* all flags flying. As he leaned over the deck railing, smiling his toothy smile, waving his big Panama hat, and, in a gesture for which he had become famous, vigorously shaking hands with himself, every watercraft in the harbor that had a whistle blew three long, joyful blasts.

Although Roosevelt's homecoming was an occasion of great joy for everyone from his wife to his children to the journalists who had followed him for decades, the sight of the former president, thin, drawn, and leaning on a cane—which he jokingly referred to as his "big stick"—came as a shock. He was, one reporter wrote, "brown as the saddle that formed part of his luggage," but his dark, tropical tan covered a face that had lost its youthful fullness and gained a network of new, deeply etched lines.

Physically at least, Theodore Roosevelt was not the same man he had been when he left New York nearly eight months earlier. Even Leo

Miller, who had endured dangers and deprivations of his own during his descent of the Gy-Paraná, had been horrified when he saw Roosevelt in Manáos, writing that his commander had "wasted to a mere shadow of his former self." For his trip from Manáos to Pará, Brazil, Roosevelt had been transported to his steamship in an ambulance and carried on board on a stretcher. He had stayed in his cabin for most of the journey, unable to talk above a whisper, and eating very little. It was not until the fourth day out that he was finally able to take a short walk on deck, but he had still needed help climbing down the ship's ladder when it reached Pará.

Once he was on board the *Aidan,* his appetite had improved tremendously—for books as well as for food. Not only did he regain twenty-five of the fifty-five pounds he had lost in the Amazon, but, in the one week that it had taken the steamship to travel from Bridgetown, Barbados, to New York, he read dozens of books. In New York Harbor, however, it was clear to everyone who had turned out to welcome him home that, while Roosevelt still had the same fighting spirit, he had lost his legendary vigor. When his oldest son, Theodore Jr., offered his father his arm to help him negotiate a gangway, Roosevelt rebuffed him, snapping, "I am all right. I can take care of myself." Every man present had been ready to offer the same aid, had Roosevelt been willing to accept it. "As he limped down the companionway . . . the impression was strong that the Colonel had endured the greatest hardships of his life," a reporter for the *New York Sun* wrote. "That was borne out when one of his friends remarked: 'I guess the Colonel will never take a trip like that again.' "

* * *

AFTER RECOVERING from the gravest and most immediate effects of his illness, Roosevelt had been eager to tell the story of his expedition's journey, but the scale of that achievement was so extraordinary that, to his surprise and outrage, he was met not with praise, but with skepticism and disbelief. Even before he had left his hospital bed in Manáos, some of the world's most prominent and respected geographers had stepped forward to question his accomplishment. Among the first to plant a seed of doubt was Sir Clements Markham, a former president of England's famed Royal Geographical Society and the man who had sent Robert Scott to the South Pole. Markham, whose area of specialty was South America, and who had traveled extensively through the continent, scoffed that Roosevelt's expedition "certainly is a very remarkable story." "I feel somewhat incredulous as to Col. Roosevelt having actually discovered a new river nearly a thousand miles long," he told a correspondent for the *New York World.*

A less eminent but arguably even more famous explorer, Henry Savage Landor, also attacked Roosevelt, even more directly and viciously. Landor, who had himself boasted of fighting his way through hundreds of miles of uncharted Brazilian wilderness—a feat that Rondon disputed—now called Roosevelt a "charlatan" and charged that his trip suspiciously mirrored Landor's own. "It seems to me he only copied the principal incidents of my voyage," he sneered. "I see he even has had the very same sickness as I experienced, and, what is more extraordinary, in the very same leg I had trouble with. These things happen very often to big explorers who carefully read the books of some of the humble travellers who preceded them. I do not want to make any comment as to so-called scientific work of Col. Roosevelt, but as far as I am concerned he makes me laugh very heartily, and I believe all those who have a little common sense will laugh just as much as I."

Roosevelt first learned of the attacks on his expedition when he was in Barbados. By the time he reached New York, he was incensed and determined to confront his detractors head-on. Several American geographers and newspapermen had leapt to his defense, including an editorial in the *New York World* that growled, "If the Colonel says the river is a thousand miles long, it's a thousand miles long. We wouldn't knock off an inch to avoid a war." Roosevelt, however, was the kind of man who fought his own battles. As for Markham, Roosevelt told the *New York Times,* the British geographer had "unconsciously paid the greatest possible tribute to what he had done." If his expedition had not been one of great importance, Markham would not have bothered to attack it. Landor, on the other hand, he dismissed as "a pure fake, to whom no attention should be paid."

These attacks on not just Roosevelt's expedition but his character only heightened the excitement surrounding the speech he agreed to give at the National Geographic Society on May 26. The society, which had fought hard—and, in Henry Fairfield Osborn's estimation, unfairly—for Roosevelt's first speech on the River of Doubt, had rented out Convention Hall, then the largest hall in Washington, D.C., for the event. Following a dinner at the New Willard Hotel, owned by Belle's father, Roosevelt rode to the lecture in a limousine— with Commander Robert Peary, the man credited with being the first to reach the North Pole, standing on the running board and leaning into an open window so that he could continue his conversation with the colonel.

As Roosevelt entered Convention Hall at 8:30 p.m., ten minutes late, an usher at the front of the auditorium caught sight of him and signaled his arrival by waving a white handkerchief. The audience leapt to its feet and erupted in thunderous cheers and applause. This was the only hall in Washington large enough to hold the society's five thousand invited guests, but it was far from luxurious. One reporter called it "dingy" and complained that it was "ill ventilated and situated on top of a huge retail market." It was also stiflingly hot on this, one of the hottest days of a notably steamy summer for Washington. As Roosevelt's venerable audience, which included everyone from ambassadors to Supreme Court justices to members of President Wilson's own Cabinet, awaited his lecture, the stench of rotting meat and vegetables thickened the air around them.

Also among the crowd seated in the auditorium were George Cherrie, Leo Miller, Anthony Fiala, and Father Zahm. Since their journey had ended, Roosevelt had done what he could for each of the men of the expedition. He had invited the camaradas into his cabin on the *Aidan,* saluting them as heroes and giving them each two gold coins as a parting gift. He had sung Colonel Rondon's praises everywhere he could be heard, ranking him as one of the four most accomplished explorers of his day. He had given Miller and Cherrie each a thousand dollars for their next expedition and had pledged to raise more. And, in an effort to soothe his friend Father Zahm's bruised ego, he had asked Gilbert Grosvenor, the chairman of the National Geographic Society, to give the priest a special seat on the platform next to him during the speech.

From the moment Roosevelt entered the hall, it was immediately apparent to his audience that he had yet to recover from the trials of his expedition. "The striking thing about Mr. Roosevelt tonight," one reporter wrote, "was that he looked tired, that his hands were cold and covered with perspiration and his voice weak. . . . His smile appeared to be forced and he gave the impression of a man who was being sustained by will power rather than by physical strength." Roosevelt, however, was also sustained by righteous anger. He was determined to set the record straight, no matter what the cost to his health. Asking the journalists in the audience to take careful notes, he snapped, "I want to call your attention to the fact that I am using my term to scientific precision, and when I say 'put it on the map,' I mean what I say. I mean that . . . [the River of Doubt] is not on any map, and that we have put it on the map."

The speech left Roosevelt's detractors mute. Despite the miserable conditions and the fact that Roosevelt was so weak that few of the men in the audience could hear a word he was saying—"I sat in the front row and could barely hear him," Grosvenor would later tell his son; "I don't think 30 people could make out his words"—not a single member of the audience left the hall during the entire hour-and-a-half lecture. After this speech, the New York Evening Journal reported the following day, "any doubts that still linger about the River of Doubt hardly are justified. . . . With a little piece of chalk Colonel Roosevelt has put the River of Doubt upon the map of South America."

Roosevelt's chance to face down his European detractors, from Markham to Landor to every chuckling newspaperman on the continent, came in mid-June, when he sailed to the continent to attend Kermit's wedding and speak before the Royal Geographical Society. As it turned out, Londoners were as eager to listen to what Roosevelt had to say as he was to be heard. Outside the front door of Burlington Gardens, five hundred men and women clamored to get into a hall that already held a thousand people and was equipped to hold, at the most, only eight hundred. Lifelong members of the Royal Geographical Society—each of whom had been guaranteed a seat at the lecture—were furious at being excluded, some even vowing to resign. A zealous suffragette held tight to the coattails of a reporter in an effort to gain entry, and one man burst into tears of frustration. Even Lord Earl Grey, a member of the Council of the Society who was to be given a place of honor on the platform with Roosevelt, was forced—much like Corinne Roosevelt Robinson at Madison Square Garden—to scale a stone wall in order to get inside.

Within the hall, every seat was taken, and the aisles were filled with the members of the council and their wives, who were forced to stand throughout the lecture. "All the benches and gangways were filled, the gallery was packed to overflowing, people sat on the front of the platform, crowded round the entrances, and occupied every available inch in their eagerness to see and hear Mr. Roosevelt," a reporter for the *Times* of London wrote.

In his opening remarks, Douglas Freshfield, the president of the Royal Geographical Society, concluded by quoting a "high testimony to Mr. Roosevelt and his companions," from Roosevelt's most notable critic, Sir Clements Markham. Markham himself had failed to appear, explaining that he was ill, but his note was a gracious, if indirect, admission of defeat. By the time Roosevelt had finished his speech—rich with tales of disease-carrying insects and man-eating fish and punctuated by his trademark high-pitched giggle, which sent his audience into roaring waves of laughter—nearly all of England had surrendered.

* * *

ROOSEVELT HAD won again. He had humiliated his enemies, defended his expedition, and restored his reputation. However, he still had one insidious foe: the fever and infection that had nearly claimed his life on the River of Doubt and which now refused to release its hold on his aging and overused body. When he docked in France, on his way to Spain for Kermit and Belle's wedding, he had "stepped briskly" and declared that he had never felt better in his life. By the time he left Europe, however, his fever had returned, and he had to admit to his old friend Arthur Hamilton Lee that he was "not in good trim."

Upon returning to the United States, Roosevelt got right back to work, writing dozens of letters and articles, attacking the Wilson administration, and giving speeches on behalf of the sinking Progressive Party. In May, *The Literary Digest* had written that he would have to "demonstrate his growing skill as an explorer and discoverer" if he hoped to find any remnants of the party that he had helped to found just a few years earlier. The Progressive Party loyalists, insisting that they had a bright future before them, had continued to resist the advances of the Republican Party. By 1916, however, the party had gasped its last, and most of its members quietly disappeared within the Republican fold.

The following year, Roosevelt's driving ambition turned from politics back to the military, and he became obsessed with leading a regiment to war, as he had done a quarter-century earlier. This time his sights were set on Europe and World War I, but President Wilson—perhaps simply believing him unfit for such a position, or perhaps fearing that his old rival would return home a reminted war hero and an unbeatable adversary in 1920—refused to let him go. Roosevelt's only consolation was that he had four young, healthy sons who could fight and, if necessary, die for their country. True to their father's ambitions and teachings, each son fought to be the first to get to the front. Each conducted himself honorably and bravely on the battlefield. Three were wounded, and the fourth, Quentin, who would always be Edith's baby, was killed.

The death of his beloved "Quenikins" devasted Roosevelt. Months after the news had reached him at Sagamore Hill, friends had glimpsed him alone in his barn one day, his arm around his horse's neck, sobbing. Death in battle was the kind of ending that Roosevelt had always imagined for himself, not for his sons, and his role in urging them to fight and risk their lives weighed heavily on him. Instead of dying in combat or on a remote, unexplored river, the ex–Rough Rider himself was destined to die slowly, ingloriously, and, for those who loved and admired him, far too soon. Early in 1917, Roosevelt had begun what was to be his final physical decline. He spent the month of February at Roosevelt Hospital in Manhattan, writing to Kermit that his ailment stemmed from his "old Brazilian trouble. Both the fever and the abscesses recurred and I had to go under the knife."

In October 1918, Roosevelt turned sixty years old. Although sick, frustrated, and brokenhearted over Quentin's death, he continued to fight, refusing to bow to the sorrow and grief that he had outrun his entire life. "When the young die at the crest of life, in their golden morning, the degrees of difference are merely degrees in bitterness," he had written to his sister Corinne. "Yet there is nothing more foolish and cowardly than to be beaten down by sorrow which nothing we can do will change." By November, he was back in the hospital, so ill he was hardly able to walk or even stand. When told that he might be confined to a wheelchair for the rest of his life, Roosevelt paused and then replied, "All right! I can work that way too."

He returned home to Sagamore Hill on Christmas Day. At 4:00 a.m. on January 6, 1919, James Amos, the man who had long been Roosevelt's loyal valet, awoke with a start from his chair near Roosevelt's bed, which had been set up in what had once been the family's busy second-story nursery. The sound that had awoken Amos was a hoarse, strangled breathing—the sound of Theodore Roosevelt dying. Amos alerted Roosevelt's nurse, who rushed to get Edith. By the time she reached her husband, he was already dead.

For the country that he had served and inspired for so many years, and which was still reeling from World War I, Roosevelt's death was as stunning as it was painful. The newspapers the next morning were filled with long obituaries, and pictures of the former president with his famous big teeth and pince-nez, but for most Americans his death still seemed impossible. A man like Roosevelt could never die. When John Burroughs was asked for a remembrance of his old friend and fellow naturalist, he spoke for a grieving nation when he wrote, "Never before in my life has it been so hard for me to accept the death of any man as it has been for me to accept the death of Theodore Roosevelt. A pall seems to settle upon the very sky. The world is bleaker and colder for his absence from it. We shall not look upon his like again."

*   *   *

OF THE men who had planned and led the descent of the River of Doubt in the spring of 1914, Roosevelt was not the first to die. Just three years after the expedition completed its journey, Rondon's faithful lieutenant and longtime companion, João Salustiano Lyra, drowned while attempting to survey the Rio Sepotuba, the river that Roosevelt and Rondon had steamed up on their way to Tapirapoan and the commencement of their overland journey. As the current swept him to his death, Lyra's last act was to throw his survey notebooks onto the riverbank so that they would be spared for posterity— a tribute to the teachings of Rondon, who had so often asked him to risk his life in the pursuit of a greater cause.

After his abrupt dismissal from the expedition, Father Zahm, the co-planner of Roosevelt's journey, continued to write about travel to distant lands, but never achieved the fame he had so long dreamed of. To the extent that his family name was to make headlines, it was his brother, Albert, rather than Father Zahm, who was to earn them, becoming a key figure in of one of the nation's most notorious attempts to rewrite history. As head of the Smithsonian Institution's aerodynamics laboratory, Albert Zahm became a principal proponent of the contention that the Smithsonian's former director, Samuel Langley, had invented the airplane before the successful flight of the Wright brothers' famous Flyer in 1903. The controversy generated by that claim—now widely discredited—so angered the Wrights that in 1928 Orville Wright chose to donate the original Wright Flyer to the Science Museum in London rather than permit it to be displayed in the United States. Only after a new regime at the Smithsonian retracted Zahm's claims was the Flyer finally returned to the United States in 1948. At work on a new travel book, Father Zahm himself fell ill and died at age seventy in Germany, and his body was returned to the United States for burial at Notre Dame, where a campus hall now bears his name.

Despite the many close calls of George Cherrie's adventure-filled life, he died in bed after a long retirement with his family on his beloved Vermont farm. After his expedition with Roosevelt, he continued his work as a field naturalist in South America for several years, collecting more than a hundred thousand birds over his lifetime. But the call to Rocky Dell had always been strong, and one day he finally went home for good. He loved fishing for brook trout in the stream that ran through one of his fields, tending his bees, and spending time with his grandchildren, who thought that he was "the biggest man in the world." He died at Rocky Dell in 1948, when he was eighty-three years old.

Only one man in the expedition lived longer than Cherrie. Despite the near-constant hardship and danger of his chosen career, Cândido Rondon lived to be ninety-two years old—thirty-two years longer than Roosevelt. Rondon's telegraph line, the central achievement of his life, was finally inaugurated on January 1, 1915, less than a year after he and Roosevelt had completed their journey. The telegraph line, however, was fated to fall obsolete in much less time than Rondon had taken to build it. The same year the line opened, radiotelegraphy found its way to Brazil, rendering unnecessary the copper telegraph wires that Rondon and his men had strung across eight hundred miles of the country's uncharted interior.

Like Roosevelt, Rondon returned home a hero and remained one

for the rest of his life. He was hounded by photographers and journalists, invited to meet the president of Brazil, asked to run for political office (an opportunity he repeatedly declined), and promoted first
to brigadier general and then, near the end of his life, to marshal. In
the 1920s, after meeting Rondon on a trip to Brazil, Albert Einstein
nominated him for the Nobel Peace Prize, and, in 1956, the Brazilian
government renamed a territory of ninety-four thousand square
miles—nearly twice the size of England—Rondônia in his honor. Two
years later, on January 19, 1958, having explored and mapped more of
the Amazon than any other man alive, and having made first contact
with dozens of isolated Indian tribes, Cândido Mariano da Silva
Rondon died in his own bed at his home in Rio de Janeiro.

Rondon today remains one of Brazil's greatest heroes, and his efforts on behalf of the Amazonian Indians have endured in the form
of the modern Indian Protection Service—the National Indian
Foundation, or FUNAI. In spite of all that he had tried to do for the
Indians he loved, however, the inroads he made into their territory
have had as devastating an impact on their survival as the rubber
boom. During Rondon's last years, in the 1950s, the path that he had
carved out of the wilderness for his short-lived telegraph line became
a road now known as BR-364. That road brought cattle ranchers, gold
prospectors, rubber-tappers, and adventurers of all grades into the interior, where they took Indian land and wiped out entire tribes. When
Rondon left the military academy in 1889, Brazil had been home to
roughly a million Indians. By the time he died sixty-nine years later,
fewer than 200,000 survived.

As the youngest American on the River of Doubt, Kermit Roosevelt
might have been expected to carry his father's legacy far into the
twentieth century. Yet somehow, for all his brilliance, courage, and
youthful Rooseveltian energy, he was never able to live up to his promise, or even his own expectations. Indeed, his death was so tragic that
the only measure of comfort his family could have found in it was the
fact that his father did not live to witness it.

The unraveling of Kermit's life began soon after he returned to

South America with his new bride. He took a job in Argentina with a branch of the National City Bank, but while building railroads and bridges in wild Indian territory had suited Kermit's adventurous spirit, banking in Buenos Aires did not. As the years passed, the young man who had once shown such promise and had impressed his father with his leadership skills and discipline became increasingly disaffected, able to cultivate an interest in little other than his wife and the son to whom she gave birth in Argentina—Kermit Jr., or Kim.

On January 6, 1919, Kermit was in Germany with the occupying army when he was handed a telegram sent by his brother Archie, who was home with severe war wounds. The telegram read simply: "The old lion is dead." Roosevelt had been a central figure in each of his children's lives, but he had been his second son's inspiration and moral compass. Without him, Kermit was lost. The next day, in a letter to his mother, Kermit confessed, "The bottom has dropped out for me."

Just as Roosevelt's only brother, Elliott, had been devastated by the death of their father, so did the death of his own father deliver a staggering blow to Kermit. His romanticism and quiet introversion had been warmly reminiscent of his uncle Elliott in his youth, but the similarities between the two men in adulthood were as striking as they were tragic. Like Elliott, Kermit never really found his footing in the world. He could not easily put aside his romantic adventures and ideals and take up his real-world responsibilities, as his father had.

Also like his ill-fated uncle, Kermit found himself turning more and more frequently to alcohol to take the edge off of real life. He often drank heavily with his brother Ted, but he was less able to hold his liquor—and less willing to stop. In the 1920s, at a party in honor of Richard Byrd, the American admiral who made the first flight over the South Pole, Kermit drank so much that he passed out, and was found the next day lying in a corner of the club. Finally, Archie had him admitted to a sanatorium against his will, just as their father had forcibly admitted Elliott to a French asylum half a century earlier.

Like everything else in Kermit's life, even the great love that had sustained him through his darkest days on the River of Doubt did not so much shatter as crumble, slowly eroding through years of neglect and betrayal. Belle's hard-edged social ambition and Kermit's dreamy, aimless approach to life left them both frustrated and sad. Kermit lost Belle's substantial inheritance after investing it in a business opportunity that failed during the Depression of the 1930s, and the couple was eventually reduced to renting out their Oyster Bay home and selling family jewelry.

Perhaps most painful of all for the proud, beautiful Belle, however, was Kermit's open infidelity. He carried out his affairs with the same unencumbered ease and shrugging disregard for the consequences not only to his wife and children but to his father's name, which seemed to pervade every aspect of his adult life. Although hurt and humiliated by the betrayal, Belle refused to let go. When Kermit disappeared in a drunken fog with his mistress, Belle asked Franklin Delano Roosevelt, her cousin by marriage and by then the president of the United States, to send the FBI to find him. When FDR committed the United States to World War II after the attack on Pearl Harbor in 1941, she asked him to give Kermit a military commission.

FDR sent Kermit to Alaska. It would prove to be his final adventure. At fifty-two years of age, just three years younger than his father had been when they had set out together down the River of Doubt, Kermit's body was so broken and ill-used that he could not do much more than sit at a local restaurant and drink wine. But he talked airmen into letting him ride along on their missions to bomb Japanese strongholds in the Aleutians, and he joined up with Muktuk Marston, a major who had organized Alaska's Tundra Army.

On the night of June 3, 1943, after making the rounds of Fort Richardson with Marston, Kermit turned to his friend and asked him what he was going to do after they returned to the post. When Marston told him that he was going to go to sleep, Kermit, haunted by all that he could have been and all that he had become, replied, "I wish I could go to sleep." He returned to his quarters alone and took out a revolver that he had carried with him during his days in the

British Army. Nearly thirty years after he had used his extraordinary physical and mental strength to prevent his father from taking his own life on the banks of the River of Doubt, Kermit, sick, tired, sad, and alone, was now too weak to save himself from that same fate. Feeling the weight of the cold, heavy revolver in his swollen and lined hands, he placed it under his chin, and pulled the trigger.

*   *   *

IN THE decades following Roosevelt's journey down the River of Doubt, others tried to duplicate his achievement. Soon after his homecoming, two expeditions set out to retrace his route. One was forced to turn back for fear of an Indian attack. The other disappeared as soon as it launched its canoes on the remote river, and its members were never seen again. It was presumed that they were all killed by the same Indians that had shadowed Roosevelt's expedition. Not until 1926 did another expedition, led by an American commander named George Miller Dyott, successfully descend the River of Doubt. Dyott returned to report that the river was just as Roosevelt had described it.

As the decades passed, the Cinta Larga Indians became increasingly bold toward outsiders. By the 1950s, they were attacking rubbertappers, gold prospectors, and settlements that had sprung up around the telegraph stations. At first, the objective of these attacks was almost always to acquire metal tools. As time passed, however, the BR-364, the road that had been constructed along Rondon's telegraph line, brought in hundreds of prospectors and adventurers who hated and feared the Indians, and who tried their best to kill as many of them as they could. The Cinta Larga's war against the outside world became a matter of self-preservation, a pitched battle against extinction. This time, the outsiders did not stop coming. They shot Indians on sight, dynamited their villages from the air, and left gifts of poisoned food on their trails. The Indians retaliated by attacking settlements, riddling men with arrows, and mutilating their corpses.

It was not until the late 1960s, more than half a century after the

Roosevelt-Rondon Scientific Expedition, that the Indians living near the River of Doubt had their first official contact with the outside world. So-called *sertanistas* from FUNAI—men who, modeling themselves and their ideals after Rondon, set out to find and pacify Amazonian Indians—tried for years to make contact, but by that time too much damage had been done. The Indians did not trust anyone outside of their own tribe, especially not white men. The *sertanistas'* advances were repeatedly repelled. The Indians kept their wives and children hidden, a clear sign of distrust, and defiantly mutilated a collection of dolls that the men had left for them as gifts. "Next day we found them ripped apart," a journalist following the *sertanistas* wrote, "the heads stuck on tree limbs, the bodies, skewered by arrows, lying beside the trail."

Steps toward pacification were slow and fearful on both sides, and when the moment of face-to-face contact finally arrived, it was fraught with emotion and heavy with the weight of two worlds colliding. This extraordinary meeting—the passing of gifts over what had seemed an unbridgeable divide—was chronicled in the pages of *National Geographic* magazine the following year, as an unarmed *sertanista* risked his life to reach out to a tribe that could easily have killed him. Standing in the rough clearing that the *sertanistas* had carved out of the forest as a place to leave gifts for the Indians, two terrified young men—one a nearly naked warrior, the other representing the Brazilian government—leaned forward, extended their right arms as far as they would reach, and exchanged gifts: a machete for a palm-frond headdress.

After the exchange was completed in silence, a series of clicks echoed in the jungle as fifty Indian warriors who had stood ready to attack withdrew their arrows from their bows. "In this manner," the magazine reported, "one of earth's last Stone Age peoples took their first fearful steps into a bewildering new world of men who know how to fly to the moon."

*   *   *

IN THE years since the Roosevelt-Rondon Scientific Expedition made
its journey, countless battles have been waged in the rain forest that
flanks the River of Doubt. Untold millions of creatures have been
born and died. They have multiplied, and they have protected, fed,
and fought for their offspring. Some species have begun to evolve to
become better predators and more elusive prey. Others have succumbed to extinction. To an outsider, this stretch of the Amazon, at
least, appears untouched and unchanging, but in the delicately balanced, constantly evolving reality of the tropical rain forest, nothing
ever remains the same.

The moment the men of the expedition pounded their camp markers into the riverbank, the Amazon began to dismantle them. The
rains expanded and warped their rough surfaces. Termites gnawed on
the soft wood. Animals and Indians carried them off for their own
uses. Even the elaborate network of fungus on the forest floor devoured the markers after they fell, reclaiming them for the jungle's intricate and tightly woven web of life. The simple tribute to Simplicio
that the men had left near the falls where the camarada had drowned
soon disappeared, as did the crude cross over Paishon's grave. Even
the brave soldier's bones were likely scavenged from their shallow resting place.

Among the most ephemeral marks the men left on the rain forest
were the ruts in the thin layer of leaf litter made by Roosevelt's cot as
he lay sweating and shaking, his voice fading in the early-morning
darkness as he instructed his friend and his son to leave him there to
die by his own hand. Had they done so, rather than resolve to find a
way to bring Roosevelt and all of the expedition out of the rain forest
alive, the former president's remains would have been scattered along
the River of Doubt—and used, like everything else in the jungle, to
protect and sustain the living.

But while the Amazon erased all evidence of the expedition, the
rain forest, the wild river that runs through it, and the former president who had led them left an indelible impression on the men who
survived. On March 1, 1919, not quite two months after Roosevelt's

death, the Explorers Club, a New York society devoted to scientific exploration, assembled at its clubhouse on Amsterdam Avenue for a memorial to the former president and fellow explorer. The club members, who included such legendary figures as Robert Peary and Roald Amundsen, invited George Cherrie to speak to them that night.

Cherrie, who felt more at home in a remote South American rain forest than he did in the rich, formal surroundings of the Explorers Club, accepted the invitation with the same wry reluctance he had felt when he had been offered a spot on Theodore Roosevelt's expedition six years earlier. Cherrie felt out of place at the black-tie affair, speaking before a gathering of some of New York's wealthiest and most powerful men, and was not convinced that he could do justice to his topic.

Stepping to the podium, his leathery skin and rugged appearance in stark contrast to the club's fine white linens, gleaming silver, and polished wood, Cherrie regaled his audience with the tales of hard adventure that were his trademark and life story. But when he came to the subject of Theodore Roosevelt, his demeanor noticeably changed, and the man who had once objected to "camping with royalty" struggled for ways to express the depth of his feelings about the former president, and their shared struggle for survival on the River of Doubt.

In the club's ornate hall, filled with mounted polar bears, Indian spears, and other trophies from across the globe, the aging naturalist became lost in the memory of a distant jungle, and a friendship forged at the limits of human endurance.

"I have always thought it strange," Cherrie said quietly, "since I had the opportunity to know him and know him intimately—because I feel that I did know him very intimately—how any man could be brought in close personal contact with Colonel Roosevelt without loving the man."

As he continued, his audience of dignitaries and socialites realized that the man before them—a man whose callused hands had fought off cavalry charges, smuggled guns, and catalogued nature's most dangerous mysteries—had begun to weep.

"I was in the consulate at La Guayra, Venezuela," the naturalist recalled, "when the Consul received the cable announcing Colonel Roosevelt's death. He handed it to me without a word.

"When I read that message," Cherrie said at last, "the tears came to my eyes. As they do now."

Notes

Manuscript Sources

Archives of the American Museum of Natural History, AMNH
Indiana Province Archives Center, IPAC
John A. Zahm Papers, CJZA, and Albert F. Zahm Papers, CAZA
Archives of the University of Notre Dame
Kermit and Belle Roosevelt Papers, KBRP
Library of Congress, Manuscript Division
National Geographic Society, NGS
Rauner Special Collections Library, RSCL
Dartmouth College Library
Theodore Roosevelt Collection, TRC
Harvard College Library, by permission of the Houghton Library, Harvard University
Theodore Roosevelt Papers, TRP, Library of Congress, Manuscript Division, Presidential Papers Series

Prologue

1. **"I don't believe"** George Cherrie, *Dark Trails* (New York, 1930), p. 250.
2. **"No civilized man"** Theodore Roosevelt, *Through the Brazilian Wilderness* (New York, 1914), p. 252.
3. **"The scene is vivid"** Kermit Roosevelt, *The Long Trail* (New York, 1921), pp. 74–75.
3. **As the fever-wracked** Ibid., p. 75.

CHAPTER 1: Defeat

7. **The doors were not scheduled to open** *New York Times,* Oct. 31, 1912.

8. **"Such unbounded energy"** John Burroughs, "Theodore Roosevelt," *Journal of the American Museum of Natural History,* Jan. 1919, p. 3.

8. **Before the doors even opened** *New York Herald,* Oct. 31, 1912.

8. **Men and boys** *New York Times,* Oct. 31, 1912.

9. **More than two thousand** Ibid.

9. **"For some unexplained"** Corinne Roosevelt Robinson, *My Brother Theodore Roosevelt* (New York, 1921), p. 275.

9. **"yelling their immortal souls"** *New York Sun,* Oct. 31, 1912.

9. **As Roosevelt passed by** Ibid.

10. **Inside the auditorium** *New York Times,* Oct. 31, 1912.

10. **Roosevelt, still famously** *New York Herald,* Oct. 31, 1912.

10. **The last time Roosevelt** Arthur MacDonald, *The Would-Be Assassin of Theodore Roosevelt* (Washington, D.C., 1914), pp. 11–12.

10. **Incredibly, Roosevelt's heavy** Stan Gores, "The Attempted Assassination of Teddy Roosevelt," in *Wisconsin Magazine of History* (Milwaukee, 1970), pp. 269–77.

10. **His coat unbuttoned** Oscar King Davis, *Released for Publication* (Boston, 1925), p. 382; Kathleen Dalton, *Theodore Roosevelt: A Strenuous Life* (New York, 2002), p. 404.

11. **At 10:03 p.m.** *New York Times,* Oct. 31, 1912.

11. **"Friends, perhaps once"** Ibid.

11. **"I know the American people"** Henry Fairfield Osborn, *Impressions of Great Naturalists* (New York, 1924), TRC.

12. **On election day** *New York Times,* Dec. 29, 1912.

12. **"a flubdub"** TR to Theodore Roosevelt Jr., Aug. 22, 1911, *The Letters of Theodore Roosevelt,* Elting E. Morison, ed. (Cambridge, Mass., 1951–1954), vol. 7, p. 336.

12. **"I suppose you will"** Quoted in Nathan Miller, *Theodore Roosevelt: A Life* (New York, 1992), p. 512.

13. **"Roosevelt goes down"** *New York Herald,* Nov. 7, 1912. (The article cites several different newspapers' editorials about the election.)

13. **"I accept the result"** Quoted in Hermann Hagedorn, *The Roosevelt Family of Sagamore Hill* (New York, 1954), p. 326.

13. **"There is no use"** TR to Arthur Hamilton Lee, Nov. 5, 1912, in *Letters,* vol. 7, pp. 633–34.

13. **Before the Republican convention** William Roscoe Thayer, *Theodore Roosevelt: An Intimate Biography* (Boston, 1919), pp. 387–88.

13. **"Many of his critics"** Ibid., p. 384.

13. **"The telephone"** Hagedorn, *Roosevelt Family,* pp. 327–28.

14. **Holed up at** Dalton, *TR: A Strenuous Life,* p. 408.

14. **"Of course I am"** TR to KR, Dec. 7, 1912, TRC.

14. **Roosevelt's family** Hagedorn, *Roosevelt Family,* p. 328.

15. **His sister Corinne** Robinson, *My Brother TR,* p. 1.

15. "regular, monotonous motion" Ibid., p. 50.

15. "One of my memories" Theodore Roosevelt, *An Autobiography* (New York, 1913), p. 17.

15. Desperate for their child David McCullough, *Mornings on Horseback* (New York, 1981), p. 94.

16. Finally, Theodore Sr. Robinson, *My Brother TR,* p. 50.

16. Early in 1879 Thayer, *TR: Intimate Biography,* p. 22.

16. "the best man" TR, *Autobiography,* p. 8.

16. "If I had very much" Quoted in McCullough, *Mornings on Horseback,* p. 187.

17. "Look out for Theodore" Quoted in ibid., p. 190.

17. He graduated Ibid., p. 222.

17. In 1884, however Edmund Morris, *The Rise of Theodore Roosevelt* (New York, 1979), p. 241.

18. "Black care" Theodore Roosevelt, *Ranch Life and the Hunting Trail* (New York, 1981), p. 59.

18. It was a transition George Washington, the United States' first president, had made a point of serving only two terms, and every president after him had followed that precedent. It was not until 1951, however, that the two-term limit was made official, by the Twenty-second Amendment, which Congress ratified after Franklin Delano Roosevelt—Theodore Roosevelt's distant cousin and nephew by marriage—was elected president four times in a row.

18. "Of course a man" Quoted in John Milton Cooper, *The Warrior and the Priest* (Cambridge, Mass., 1983), p. 118.

18. "My dear fellow" TR to Paul Martin, March 2, 1909, in *Letters,* vol. 6, p. 1541.

CHAPTER 2: Opportunity

19. "bringing together men" Emilio Frers to TR, Jan. 28, 1913, TRP.

20. Frers's words must Ibid.

20. Although Frers could not have "I have always felt a little uneasy on account of all you children because I have not made money," Roosevelt wrote to Kermit just days after the election. "It may be that my reluctance to do the well-paid things I am asked to do represents mere Quixotic fastidiousness on my part, for there is no moral wrong in them. But I shrink to a degree greater than I can express from commercializing what I did as President or the reputation I have gained in public service." (TR to KR, Nov. 11, 1912, TRC.)

20. "You blessed fellow" TR to KR, April 23, 1908, TRC.

21. Although he suffered TR to Anna Cowles, Nov. 11, 1913, TRC.

21. "I am greatly pleased" TR to Emily Tyler Carow, Jan. 4, 1913, in *Letters,* vol. 7, pp. 688–89.

21. In fact, at that time Even a decade later, the Pan American Society was still trying to entice Americans to visit their neighbor to the south. Toward that end, the society published a twenty-four-page pamphlet titled *The Call of South America.* (John Barrett, *The Call of South America* [New York, 1922], p. 1.)

22. "They were bearded" H. M. Tomlinson, *The Sea and the Jungle* (Evanston, Ill., 1999), p. 203.

22. Nicknamed "Mad Maria" Alain Gheerbrant, *The Amazon* (New York, 1988), p. 91.

23. Looking back TR, *Autobiography,* pp. 17–18.

23. Captivated by the thrill Ibid., p. 18.

23. When Roosevelt was only Geoffrey Hellman, *Bankers, Bones and Beetles* (New York, 1968), p. 23.

23. He entered college TR, *Autobiography,* pp. 28–29.

24. During his last term John Burroughs, "Theodore Roosevelt," *Journal of the American Museum of Natural History,* Jan. 1919, p. 3.

24. "by far the most successful" Henry Fairfield Osborn, "Theodore Roosevelt, Naturalist," *Journal of the American Museum of Natural History,* Jan. 1919, p. 8.

25. Roosevelt had known As a child, Roosevelt had been close friends with Henry Fairfield Osborn's older brother Frederick, a bright little boy who had a passion for birds that rivaled Roosevelt's own. The two boys had been known to spend entire days together tramping through forests in search of interesting animals. On one such day, young Roosevelt, to his delight, had spotted what he believed was a new species of frog. His pockets already bulging with other specimens, he placed the frog on his head and clapped his hat down over it. The temporary measure seemed satisfactory until Secretary of State Hamilton Fish and his wife appeared on their afternoon drive along the river. As soon as they saw the carriage coming toward them, both boys obediently doffed their hats, and the frog, taking advantage of the situation, leapt off Roosevelt's head and made good his escape. Frederick Osborn, as Roosevelt would sadly recall many years later, drowned "in his gallant youth." But Roosevelt never forgot his boyhood friend, and he went on to form a lifelong friendship with his younger brother. (Henry Fairfield Osborn, *Impressions of Great Naturalists* [New York, 1924], p. 168, TRC; Theodore Roosevelt, "My Life as a Naturalist," *Natural History,* April 1980, p. 84.)

25. "I can hardly" Osborn to TR, June 25, 1913, TRP.

26. A priest since Ralph E. Weber, "Father Zahm," *Catholic World,* Feb. 1922, p. 3.

26. But, paradoxically "Priest and Scientist," *Indianapolis Journal,* Jan. 16, 1898, IPAC.

26. In 1896, while still John Zahm, *Evolution and Dogma* (Chicago, 1896), p. xviii.

27. "keep yourself before" Ralph E. Weber, *Notre Dame's John Zahm* (Notre Dame, Ind., 1961), p. 19.

27. "the chummiest of chums" John Zahm to Albert Zahm, Oct. 17, 1913, CAZA 4/09.

27. "Where was I to find" John Zahm, *Through South America's Southland* (New York, 1916), p. 4.

27. Finally, in the summer Ibid., p. 8.

27. In an extraordinary Ibid.

28. "You may save" Quoted in ibid., p. 9.

28. **"By George!"** Ibid., p. 8.

29. **"With a wide knowledge"** Frank Chapman, *Autobiography of a Bird Lover* (New York, 1933), p. 215.

29. **"[I] would like"** TR to John Zahm, June 10, 1913, TRP.

CHAPTER 3: Preparation

30. **"delightful holiday"** TR to John Zahm, July 7, 1913, TRP.

30. **"a funny little Catholic priest"** TR to Arthur Hamilton Lee, July 7, 1913, in *Letters,* vol. 7, pp. 738–41.

30. **In July** Frank Chapman, introduction to Theodore Roosevelt, *Through the Brazilian Wilderness* (New York, 1924), p. xiii.

31. **Fiala's first trip** Herman R. Friis, ed., *The Arctic Diary of Russell Williams Porter* (Charlottesville, Va., 1976), p. 76. Both expeditions were sponsored by William Ziegler, the wealthy president of the Royal Baking Powder Company, and, in part, the National Geographic Society. The Fiala-Ziegler Expedition was the first to take the society's flag—with its famous blue, brown, and green bands representing the sky, earth, and sea—on assignment.

31. **The renamed** Anthony Fiala, "Two Years in the Arctic," *McClure's Magazine,* Feb. 1906, pp. 341–57.

31. **On Fiala's orders** George Shorkley, "Medical Records—Ziegler Polar Expedition," Jan. 23, 1904, Courtesy of Dartmouth College Library.

32. **"an ill conceived"** Quoted in Fergus Fleming, *Ninety Degrees North* (New York, 2001), p. 315.

32. **"I would give anything"** John Zahm, *Through South America's Southland* (New York, 1916), p. 11.

32. **"A better man"** Ibid., p. 12.

32. **The expedition's tentative plan** Frank Chapman to Henry Fairfield Osborn, June 24, 1913, AMNH; Frank Chapman, *Autobiography of a Bird Lover* (New York, 1933), p. 216.

33. **Fiala was looking forward** Fiala would later explain his theory in an interview with *The Saturday Evening Post:* "The South American Indian goes practically naked, has few possessions, and the water of the rivers is always warm. So, when he comes to a cataract, he usually doesn't try to portage; and if the canoe upsets, it doesn't matter much. He has never had any stimulus to build a better boat. But the North American Indian wore furs and navigated rivers that were always cold. So he developed a light, buoyant canoe, hard to upset, easy to portage." (Webb Waldron, "Making Exploring Safe for Explorers," *Saturday Evening Post,* Jan. 30, 1932, p. 38.)

33. **The canoes he ordered** Anthony Fiala, Appendix B, in TR, *Through the Brazilian Wilderness,* pp. 371–72.

33–34. **Father Zahm, meanwhile** John Zahm to George Curtiss, Aug. 16, 1913, IPAC.

34. **Characteristically** Ibid.

34. **He also ordered** Rogers Peet Company invoices, IPAC.

34. **Fiala ordered** Austin, Nichols & Co., Inc., invoices, IPAC.

34. **"I am sending you"** Anthony Fiala to TR, Sept. 5, 1913, TRP.

35. **"I'll reply to you"** Quoted in Chapman, introduction to TR, *Through the Brazilian Wilderness*, 1924, p. xiii.

36. **Chapman had known Cherrie** Ibid., p. ix.

36. **Cherrie received** George Cherrie, *Dark Trails* (New York, 1930), p. 247.

36. **Besides his reluctance** Chapman, *Autobiography of a Bird Lover*, p. 214.

36. **$150 per month** Paul H. Douglas, *Real Wages in the United States, 1890–1926* (Boston, 1930), p. 392, table insert.

36. **As extra insurance** Frank Chapman to Henry Fairfield Osborn, June 24, 1913, AMNH.

36. **This division of labor** Frank Chapman to Henry Fairfield Osborn, Aug. 1, 1913, AMNH.

37. **"prepared with the utmost"** Henry Fairfield Osborn, "Theodore Roosevelt, Naturalist," *Journal of the American Museum of Natural History*, Jan. 1919, p. 8.

CHAPTER 4: On the Open Sea

38. **On the morning of October 4, 1913** Unnamed newspaper, Oct. 5, 1913, TRC.

38. **As soon as Roosevelt** *New York Times,* Oct. 5, 1913.

38. **Among those waiting** Although Roosevelt would not be visiting his country, Minister Federico Alfonso Pezet of Peru also went to the pier to wish the former president a safe trip and assure him that "a most cordial welcome awaited him if any change of plans would cause him to enter Peruvian territory." (Unnamed newspaper, Oct. 5, 1913, TRC.)

38. **For the ambassadors** As Roosevelt gave Brazil's Ambassador Don Domicio da Gama's hand a vigorous shake, he said, "Good-bye, Mr. Ambassador," then reassured him, "I've changed that sentence." Da Gama must have been relieved to hear those words. Two months earlier, Roosevelt had sent copies of the speeches he intended to give in South America to each of the ambassadors. Well aware that they were concerned that he would discuss the Monroe Doctrine, which was a highly sensitive topic throughout the continent, Roosevelt had set nerves on edge by declaring, "That is exactly what I am going to talk about." (Chapman, introduction to Theodore Roosevelt, *Through the Brazilian Wilderness* [New York, 1924], p. xv; Frank Chapman, *Autobiography of a Bird Lover* [New York, 1933], p. 216.)

39. **A few weeks before** Lemuel Quigg had been in South America twenty years earlier, and he admitted that "things must have changed immensely since then," but he predicted that attitudes toward the United States had not. "From Venezuela, on either coast, to Patagonia, they were against the Monroe Doctrine. They did not at all understand it," he wrote. To South Americans, he explained, the doctrine meant "that we assumed the position of patron and that we were entitled to step in and say who should or who should not run for President, and that

we arrogated to ourselves functions of that kind. I predict that you will find this notion everywhere you stop, and . . . you will have the damnedest time explaining the Monroe Doctrine that any man ever had since Socrates undertook his defense." (Lemuel Quigg to TR, Sept. 24, 1913, TRP.)

40. **"bubbling like a frying-pan"** TR to KR, Feb. 14, 1913, TRC.

41. **"I should regard it"** TR to George Otto Trevelyan, Oct. 1, 1911, in *Letters,* vol. 7, p. 392.

41. **Kermit spoke Arabic** Will Irwin, ed., Introduction to *Letters to Kermit from Theodore Roosevelt* (New York, 1946), p. 3.

41. **"the soul of a poet"** Author's interview with Kermit Roosevelt, grandson of the late Kermit Roosevelt.

41. **"He is very interested"** KR to Belle Willard, 1912, KBRP.

42. **"For there is neither"** William Roscoe Thayer, *Theodore Roosevelt: An Intimate Biography* (Boston, 1919), p. 375.

42. **Concerned that his son** TR to KR, April 20, 1913, TRC.

42. **"Unless things go"** KR to TR, July 31, 1913, KBRP.

42. **"Twice it was"** KR to Belle Willard, Sept. 15, 1912, KBRP.

43. **"for the Indians are up"** KR to Belle Willard, Oct. 10, 1912, KBRP.

43. **That summer, Kermit** KR to TR, July 31, 1913, TRP.

43. **"Kermit was a very"** Theodore Roosevelt, Jr., *All in the Family* (New York, 1929), p. 29.

44. **"tremendously homesick"** KR to TR, 1913, KBRP.

44. **Her name was Belle** Unnamed newspaper, Jan. 15, 1913, KBRP.

44. **Petite and blonde** *New York Times,* Jan. 4, 1913, KBRP. Belle's father owned the highly fashionable Willard Hotel on Pennsylvania Avenue in Washington, D.C.—a luxurious establishment just down the street from the White House, which had become a landmark in the capital's social and political life. The hotel had been one of Ulysses S. Grant's favorite places to have an after-work cigar when he was in office. Julia Ward Howe wrote "The Battle Hymn of the Republic" at the Willard in 1861, and Martin Luther King, Jr., would write parts of his historic "I Have a Dream" speech there a century later. Even Alice Roosevelt, Theodore's older daughter, was known to drop by the Willard on occasion, where she scandalized patrons in the hotel dining room by smoking in public.

44. **Kermit had met Belle** Belle had been in Paris, ensconced in opulent comfort at the Hotel Astoria on the Champs-Élysées, that summer when she had received news of Kermit's fall from the bridge. She had been relieved to hear that he had recovered fully, but she could not resist teasing him just a little. "I am glad to hear that you are quite well again. Broken ribs, and knee caps and 'other injuries,' especially other injuries, sounded very serious and I had visions of long weeks of suffering flat on your back, instead of which you've apparently been having glorious sport, hunting and riding etc.—so much for sympathy waisted! [sic]" (Belle Willard to KR, n.d., KBRP.)

44. **"No letter from"** KR to Belle Willard, March 1913, KBRP.

44. **"I don't want"** KR to Belle Willard, Dec. 1912, KBRP.

44. **Kermit planned to** Bahia is present-day Salvador.

45. "It won't be anything" TR to KR, June 23, 1913, in *Letters,* vol. 7, p. 732.

45. "a sort of grim pride" Theodore Roosevelt, Jr., to KR, Sept. 9, 1913, KBRP.

45. "I have not been able" Quoted in Sylvia Jukes Morris, *Edith Kermit Roosevelt: Portrait of a First Lady* (New York, 1980), p. 391.

45. "all right again" KR to Edith Roosevelt, Aug. 1913, KBRP.

46. "Father needs" Quoted in Morris, *Edith Kermit Roosevelt,* p. 397.

46. "sphinx-like silence" Ibid.

46. "I can but" Edith Roosevelt to KR, Sept. 14, 1913, KBRP.

46. frantic telephoning John Zahm, *Through South America's Southland* (New York, 1916), p. 14.

46. Jacob Sigg Ibid., pp. 13–14.

47. At 1:00 p.m. George Cherrie, *Diary,* Oct. 11, 1913, AMNH.

47. "I think he feels" Edith Roosevelt to Anna Roosevelt Cowles, Oct. 15, 1913, TRC.

47. "If we have" TR to Ethel Roosevelt Derby, Oct. 8, 1913, TRC.

48. "Ask [Gilbert] Grosvenor" John Zahm to Albert Zahm, Oct. 17, 1913, CAZA 4/09.

48. Most days she TR to Ethel Roosevelt Derby, Oct. 8, 1913, TRC.

48. Twenty-five years old Unnamed newspaper, Jan. 3, 1913, TRC.

48. Lately, she had become Morris, *Edith Kermit Roosevelt,* p. 395.

48. "Margaret has proved" TR to Ethel Roosevelt Derby, Oct. 8, 1913, TRC.

48. Margaret was looking forward Morris, *Edith Kermit Roosevelt,* p. 399.

48. The men of the Zahm, *Through South America's Southland,* p. 15.

49. "I am pleased" TR to Frank Chapman, Oct. 15, 1913, TRP.

49. "The Colonel's friendly" George Cherrie, *Dark Trails* (New York, 1930), p. 255.

49. During the voyage Ibid.

50. "Dear Belle" KR to Belle Willard, n.d., KBRP.

CHAPTER 5: A Change of Plans

52. 15 percent Michael Goulding, Ronaldo Barthem, and Efrem Ferreira, *The Smithsonian Atlas of the Amazon* (Washington, D.C., 2003), pp. 28–30.

53. The river's mouth Ibid., pp. 29–30.

53. When the two The Nazca Plate continues to slide under South America at the geologically lightning-fast pace of eight to ten centimeters per year.

55. The potential political Donald F. O'Reilly, "Rondon: Biography of a Brazilian Republican Army Commander," Ph.D. dissertation, New York University, 1969, p. 39.

56. Rio de Janeiro In the mid-1950s, Brazil decided that it needed a capital in the interior of the country, so it began building a city named Brasilia in the cool, arid highlands. Construction began in 1956, and the capital was moved from Rio to Brasilia four years later.

56. A week earlier TR to Lauro Müller, Oct. 14, 1913, TRP.

56. The forty-eight-year-old Theodore Roosevelt, *Through the Brazilian Wilderness* (New York, 1914), p. 50.

56. **On October 4** Todd A. Diacon, *Stringing Together a Nation* (Durham, N.C., 2004) p. 32.

56. **Rondon had not been** Amilcar Botelho de Magalhães, *Impressão da Commissão Rondon*, p. 210.

57. **Rondon had accepted** Cândido Mariano da Silva Rondon, *Lectures Delivered on the 5th, 7th, and 9th of October, 1915* (Rio de Janeiro, 1916), p. 10.

57. **"The fact is,"** Magalhães, *Impressão da Commissão Rondon*, p. 210.

57. **"The ordinary traveller"** TR, *Through the Brazilian Wilderness*, pp. 171–72.

57. **Müller, a sophisticated** Ibid., p. 8.

57. **"Colonel Roosevelt"** George Cherrie, *Dark Trails* (New York, 1930), pp. 259–60.

58. **Rondon had stumbled** Ibid., p. 259.

58. **When he was told** Rondon, *Lectures*, pp. 11–12.

58. **Francisco de Orellana** Anthony Smith, *Explorers of the Amazon* (Chicago, 1990), pp. 39–73.

59. **"eating nothing but leather"** Gaspar de Carvajal, *The Discovery of the Amazon*, trans. Bertram T. Lee, ed. H. C. Heaton (New York, 1934), p. 172.

59. **Once on the river** Smith, *Explorers of the Amazon*, pp. 84–88; Edward J. Goodman, *The Explorers of South America* (Norman, Okla., 1972), pp. 66–71.

59. **Thirteen years later** Smith, *Explorers of the Amazon*, pp. 91–135.

59. **Colonel Teles Pires** TR, *Through the Brazilian Wilderness*, p. 301.

60. **"Now, we will"** *New York Times*, May 27, 1914.

60. **Osborn was thunderstruck** Henry Fairfield Osborn, "Theodore Roosevelt, Naturalist," *Journal of the American Museum of Natural History*, Jan. 1919, p. 7.

60. **Roosevelt's admission** TR to Frank Chapman, Nov. 4, 1913, in *Letters*, vol. 7, p. 753.

60. **"In a word"** Frank Chapman, introduction to TR, *Through the Brazilian Wilderness*, 1924 p. xviii. (Chapman used the river's current name: Rio Roosevelt.)

60. **"If they had the slightest"** Ibid., pp. xiv–xv.

61. **"last chance to be"** Quoted in Edward Wagenknecht, *The Seven Worlds of Theodore Roosevelt*, p. 11.

61. **"The little boy"** Corinne Roosevelt Robinson, *My Brother Theodore Roosevelt*, (New York, 1921) p. 277.

61. **In 1909** The American physician Frederick Albert Cook claimed to have reached the North Pole first, but most historians credit Peary and Henson with the accomplishment.

62. **"Tell Osborn"** Osborn, "Theodore Roosevelt, Naturalist"; Henry Fairfield Osborn, *Impressions of Great Naturalists* (New York, 1924), p. 180, TRC.

62. **"Father Zahm is"** Chapman, introduction to TR, *Through the Brazilian Wilderness*, 1924, pp. xiv–xv.

62. **"most eager to begin"** John Zahm to Albert Zahm, Nov. 16, 1913, CAZA 4/09.

63. **Brazilians who had** traveled Chapman, introduction to TR, *Through the Brazilian Wilderness*, 1924, p. xv.

63. **When Roosevelt's party** Cherrie, *Dark Trails*, p. 261.

63. "appalling amount of luggage" Leo E. Miller, *In the Wilds of South America* (New York, 1918), p. 198.

64. "I loathe state-travelling" TR to Ethel Roosevelt Derby, Dec. 10, 1913, TRC.

64. "As you will see" John Zahm to Albert Zahm, Nov. 27, 1913, CAZA 4/09.

64. "continuous ovation" John Zahm to Albert Zahm, Dec. 12, 1913, CAZA 4/09; "Roosevelt's Visit to South America," *American Review of Reviews,* July 1914.

65. Roosevelt had offered Colombia Thomas Bailey, *A Diplomatic History of the American People,* 10th ed. (Englewood Cliffs, N.J., 1980).

65. He wrote to his Quoted in Kathleen Dalton, *Theodore Roosevelt: A Strenuous Life* (New York, 2002), p. 255.

65. "Don't you know" Jose Custodio Alves de Lima, "Reminiscences of Roosevelt in Brazil," *Brazilian American,* Jan. 29, 1927, p. 8.

65. "The human multitude" Quoted in *North American Review,* March 1914, TRC.

66. "As soon as" John Zahm, *Through South America's Southland* (New York, 1916), p. 280.

66. "I love peace" Ibid., p. 281.

67. While in Buenos Aires Sylvia Jukes Morris, *Edith Kermit Roosevelt: Portrait of a First Lady* (New York, 1980), p. 399.

67. While working on KR to Belle Willard, Sept. 15, 1912, KBRP.

67. "in quite as good health" TR to Anna Roosevelt Cowles, Nov. 11, 1913, TRC.

67. "Dear Kermit" Belle Willard to KR, Nov. 3, 1913, KBRP.

68. "I don't remember" KR to Belle Willard, n.d., KBRP.

68. "Kermit is as much" TR to Eleanor Roosevelt, Dec. 10, 1913, TRC.

68. Edith, however Morris, *Edith Kermit Roosevelt,* p. 399.

68. While they were still in Bahia KR to Belle Willard, n.d., KBRP.

69. Roosevelt had always seemed Ethel, Roosevelt's younger daughter, had been in New York with Belle when she had heard the news, cried out by a paperboy hawking the "extras," or special editions, that indicated urgent dispatches. "We had been to the theater," Belle wrote Kermit soon afterward, "and after we got back heard an 'Extra' called. Ethel went to the window but couldn't make out what it was. She said, 'Extras frighten me so but I will not be foolish about it this time. Let's go to bed.' The next morning I woke only to find her dressed. She had just gotten a note . . . telling her not to worry as they did not think her father was seriously hurt. I shall never forget Ethel's face as she dashed out." (Belle Willard to KR, Oct. 1912, KBRP.)

69. "It was a bad" KR to Belle Willard, Nov. 26, 1912, KBRP.

69. "I did not like" TR to Eleanor Roosevelt, Dec. 10, 1913, TRC.

69. "It just doesn't seem" KR to Belle Willard, n.d., KBRP.

70. "We would have" KR to Belle Willard, Nov. 26, 1913, KBRP.

CHAPTER 6: Beyond the Frontier

73. On the morning Cândido Mariano da Silva Rondon, *Lectures Delivered on the 5th, 7th, and 9th of October, 1915* (Rio de Janeiro, 1916), p. 14.

74. **Born in the remote** Donald F. O'Reilly, "Rondon: Biography of a Brazilian Republican Army Commander," Ph.D. dissertation, New York University, 1969, pp. 1–5.

74. **The War of the Triple Alliance** Ibid.

75. **Orphaned at the age** Lucien Bodard, *Green Hell* (New York, 1971), p. 10.

75. **He woke up** O'Reilly, "Rondon," pp. 14–16.

76. **Rondon lost an entire year** Bodard, *Green Hell,* p. 11.

76. **"I want to bring"** Quoted in ibid.

76. **Rondon was a member** João Cruz Costa, *A History of Ideas in Brazil* (Berkeley, Calif., 1964), p. 82.

76. **"the respectful heirs"** O'Reilly, "Rondon," p. 22.

76. **His math teacher** Ibid., p. 18; Costa, *History of Ideas,* p. 87.

77. **Although he was** E. Bradford Burns, *A History of Brazil* (New York, 1993), p. 232.

77. **Less than six months** O'Reilly, "Rondon," pp. 39–40.

77. **Rondon was supposed to have** Ibid., p. 67.

78. **In 1903** Ibid., p. 77.

78. **Assignment to Rondon's unit** Todd A. Diacon, *Stringing Together a Nation* (Durham, N.C., 2004), pp. 54–55.

78. **He had started out** O'Reilly, "Rondon," pp. 115–16.

78. **"monstrously fecund"** Ibid., p. 119.

78. **In some places** Rondon, *Commissão de Linhas Telegraphicas Estrategicas de Matto Grosso ao Amazonas,* vol. 1, p. 223.

79. **By late August** O'Reilly, "Rondon," p. 127; Theodore Roosevelt, *Through the Brazilian Wilderness* (New York, 1914), p. 52.

79. **By the time** Rondon, *Relatório,* vol. 1, p. 233; TR, *Through the Brazilian Wilderness,* pp. 263–64.

79. **237 days** O'Reilly, "Rondon," p. 131.

79. **Rondon was not** Rondon, *Lectures,* p. 18.

80. **Roosevelt had learned** Bodard, *Green Hell,* p. 13.

80. **"as if it were"** Kermit Roosevelt, *The Long Trail* (New York, 1921), pp. 68–69.

80. **It would be a measure** Joseph R. Ornig, *My Last Chance to Be a Boy* (Mechanicsburg, Pa., 1994), p. 223.

81. **"bathed in the"** Cherrie, *Dark Trails,* p. 267.

81. **Although Corumbá** J. C. Oakenfull, *Brazil in 1913* (Frome, England, 1914), p. 548.

81. **"For ambulance service"** Cherrie, *Dark Trails,* p. 268.

81. **"It was a brilliantly"** TR, *Through the Brazilian Wilderness,* p. 95.

82. **Rondon had gone** Cherrie, *Dark Trails,* p. 274.

82. **"What a Xmas Eve!"** George Cherrie, *Diary,* Dec. 24, 1913, AMNH.

82. **Kermit confessed** KR to Belle Willard, Dec. 24, 1913, KBRP.

82. **"The priest is"** Ibid.

83. **"On several occasions"** Theodore Roosevelt, *An Autobiography* (New York, 1913), p. 52.

83. **"We did not hear"** "Personal Glimpses," *Literary Digest,* May 16, 1914, TRC.

CHAPTER 7: Disarray and Tragedy

85. **Tapirapoan consisted** Leo E. Miller, *In the Wilds of South America* (New York, 1918), p. 223.

85. **"almost at will"** Theodore Roosevelt, *Through the Brazilian Wilderness* (New York, 1914), p. 160.

85. **Rondon had arranged** Cândido Mariano da Silva Rondon, *Lectures Delivered on the 5th, 7th, and 9th of October, 1915* (Rio de Janeiro, 1916), p. 37.

86. **The problem was** Todd A. Diacon, *Stringing Together a Nation* (Durham, N.C., 2004), p. 36.

86. **Amilcar, despite his** Amilcar Botelho de Magalhães, *Impressão da Commissão Rondon*, p. 225.

86. **"apparently fresh from"** Miller, *In the Wilds*, p. 225.

86. **"constantly engaged"** John Zahm, *Through South America's Southland* (New York, 1916), p. 473.

86. **"The oxen aren't"** KR to Belle Willard, Jan. 20, 1914, KBRP.

87. **"Intervention must"** Quoted in Frederick S. Calhoun, *Power and Principle: Armed Intervention in Wilsonian Foreign Policy* (Kent, Ohio, 1986), p. 40.

87. **"constant preoccupation"** Rondon, *Lectures*, p. 29.

87. **Not only were the** Ibid., p. 37. In a letter to John Scott Keltie, the secretary of the Royal Geographical Society, Roosevelt admitted that he thought the lavish saddle and bridle among these gifts were "exquisitely unfit for such a trip," but he had no choice but to accept them graciously. "I would have given deep offense to very good and kind people if I had not used them," he wrote. (TR to Keltie, Feb. 25, 1915, in *Letters*, vol. 8, p. 905.)

88. **On January 19** TR, *Through the Brazilian Wilderness*, p. 170.

88. **But Rondon also wanted** Rondon, *Lectures*, pp. 37–38.

89. **"Away from the broad"** TR, *Through the Brazilian Wilderness*, p. 165.

89. **By the next morning** Zahm, *Through South America's Southland*, p. 480; TR, *Through the Brazilian Wilderness*, p. 182.

89. **"The whole region"** Theodore Roosevelt, Address to National Geographic Society, May 26, 1914, NGS.

90. **"Until Tapirapoan"** Cajazeira, *Relatório*, Museu do Índio, Rio de Janeiro.

90. **Meals usually consisted** TR, *Through the Brazilian Wilderness*, p. 181; KR to Edith Roosevelt, Feb. 8, 1914, KBRP.

90. **"all nearly famished"** George Cherrie, *Diary*, Jan. 21, 1914, AMNH.

90. **"It was rarely"** Zahm, *Through South America's Southland*, p. 479.

90. **There was no way** Miller, *In the Wilds*, p. 231.

90. **For the men in** Zahm, *Through South America's Southland*, p. 479.

91. **Strewn across** Ibid., p. 480.

91. **"What became of"** Ibid.

91. **Three Brazilians** Rondon, *Lectures*, p. 39.

91. **Julio de Lima** In his official military report on the expedition, Amilcar would

sum Julio up in four simple words: "Beautiful muscles, dreadful feelings!" (Magalhães, *Impressão da Commissão Rondon*, p. 216.)

92. "squatted in the Yedo" Rondon, *Lectures*, p. 39.

92. "English, Portuguese" TR, *Through the Brazilian Wilderness*, p. 157.

93. "told of the stone gods" Ibid., p. 223.

93. "It was while" Ibid., p. 180.

94. The supply ship Anthony Fiala, "Two Years in the Arctic," *McClure's Magazine*, Feb. 1906, pp. 471–84.

94. The trucks, which belonged Miller, *In the Wilds*, p. 227.

95. According to Rondon Esther de Viveiros, *Rondon: Conta Sua Vida* (Rio de Janeiro, 1958), p. 389.

95. "Truth to tell" Zahm, *Through South America's Southland*, p. 41.

95. "Whites, Indians" Ibid., p. 40.

95. "ignorant and careless negro" John Zahm to TR, March 14, 1914, TPR.

95. "measure of how much" Viveiros, *Rondon: Conta Sua Vida*, p. 389.

95. "The colonel possesses" Todd A. Diacon, "Are the Good Guys Always Bad?" Annual Meeting of the Southern Historical Association, Alabama, 1998, p. 17.

95. "Our great" John Zahm, *Evolution and Dogma* (Chicago, 1896), p. xxi.

96. "Although the Indian Service" Viveiros, *Rondon: Conta Sua Vida*, p. 394.

96. Three had drowned TR, *Through the Brazilian Wilderness*, p. 154.

97. "A good doctor" Ibid., p. 309.

97. More than a decade earlier Quoted in Kathleen Dalton, *Theodore Roosevelt: A Strenuous Life* (New York, 2002), p. 234.

98. "never gotten over" Kermit Roosevelt, *The Long Trail* (New York, 1921), p. 37.

98. "must be on hand" Quoted in Dalton, *TR: A Strenuous Life*, p. 234.

98. "You see he" KR to Belle Willard, n.d., KBRP.

98. "utterly miserable" TR to Quentin Roosevelt, Jan. 16, 1914, in *Letters*, vol. 7, p. 757.

99. The young woman Unnamed newspaper, Jan. 3, 1914, TRC.

99. "Margaret drank only" Quoted in Sylvia Jukes Morris, *Edith Kermit Roosevelt: Portrait of a First Lady* (New York, 1980), p. 552.

99. "Poor Henry Hunt" Edith Roosevelt, *Diary*, Jan. 5, 1914, TRP.

CHAPTER 8: Hard Choices

100. Heavy sheets of rain Theodore Roosevelt, *Through the Brazilian Wilderness* (New York, 1914), p. 198.

100. Little more than a clearing John Zahm, *Through South America's Southland* (New York, 1916), p. 494.

101. Whenever the downpour TR, *Through the Brazilian Wilderness*, pp. 192–93.

101. "Why they do not" Ibid., p. 193.

102. Even before reaching Leo E. Miller, *In the Wilds of South America* (New York, 1918), p. 240.

102. **In Tapirapoan alone** Joseph R. Ornig, *My Last Chance to Be a Boy* (Mechanicsburg, Pa., 1994), p. 100.

102. **Only one of the men** TR, *Through the Brazilian Wilderness*, p. 153. Today, the river's name is spelled "Jiparaná."

103. **"It seemed to me"** Miller, *In the Wilds*, p. 240.

103. **"When I get back"** TR to Henry Fairfield Osborn, Jan. 5, 1914, AMNH.

103. **"Father Zahm has now"** KR to Edith Roosevelt, Jan. 3, 1914, KBRP.

103. **"All for each"** Theodore Roosevelt, *An Autobiography* (New York, 1913), p. vi.

103. **"no real harm"** KR to Edith Roosevelt, n.d., KBRP.

103. **"Of our whole expedition"** TR to Edith Roosevelt, Dec. 1913, TRP.

104. **Borrowing from Psalm 44** John Zahm to TR, June 3, 1912, TRP.

104. **"Win or lose"** TR to John Zahm, June 6, 1912, TRP.

104. **Manáos** Modern-day Manaus.

104. **"through the heart"** John Zahm to Albert Zahm, Jan. 5, 1914, CAZA 4/09.

105. **Given the discomforts** Cândido Mariano da Silva Rondon, *Lectures Delivered on the 5th, 7th, and 9th of October, 1915* (Rio de Janeiro, 1916), pp. 46–47.

105. **Father Zahm reassured him** Ibid.

105. **"Indians are meant to carry"** Esther de Viveiros, *Rondon: Conta Sua Vida* (Rio de Janeiro, 1958), p. 394.

106. **"The colonel's Positivism"** TR, *Through the Brazilian Wilderness*, p. 77.

106. **One night during** Rondon, *Lectures*, p. 39.

106. **Finally, after what** Viveiros, *Rondon: Conta Sua Vida*, p. 394.

106. **"Father Zahm is being"** KR to Belle Willard, Jan. 31, 1914, KBRP.

106. **The next day** Roosevelt memo, Feb. 1, 1914, TRP. Euzebio Paul was a Brazilian member of the expedition. L. Oliveira was a geologist.

107. **First a team of** Todd A. Diacon, *Stringing Together a Nation* (Durham, N.C., 2004), p. 31.

108. **"as big-hearted"** Miller, *In the Wilds*, p. 230.

108. **In the tender light** TR, *Through the Brazilian Wilderness*, p. 181.

108. **Before they left camp** Miller, *In the Wilds*, p. 230.

108. **Kermit had developed** Kermit Roosevelt, *Diary*, Feb. 10, 1914, KBRP.

108. **Early in the overland journey** George Cherrie, *Diary*, Jan. 18, 1914, AMNH.

109. **"death to being dislodged"** H. M. Tomlinson, *The Sea and the Jungle* (Evanston, Ill., 1999), p. 164.

109. **"mournfully, dismally"** KR to Edith Roosevelt, Feb. 8, 1914, KBRP.

109. **Their mules slipped** Cherrie, *Diary*, Feb. 6, 1914, AMNH.

109. **"Everything became mouldy"** TR, *Through the Brazilian Wilderness*, pp. 198–99.

109. **"It is hard"** TR to Theodore Roosevelt Jr., May 17, 1909, in *Letters*, vol. 7, p. 10.

110. **After they made camp** Cherrie, *Diary*, Feb. 4, 1914, AMNH.

110. **Miller dismissed Fiala** Leo Miller to Frank Chapman, Feb. 25, 1914, AMNH.

110. **"I have not written"** Cherrie, *Diary*, Nov. 25, 1914, AMNH.

111. **Roosevelt made an effort** Anthony Fiala, Theodore Roosevelt Memorial Meeting, March 1, 1919, TRC.

111. **"Fiala left us"** Cherrie, *Diary*, Feb. 4, 1914, AMNH.

CHAPTER 9: Warnings from the Dead

112. **"The oxen have"** Kermit Roosevelt, Diary, Feb. 6, 1914, KBRP.

112. **Since Tapirapoan** KR, *Diary,* Feb. 6, 1914, KBRP; Theodore Roosevelt, *Through the Brazilian Wilderness* (New York, 1914).

112. **"enormously heavy"** TR to John Scott Keltie, Feb. 25, 1915, in *Letters,* vol. 8, pp. 904–5.

113. **Two oxcarts** George Cherrie, *Diary,* Feb. 6, 1914, AMNH.

113. **The naturalists were even** Leo E. Miller, *In the Wilds of South America* (New York, 1918), p. 232.

113. **"the sheer necessities"** TR, *Through the Brazilian Wilderness,* p. 209.

113. **He counted as necessities** KR to Belle Willard, Feb. 10, 1914, KBRP.

113. **"Through all the"** KR to Belle Willard, Feb. 8, 1914, KBRP.

113. **The poems were** TR to Thomas Herbert Warren, June 7, 1916, in *Letters,* vol. 8, p. 1056.

113. **Before they began** TR to John Scott Keltie, Feb. 25, 1915, in *Letters,* vol. 8, pp. 904–5.

114. **Pausing on a hilltop** TR, *Through the Brazilian Wilderness,* p. 213.

114. **Farther north** Ibid., p. 214.

114. **When they reached** Ibid., pp. 214–15.

114. **From a telegram** Anthony Fiala, Appendix B, in ibid., p. 361.

114. **Not long after** Cândido Mariano da Silva Rondon, *Lectures Delivered on the 5th, 7th, and 9th of October, 1915* (Rio de Janeiro, 1916), pp. 50–51.

114. **"I just saved myself"** Quoted in "Personal Glimpses," *Literary Digest,* May 16, 1914, TRC.

115. **It was true that** Rondon, *Lectures,* pp. 50–51.

115. **Fiala blamed** Webb Waldron, "Making Exploring Safe for Explorers," *Saturday Evening Post,* Jan. 30, 1932, p. 38.

115. **"how buoyantly"** Ibid.

116. **"in a still wilder region"** TR, *Through the Brazilian Wilderness,* p. 203.

116. **Rondon had made** Donald F. O'Reilly, "Rondon: Biography of a Brazilian Army Commander," Ph.D. dissertation, New York University, 1969, pp. 94–95.

116. **Ordering his men** Ibid.; Kalvero Oberg, "Indian Tribes of Northern Mato Grosso, Brazil," *Institute of Social Anthropology,* Pub. 15, 1953, p. 93.

116. **For weeks, the Nhambiquara** Miller, *In the Wilds,* p. 232.

117. **"Someone may recall"** Claude Lévi-Strauss, *Tristes Tropiques* (New York, 1992), p. 273.

117. **"A Protestant mission"** Ibid., p. 263. "Nambikwara": Over the decades since Rondon first made contact with the Nhambiquara, the tribe's name has been spelled several different ways. This book will use Rondon's spelling throughout, except when quoting a source that uses an alternate.

118. **In Utiarity** TR, *Through the Brazilian Wilderness,* p. 190.

118. **He even hired** Ibid., p. 188.

118. **They were still largely** Julian H. Steward, ed., *Handbook of South American Indians,* vol. 3 (Washington, D.C., 1948), pp. 363–64.

118. **Some of the Pareci** TR, *Through the Brazilian Wilderness,* pp. 217–18.

119. **Shortly before** Ibid., p. 194.

120. **"I feel for them"** O'Reilly, "Rondon," pp. 142–43.

120. **Outraged by** Todd A. Diacon, "Are the Good Guys Always Bad?" Annual Meeting of the Southern Historical Association, Alabama, 1998, p. 19.

120. **In 1910** The SPI still exists today, but under a different name. In the late 1960s, after several of its directors were charged with exploiting the very Indians whom they had been hired to protect, the agency was reorganized and renamed. It is now known as the Fundaçao Nacional do Índio, or FUNAI.

120. **In fact, so infamous** TR, *Through the Brazilian Wilderness,* p. 155.

120. **"Sir! I have"** Esther de Viveiros, *Rondon: Conta Sua Vida* (Rio de Janeiro, 1958), p. 386.

120. **"Let us weep"** Quoted in Lucien Bodard, *Green Hell* (New York, 1971), p. 13.

121. **"I don't go so far"** Michael McGerr, *A Fierce Discontent* (New York, 2003), pp. 205–7.

121. **"There were still"** Theodore Roosevelt, *An Autobiography* (New York, 1913), p. 123.

122. **"friends proclaim their presence"** TR, *Through the Brazilian Wilderness,* p. 224.

122. **"When preparing for"** Oberg, "Indian Tribes," p. 98.

122. **Conversely, to show** TR, *Through the Brazilian Wilderness,* p. 224.

123. **Once in the camp** Ibid., p. 218.

123. **"a very pleasant set"** KR to Belle Willard, Feb. 8, 1914, KBRP.

123. **"They had the unpleasant habit"** Miller, *In the Wilds,* p. 233.

123. **"They laughed at"** TR, *Through the Brazilian Wilderness,* p. 235.

124. **"light-hearted robbers"** Ibid., p. 240.

124. **Not far from the** Miller, *In the Wilds,* p. 235.

125. **At the very outset** TR to John Scott Keltie, Feb. 25, 1915, *Letters,* vol. 8, pp. 904–5.

CHAPTER 10: The Unknown

130. **Rondon had instructed Pyrineus** Cândido Mariano da Silva Rondon, *Lectures Delivered on the 5th, 7th, and 9th of October, 1915* (Rio de Janeiro, 1916), p. 68.

130. **"river whose importance"** Ibid., p. 69.

131. **The Madeira, which starts** Michael Goulding, Ronaldo Barthem, and Efrem Ferreira, *The Smithsonian Atlas of the Amazon* (Washington, D.C., 2003), p. 151.

131. **On the spot** Rondon, *Lectures,* pp. 70–71.

132. **Unknown to Roosevelt** Todd A. Diacon, *Stringing Together a Nation* (Durham, N.C., 2004), pp. 36–37.

134. **"recently built"** Rondon, *Lectures,* p. 70.

134. **"One was small"** Theodore Roosevelt, *Through the Brazilian Wilderness* (New York, 1914), p. 243.

135. **At up to twenty-five hundred** Anthony Fiala, Appendix B, ibid., p. 355.

137. **He had been fighting** Diacon, *Stringing Together a Nation,* p. 32.

137. **"Most of his equipment"** Leo Miller to Frank Chapman, Feb. 25, 1914, AMNH.

138. **"We discovered here"** Ibid.

138. **"For meat"** Fiala, Appendix B, in TR, *Through the Brazilian Wilderness,* pp. 359–60.

138. **They finally decided** George Cherrie, *Diary,* Feb. 26, 1914, AMNH.

139. **"If our canoe voyage"** TR, *Through the Brazilian Wilderness,* pp. 241–42.

139. **"We had looked forward"** Leo E. Miller, *In the Wilds of South America* (New York, 1918), p. 240.

139. **In a gesture** Leo Miller to Frank Chapman, Feb. 25, 1914, AMNH.

139. **"Roosevelt asked me"** George Cherrie to Stella Cherrie, Feb. 26, 1914, AMNH.

140. **"For several minutes"** Miller, *In the Wilds,* pp. 241–42.

CHAPTER 11: Pole and Paddle, Axe and Machete

141. **From his position** Cândido Mariano da Silva Rondon, *Lectures Delivered on the 5th, 7th, and 9th, of October, 1915* (Rio de Janeiro, 1916), p. 70.

141. **"As we drifted"** Theodore Roosevelt, *Through the Brazilian Wilderness* (New York, 1914), p. 247.

142. **"fragrant scents"** Ibid., p. 246.

142. **"Very little animal life"** George Cherrie, *Diary,* Feb. 27, 1914, AMNH.

142. **While Roosevelt and Cherrie** TR, *Through the Brazilian Wilderness,* p. 246.

142. **Pulling the dugout** Rondon, *Lectures,* p. 71.

142. **"the muscles stood out"** TR, *Through the Brazilian Wilderness,* p. 245.

142. **"strapping set"** Ibid., p. 244.

143. **"like pirates"** Ibid.

143. **Roosevelt's own boatmen** Ibid.

144. **Alexander von Humboldt** John Noble Wilford, *The Mapmakers* (New York, 2000), pp. 280–81.

145. **Kermit and his paddlers** George Cherrie, *Dark Trails* (New York, 1930), p. 278.

145. **"literally toward"** TR, *Through the Brazilian Wilderness,* p. 245; Rondon, *Lectures,* p. 71.

145. **"close supervision"** TR to John Scott Keltie, Feb. 25, 1915, in *Letters,* vol. 8, p. 905.

145. **After only two hours** TR, *Through the Brazilian Wilderness,* p. 246.

146. **After making their way** Ibid.

CHAPTER 12: The Living Jungle

151. **Soaring more than** John Terbough, *Diversity and the Tropical Rain Forest* (New York, 1992), pp. 108–9.

151. **Unable to sink** Edward S. Ayensu, *The Life and Mysteries of the Jungle* (New York, 1980), p. 39.

151. **The most obvious** Adrian Forsyth and Kenneth Miyata, *Tropical Nature* (New York, 1984), pp. 47–49.

151. **While most plants** Ibid., p. 47.

152. **A principal risk** Ibid., p. 50. This book offers a fascinating and more detailed discussion of the relationship of vines, epiphytes, and trees.

152. **Another adaptation** Edgar Aubert De La Rüe, *The Tropics* (New York, 1957), pp. 51–55; Ayensu, *Life and Mysteries*, p. 32.

152. **Some have developed** Forsyth and Miyata, *Tropical Nature*, p. 46; Francis E. Putz, *The Biology of Vines* (Cambridge, Mass., 1991), pp. 366–70.

152. **Its shading action** Ayensu, *Life and Mysteries*, p. 31.

153. **If Roosevelt had been** John Kricher, *A Neotropical Companion* (Princeton, 1997), p. 49.

153. **Every morning** George Cherrie, *Dark Trails* (New York, 1930), pp. 279–80.

154. **"The ragged bugler"** Theodore Roosevelt, *Through the Brazilian Wilderness* (New York, 1914), p. 264.

154. **The colonel still woke** Donald F. O'Reilly, "Rondon: Biography of a Brazilian Army Commander," Ph.D. dissertation, New York University, 1969, pp. 41–42.

155. **He was, Rondon wrote** "Col. Roosevelt as His Guide Remembers Him," *New York Times*, Jan. 6, 1929.

155. **Although they had risen** TR, *Through the Brazilian Wilderness*, pp. 246–47.

155. **Hour after hour passed** Cherrie, *Dark Trails*, p. 280.

155. **He drank in** TR, *Through the Brazilian Wilderness*, p. 247.

156. **"There would be"** Kermit Roosevelt, *The Long Trail* (New York, 1921), p. 72.

156. **"Our clothes"** TR, *Through the Brazilian Wilderness*, p. 266.

156. **That afternoon** Kermit Roosevelt, Diary, Feb. 28, 1914, KBRP; TR, *Through the Brazilian Wilderness*, p. 247.

157. **"Often, even in"** Henry Walter Bates, *The Naturalist on the River Amazons* (London, 1864), pp. 40–43.

157. **This blindness left them** TR, *Through the Brazilian Wilderness*, p. 248.

157. **"Frequently at night"** Cherrie, *Dark Trails*, p. 15.

158. **"Let there be"** Ibid.

CHAPTER 13: On the Ink-Black River

161. **The river had been** George Cherrie, *Dark Trails* (New York, 1930), p. 83.

161. **Floating in the shallow** *New York Times*, Jan. 6, 1929.

162. **During telegraph line expeditions** Todd A. Diacon, *Stringing Together a Nation* (Durham, N.C., 2004), p. 23.

162. **One morning during** Theodore Roosevelt, *Through the Brazilian Wilderness* (New York, 1914), p. 51.

162. **While crossing a river** John Hemming, *Die If You Must* (London, 2003), pp. 6–7.

162. **"the fish that eats men"** Ibid., p. 41.

162. **"ferocious little monsters"** Ibid., p. 133.

162–63. **"The [piranha's] rabid"** Ibid., p. 42.

163. "Suddenly I heard" Cherrie, *Dark Trails*, p. 265.

163. "As I fell" Ibid., pp. 72–74.

164. This sharp-spined fish Stephen Spotte, *Candiru: Life and Legend of the Bloodsucking Catfishes* (Berkeley, Calif., 2002), p. ix.

165. In 1897, George Boulenger Ibid., pp. 20–21.

165. Instances of candirus parasitizing Ibid., pp. 211–16.

166. On the morning of March 1 George Cherrie, *Diary*, March 1, 1914, AMNH.

166. As they moved TR, *Through the Brazilian Wilderness*, p. 248.

166. Around another bend Ibid., pp. 248–49.

167. The village Kermit Roosevelt, *Diary*, March 1, 1914, KBRP.

167. In fact, Rondon speculated Cândido Mariano da Silva Rondon, *Lectures Delivered on the 5th, 7th, and 9th of October, 1915* (Rio de Janeiro, 1916), p. 72.

168. Moments later, a monkey Cherrie, *Dark Trails*, p. 281.

168. In 1931, Clodomiro Picado Harry W. Greene, *Snakes: The Evolution of Mystery in Nature* (Berkeley, Calif., 1997), p. 76.

169. No antivenom existed The problem was so serious that one of Brazil's scientific research centers was devoted to venom research. A few months earlier, soon after his arrival in Brazil, Roosevelt had been given a tour of this center, the Instituto Serumthérapico. The institute, which was situated just outside of São Paulo, had been founded twelve years earlier in response to an outbreak of bubonic plague, but snakebites had become such an overwhelming national problem—at that time, roughly twenty thousand Brazilians were bitten by venomous snakes each year, and five thousand died from their wounds—that much of its scientists' time was now devoted to producing snakebite serum. The institute had successfully developed an antivenom for the bite of the fer-de-lance, a particularly powerful and dangerous species of pit viper, but despite its best efforts, it had yet to find a formula that would fend off death after a coral-snake bite. (TR, *Through the Brazilian Wilderness*, p. 15.)

169. While the camaradas noisily TR, *Through the Brazilian Wilderness*, p. 249.

169. "Despite his two hundred" Cherrie, *Dark Trails*, p. 282.

169. When Roosevelt's foot TR, *Through the Brazilian Wilderness*, p. 249.

CHAPTER 14: Twitching Through the Woods

171. "The number of twists" George Cherrie, *Dark Trails* (New York, 1930), p. 282.

171. When they set off George Cherrie, *Diary*, March 2, 1914, AMNH.

172. Scientists have divided Milky rivers are also frequently referred to as "whitewater" rivers, a potentially confusing terminology that has nothing to do with the more colloquial use of that adjective to refer to churning, rapids-filled rivers. To avoid confusion, the term "whitewater" will be used in this book only in the latter, layman's meaning.

172. Alfred Russel Wallace Michael Goulding, Ronaldo Barthem, and Efrem Ferreira, *The Smithsonian Atlas of the Amazon* (Washington, D.C., 2003), p. 41.

173. "Instead of finding" Cherrie, *Dark Trails*, p. 282.

173. **Stretching before them** Theodore Roosevelt, *Through the Brazilian Wilderness* (New York, 1914), p. 251.

174. **"with enormous velocity"** Cândido Mariano da Silva Rondon, *Lectures Delivered on the 5th, 7th, and 9th of October, 1915* (Rio de Janeiro, 1916), pp. 72–73.

174. **"the last stronghold"** Ibid., p. 73.

174. **The water channel** TR, *Through the Brazilian Wilderness*, p. 251.

174. **"It seemed extraordinary"** Ibid., pp. 251–52.

174. **"No canoe could"** Cherrie, *Dark Trails*, p. 283.

174. **Even Kermit** Kermit Roosevelt, *Diary*, March 2, 1914, KBRP.

175. **The camaradas had already** TR, *Through the Brazilian Wilderness*, pp. 253–54.

175. **"bumping and sliding"** Ibid., 254.

176. **The tent-making bat** Louise H. Emmons, *Neotropical Rainforest Mammals* (Chicago, 1997), pp. 79–80; Ronald M. Nowak, *Walker's Bats of the World* (Baltimore, 1994), p. 154.

176. **The lumbering armadillo** Emmons, *Neotropical Rainforest Mammals*, p. 47.

177. **Aspredinidae and Anabantidae** Author's interview with Marcelo de Carvalho, ichthyologist with the American Museum of Natural History and the University of São Paulo.

177. **The three-toed sloth** Emmons, *Neotropical Rainforest Mammals*, p. 42.

177. **The mere fact** Ibid., pp. 42–43.

177. **So perfectly has the sloth** Ibid., p. 42.

178. **The caterpillar of certain sphinx moths** Adrian Forsyth and Kenneth Miyata, *Tropical Nature* (New York, 1984), p. 126.

178. **After killing an ant** William Agosta, *Thieves, Deceivers and Killers: Tales of Chemistry in Nature* (Princeton, 2001), pp. 106–7.

178. **Certain orchids** Forsyth and Miyata, *Tropical Nature*, p. 72.

178. **Some of the most** Erica Lynn Hardy, Online article, "Phyllobates Terribilis," University of Michigan Museum of Zoology, Animal Diversity Web; Chris Harman, "Frogs with a Toxic Taste," *Americas*, Jan. 2000, p. 3.

179. **Although the reasons** Jared Diamond, *Guns, Germs, and Steel* (New York, 1999), pp. 42–43.

179. **"Few people have heard"** Cherrie, *Dark Trails*, p. 186.

180. **"utterly trivial"** TR, *Through the Brazilian Wilderness*, p. 53.

180. **So important and ubiquitous** Edward O. Wilson, *The Diversity of Life* (Cambridge, Mass., 1992), p. 5.

180. **giant six-inch** Mark W. Moffett, *The High Frontier* (Cambridge, 1993), p. 103.

181. **biting with pincerlike** John Kricher, *A Neotropical Companion* (Princeton, 1997), p. 327.

181. **The Brazilian wasp** William Agosta, *Bombadier Beetles and Fever Trees* (Reading, Penn., 1996), pp. 36–37.

181. **Ants of the neotropical genus** Bert Hölldobler and Edward O. Wilson, *The Ants* (Cambridge, Mass., 1990), p. 571.

181. **Acting in concert** Ibid., pp. 573–76.

182. **Many tropical trees** Forsyth and Miyata, *Tropical Nature*, pp. 108–9. For

more on the symbiotic relationship between plants and ants, see Hölldobler and Wilson, *The Ants,* pp. 530–35.

182. **As a result of such** Kricher, *Neotropical Companion,* p. 36.

182. **On the morning of March 4** Cherrie, *Dark Trails,* p. 284.

182. **The mass swarming** Kricher, *Neotropical Companion,* p. 10.

182. **The termites ate** Cherrie, *Dark Trails,* pp. 284–85.

182. **One night near Utiarity** TR, *Through the Brazilian Wilderness,* p. 193.

182. **"Our hands"** Ibid., pp. 255–56.

182. **Each night when** Ibid., p. 253.

183. **"I had never before"** Ibid., p. 253.

183. **In their hunt for food** Forsyth and Miyata, *Tropical Nature,* p. 128.

183. **Some of the hawk moths** Ibid., p. 70.

183. **The leaf-cutting ants** Hölldobler and Wilson, *The Ants,* pp. 596–603.

184. **Pink-faced capuchin** Moffett, *High Frontier,* pp. 120–22; Emmons, *Neotropical Rainforest Mammals,* pp. 129–30.

184. **Millions of bats** Emmons, *Neotropical Rainforest Mammals,* p. 59.

184. **Snakes, spiders** Wilson, *Diversity of Life,* p. 4.

184. **The rubber tree** Kricher, *Neotropical Companion,* p. 148.

184. **The army ants** Hölldobler and Wilson, *The Ants,* pp. 576–77; Wilson, *Diversity of Life,* p. 6.

CHAPTER 15: The Wild Water

186. **"and therefore more picturesque"** Cândido Mariano da Silva Rondon, *Lectures Delivered on the 5th, 7th, and 9th of October, 1915* (Rio de Janeiro, 1916), p. 75.

186. **"We held endless discussions"** Theodore Roosevelt, *Through the Brazilian Wilderness* (New York, 1914), p. 255.

186. **It could swing** Rondon, *Lectures,* p. 65.

187. **"We did not know"** TR, *Through the Brazilian Wilderness,* p. 255.

187. **Around three o'clock** Ibid., p. 258.

187. **What they saw** Rondon, *Lectures,* p. 77.

187. **During the first portage** TR, *Through the Brazilian Wilderness,* p. 255.

187. **Kermit had gone** Kermit Roosevelt, *Diary,* March 7, 1914, KBRP.

188. **"very good eating"** TR, *Through the Brazilian Wilderness,* p. 249.

188. **Lyra and Kermit divided** Ibid., pp. 259–60.

188. **One group** George Cherrie, *Diary,* March 10, 1914, AMNH.

188. **Desperate not to** Ibid.

188. **In the process** TR, *Through the Brazilian Wilderness,* p. 261.

189. **"dressed substantially like"** Ibid.

189. **After twelve days** Rondon, *Lectures,* p. 78.

189. **Slowly, inch by inch** TR, *Through the Brazilian Wilderness,* p. 262.

189. **At some point** Rondon, *Lectures,* p. 78; TR, *Through the Brazilian Wilderness,* p. 262.

190. **"Rolling over the bowlders"** TR, *Through the Brazilian Wilderness,* p. 262.

Chapter 16: Danger Afloat, Danger Ashore

191. "That means time" George Cherrie, *Diary,* March 11, 1914, AMNH.

191. Each tin box Anthony Fiala, Appendix B, in Theodore Roosevelt, *Through the Brazilian Wilderness* (New York, 1914), p. 360.

192. "There were sufficient" George Cherrie, "The Birds of Matto Grosso, Brazil," *Bulletin of the American Museum of Natural History,* vol. 60 (1930), p. 12.

192. Not only had they Kermit Roosevelt, *Diary,* March 2, 1914, KBRP.

193. "it had some special" TR, *Through the Brazilian Wilderness,* p. 252.

193. "No one of us" Ibid., p. 255.

193. As the rain fell Ibid., p. 262.

193. It was a species Cândido Mariano da Silva Rondon, *Lectures Delivered on the 5th, 7th, and 9th of October, 1915* (Rio de Janeiro, 1916), p. 79; TR, *Through the Brazilian Wilderness,* p. 262.

193. The men measured George Cherrie, *Dark Trails* (New York, 1930), p. 286.

194. They worked in shifts Cherrie, "Birds of Matto Grosso," p. 12.

194. The toll on the camaradas Ibid., p. 11.

194. Even after the sun set TR, *Through the Brazilian Wilderness,* p. 266.

194. "Looking at the way" Ibid., p. 254.

194. "utterly worthless" Ibid., p. 290.

194. "When we were able" Rondon, *Lectures,* p. 105.

195. "In the Expedition" Ibid., p. 106.

195. "inborn, lazy shirk" TR, *Through the Brazilian Wilderness,* p. 290.

195. But Rondon was determined Rondon, *Lectures,* p. 106.

195. Twenty years earlier Todd A. Diacon, *Stringing Together a Nation* (Durham, N.C., 2004), p. 67.

195. Such punishment Donald F. O'Reilly, "Rondon: Biography of a Brazilian Republican Army Commander," Ph.D. dissertation, New York University, 1969, pp. 58–59.

195. Although Rondon deeply Rondon was put on trial in Rio de Janeiro for the caning incident, but the case was ultimately filed (ibid., p. 61).

196. Six years earlier Ibid., p. 100.

196. Kermit shot TR, *Through the Brazilian Wilderness,* p. 265. KR, *Diary,* March 13, 1914, KBRP.

196. "I spent the day" TR, *Through the Brazilian Wilderness,* p. 265.

196. "He was always alone" Rondon, *Lectures,* p. 77.

196. "Quite unknown" Theodore Roosevelt, *An Autobiography* (New York, 1913), p. 22.

197. "It was a continual" Kermit Roosevelt, *The Long Trail* (New York, 1921), p. 37.

197. On March 13 Cherrie, *Diary,* March 12, 1914, AMNH.

197. It took all twenty-two men Cherrie, *Dark Trails,* p. 287.

198. "Of the two hazards" TR, *Through the Brazilian Wilderness,* p. 267.

198. "one set of big ripples" Ibid.

198. It began to fill Cherrie, *Dark Trails,* p. 287.

199. "We had already met" Ibid., p. 288.

CHAPTER 17: Death in the Rapids

200. **When they climbed aboard** Theodore Roosevelt, *Through the Brazilian Wilderness* (New York, 1914), p. 268.

201. **Like the first set** Ibid.

201. **Pushing past the island** Cândido Mariano da Silva Rondon, *Lectures Delivered on the 5th, 7th, and 9th of October, 1915* (Rio de Janeiro, 1916), p. 80.

201. **Rondon quickly ordered** Ibid., p. 82.

201. **Sitting in his cramped** TR, *Through the Brazilian Wilderness*, p. 268.

202. **"rather one of them"** Quoted in Kathleen Dalton, *Theodore Roosevelt: A Strenuous Life* (New York, 2002), p. 134.

202. **Most of these tests** Theodore Roosevelt Jr., *All in the Family* (New York, 1929), p. 88.

202. **"a state of intense"** Theodore Roosevelt, *An Autobiography* (New York, 1913), p. 38.

202. **On one occasion** Hermann Hagedorn, *The Roosevelt Family of Sagamore Hill* (New York, 1954), p. 33.

203. **"Dive, Alice!"** Ibid., p. 32.

203. **"Kermit is a great pleasure"** TR to Corinne Roosevelt Robinson, June 21, 1909, in *Letters*, vol. 7, p. 17.

203. **He had disappeared** TR to Anna Roosevelt Cowles, Oct. 17, 1909, in *Letters*, vol. 7, p. 38.

203. **"Since I have been"** TR to Corinne Roosevelt Robinson, July 27, 1909, in *Letters*, vol. 7, p. 26.

203. **"great comfort and help"** TR, *Through the Brazilian Wilderness*, p. 270.

204. **The three men successfully rode** Rondon, *Lectures*, p. 82.

204. **"exceptionally good men"** TR, *Through the Brazilian Wilderness*, p. 268; see also Rondon, *Lectures*, p. 82.

204. **"the least seaworthy of all"** TR, *Through the Brazilian Wilderness*, p. 268.

204. **Realizing that their only** Ibid., pp. 268–69.

204. **Fighting to save** Rondon, *Lectures*, p. 82.

205. **From their canoe above** George Cherrie, *Dark Trails* (New York, 1930), p. 289.

CHAPTER 18: Attack

209. **When his dugout was swept** Theodore Roosevelt, *Through the Brazilian Wilderness* (New York, 1914), p. 269.

209. **"beaten out on the bowlders"** Ibid.

210. **As he approached** Cândido Mariano da Silva Rondon, *Lectures Delivered on the 5th, 7th, and 9th of October, 1915* (Rio de Janeiro, 1916), p. 80.

210. **Furious, and worried** Ibid., pp. 80–81.

210. **Rushing past the dog** Ibid., p. 81.

210. **After he was driven** TR, *Through the Brazilian Wilderness*, pp. 269–70.

211. **As valuable as** George Cherrie, *Diary*, March 15, 1914, AMNH.

211. **No sooner had** Rondon, *Lectures,* p. 82.

211. **"one hope left"** Ibid.

211. **After a frantic search** George Cherrie, *Dark Trails* (New York, 1930), p. 289; Kermit Roosevelt, *Diary,* March 15, 1914, KBRP.

211. **"Unfortunately the moment"** Rondon, *Lectures,* p. 82.

212. **"very narrow escape"** TR, *Through the Brazilian Wilderness,* p. 270.

212. **Although Kermit had joined** Ibid.

212. **"Simplicio was drowned"** KR, *Diary,* March 15, 1914, KBRP.

212. **"The loss of a human life"** Cherrie, *Dark Trails,* p. 289.

213. **"We may reach New York"** George Cherrie to Stella Cherrie, Feb. 26, 1914, AMNH.

213. **"Certainly no one"** Rondon, *Lectures,* pp. 82–83.

213. **"lets his soldiers die"** Quoted in Todd A. Diacon, "Are the Good Guys Always Bad?" Annual Meeting of the Southern Historical Association, Alabama, 1998, p. 17.

213. **"Death and dangers"** Esther de Viveiros, *Rondon: Conta Sua Vida* (Rio de Janeiro, 1958), p. 409.

214. **"perpetuated the name"** Rondon, *Lectures,* p. 83.

214. **"In these rapids"** TR, *Through the Brazilian Wilderness,* p. 270.

214. **The day before** Cherrie, *Dark Trails,* p. 290.

214. **At 7:00 a.m.** TR, *Through the Brazilian Wilderness,* pp. 271–72.

214. **Having satisfied himself** Rondon, *Lectures,* pp. 83–84.

215. **She had been raised** Donald F. O'Reilly, "Rondon: Biography of a Brazilian Republican Army Commander," Ph.D. dissertation, New York University, 1969, pp. 52, 62.

215. **She finally taught herself** Author's interview with Rondon's grandchildren, March 25, 2003.

215. **"This day brings us"** O'Reilly, "Rondon," p. 70.

215. **At times he had** Todd A. Diacon, *Stringing Together a Nation* (Durham, N.C., 2004), pp. 69–71.

216. **Now, contentedly walking** Rondon, *Lectures,* p. 84.

216. **The forest was** Ibid.

216. **Certain that Lobo** Ibid.

216. **Suddenly Lobo reappeared** Ibid., p. 85. In retrospect, Rondon concluded that the whinny he had heard had been not a spider monkey but an Indian imitating its call. He also realized that, by running ahead of him, Lobo had saved his life. (TR, Address to National Geographic Society, May 26, 1914, NGS.)

217. **He found the rest** Cherrie, *Dark Trails,* p. 291.

217. **While Rondon was gone** TR, *Through the Brazilian Wilderness,* p. 273.

217. **Rondon was deeply concerned** Rondon, *Lectures,* p. 84.

217. **By the time the five men** Ibid., pp. 85–86.

218. **Scanning the forest** Ibid., p. 86.

218. **That arrow had been launched** Cherrie, *Dark Trails,* pp. 291–92.

218. **"These melancholic reflections"** Viveiros, *Rondon,* p. 409.

218. **In fact, he claimed** O'Reilly, "Rondon," p. 146. Four years earlier, after a

group of Kayabi Indians had killed a rubber-tapper, Rondon had staunchly defended the Kayabi, pointing out that the tapper had had a long history of terrorizing these Indians. "I can assure you," he had written the tapper's employer, "that Indians never attack without a reason; they attack for no other reason than to defend themselves against treason and falsehoods." (Diacon, *Stringing Together a Nation,* p. 109.)

218. **"If you are shot"** TR, Address to National Geographic Society, May 26, 1914, NGS.

219. **But as he examined these arrows** Rondon, *Lectures,* p. 86.

CHAPTER 19: The Wide Belts

220. **Because they did not yet** Although it is believed that humans did use boats in their occupation of Australia and New Guinea, there is no substantial evidence of watercraft anywhere else in the world for another thirty thousand years. (Jared Diamond, *Guns, Germs, and Steel* [New York, 1999], p. 41.)

220. **Some twelve thousand years ago** Anna Roosevelt, ed., *Amazonian Indians: From Prehistory to the Present* (Tucson, 1994), p. 1.

221. **After the Spanish explorer** Alain Gheerbrant, *The Amazon* (New York, 1988), p. 27.

221. **Orellana named these women** John Kricher, *A Neotropical Companion* (Princeton, 1997), p. 198.

221. **While traveling down** Barbara Weinstein, *The Amazon Rubber Boom* (Stanford, Calif., 1983), p. 8.

222. **Julio César Arana** Wade Davis, *One River* (New York, 1996), pp. 236–39.

222. **Their best hope** Alex Shoumatoff, *The Rivers Amazon,* p. 42.

223. **"Such isolation"** George Cherrie, *Dark Trails* (New York, 1930), p. 217.

223. **The mysterious Indians** Author's interview with Cinta Larga.

224. **Their axes were ground** W. Jesco von Puttkamer, "Brazil Protects Her Cinta Largas," *National Geographic,* Sept. 1971; author's interview with Dr. Robert Carneiro. Roosevelt had known about and used matches his entire life. John Walker, an English chemist, had sold the first friction matches in 1827.

224. **So cut off from** Author's interview with Cinta Larga. The Roosevelt-Rondon Scientific Expedition was a momentous event in the lives of the Indians of this isolated tribe, and so the story has become part of the Cinta Larga's tribal lore and, over the intervening ninety-one years, has been passed down from generation to generation.

224. **Although they lived on** George Cherrie, *Diary,* April 12, 1914, AMNH; author's interview with Cinta Larga.

225. **The women, who wore their hair** Richard Chapelle, *Les Hommes à la Ceinture d'Écorce* (Paris, 1978), p. 100; von Puttkamer, "Brazil Protects Her Cinta Largas," p. 425.

225. **The tribe's trails were marked** "Cinta Larga," *Encyclopedia of Indigenous Peoples in Brazil* (Oct. 2003); Chapelle, *Les Hommes,* p. 117.

226. **In fact, so familiar** Chapelle, *Les Hommes,* p. 195; "Cinta Larga," *Encyclopedia of Indigenous Peoples in Brazil* (Oct. 2003).

226. **This milky liquid** Von Puttkamer, "Brazil Protects Her Cinta Largas," p. 435.

227. **Clearing the land** Robert L. Carneiro, "Indians of the Amazonian Forest," in *People of the Tropical Rain Forest* (Berkeley, Calif., 1988), pp. 80–82.

227. **Each Cinta Larga village** "Cinta Larga," *Encyclopedia of Indigenous Peoples in Brazil* (Oct. 2003).

227. **The chief had to exhibit** Ibid.

227. **The Cinta Larga would not** Chapelle, *Les Hommes,* pp. 104, 165–66.

227. **Not only did the chief** Ibid., pp. 179–82.

227. **Girls were considered** "Cinta Larga," *Encyclopedia of Indigenous Peoples in Brazil* (Oct. 2003).

227. **In such small** Chapelle, *Les Hommes,* pp. 179–82.

228. **Like women in most** Ibid., p. 181.

228. **As important as children were** Ibid., pp. 102–4.

228. **Because the Indians** Author's interview with Cinta Larga.

228. **War was not a rare event** Dal Poz, "No País dos Cinta Larga: Uma Etnografia do Ritual," Dissertação de Mestrado, University of São Paulo, 1991, p. 56; Chapelle, *Les Hommes,* p. 197.

229. **The Cinta Larga also occasionally** Dal Poz, "No País dos Cinta Larga," p. 60.

229. **They would cut their hair** Ibid., p. 57.

229. **The men were sometimes forced** Chapelle, *Les Hommes,* p. 165.

229. **Although skilled with** Dal Poz, "No País dos Cinta Larga," p. 58.

230. **They could eat** Ibid., pp. 276, 279.

230. **The tribe drew a clear distinction** Ibid., pp. 275–76.

231. **The Cinta Larga often tossed** Ibid., p. 274.

CHAPTER 20: Hunger

232. **There were no trees** Cândido Mariano da Silva Rondon, *Lectures Delivered on the 5th, 7th, and 9th of October, 1915* (Rio de Janeiro, 1916), p. 86.

233. **"We left all"** Theodore Roosevelt, *Through the Brazilian Wilderness* (New York, 1914), p. 274.

233. **"The only way"** Ibid.

233. **For better stability** Ibid.

233. **Their misery growing** Ibid., p. 275.

233. **They had already consumed** Ibid., p. 273.

234. **They limited themselves** Ibid., p. 287.

234. **"taste was not unpleasant"** Ibid., p. 257.

234. **Although raw** *palmito* George Cherrie, Memorial Meeting, March 1, 1919, TRC.

235. **So hard that they** "Tasty Brazil Nuts Stun Harvesters and Scientists," *Smithsonian,* April 1999.

236. **Because it touches** Adrian Forsyth and Kenneth Miyata, *Tropical Nature* (New York, 1984), pp. 66–71.

236. These specialized strategies John Kricher, *A Neotropical Companion* (Princeton, 1997), p. 128.

237. Even when they are mature Forsyth and Miyata, *Tropical Nature*, pp. 84–85.

238. "A curious effect" George Cherrie, *Dark Trails* (New York, 1930), p. 306.

238. When the conversations Cherrie, Memorial Meeting, March 1, 1919, TRC.

238. "When food was scarcest" Ibid.

239. On March 16 George Cherrie, *Diary*, March 16, 1914, AMNH.

239. The very next day Cherrie, *Diary*, March 17, 1914, AMNH.

239. "Up to this point" Rondon, *Lectures*, p. 88.

239. Not only did they find Kermit Roosevelt, *Diary*, March 17, 1914, KBRP.

239. Even better TR, *Through the Brazilian Wilderness*, p. 276.

240. The good mood Rondon, *Lectures*, p. 89.

240. "I had urged" TR, *Through the Brazilian Wilderness*, pp. 278–79.

240. "The camaradas" Ibid.

241. The men felt Cherrie, *Diary*, March 18, 1914, AMNH.

241. Rounding a bend Rondon, *Lectures*, p. 90.

242. While the Cinta Larga Cherrie, *Diary*, March 18, 1914, AMNH.

242. One night Cherrie, *Diary*, March 19, 1914, AMNH.

243. "could only make a small" Rondon, *Lectures*, p. 91.

243. They had not chosen Cherrie, *Dark Trails*, p. 297.

244. The trees that they TR, *Through the Brazilian Wilderness*, p. 280.

244. As the camaradas began Cherrie, *Dark Trails*, p. 298.

244. "had kept in full flesh" TR, *Through the Brazilian Wilderness*, p. 303.

244. The very next day Cherrie, *Diary*, March 21, 1914, AMNH; KR, *Diary*, March 21, 1914, KBRP.

245. The tension between TR, *Through the Brazilian Wilderness*, p. 284.

245. After the men had set up Rondon, *Lectures*, p. 92.

245. They had found KR, *Diary*, March 21, 1914, KBRP.

245. "Mr. Roosevelt asked me" Rondon, *Lectures*, p. 92.

246. The point of Roosevelt's talk Ibid.

246. "Kermit was extraordinarily" Esther de Viveiros, *Rondon: Conta Sua Vida* (Rio de Janeiro, 1958), p. 409.

246. "Mr. Kermit will not" Ibid.

246. "The topographical survey" Rondon, *Lectures*, p. 92.

CHAPTER 21: The Myth of "Beneficent Nature"

247. At 7:00 a.m. Theodore Roosevelt, *Through the Brazilian Wilderness* (New York, 1914), pp. 285–86.

247. "On all sides" Cândido Mariano da Silva Rondon, *Lectures Delivered on the 5th, 7th, and 9th of October, 1915* (Rio de Janeiro, 1916), p. 92.

248. The Brazilian colonel did not Ibid., pp. 92–93.

248. "Our position" George Cherrie, *Diary*, March 23, 1914, AMNH.

248. As Rondon had learned TR, *Through the Brazilian Wilderness*, p. 147.

249. **As big as a bumblebee** Andrew Speilman and Micheal D'Antonio, *Mosquito* (New York, 2001), pp. xvi–xvii.

249. **A botfly maggot** John Kricher, *A Neotropical Companion* (Princeton, 1997), pp. 379–80.

249. **The real menace** Speilman and D'Antonio, *Mosquito,* pp. 74–104.

250. **Once she has found** Ibid., pp. 13–16.

250. **Malaria was the danger** Todd A. Diacon, *Stringing Together a Nation* (Durham, N.C., 2004), p. 63.

250. **Just four years earlier** Ibid., pp. 63–65.

250. **He had only one** Robert S. Desowitz, *The Malaria Capers: Tales of Parasites and People* (New York, 1991), pp. 199–202.

250. **The Brazilian doctor** TR, *Through the Brazilian Wilderness,* p. 275.

251. **To be truly effective** Desowitz, *Malaria Capers,* pp. 202–3.

251. **The first sign of malaria** Speilman and D'Antonio, *Mosquito,* p. 84.

251. **Since contracting the disease** Will Irwin, ed., Introduction, *Letters to Kermit from Theodore Roosevelt* (New York, 1946), p. 2.

251. **He had had several attacks** Kermit Roosevelt, *Diary,* March 19, 1914, KBRP.

251. **Until the expedition reached** Cajazeira, *Relatório,* Museu do Índio, Rio de Janeiro.

252. **"The very pathetic myth"** TR, *Through the Brazilian Wilderness,* p. 147.

252. **"There is a universal saying"** Kermit Roosevelt, *The Long Trail* (New York, 1921), p. 9.

252. **"responsible to the law"** Ibid., p. 11.

252. **Roosevelt had witnessed** Ibid., p. 10.

253. **"Their clothes were"** TR, *Through the Brazilian Wilderness,* p. 302.

253. **"He wrote every day"** "Col. Roosevelt As His Guide Remembers Him," *New York Times,* Jan. 6, 1929, TRC.

254. **"the best camp companion"** George Cherrie, "Roosevelt in the Field," May 26, 1927, AMNH.

254. **Cherrie had just taken** George Cherrie, *Dark Trails* (New York, 1930), pp. 300–301.

254. **"Day after day"** Cherrie, "Roosevelt in the Field," AMNH.

254–55. **"We talked together often"** TR, *Through the Brazilian Wilderness,* p. 297.

255. **He had gone to work** Cherrie, *Dark Trails,* p. 5.

255. **Cherrie took a bland** Ibid.

255. **South American insurrections** TR, *Through the Brazilian Wilderness,* pp. 3–4.

256. **"They say that"** Rondon, *Lectures,* p. 109.

256. **He was a sergeant** Ibid., p. 107.

256. **When Paishon accepted** Esther de Viveiros, *Rondon: Conta Sua Vida* (Rio de Janeiro, 1958), pp. 414–15.

256. **In fact, since the expedition** TR, *Through the Brazilian Wilderness,* p. 303.

256. **He shamelessly begged** Ibid., p. 303.

256. **The only incentive** Rondon, *Lectures,* pp. 105–6.

257. **"Julio came crying"** TR, *Through the Brazilian Wilderness,* p. 303.

257. **"On such an expedition"** Ibid., p. 303.

CHAPTER 22: "I Will Stop Here"

258. **Antonio Correia** Theodore Roosevelt, *Through the Brazilian Wilderness* (New York, 1914), p. 288.

259. **"probably means many more"** George Cherrie, *Diary*, March 25, 1914, AMNH.

259. **The skies had been clear** Cherrie, *Diary*, March 26, 1914, AMNH.

259. **"as big as cables"** TR, *Through the Brazilian Wilderness*, p. 291.

259. **On that day** Ibid., pp. 291–92.

259. **One of the camaradas also caught** Cherrie, *Diary*, March 26, 1914, AMNH.

259. **Rondon's meticulous charting** Cherrie, *Diary*, March 24, 1914, AMNH.

260. **On the day after** TR, *Through the Brazilian Wilderness*, p. 293.

260. **Cherrie had wandered** Cherrie, *Diary*, March 27, 1914, AMNH.

260. **The two boats were pinned** Ibid.

261. **Roosevelt was the first** George Cherrie, *Dark Trails* (New York, 1930), p. 253.

261. **Six years later, while he was riding** Kermit Roosevelt, *The Long Trail* (New York, 1921), p. 38.

261. **Although the water level** George Cherrie, Memorial Meeting, March 1, 1919, TRC.

262. **When they reached** TR, *Through the Brazilian Wilderness*, p. 293.

262. **As the river roared** KR, *Long Trail*, p. 72.

262. **"From that time on"** Cherrie, Memorial Meeting, March 1, 1919, TRC.

262. **When the men had finally** Cherrie, *Dark Trails*, p. 253; TR, *Through the Brazilian Wilderness*, p. 293.

262. **It was 4:00 p.m.** TR, *Through the Brazilian Wilderness*, pp. 293–94.

262. **"Practically everything"** Cherrie, *Dark Trails*, p. 303.

263. **After fighting their way** Kermit Roosevelt, *Diary*, March 28, 1914, KBRP.

263. **Within this gorge** Cândido Mariano da Silva Rondon, *Lectures Delivered on the 5th, 7th, and 9th of October, 1915* (Rio de Janeiro, 1916), pp. 98–99.

263. **It was immediately apparent** Ibid.

264. **Cherrie wrote that he** Cherrie, *Dark Trails*, pp. 307–8.

264. **"Many cases have been"** Arkady Fiedler, *The River of Singing Fish* (London, 1951), pp. 102–3.

264. **did not "utter a word"** Cherrie, *Dark Trails*, pp. 253, 308.

265. **"No man has any business"** TR, *Through the Brazilian Wilderness*, p. 319.

265. **When he was a rancher** Theodore Roosevelt, *An Autobiography* (New York, 1913), pp. 118–19.

265. **"Both the men of my"** Ibid., p. 140.

265. **When a doctor** John Milton Cooper, *The Warrior and the Priest* (Cambridge, Mass., 1983), p. 14.

266. **"quite content to go now"** Kathleen Dalton, *Theodore Roosevelt: A Strenuous Life* (New York, 2002), p. 176.

266. **"I had always felt"** TR, *Autobiography*, p. 222.

266. **"The truth is"** Quoted in Cooper, *The Warrior and the Priest*, p. 154.

266. **To John Barrett** John Barrett, *The Call of South America* (New York, 1922), p. 5.

266. "I have always" Oscar King Davis, *Released for Publication* (Boston, 1925), p. 434.

267. Just before dawn Cherrie, *Dark Trails*, pp. 308–9.

Chapter 23: Missing

271. They were not prepared *New York Times,* March 23, 1914.

271. The article had been sparked Ibid.

272. The newspaper did its best Ibid.

272. Earlier in the year Sylvia Jukes Morris, *Edith Kermit Roosevelt: Portrait of a First Lady* (New York, 1980), p. 402.

273. "Can you obtain" Quoted in *New York Times,* March 24, 1914.

273. Spanish-American War Edward Renehan, *The Lion's Pride* (New York, 1999), p. 27.

274. Kermit had succeeded TR to Ethel Roosevelt Derby, Dec. 10, 1913, TRC.

274. From her hotel in Madrid *New York Times,* Jan. 4, 1914, KBRP.

274. A few days after Fiala's *Washington Post,* March 28, 1914, KBRP.

275. "I have sent you" Belle Willard to KR, n.d., KBRP.

275. On the overland journey Theodore Roosevelt, *Through the Brazilian Wilderness* (New York, 1914), p. 177.

275. "The desert has always" KR to Belle Willard, Nov. 20, 1913, KBRP.

275. "You must be getting" KR to Belle Willard, Jan. 31, 1913, KBRP.

276. Even Roosevelt's sister Bamie Quoted in Kathleen Dalton, *Theodore Roosevelt: A Strenuous Life* (New York, 2002), p. 134.

276. Kermit, who had been Quoted in J. J. Perling, *Presidents' Sons: The Prestige of Name in a Democracy* (New York, 1947), pp. 253–54.

276. "melancholic streak" Quoted in Dalton, *TR: A Strenuous Life,* p. 197.

276. "one with the white head" Edith Roosevelt to Anna Roosevelt Cowles, Oct. 5, 1913, TRC.

276. "odd and independent" Quoted in Peter Collier with David Horowitz, *The Roosevelts: An American Saga* (New York, 1994), p. 117.

276. "He never need retire" Quoted in Hermann Hagedorn, *The Roosevelt Family of Sagamore Hill* (New York, 1954), p. 22.

277. While at Groton Quoted in Dalton, *TR: A Strenuous Life,* p. 326.

277. In childhood, Elliott Blanche Wiesen Cook, *Eleanor Roosevelt,* vol. 1 (New York, 1992), p. 32.

277. When their father died David McCullough, *Mornings on Horseback* (New York, 1981), p. 187.

277. "Elliott gave unstintedly" Corinne Roosevelt Robinson, *My Brother Theodore Roosevelt* (New York, 1921), p. 104.

277. "He was so mad" Quoted in Edmund Morris, *The Rise of Theodore Roosevelt* (New York, 1979), p. 94.

277. Four years later Cook, *Eleanor Roosevelt,* vol. 1, p. 43.

278. **Theodore wrote to Bamie** TR to Anna Roosevelt Cowles, July 29, 1894, in *Letters,* vol. 1, p. 392.

278. **"I only need"** Quoted in McCullough, *Mornings on Horseback,* p. 369.

278. **"more overcome"** Quoted in Dalton, *TR: A Strenuous Life,* p. 140.

279. **When Kermit was at Groton** In 1902, after receiving several reports on Kermit's schoolwork that were less than sterling, Roosevelt had sent his then thirteen-year-old son a letter clearly intended to shake him out of his lethargy. "I do not like your having so many black marks," he had written from the White House. "As you know, I have much sympathy for some kinds of mischief, but there are other kinds with which I have no sympathy at all." (TR to KR, Nov. 24, 1902, TRC.)

279. **After leaving Harvard** Morison, *The Letters of Theodore Roosevelt,* Elting E. Morris, ed. (Cambridge, Mass., 1951–1954), p. 1145 n.

279. **"I do not like"** Quoted in Collier with Horowitz, *The Roosevelts,* p. 129.

279. **"We worked hard"** TR to Archie Roosevelt, Feb. 27, 1910, in *Theodore Roosevelt's Letters to His Children* (New York, 1919), pp. 239–40.

280. **"It came to me"** Oscar King Davis, *Released for Publication* (Boston, 1925), pp. 434–35.

CHAPTER 24: The Worst in a Man

281. **"Kermit," Roosevelt would later** Theodore Roosevelt, *Through the Brazilian Wilderness* (New York, 1914), p. 294.

282. **Lyra had come to respect** Ibid., p. 302.

282. **"everything except the food"** Kermit Roosevelt, *Diary,* March 28, 1914, KBRP.

282. **Roosevelt kept only** TR, *Through the Brazilian Wilderness,* p. 295.

283. **"The work was not only"** Ibid., p. 295.

283. **The men understood** Cândido Mariano da Silva Rondon, *Lectures Delivered on the 5th, 7th, and 9th of October, 1915* (Rio de Janeiro, 1916), p. 100.

283. **While Kermit and Lyra struggled** George Cherrie, *Dark Trails* (New York, 1930), p. 305.

283. **On the third day** George Cherrie, *Diary,* March 30, 1914, AMNH.

284. **To add to** Rondon, *Lectures,* p. 103.

284. **The storm even** TR, *Through the Brazilian Wilderness,* p. 298.

284. **The men began** Cherrie, *Diary,* April 2, 1914, AMNH.

284. **"Instead of getting out"** Ibid.

284. **During that month** TR, *Through the Brazilian Wilderness,* pp. 298–99.

284. **"No one can tell"** Ibid., p. 301.

285. **"We had to cheer them"** Ibid., p. 299.

285. **"In the weeks"** Cherrie, *Dark Trails,* p. 253.

285. **Early on, Roosevelt** *New York Times,* Jan. 6, 1929, TRC.

285. **He began to give** George Cherrie, Memorial Meeting, March 1, 1919, TRC.

285. **"A sense of gloom"** Cherrie, *Dark Trails,* p. 303.

285. On March 30 KR, *Diary,* March 30, 1914, KBRP.

286. "considerable suffering" Rondon, *Lectures,* p. 102.

286. During an earlier expedition, Cherrie, *Dark Trails,* p. 114.

286. "Under such conditions" TR, *Through the Brazilian Wilderness,* p. 302.

287. While Antonio Correia Cherrie, *Diary,* April 3, 1914, AMNH.

287. While Lyra and his men Ibid.

287. Only one man TR, *Through the Brazilian Wilderness,* p. 304; Cherrie, *Dark Trails,* p. 311.

288. It was not long TR, *Through the Brazilian Wilderness,* p. 304.

288. At the intermediate Cherrie, *Diary,* April 3, 1914, AMNH.

288. After Julio had set TR, *Through the Brazilian Wilderness,* p. 304.

288. "I wonder what" Cherrie, *Dark Trails,* pp. 310–11.

288. The men's voices Cherrie, *Diary,* April 3, 1914, AMNH.

Chapter 25: "He Who Kills Must Die"

289. "We all felt" George Cherrie, *Dark Trails* (New York, 1930), p. 311.

289. At the intermediate station George Cherrie, *Diary,* April 3, 1914, AMNH.

290. To Kermit and Cherrie's Cherrie, *Dark Trails,* p. 311.

290. The young man lay Cândido Mariano da Silva Rondon, *Lectures Delivered on the 5th, 7th, and 9th of October, 1915* (Rio de Janeiro, 1916), p. 105.

290. Julio had shot Theodore Roosevelt, *Through the Brazilian Wilderness* (New York, 1914), p. 304.

290. "My eyes are better" Ibid.

290. It had taken Lyra Rondon, *Lectures,* pp. 104–5.

291. "in a blind rage" Kermit Roosevelt, *Diary,* April 7, 1914, KBRP.

291. "When I met him" Esther de Viveiros, *Rondon: Conta Sua Vida* (Rio de Janeiro, 1958), p. 416.

291. "that the evil doer" Amilcar Botelho de Magalhães, *Impressão da Comissão Rondon,* p. 210.

292. As they argued Viveiros, *Rondon,* p. 416.

292. The two camaradas Cherrie, *Dark Trails,* p. 312.

292. "Perhaps hearing" Ibid., p. 305.

292. "His murderous hatred" Ibid., p. 305.

292. "the poor body" Ibid., p. 308.

293. "the bad destiny" Rondon, *Lectures,* p. 107.

293. While the officers stood Cherrie, *Dark Trails,* p. 312.

293. "reverently and carefully" Cherrie, *Diary,* April 3, 1914, AMNH.

293. Together they laid Rondon, *Lectures,* p. 108.

293. "Then we left him" TR, *Through the Brazilian Wilderness,* p. 308.

293. One man was stationed Cherrie, *Diary,* April 3, 1914, AMNH.

294. Since they could not risk Cherrie, *Dark Trails,* p. 314.

294. As his chest heaved Rondon, *Lectures,* p. 108.

294. "As he and I went" Cherrie, *Dark Trails,* p. 306.

295. **Kermit was acutely aware** KR, *Diary,* April 2, 1914, KBRP.

295. **"There were a good many"** George Cherrie, Memorial Meeting, March 1, 1919, p. 28, TRC.

295. **"with the fire of decision"** Cherrie, *Dark Trails,* pp. 5–6.

295. **So closely did** Cajazeira, *Relatório,* Museo do Índio, Rio de Janeiro, p. 39.

296. **As an added precaution** Cherrie, *Diary,* April 4, 1914, AMNH.

296. **Cajazeira wrapped Roosevelt** Cajazeira, *Relatório,* p. 39.

296. **Roosevelt's condition** Ibid.

296. **Every six hours** Exhibit, Relatório Geral, Museu de Republic.

296. **"only a few fractions"** Cajazeira, *Relatório,* p. 39.

297. **As his temperature** Kermit Roosevelt, *The Long Trail* (New York, 1921), pp. 74–75.

297. **As the night wore on** Ibid., pp. 75–76.

297. **At about 2:00 a.m.,** Viveiros, *Rondon,* p. 416. Rondon tried to reason with Roosevelt, but he was, the Brazilian colonel would later write, "restless and irritated by my resistance." Finally, Rondon pointed out to Roosevelt that the expedition had both of their names on it. "For that reason," the Brazilian said, "it is impossible for us to be separate." (Viveiros, *Rondon,* p. 416.)

297. **Rondon immediately ordered** Rondon, *Lectures,* p. 109.

298. **Cajazeira planned** Cajazeira, *Relatório,* p. 39.

298. **"I have fever"** KR, *Diary,* April 5, 1914, KBRP.

298. **Later, when Antonio** Cherrie, *Diary,* April 5, 1914, AMNH.

299. **Notwithstanding the monkeys'** TR, *Through the Brazilian Wilderness,* p. 310.

299. **"I found"** KR, *Diary,* April 5, 1914, KBRP.

299. **"The fresh meat"** Cherrie, *Dark Trails,* p. 315.

299. **"For the most part"** Cherrie, *Diary,* April 6, 1914, AMNH.

300. **"Senhor Coronel!"** Viveiros, *Rondon,* p. 416.

300. **Rondon looked up** Rondon, *Lectures,* p. 114.

CHAPTER 26: Judgment

301. **"imploring for mercy"** Cândido Mariano da Silva Rondon, *Lectures Delivered on the 5th, 7th, and 9th of October, 1915* (Rio de Janeiro, 1916), p. 114.

301. **"an arrant craven"** Theodore Roosevelt, *Through the Brazilian Wilderness* (New York, 1914), p. 307.

301. **"It is not possible"** Esther de Viveiros, *Rondon: Conta Sua Vida* (Rio de Janeiro, 1958), p. 314.

301. **Having said all** Amilcar Botelho de Magalhães, *Impressão da Commissão Rondon,* p. 210.

302. **They refused to look** TR, *Through the Brazilian Wilderness,* p. 307.

302. **Seated in different dugouts** Rondon named the tributary the Rio Capitão Cardoso, in honor of one of his most valued soldiers, the man who had died from beriberi just before the expedition had reached the telegraph station at Cáceres. It was, he wrote, "a modest homage of the gratitude . . . which I owe to an old and constant companion in my work in the wilderness." (Rondon, *Lectures,* p. 111.)

302. "Rondon," Kermit wrote Kermit Roosevelt, *Diary,* April 6, 1914, KBRP.

302. "the duty of a Brazilian officer" Rondon, *Lectures,* p. 114.

303. "What was our astonishment" George Cherrie, *Diary,* April 7, 1914, AMNH.

303. "the clash was tremendous" Viveiros, *Rondon,* p. 416.

303. "could not legally" Ibid.

303. "He, Colonel Rondon" TR, *Through the Brazilian Wilderness,* p. 307.

304. "To take the greatest advantage" Rondon, *Lectures,* p. 115.

304. "Today Col. Rondon" Cherrie, *Diary,* April 7, 1914, AMNH.

304. When the camarada returned George Cherrie, *Dark Trails* (New York, 1930), p. 316.

304. "It may well be" Cherrie, *Diary,* April 7, 1914, AMNH.

304. However, as well as Ibid.

305. Slicing open its belly TR, *Through the Brazilian Wilderness,* p. 311.

305. For the Brazilians, such There is no modern scientific evidence that piraíba are man eaters.

305. Cajazeira himself TR, *Through the Brazilian Wilderness,* pp. 311–12.

306. Night had fallen Rondon, *Lectures,* p. 115.

306. "It was questionable" TR, *Through the Brazilian Wilderness,* p. 305.

306. According to one account Richard Chapelle, *Les Hommes à la Ceinture d'Écorce* (Paris, 1978), p. 160.

CHAPTER 27: The Cauldron

307. In a rare moment Anthony Fiala, Appendix B, in Theodore Roosevelt, *Through the Brazilian Wilderness* (New York, 1914), p. 363.

307. Any hope that George Cherrie, *Diary,* April 9, 1914, AMNH.

308. "On the 10th" TR, *Through the Brazilian Wilderness,* p. 313.

308. "How I longed" Ibid.

308. "My supper" Cherrie, *Diary,* April 8, 1914, AMNH.

308. The officers did their best TR, *Through the Brazilian Wilderness,* p. 314.

308. "The lack of" Cherrie, *Diary,* April 8, 1914, AMNH.

308. "A long further delay" TR, *Through the Brazilian Wilderness,* p. 309.

309. "scarce able to stand" Cherrie, *Diary,* April 9, 1914, AMNH.

309. Deeply concerned Kermit Roosevelt, *Diary,* April 15, 1914, KBRP.

309. Kermit was so sick Cherrie, *Diary,* April 10, 1914, AMNH.

309. Kermit had even written KR to Belle Willard, Jan. 2, 1914, KBRP.

310. "something began to" Arkaday Fiedler, *The River of Singing Fish* (London, 1951), p. 76.

310. "The forest of the Amazons" H. M. Tomlinson, *The Sea and the Jungle* (Evanston, Ill., 1999), p. 138.

310. Cherrie discovered Cherrie, *Diary,* April 10, 1914, AMNH.

311. "No sign of mental depression" Cândido Mariano da Silva Rondon, *Lectures Delivered on the 5th, 7th, and 9th of October, 1915* (Rio de Janeiro, 1916), p. 116.

311. For his trip to Africa Kermit Roosevelt, *The Long Trail* (New York, 1921), p. 52.

311. "The plans for the Brazilian" Ibid., p. 50.

311. Among the books TR, *Through the Brazilian Wilderness*, p. 241.

312. "These and many others" Ibid., pp. 260–61.

312. "The choice from Longfellow's" KR, *The Long Trail*, p. 52.

312. "For French verse" Ibid., p. 53.

312. On April 11, he finished KR, *Diary*, April 11, 1914, KBRP.

313. "felt the need of" George Cherrie, Memorial Meeting, March 1, 1919, p. 28, TRC.

313. "Personally I feel" Cherrie, *Diary*, April 11, 1914, AMNH.

313. "A precedence" Ibid.

314. While waiting Cherrie, *Diary*, April 12, 1914, AMNH.

314. Not only did the Ibid.

CHAPTER 28: The Rubber Men

318. "It is blasphemous" H. M. Tomlinson, *The Sea and the Jungle* (Evanston, Ill., 1999), p. 149.

318. "Into this rubbery wilderness" John Muir, *John Muir's Last Journey,* Michael P. Branch, ed. (Washington, D.C., 2001), p. 54.

318. Thirty-six years earlier Barbara Weinstein, *The Amazon Rubber Boom* (Stanford, Calif., 1983), p. 219.

318. Labor in Malaysia Alex Shoumatoff, *The Rivers Amazon* (San Francisco, 1978), p. 99.

318. Because of the cost It was not until later that scientists realized that rubber tree cultivation would never work in the Amazon because the trees have too many natural enemies. In the wild, they protect themselves as a species by never living in a stand, thus making it difficult for a blight to spread from one tree to another. It is rare to find more than a single rubber tree per acre in the Amazon. (Weinstein, *Amazon Rubber Boom*, p. 14.)

319. By the time Roosevelt's Theodore Roosevelt, *Through the Brazilian Widerness* (New York, 1914), p. 325.

319. "Such a man" Ibid., p. 324.

319. The *seringueiro's* day Claude Lévi-Strauss, *Tristes Tropiques* (New York, 1992), p. 367.

319. By 10:00 a.m. Weinstein, *Amazon Rubber Boom*, p. 16; Lévi-Strauss, *Tristes Tropiques*, pp. 367–68.

320. "red-letter day" TR, *Through the Brazilian Wilderness*, p. 315.

320. After launching their boats Cândido Mariano da Silva Rondon, *Lectures Delivered on the 5th, 7th, and 9th of October, 1915* (Rio de Janeiro, 1916), p. 118.

320. An hour later George Cherrie, *Diary*, April 15, 1914, AMNH.

321. The house belonged TR, *Through the Brazilian Wilderness,* p. 316.

321. "So none of the provisions" Cherrie, *Diary*, April 15, AMNH.

321. Little more than a mile Rondon, *Lectures*, p. 119.

321. When Rondon saw Marques Ibid.

322. The former president Cajazeira, *Relatório*, Museo do Índio, Rio de Janeiro, p. 42.

322. The canvas would have Ibid.

322. The skin around his wound Ibid.

323. "We administered the palliative" Ibid.

323. "As was only natural" Ibid.

323. So sick was the former president Rondon, *Lectures,* p. 119.

324. Marques, who was among Ibid.

324. A frightened *seringueiro* Ibid., pp. 121–22.

325. From their canoes George Cherrie, *Dark Trails* (New York, 1930), p. 320.

325. Seeing his opportunity Rondon, *Lectures,* p. 120.

325. So deep-seated Ibid.

325. As soon as she could talk Cherrie, *Diary,* April 15, 1914, AMNH.

325. He and three of his neighbors Cherrie, *Dark Trails,* p. 321.

326. Honorato began to realize Ibid.

326. "most hospitable" TR, *Through the Brazilian Wilderness,* p. 316.

326. "like a dream" Ibid., p. 316.

326. Even the sight Cherrie, *Diary,* April 15, 1914, AMNH.

327. Sitting outside after Ibid.

328. From the start Author's interview with Cinta Larga.

CHAPTER 29: A Pair of Flags

330. According to the expedition's Theodore Roosevelt, *Through the Brazilian Wilderness* (New York, 1914), p. 316.

330. "working poorly" Kermit Roosevelt, *Diary,* April 16, 1914, KBRP.

330. "retained their original" TR, *Through the Brazilian Wilderness,* p. 319.

331. Just two days earlier KR, *Diary,* April 14, 1914, KBRP.

331. "in worse shape" TR, *Through the Brazilian Wilderness,* p. 319.

331. "If I am to go" *New York Times,* Jan. 7, 1919.

331. Using only the simplest Cajazeira, *Relatório* Museo do Índio, Rio de Janeiro, p. 42.

331. As the doctor worked TR, *Through the Brazilian Wilderness,* p. 319.

331. "Father's courage" Kermit Roosevelt, *The Long Trail* (New York, 1921), p. 76.

332. "dusky cigar-smoking wife" TR, *Through the Brazilian Wilderness,* p. 322.

332. Although the operation George Cherry, *Diary,* April 21, 1914, AMNH.

332. The bacterial infection Cajazeira, *Relatória,* p. 43.

332. "He eats very little" Cherry, *Diary,* April 21, 1914, AMNH.

332. They rejoiced when TR, *Through the Brazilian Wilderness,* p. 325.

332. At exorbitant cost Cherry, *Diary,* April 20, 1914, AMNH.

333. "In this land of plenty" TR, *Through the Brazilian Wilderness,* p. 325.

333. The only food Cherrie, *Diary,* April 23, 1914, AMNH.

333. After months of worrying KR, *Diary,* April 20, 1914, KBRP.

333. Concern over Roosevelt's condition Cherrie, *Diary,* April 24, 1914, AMNH.

333. These falls TR, *Through the Brazilian Wilderness,* p. 328.

333. Men much younger Ibid.

333. "the 'king' " Cherrie, *Diary,* April 24, 1914, AMNH.

334. Caripe was exactly TR, *Through the Brazilian Wilderness,* pp. 328–29.

334. The Carupanan falls demanded KR, *Diary,* April 25, 1914, KBRP.

334. On the afternoon of April 26 TR, *Through the Brazilian Wilderness,* pp. 329–30.

334. When the men on the river Ibid., p. 330.

EPILOGUE

336. On the afternoon of May 19, 1914 *New York Times,* May 20, 1914.

336. "brown as the saddle" *New York World,* May 20, 1914.

337. "wasted to a mere shadow" Leo E. Miller, *In the Wilds of South America* (New York, 1918), p. 264.

337. For his trip from Manáos *New York World,* May 20, 1914.

337. It was not until *New York Times,* May 19, 1914.

337. Not only did he regain *New York Times,* May 20, 1914.

337. "I am all right" *New York Sun,* May 20, 1914.

338. "certainly is a very remarkable" *New York World,* May 7, 1914.

338. "charlatan" *New York World,* May 9, 1914.

338. "If the Colonel says" *New York World,* May 8, 1914.

338. "unconsciously paid" *New York Times,* May 14, 1914.

339. "a pure fake" TR to Arthur Hamilton Lee, May 23, 1914, TRC. Rondon had traveled with Landor during his visit to Brazil, and he wrote Roosevelt a letter stating that the self-proclaimed explorer had not entered any uncharted territory. Roosevelt later published this letter in *Le Matin,* one of the largest newspapers in Paris, where Landor was living. "I think that I have definitely put a stop to all serious considerations of his claims as an explorer so far as competent observers and witnesses are concerned," Roosevelt later wrote to Rondon. *(New York Times,* June 13, 1914; TR to Rondon, Nov. 5, 1914, TRP.)

339. The society, which had fought *New York Times,* May 27, 1914.

339. Following a dinner Gilbert Grosvenor to Melville Grosvenor, Dec. 29, 1962, NGS.

339. As Roosevelt entered *New York Sun,* May 27, 1914.

340. "The striking thing" *New York World,* May 27, 1914.

340. Asking the journalists Theodore Roosevelt, Address to National Geographic Society, May 26, 1914, NGS.

340. "I sat in the front row" Gilbert Grosvenor to Melville Grosvenor, Dec. 29, 1962, NGS.

340. "any doubts that *New York Evening Journal,* May 27, 1914.

340. Roosevelt's chance Belle had been forced to move her wedding date from April to June because of the late arrival of the expedition, but it still took place in Madrid.

341. Outside the front door *New York Times,* June 17, 1914.

341. Lifelong members *New York Tribune,* June 17, 1914.

341. Even Lord Earl Grey *Times of London,* June 17, 1914.

341. "All the benches" Ibid.

341. In his opening remarks Ibid.

342. "stepped briskly" Unnamed newspaper, June 5, 1914, TRC.

342. "not in good trim" TR to Arthur Hamilton Lee, June 29, 1914, in *Letters*, vol. 8, p. 769.

342. "demonstrate his growing skill" *Literary Digest*, May 23, 1914, TRC.

343. Months after the news Kathleen Dalton, *Theodore Roosevelt: A Strenuous Life* (New York, 2002), p. 507.

343. "old Brazilian trouble" TR to KR, Feb. 18, 1917, in *Letters*, vol. 8, p. 1286.

343. "When the young die" TR to Corinne Roosevelt Robinson, Aug. 3, 1918, in *Letters*, vol. 8, pp. 1356–57.

343. "All right!" Quoted in Hermann Hagedorn, *The Roosevelt Family of Sagamore Hill* (New York, 1954), p. 423.

344. "Never before" John Burroughs, "Theodore Roosevelt," *Journal of the American Museum of Natural History*, Jan. 1919, TRC.

344. Just three years after Amilcar Botelho de Magalhães, *Impressão da Commissão Rondon*, p. 133.

344. Albert Zahm became Fred Howard, *Wilbur and Orville: A Biography of the Wright Brothers* (New York, 1987).

345. Father Zahm himself Ralph E. Weber, *Notre Dame's John Zahm* (Notre Dame, 1961), p. 196.

345. After his expedition Joseph R. Ornig, *My Last Chance to Be a Boy* (Mechanicsburg, Pa., 1994), p. 222.

345. He loved fishing Author's interview with Hubert Cherrie, George and Stella Cherrie's grandson.

345. The same year Todd A. Diacon, *Stringing Together a Nation* (Durham, N.C., 2004), p. 49.

346. He was hounded Donald F. O'Reilly, "Rondon: Biography of a Brazilian Republican Army Commander," Ph.D. dissertation, New York University, 1969, pp. 187, 192.

346. When Rondon left Mac Margolis, *The Conquest of the Amazon Frontier* (New York, 1992), p. 92.

347. He took a job Unnamed newspaper, July 30, 1914, TRC.

347. "The bottom has dropped" Quoted in Edward Renehan, *The Lion's Pride* (New York, 1998), p. 223.

347. In the 1920s Peter Collier with David Horowitz, *The Roosevelts: An American Saga* (New York, 1994), pp. 381, 398.

348. Kermit lost Belle's Collier with Horowitz, *The Roosevelts*, p. 380.

348. When Kermit disappeared Ibid., p. 411.

348. At fifty-two Renehan, *Lion's Pride*, pp. 231–32.

348. On the night of June 3, 1943 Collier with Horowitz, *The Roosevelts*, p. 413; Renehan, *Lion's Pride*, p. 232.

349. Not until 1926 *New York Times*, June 26, 1927.

349. By the 1950s W. Jesco von Puttkamer, "Brazil Protects Her Cinta Largas," *National Geographic*, Sept. 1971, p. 421.

349. **It was not until** Initially, FUNAI officials were uncertain how many tribes and sub-tribes lived along the River of Doubt and so classified them all as Cinta Larga. As contact with the tribesmen grew, experts later distinguished between the tribe that lives to the west of the river and the tribe that lives to the east. The former calls itself the Paiter, and is now officially known as the Suruí. The latter refers to itself as the Matétamãe, and is known to the outside world as the Cinta Larga. (For excellent descriptions of FUNAI's first contact with the Suruí and Cinta Larga, see John Hemming, *Die If You Must* [London, 2003], pp. 301–7, and Von Puttkamer, "Brazil Protects Her Cinta Largas."

350. **The Indians kept** Von Puttkamer, "Brazil Protects Her Cinta Largas," p. 428.

350. **Steps toward pacification** Ibid., p. 420.

350. **After the exchange** Ibid.

351. **On March 1, 1919** George Cherrie, Memorial Meeting, March 1, 1919, TRC.

352. **"I have always thought"** Ibid., pp. 21, 28.

SELECT BIBLIOGRAPHY

Abbott, Lawrence F. *Impressions of Theodore Roosevelt.* New York: Doubleday, Page & Company, 1919.

Agosta, William. *Bombardier Beetles and Fever Trees: A Close-up Look at Chemical Warfare and Signals in Animals and Plants.* New York: Addison-Wesley Publishing, 1995.

———. *Thieves, Deceivers and Killers: Tales of Chemistry in Nature.* Princeton: Princeton University Press, 2001.

Angle, Paul M. *Crossroads: 1913.* Chicago: Rand McNally & Company, 1963.

Anthony, H. E. "The Capture and Preservation of Small Mammals for Study." *The American Museum of Natural History, Science Guide No. 61, 1950.*

Appleby, R. Scott. "Between Americanism and Modernism: John Zahm and Theistic Evolution." *Church History,* 1987.

Attenborough, David. *The Private Life of Plants.* Princeton: Princeton University Press, 1995.

Ayensu, Edward S. *The Life and Mysteries of the Jungle.* New York: Crescent Books, 1980.

Barrett, John. *The Call of South America.* New York: Members of the Pan American Society of the United States, 1922.

Bartlett, R. D., and Patricia Bartlett. *Reptiles and Amphibians of the Amazon.* Gainesville: University Press of Florida, 2003.

Bates, Henry Walter. *The Naturalist on the River Amazons.* London: John Murray, 1864.

Bierregaard, Richard O., Jr., et al. *Lessons from Amazonia: The Ecology and Conservation of a Fragmented Forest.* New Haven, Conn.: Yale University Press, 2001.

Bodard, Lucien. *Green Hell: Massacre of the Brazilian Indians,* trans. Jennifer Monaghan. New York: Outerbridge & Dienstfrey, 1971.

Brands, H. W. *T. R.: The Last Romantic*. New York: Basic Books, 1997.

Brooks, Edwin, et al. *Tribes of the Amazon Basin in Brazil 1972*. London: Charles Knight & Co., 1973.

Burns, E. Bradford. *A History of Brazil*. New York: Columbia University Press, 1993.

Burroughs, John. "Theodore Roosevelt: His Americanism Reached into the Marrow of His Bones." *Natural History*, January 1919.

Chace, James. *1912: Wilson, Roosevelt, Taft and Debs—The Election That Changed the Country*. New York: Simon & Schuster, 2004.

Chapelle, Richard. *Les Hommes à la Ceinture d'Écorce*. France: Flammarion, 1978.

Chapman, Frank M. *Autobiography of a Bird Lover*. New York: D. Appleton-Century Company, 1933.

Cherrie, George. *Dark Trails: Adventures of a Naturalist*. New York: G. P. Putnam's Sons, 1930.

———. "Theodore Roosevelt Memorial Meeting at The Explorers Club." March 1, 1919.

———. "Through the Brazilian Wilderness with Colonel Roosevelt." In *Exploration Tales for Soldiers and Sailors*.

———. "To South America for Bird Study." *The American Museum Journal*, April 1917.

"Cinta Larga," *Indigenous Peoples in Brazil*, www.socioambiental.org/website/pib/epienglish/cintalarga.

Collier, Peter, with David Horowitz. *The Roosevelts: An American Saga*. New York: Simon & Schuster, 1994.

Cook, Blanche Wiesen. *Eleanor Roosevelt, Volume 1: 1884–1933*. New York: Penguin Books, 1992.

Cooper, John Milton, Jr. *Pivotal Decades: The United States, 1900–1920*. New York: W. W. Norton & Company, 1990.

———. *The Warrior and the Priest: Woodrow Wilson and Theodore Roosevelt*. Cambridge, Mass.: Belknap Press of Harvard University Press, 1983.

Costa, João Cruz. *A History of Ideas in Brazil*, trans. Suzette Macedo. Berkeley, University of California Press, 1964.

Czaya, Eberhard. *Rivers of the World*. New York: Van Nostrand Reinhold Company, 1981.

Dalton, Kathleen. *Theodore Roosevelt: A Strenuous Life*. New York: Alfred A. Knopf, 2002.

Daly, Douglas. "The Perils of Collecting." *Audubon*, January–February 1995.

Davis, Oscar King. *Released for Publication: Some Inside Political History of Theodore Roosevelt and His Times, 1898–1918*. Boston: Houghton Mifflin Company, 1925.

Davis, Wade. *One River: Explorations and Discoveries in the Amazon Rain Forest*. New York: Touchstone, 1997.

Degraaf, Richard M., and John H. Rappole. *Neotropical Migratory Birds: Natural History, Distribution, and Population Change*. London: Comstock Publishing Associates, 1995.

Denslow, Julie Sloan, and Christine Padoch, eds. *People of the Tropical Rain Forest.* Berkeley: University of California Press, 1988.

Desowitz, Robert S. *The Malaria Capers: Tales of Parasites and People.* New York: W. W. Norton & Company, 1991.

Diacon, Todd A. *Stringing Together a Nation: Cândido Mariano da Silva Rondon and the Construction of a Modern Brazil, 1906–1930.* Durham, N.C.: Duke University Press, 2004.

Diamond, Jared. *Guns, Germs, and Steel: The Fates of Human Societies.* New York: W. W. Norton & Company, 1999.

Dolnick, Edward. *Down the Great Unknown: John Wesley Powell's 1869 Journey of Discovery and Tragedy Through the Grand Canyon.* New York: HarperCollins Publishers, 2001.

Douglas, Paul H. *Real Wages in the United States, 1890–1926.* Boston: Houghton Mifflin Company, 1930.

Eisenhower, John S. D. *Intervention!: The United States and the Mexican Revolution, 1913–1917.* New York: W. W. Norton & Company, 1993.

Emmons, Louise H. *Neotropical Rainforest Mammals: A Field Guide.* Chicago: University of Chicago Press, 1990.

Fiedler, Arkady. *The River of Singing Fish.* London: Reader's Union, 1951.

Fleming, Fergus. *Ninety Degrees North: The Quest for the North Pole.* New York: Grove Press, 2001.

Forsyth, Adrian, and Ken Miyata. *Tropical Nature: Life and Death in the Rain Forests of Central and South America.* New York: Charles Scribner's Sons, 1984.

Friis, Herman, ed. *The Arctic Diary of Russell Williams Porter.* Charlottesville: University Press of Virginia, 1976.

Gable, John Allen. *The Bull Moose Years: Theodore Roosevelt and the Progressive Party.* Port Washington, N.Y.: Kennikat Press, 1978.

Gardner, Joseph L. *Departing Glory: Theodore Roosevelt as Ex-President.* New York: Charles Scribner's Sons, 1973.

Gheerbrant, Alain. *The Amazon: Past, Present, and Future,* trans. I. Mark Paris. New York: Harry N. Abrams, 1988.

Giller, Paul S., and Björn Malmqvist. *The Biology of Streams and Rivers.* Oxford: Oxford University Press, 1998.

Goodman, Edward J. *The Explorers of South America.* Norman: University of Oklahoma Press, 1972.

Gores, Stan. "The Attempted Assassination of Teddy Roosevelt." *Wisconsin Magazine of History,* Summer 1970.

Goulding, Michael. *The Fishes and the Forest: Explorations in Amazonian Natural History.* Berkeley: University of California Press, 1980.

Goulding, Michael, and Ronaldo Barthem. *The Catfish Connection: Ecology, Migration, and Conservation of Amazon Predators.* New York: Columbia University Press, 1997.

Goulding, Michael, Ronaldo Barthem, and Efrem Ferreira. *The Smithsonian Atlas of the Amazon.* Washington, D.C.: Smithsonian Books, 2003.

Goulding, Michael, Nigel J. H. Smith, and Dennis J. Mahar. *Floods of Fortune: Ecology and Economy Along the Amazon*. New York: Columbia University Press, 1996.

Greene, Harry W. *Snakes: The Evolution of Mystery in Nature*. Berkeley: University of California Press, 1997.

Hagedorn, Hermann. *The Roosevelt Family of Sagamore Hill*. New York: Macmillan Company, 1954.

Hellman, Geoffrey. *Bankers, Bones and Beetles: The First Century of the American Museum of Natural History*. New York: Natural History Press, 1968.

Hemming, John. *Die If You Must*. London: Pan Books, 2004.

———. *Red Gold: The Conquest of the Brazilian Indians, 1500–1760*. Cambridge, Mass.: Harvard University Press, 1978.

Hollander, Zander. *Madison Square Garden: A Century of Sport and Spectacle on the World's Most Versatile Stage*. New York: Hawthorn Books, 1973.

Hölldobler, Bert, and Edward O. Wilson. *The Ants*. Cambridge, Mass.: Belknap Press of Harvard University Press, 1990.

———. *Journey to the Ants: A Story of Scientific Exploration*. Cambridge, Mass.: Belknap Press of Harvard University Press, 1994.

Homberger, Eric. *The Historical Atlas of New York City*. New York: Henry Holt & Company, 1994.

Hopkins, Robert S. *Darwin's South America*. New York: John Day Company, 1969.

Howard, Fred. *Wilbur and Orville: A Biography of the Wright Brothers*. New York: Alfred A. Knopf, 1987.

Joerg, W. L. G., ed. *The Discovery of the Amazon According to the Account of Friar Gaspar de Carvajal and Other Documents*, trans. Bertram T. Lee. New York: American Geographical Society, 1934.

Kozák, Vladimír. "Ritual: A Simple Interment." *Natural History*, January 1963.

Kricher, John. *A Neotropical Companion: An Introduction to the Animals, Plants, and Ecosystems of the New World Tropics*. Princeton: Princeton University Press, 1997.

Lévi-Strauss, Claude. *Tristes Tropiques*, trans. John and Doreen Weightman. New York: Penguin Books, 1992.

Lundberg, John G., et al. "The Stage for Neotropical Fish Diversification: A History of Tropical South American Rivers." In *Phylogeny and Classification of Neotropical Fishes*. Pôrto Alegre, Brazil: Edipucrs, 1998.

Mabberley, D. J. *Tropical Rainforest Ecology*. New York: Chapman & Hill, 1992.

Macdonald, Arthur. "The Would-be Assassin of Theodore Roosevelt." *Medical Times*, April 1914.

Magalhães, Amilcar Botelho de. *Impressões da Commissão Rondon*. São Paulo: Companhia Editoria Nacional, 1942.

Margolis, Mac. *The Last New World: The Conquest of the Amazon Frontier*. New York: W. W. Norton & Company, 1992.

McCullough, David. *Mornings on Horseback*. New York: Simon & Schuster, 1981.

McGerr, Michael. *A Fierce Discontent: The Rise and Fall of the Progressive Movement in America, 1870–1920*. New York: Free Press, 2003.

Meeuse, Bastiaan, and Sean Morris. *The Sex Life of Flowers*. London: Faber & Faber, 1984.

Meggers, Betty J. *Amazonia: Man and Culture in a Counterfeit Paradise*. Chicago: Aldine Atherton, 1971.

Miller, Leo E. *In the Wilds of South America*. New York: Charles Scribner's Sons, 1918.

Miller, Nathan. *Theodore Roosevelt: A Life*. New York: William Morrow & Company, 1992.

Moffett, Mark W. *The High Frontier: Exploring the Tropical Rainforest Canopy*. Cambridge, Mass.: Harvard University Press, 1993.

Morris, Edmund. *The Rise of Theodore Roosevelt*. New York: Ballantine Books, 1979.

———. *Theodore Rex*. New York: Random House, 2001.

Morris, Sylvia Jukes. *Edith Kermit Roosevelt: Portrait of a First Lady*. New York: Coward, McCann & Geoghegan, 1980.

Mowry, George E. *The Era of Theodore Roosevelt and the Birth of Modern America, 1900–1912*. New York: Harper & Row, 1958.

Mozans, H. J. *Along the Andes and Down the Amazon*. New York: D. Appleton & Company, 1912.

Muir, John. *John Muir's Last Journey: South to the Amazon and East to Africa*. Washington, D.C.: Island Press, 2001.

Myers, Norman. *The Primary Source: Tropical Forests and Our Future*. New York: W. W. Norton & Company, 1984.

Naumburg, Elsie M. B. "The Birds of Matto Grosso, Brazil: A Report on the Birds Secured by the Roosevelt-Rondon Expedition," with field notes by George K. Cherrie. *Bulletin of the American Museum of Natural History*, 1930.

Neuweiler, Gerhard. *The Biology of Bats*, trans. Ellen Covey. Oxford: Oxford University Press, 2000.

Oakenfull, J. C. *Brazil in 1913*. Frome, England: Selwood Press, 1914.

O'Reilly, Donald F. "Rondon: Biography of a Brazilian Republican Army Commander." Ph.D. dissertation. New York University, 1969.

Ornig, Joseph R. *My Last Chance to Be a Boy*. Mechanicsburg, Pa..: Stackpole Books, 1994.

Osborn, Henry Fairfield. *Impressions of Great Naturalists*. New York: Charles Scribner's Sons, 1924.

O'Toole, Patricia. *When Trumpets Call: Theodore Roosevelt After the White House*. New York: Simon & Schuster, 2005.

Owen, Denis. *Camouflage and Mimicry*. Chicago: University of Chicago Press, 1980.

Patterson, Jerry E. *The City of New York: A History Illustrated from the*

Collections of The Museum of the City of New York. New York: Harry N. Abrams, 1978.

Penny, Norman D., and Jorge R. Arias. *Insects of an Amazon Forest.* New York: Columbia University Press, 1982.

Perling, J. J. *Presidents' Sons: The Prestige of Name in a Democracy.* New York: Odyssey Press, 1947.

Plotkin, Mark J. *Tales of a Shaman's Apprentice: An Ethnobotanist Searches for New Medicines in the Amazon Rain Forest.* New York: Penguin Books, 1993.

Price, David. *Before the Bulldozer: The Nambiquara Indians and the World Bank.* Washington, D.C.: Steven Locks Press, 1989.

Putz, Francis E. *The Biology of Vines.* Cambridge, Mass.: Cambridge University Press, 1991.

Quinn, Sandra L., and Sanford Kanter. *America's Royalty: All the Presidents' Children.* Westport, Conn.: Greenwood Press, 1983.

Ramos, Alcida R. *Frontier Expansion and Indian Peoples in the Brazilian Amazon.* Gainesville: University Press of Florida, 1984.

Renehan, Edward J., Jr. *The Lion's Pride: Theodore Roosevelt and His Family in Peace and War.* Oxford: Oxford University Press, 1998.

Revkin, Andrew. *The Burning Season: The Murder of Chico Mendes and the Fight for the Amazon Rain Forest.* Boston: Houghton Mifflin Company, 1990.

Ribeiro, Darcy. *O Indigenista Rondon.* Rio de Janeiro, 1958.

Ridgway, Robert. "Directions for Collecting Birds." *Bulletin of the United States National Museum,* 1891.

Robinson, Corinne Roosevelt. *My Brother Theodore Roosevelt.* New York: Charles Scribner's Sons, 1921.

Rocco, Fiammetta. *The Miraculous Fever-Tree: Malaria and the Quest for a Cure That Changed the World.* New York: HarperCollins, 2003.

Rondon, Colonel Cândido Mariano da Silva. *Lectures Delivered on the 5th, 7th and 9th of October 1915 at the Phenix Theatre of Rio de Janeiro on The Roosevelt-Rondon Scientific Expedition and The Telegraph Line Commission,* trans. R. G. Reidy and Ed. Murray. Rio de Janeiro: Typographia Leuzinger, 1916.

Roosevelt, Anna, ed. *Amazonian Indians from Prehistory to the Present.* Tucson: University of Arizona Press, 1994.

Roosevelt, Kermit. *The Long Trail.* New York: Metropolitan Publications, 1921.

Roosevelt, Theodore. *All in the Family.* New York: G. P. Putnam's Sons, 1929.

———. *An Autobiography.* New York: The Macmillan Company, 1913.

———. *The Letters of Theodore Roosevelt,* ed. Elting E. Morison, John Morton Blum, and Alfred Chandler. 8 vols. Cambridge, Mass.: Harvard University Press, 1951–54.

———. "My Life as a Naturalist." *Natural History,* April 1980.

———. *Ranch Life and the Hunting-Trail.* New York: Century Co., 1888.

———. *Theodore Roosevelt: An American Mind,* ed. Mario R. DiNunzio. New York: Penguin Books, 1995.

————. *Theodore Roosevelt's Letters to His Children,* ed. Joseph Bucklin Bishop. New York: Charles Scribner's Sons, 1919.

————. *Through the Brazilian Wilderness.* New York: Charles Scribner's Sons, 1914.

Royte, Elizabeth. *The Tapir's Morning Bath: Mysteries of the Tropical Rain Forest and the Scientists Who Are Trying to Solve Them.* Boston: Houghton Mifflin Company, 2001.

Schilthuizen, Menno. *Frogs, Flies, and Dandelions: Speciation—The Evolution of New Species.* Oxford: Oxford University Press, 2001.

Schreider, Helen, and Frank Schreider. *Exploring the Amazon.* Washington, D.C.: National Geographic Society, 1970.

Shoumatoff, Alex. *The Rivers Amazon.* San Francisco: Sierra Club Books, 1978.

Simpson, George Gaylord. *Splendid Isolation: The Curious History of South American Mammals.* New Haven: Yale University Press, 1980.

Smith, Anthony. *Explorers of the Amazon.* Chicago: University of Chicago Press, 1990.

Smith, Nigel J. H. *The Amazon River Forest: A Natural History of Plants, Animals, and People.* Oxford: Oxford University Press, 1999.

Spielman, Andrew, and Michael D'Antonio. *Mosquito: A Natural History of Our Most Persistent and Deadly Foe.* New York: Hyperion, 2001.

Spotte, Stephen. *Candiru: Life and Legend of the Bloodsucking Catfishes.* Berkeley, Calif.: Creative Arts Book Company, 2002.

St. Clair, David. *The Mighty, Mighty Amazon.* London: Souvenir Press, 1968.

Steward, Julian H. *Handbook of South American Indians, Volume 3: The Tropical Forest Tribes.* Washington, D.C.: United States Government Printing Office, 1948.

Stotz, Douglas F., et al. *Neotropical Birds: Ecology and Conservation.* Chicago: University of Chicago Press, 1996.

Terbough, John. *Diversity and the Tropical Rain Forest.* New York: Scientific American Library, 1992.

Thayer, William Roscoe. *Theodore Roosevelt: An Intimate Biography.* Boston: Houghton Mifflin Company, 1919.

Tomlinson, H. M. *The Sea and the Jungle.* Evanston, Ill.: Marlboro Press/Northwestern, 1999.

Tourtellot, Jonathan B. "The Amazon: Sailing a Jungle Sea." In *Great Rivers of the World.* Washington, D.C.: National Geographic, 1984.

Viveiros, Esther de. *Rondon: Conta Sua Vida.* Rio de Janeiro: Livraria São José, 1958.

Von Puttkamer, W. Jesco. "Brazil Protects Her Cinta Largas." *National Geographic,* September 1971.

Wagenknecht, Edward. *The Seven Worlds of Theodore Roosevelt.* New York: Longmans, Green & Co., 1958.

Waldron, Webb. "Making Exploring Safe for Explorers." *Saturday Evening Post,* January 30, 1932.

Watts, Sarah. *Rough Rider in the White House*. Chicago: University of Chicago Press, 2003.

Weber, Ralph E. *Notre Dame's John Zahm: American Catholic Apologist and Educator*. Notre Dame, Ind.: University of Notre Dame Press, 1961.

Weinstein, Barbara. *The Amazon Rubber Boom, 1850–1920*. Stanford, Calif.: Stanford University Press, 1983.

Whitmore, T. C. *An Introduction to Tropical Rain Forests*. Oxford: Oxford University Press, 1998.

Wickler, Wolfgang. *Mimicry in Plants and Animals*. Toronto: McGraw-Hill, 1968.

Wilford, John Noble. *The Mapmakers*. New York: Vintage Books, 1981.

Wilson, Edward O. *The Diversity of Life*. Cambridge, Mass.: Belknap Press of Harvard University Press, 1992.

Worcester, Donald E. *Makers of Latin America*. New York: E. P. Dutton & Co., 1966.

Zahm, John A. *Evolution and Dogma*. New York: Regina Press, 1975.

———. *Through South America's Southland*. New York: D. Appleton & Company, 1916.

ACKNOWLEDGMENTS

After completing this book, I have more people to thank than there are miles on the River of Doubt. To no one, however, do I owe a greater debt of gratitude than to my husband, Mark Uhlig. Mark inspired me not only to work hard but to think hard, to expand my vision of this book until it far exceeded even my earliest dreams for it. Without his invaluable advice and unfailing support, this book would be much smaller in scope and spirit than it is—as would my life.

I am also deeply indebted to James Chace, who first introduced me to the River of Doubt and encouraged me to write about it. James was a constant source of help and inspiration during his lifetime, and continues to be one even now, after his untimely death. For decades, countless writers, editors, policymakers, and students gravitated to him, drawn to his keen intellect, rare originality, and remarkable generosity. Like all great teachers, his influence will be felt for generations to come.

As an editor at *National Geographic* magazine, I was always impressed by the dedication of scientists and other specialists who would spare no effort to ensure that the magazine got everything right, down to the last detail. As a writer, struggling to understand the intricacies of the Amazon rain forest, I was thrilled and grateful to find that those same experts—men and women at the top of their professions—were as willing to help an individual as they were a venerable institution like the National Geographic Society. Time and again, scientists who did not know me, and who had no personal stake in my work, generously volunteered their time to answer my endless questions, recommend the best books and journals, and introduce me to other experts in their field. They never complained when I called back for the thousandth time with "just one more question," and they never failed to amaze me with the breadth and depth of their knowledge.

Robert Carneiro, one of the world's pre-eminent anthropologists and the American Museum of Natural History's specialist on South America's indigenous peoples, not only patiently explained man's earliest migrations into and throughout South America but made inquiries on my behalf, introduced me to people connected to Cândido Rondon, and, later, carefully read my manuscript and offered valuable insights and suggestions. Marcelo de Carvalho, a Brazilian ichthyologist also on the staff of the American Museum of Natural History, helped me peer into the fascinating depths of the South American rivers he knows so well. Douglas Daly, the respected curator of Amazonian botany at the New York Botanical Garden, graciously answered my many questions about the Amazon's most influential inhabitants—its trees and other plant life. Flávio Lima of the Museu de Zoologia da USP provided me with critical information that I could not have found anywhere else, and was my best source on a river whose remoteness has deterred many other scientists. Douglas Stotz, an ornithologist at Chicago's Field Museum who has often worked along the banks of the Aripuanã, described to me the joys and challenges of collecting birds in the Amazon. He is, in many ways, a modern-day George Cherrie. Doctors Paul Uhlig and Stephen Calderwood, with Massachusetts General Hospital, generously gave their time and considerable expertise to help me better understand tropical illnesses and bacterial infections.

The children, grandchildren, and great-grandchildren of the men of the Roosevelt-Rondon Scientific Expedition were also, without exception, kind, generous, and immensely helpful. Of Roosevelt's descendants, I owe the greatest thanks to Tweed Roosevelt, who in 1992, with a team of twenty men and women, successfully retraced his great-grandfather's expedition from the River of Doubt's deadly serpentine headwaters to its juncture with the Aripuanã. Sincere thanks also go to Willard Roosevelt, Kermit's only surviving child; Kermit Roosevelt III, Kermit's grandson and namesake; Edith Williams; Sarah Chapman; and Elizabeth Aldred. Many thanks too to Deb Cherrie, George Cherrie's great-granddaughter-in-law, and Hubert Cherrie, the ornithologist's grandson, who has inherited his grandfather's wit and courage.

While in Rio de Janeiro, I also had the good fortune to meet several of Marshal Cândido Rondon's grandchildren. Maria Beatriz Rondon Amarante generously invited me to her home, where she and her cousins, Maria Ignez Rondon Amarante, Angelo Christiano Rondon Amarante, and Pedro Henrique Bernardes Rondon, answered my questions and shared with me illuminating and little-known details about their grandfather and his beloved Chiquita.

For introducing me to Marshal Rondon's grandchildren and explaining the design of Rondon's telegraph stations, I thank Patricia and Mario Civelli. I am grateful to Lucrecia Franco for being my knowledgeable and cheerful guide through the libraries and museums of Rio de Janeiro, and to the intrepid Pedro Varela for traveling with me to remote and inhospitable stretches of the Amazon and helping me find and interview a group of Cinta Larga who remember well their tribal history. For helping me find translators and experts and track down last-minute letters and elusive facts, I am grateful to Kathryn Bard, Karen Courtnage, Mery Galanternick, Lisa Grossman, Pamela Muraski, Rani Shanker, Anna Uhlig, and Sandra Wellington. For his generous help, and for keeping me, as well as the rest of the world, informed about everything that is happening in South America—from politics to culture to conservation—I thank Larry Rohter, the *New York Times* bureau chief in Rio de Janeiro.

I am indebted to Marilia Rebello and Erin Schneider for French and Portuguese translations that are as lyrical as they are precise. Heartfelt thanks to David Uhlig for volunteering his talent as a photographer and graphic designer, to Myron Pitts for being unfailingly helpful, and to Richard Oller, Darren Sextro, Kevin Childress, and Lora Uhlig for offering advice as early readers.

For introducing me to the manuscripts and archival objects that breathed life into this book—from published books and articles to private journals and letters to equipment invoices, medical reports, splintered arrows, and rusted surgical knives—I am grateful to Elizabeth Bré, Denise Portugal Lamar, and the entire staff of the Museu do Índio; Jacqueline Dougherty and Reverend William B. Simmons, Indiana Province Archives Center of the Congregation of Holy Cross; Karla Estelita Godoy, Museu da República; Angela Kindig, Peter Lysy, and Sharon Sumpter, Notre Dame University Archives; Mary LeCroy, Ornithology Department of the American Museum of Natural History; Antonio Carlos de Souza Lima and Fátima Nascimento, Museu Nacional; Eileen Morales, Museum of the City of New York; and Liisa Morton, executive director of the Museum of Surveying. In the tradition of saving the best for last, I would like to offer a special thanks to Wallace Finley Dailey, the curator of the Theodore Roosevelt Collection at Harvard, whose work has helped define modern scholarship in this area.

I thank Sydney Possuelo, the world's greatest living *sertanista,* and João Dal Poz, the Cinta Larga's devoted and accomplished anthropologist, for giving me invaluable insight into the lives of indigenous Amazonians in general and the Cinta Larga in particular, and I am grateful to Oitamina Cinta Larga and Tatataré Cinta Larga, two of the tribe's former chiefs, for a firsthand introduction to the Cinta Larga, its way of life as well as its tribal history.

For giving me my first opportunities as a writer and editor, and for making this book possible by teaching me their craft through example and patient instruction, I would like to thank Donald Belt, Dean Bevan, Robert Booth, Judith Brown, Preston and Virginia Fambrough,

Steven Gerson, Jon Goodman, David Jeffrey, Jude Nixon, Bernard Ohanian, Robert Poole, Lucy Price, Mary Singh, Rhonda Wickham, and Scott Wyerman. For their encouragement and support on this project, I thank Molly Crosby, Jennifer Fox, David and Martha Ives, Davida Kales, Jodi Lewis, Keith Moore, and Don Wilson. Thanks also to Adam Bellow for his generous advice and guidance, and to the staff of the National Geographic Society, who inspired and encouraged my interest in exploration and natural history.

Every writer hopes to have in her corner an agent and editor upon whose talent and wisdom she can depend. I have been fortunate to find two of the industry's best in Suzanne Gluck and Bill Thomas. Suzanne not only agreed to take on an unknown writer but came through for me at every turn with power and grace. Bill is the consummate editor, and I am extremely grateful that my book landed in his experienced hands.

For being a model of patience and a source of inspiration over the past three years—the span of her lifetime—I am indebted to my daughter, Emery Millard Uhlig, and for enduring research trips and long hours at the office, I thank her new little sister, Petra Tihen Uhlig, who has timed her arrival to coincide with the publication of this book. For the invaluable knowledge that, while I researched and wrote, Emery was in the very best of hands, I thank our dear friend and beloved family member, Betty Jacobs. I also owe a lifetime of gratitude to my mother-in-law, Doris Uhlig, for welcoming me wholeheartedly into her family. For their flawless example, I thank George Emery Millard, Mable Mitchel, Lora Tihen, and Ethel Wright, and for making me proud beyond measure to be their sister, I thank Kelly Sandvig, Anna Shaffer, and Nichole Millard. Finally, for giving me a lifetime of unconditional love and for making whatever I have achieved in my life possible, I am deeply grateful to my parents, Lawrence and Constance Millard.

INDEX

CREDITS

The author and publisher gratefully acknowledge the American Museum of Natural History Library, the Theodore Roosevelt Collection, Harvard College Library, and The Explorer's Club for permission to print the following photos, which appear in inserts pages 1–16:

Specific credits:

Theodore Roosevelt Collection, Harvard College Library: page 1, all; page 2, all; page 3, all; page 5, bottom; page 6, all; page 7, all; page 8, all; page 9, top; page 10, bottom; page 11, middle; page 12, top; page 13, top and bottom; page 14, top; page 15, bottom; page 16, all.

American Museum of Natural History Library: page 4, bottom; page 5, top; page 9, middle and bottom; page 10, top; page 11, top and bottom; page 12, middle and bottom; page 13, middle; page 14, bottom; page 15, top.

The Explorer's Club: page 4, top.